Escaping Nazi Germany

Escaping Nazi Germany

One Woman's Emigration from Heilbronn to England

Joachim Schlör

BLOOMSBURY ACADEMIC
LONDON • NEW YORK • OXFORD • NEW DELHI • SYDNEY

BLOOMSBURY ACADEMIC
Bloomsbury Publishing Plc
50 Bedford Square, London, WC1B 3DP, UK
1385 Broadway, New York, NY 10018, USA
29 Earlsfort Terrace, Dublin 2, Ireland

BLOOMSBURY, BLOOMSBURY ACADEMIC and the Diana logo
are trademarks of Bloomsbury Publishing Plc

First published in Great Britain 2021
This paperback edition published in 2022

Copyright © Joachim Schlör, 2021

Joachim Schlör has asserted his right under the Copyright, Designs and
Patents Act, 1988, to be identified as Author of this work.

This book has first been published in German as "Liesel, it's time for you to leave". Von Heilbronn nach London.
Die Flucht der Familie Rosenthal vor der nationalsozialistischen Verfolgung. Stadtarchiv Heilbronn 2016.

Translation from the German original: Christopher Lutton.

For legal purposes the Acknowledgements on pp.viii–ix constitute
an extension of this copyright page.

Cover image: Portrait of young Liesel Rosenthal (© Stadtarchiv Heilbronn)

All rights reserved. No part of this publication may be reproduced or transmitted
in any form or by any means, electronic or mechanical, including photocopying,
recording, or any information storage or retrieval system, without prior
permission in writing from the publishers.

Bloomsbury Publishing Plc does not have any control over, or responsibility for,
any third-party websites referred to or in this book. All internet addresses given
in this book were correct at the time of going to press. The author and publisher
regret any inconvenience caused if addresses have changed or sites have
ceased to exist, but can accept no responsibility for any such changes.

Every effort has been made to trace copyright holders and to obtain their
permissions for the use of copyright material. The publisher apologizes for any
errors or omissions and would be grateful if notified of any corrections that
should be incorporated in future reprints or editions of this book.

A catalogue record for this book is available from the British Library.

Library of Congress Cataloging-in-Publication Data
Names: Schlör, Joachim, 1960-author. | Lutton, Christopher, Translator.
Title: Escaping Nazi Germany: one woman's emigration from Heilbronn to
England / Joachim Schlör; [translated by] Christopher Lutton.
Other titles: "Liesel, it's time for you to leave." English | One woman's emigration from Heilbronn to England
Description: London, UK; New York, NY: Bloomsbury Academic, 2020. |
Includes bibliographical references and index.
Identifiers: LCCN 2020030996 (print) | LCCN 2020030997 (ebook) | ISBN 9781350154124 (hardback) |
9781350232099 (paperback) | ISBN 9781350154131 (ebook) | ISBN 9781350154148 (epub)
Subjects: LCSH: Rosenthal, Liesel, 1915-2001–Correspondence. | Rosenthal family. |
Jews–Germany–Heilbronn–20th century–Biography. | Holocaust, Jewish (1939-1945)–Germany–Heilbronn. |
Holocaust survivors–Germany–Heilbronn–Biography. | Antisemitism–Germany–Heilbronn–History. |
Jews–England–London–20th century–Biography. | Jewish refugees–England–London–20th
century–Biography. | Heilbronn (Germany)–Biography.
Classification: LCC DS134.4 .S3513 2020 (print) | LCC DS134.4 (ebook) | DDC 940.53/18092 [B]–dc23
LC record available at https://lccn.loc.gov/2020030996
LC ebook record available at https://lccn.loc.gov/2020030997

ISBN: HB: 978-1-3501-5412-4
PB: 978-1-3502-3209-9
ePDF: 978-1-3501-5413-1
eBook: 978-1-3501-5414-8

Typeset by Integra Software Services Pvt. Ltd.

To find out more about our authors and books visit www.bloomsbury.com
and sign up for our newsletters.

Contents

Illustrations	vi
Acknowledgements	viii
Introduction	1
1 'Liesel, it's time for you to leave.' Departure	9
2 Digression: 'Dear Liesel, there are still so many questions.' A trip to Bombay	47
3 'This morning I got a letter from Jack.' A way out for Helmut	63
4 'Dear Liesel, Urug. is no longer an option.' What happened to the parents?	81
5 'An alien of a most excellent type.' The war years in London	119
6 'Thinking of Germany.' From a broken picture book	159
7 'Your home' ['Ihre Heimat']. Reconnecting	179
8 Digression: 'Now in ruins.' The house in the Götzenturmstraße	193
9 'How was the wine harvest?' Heilbronn from afar	199
Notes	224
Bibliography	244
Index	257

Illustrations

1	Postcard from Ludwig Rosenthal to his daughter Liesel, 17 January 1939	1
2	Liesel Rosenthal, *c.* 1937	12
3	Rabbi Dr Moses Engelbert	14
4	Hermine Rothschild before her marriage to Ludwig Rosenthal	15
5	The house on Staufenbergstraße 12	18
6	Siegfried Gumbel visiting his son Erich in Jerusalem	26
7	The Wertheimer family	32
8	The street with the Heilbronn synagogue and the new post office, *c.* 1930	35
9	The ticket to Bombay	54
10	The house on Mozartstraße 10 (around 1910) where the family lived from January 1933	74
11	Liesel's brother Helmut, who now called himself Jack Rosen	79
12	The Heilbronn synagogue on the day of the fire, 10 November 1938	84
13	The burned-out synagogue, 1939	86
14	Letter from Hermine Rosenthal to her daughter Liesel, early 1939	110
15	Postcard from Hermine to her daughter Liesel from 25 March 1939	115
16	German POWs in Marseille, photographed in August 1919.	117
17	David (Heinz) Gumbel in Jerusalem, 1963	122
18	Liesel Rosenthal, photographed by Jack Paynton, London 1939	133
19	The Rosenthal and Schwab families, *c.* 1945	153
20	A view from Götzenturmstraße in the northern direction	162
21	Code of conduct for German refugees	166
22	Jack Rosen (Helmut Rosenthal) as a soldier	167
23	Liesel Schwab with her daughter Julia, 1950	172
24	The Götzenturmstraße, as seen in a postcard from the 1930s	181
25	Mayor Paul Meyle	188
26	Letterhead of Rosenthal and Dornacher Wine Wholesalers, 43 Götzenturmstraße, 1919	196
27	List of the Heilbronn wine merchants	197
28	Fritz Wolf during his visit to Heilbronn in 1985	217
29	Alice Schwab with her daughter Julia, 1955	222

Illustrations

*

Illustrations have been reproduced with the kind permission from the following private collections and institutions:
Baroness Julia Neuberger, Private Collections
Stadtarchiv Heilbronn, Archivalien
Stadtarchiv Heilbronn, Fotosammlung

Acknowledgements

This is the story of a young woman who left her hometown of Heilbronn, Germany, in 1937 and emigrated to England as a domestic servant. The anti-Jewish measures of the Nazi regime made life in Germany impossible for her. In the long and complicated process during which Fräulein Alice Rosenthal, known as Liesel, became Mrs Alice Schwab, she managed to bring her brother Helmut and her parents, Hermine and Ludwig Rosenthal, out of Germany – there were, however, other members of the wider family who did not survive the Holocaust. In England, Liesel began to build up her own life, with a circle of friends and a degree of independence that worried her parents. In a certain way, for her emigration meant emancipation.

The worries, and the sorrows, and the anxieties of all family members, relatives and friends have been expressed in several hundreds of postcards and letters. These written testimonies contain, and report on, world history in general and one family's very specific history at the same time. After her marriage to Walter Schwab, some years after the end of the Second World War, and before the birth of her daughter Julia, Alice Schwab bundled the letters together and stowed them in boxes where they remained until Julia – now Baroness Julia Neuberger DBE – and I opened them in 2012.

Her mother's life needs to be regarded and studied in the context of German-Jewish history, with a specific interest in the lives of Jews in Southwest Germany and those families active in the wine trade, but also in the context of anti-Semitism in Germany and the path to destruction, as well as in the context of Jewish immigration into the UK and Palestine. In this sense, it is just one of many thousands of similar stories. Still, it is unique. We hear authentic voices discussing questions of the emigration process, visas, visits to consulates, the packing of suitcases and the loss of property; we learn about personal friendships and marriage plans, about a trip to Bombay and about the fate of relatives who had found their way to places all over the world, from Jerusalem to Sydney, from Buenos Aires to New York; and we see the core family arrive in England and try to integrate into British society.

From there, and as British citizens, they discuss their relationship to the city where they all had come from: Heilbronn. Again, Heilbronn is just one of many German cities that once had an established Jewish community and allowed – and witnessed, and participated in – their destruction under the Nazi regime: forced emigration, the burning of the synagogue, deportation to the death camps, the theft of property. And again, in some ways Heilbronn is unique. It had a longstanding democratic and liberal tradition, which might be one reason for the very violent anti-Semitism of the local Nazis – that in turn shocked and shamed those local actors who did not agree with the regime. On 4 December 1944, the city was destroyed nearly completely in a British air raid, resulting in the loss of more than 7,000 lives. Earlier than other German municipalities the city administration (Mayor Paul Meyle), together with a group of local activists, saw the need to get in touch with Heilbronner Jews who had emigrated between 1933 and 1939. And earlier than other German municipalities (in 1963) the city archives decided to publish a book on the history and the fate of the local Jewish community.

The Rosenthal family and their circle of friends and acquaintances retained a strong interest in their former hometown. Opening the perspective from the core family to the wider world of 'Auslandsheilbronner' allows us to continue the story beyond the end of the war and to integrate questions of memory culture and politics into the narrative of emigration and immigration, and of war, internment and survival. It also allows us to read and discuss the letters of Fritz Wolf, a childhood friend of Liesel, an unpublished author of a very high quality, a Heilbronner who ended up in Nahariya in Northern Israel, and who – from there, in his letters to Heilbronn's post–War Mayor Meyle – discusses history, memory, guilt and responsibility, and asks questions whose urgency and relevance go far beyond the local background of a South West German city of many winegrowers and few wine merchants.

I wish to thank Julia Neuberger for giving me access to the letters and for providing me with information about her family. Furthermore, I thank the City Archives of Heilbronn, Professor Christhard Schrenk and Dr Annette Geisler, for publishing the German original of this book, for hosting us at a very moving launch event in early 2016 and for keeping this story alive through scenic readings at local schools. Now I hope that Liesel's story will find readers in the country she made her home, and I want to thank Christopher Lutton for his translation.

Introduction

Dear Liesel!
First of all you must ask the Uruguay[an] consulate <u>immediately</u> if it is possible for us to travel from Engl[and] to Urug[uay]. We will of course take our own furniture with us, just as [we] would sort out our boat tickets here. If not then you must next try to arrange Australia for us, but I fear that this project is dragging on so long, and we urgently need a tangible, quick solution. There is no need to telegraph us, save your money, but please try to do more for us. Let us know as soon as you can about Uruguay, as d[ear] Mother may have to go to Berlin on that account next week. W[ith] love and kisses for you and Heller. Father.

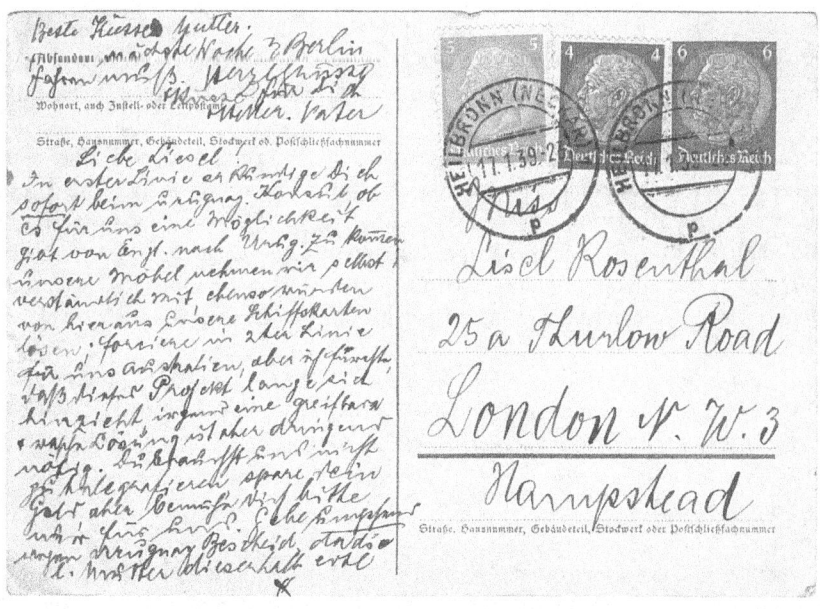

Figure 1 Postcard from Ludwig Rosenthal to his daughter Liesel, 17 January 1939. © Baroness Julia Neuberger, Private Collection

The postcard with this news, including stamps of four, five and six German Pfennigs (with Paul von Hindenburg on them), was postmarked on 17 January 1939 in Heilbronn (Neckar) and sent to 'Miss Lisel Rosenthal, 25a Thurlow Road, London N.W.3, Hampstead'. The following story is about the fate of these four members of the Rosenthal family: Ludwig, the father; Hermine, the mother; Alice (Lisel or Liesel), the daughter; and Helmut (Heller, later Jack), the son. It is based on a reading and critical analysis of several hundred letters and postcards exchanged between the four family members – as well as a large number of relatives, friends, acquaintances old and new, plus various authorities and institutions – over a period of roughly ten years between 1937 and 1947.[1] Liesel, only ever called Alice, her birth name, by strangers, is the focal point of all these letters. On 17 May 1937, seven days after her 22nd birthday, she emigrated from her (and my) home city of Heilbronn to England, initially to Birmingham and then to London. From there she attempted to get her brother and parents out of Nazi Germany.

From the day of Liesel's emigration until the spring of 1939, Ludwig Rosenthal (born 6 February 1880), 'Wine and Spirit Specialist', as he described himself on his headed paper, and his wife Hermine (born 19 April 1892 in Bad Cannstatt), from the Rothschild family, made efforts to organize their own emigration. As this postcard shows, they considered various countries and 'projects'. Life was becoming increasingly difficult for them in Heilbronn and they had been familiarizing themselves with living conditions in England, Chile, Uruguay, South Africa and Australia. They were worried about their children's wellbeing, but also about their possessions, their flat, their 'things' [*Sachen*], as they say in Swabia.

The letters document both world and family history. The 'great' political events, such as the Nazi dictatorship, then in its fifth year, the increasing persecution of Jews in Germany and Europe, the outbreak and progress of the Second World War, even the imminent upheaval in the British Empire, including in the British Mandate of Palestine, do more than merely frame the family's story: they actively shape it, and are reflected in it. Carefully written, they put the family members' relationships with each other to the test, as 'please try to do more for us' from the above excerpt shows. Through specific phrases, abbreviations ('d[ear] Mother', 'w[ith] love') and expressions, through tone and emphasis, through their Swabian dialect and through switching between German and English, the letters also reveal much about each individual's efforts to survive these global events, to preserve their sense of worth and to justify their actions:[2]

> *Ich mache mir so Vorwürfe, daß ich nicht gleich von hier aus n/Uruguay ging, wo ich doch alle meine Papiere ready für dort hatte, das Geld deponiert war u. meine 2 Lifts für Montevideo bezahlt waren. Dort hätten wir von meinen Zinsen schön leben können, ich hätte arbeiten dürfen u. jetzt lebe nur in Sorgen u. verbrauche mich vollständig auf.*

> *I am so cross with myself that I did not go straight from here to Uruguay, where I had all my papers ready, where I had sent my money and where my two lifts to Montevideo were paid for. We could have lived there quite nicely from the interest and I could have found a job. Now I live in a constant state of worry and I am using myself up completely.*

This note from Hermine is undated, but was attached to Ludwig's letter dated 23 June 1940 (56 Worple Road, Wimbledon) and is likely to come from the same day. This is indicative of the problematic nature of the sources on which this story is based. Alice Schwab, as she was known after her marriage to Walter Schwab in London in 1942, kept the letters and postcards in bundles packed away in boxes until her death in 2001. Her daughter Julia Neuberger never opened them and only showed them to me in June 2012. After a while, when she saw how moved I was by even a short and superficial reading of the letters which she herself could not decipher, she gave them to me and neither of us knew where this would lead us. Liesel was the addressee of almost all the letters, but very few documents written by her have been preserved. In 1990, at the age of seventy-five she gave an interview for the National Life Story Collection of the British Library in London, now stored under the Sounds archive, 'Jewish Survivors of the Holocaust'.[3] The printed summary is entitled 'Thank You for Everything'; in the family this document has been termed 'Liesel's memoirs'. Unsurprisingly given how much time had elapsed, although these memoirs offer an impressive insight into how she looked back at her life as a mother and a grandmother to her daughter Julia and her grandchildren Harriet and Matthew, in terms of detail and chronology they are extremely unreliable.[4] In the collection of letters itself she is, although the focal point, remarkably absent, her personality being apparent in the image of her developed by others through contact with her. Moreover, and entirely to be expected given the circumstances, the documents are incomplete: some are ripped, splotchy and difficult to decipher. There are undated letters which are almost impossible to put into order, and there are very private letters, of which I have used the ones which are important in telling the story or for giving an impression of Liesel's personality. And there are many inconsequential letters, slips of paper, bills and notes referring to daily things written by seamstresses or work colleagues: these are aspects of a correspondence just as much about trivial matters as important ones. This makes them of particular value. In many historical accounts human beings are portrayed as mere objects of what happens to them, and in many memoirs personal experience is foregrounded rather too prominently.[5] In these letters the one is inconceivable without the other.

Letters have always been an important source for cultural and historical research. In the past few years, as was described at a recent conference, 'our understanding of the letter as a form of text, as a material object, and as a generator or reflector of social norms and cultural practices has become more nuanced,'[6] but many questions remain open. How – if at all – can we conceptualize letters as a genre, and what is to be gained from that?

> In what ways do variable transmission processes – including the collection, archiving, editing, or exhibition of letters – influence our perception of the epistolary? Finally, and this is perhaps the most important question, how does one approach a type of text which is used both as a pragmatic and as a literary form and which is rooted in historical reality while at the same time retaining its potential to deploy fictional qualities?[7]

The writing habits of the people involved are hardly known. What previously had been discussed at the kitchen table face to face, before the family relationship was broken apart, had now to be conveyed in letters and postcards – under the watchful eye of the censor. As a 'place' of exchange and resolution of problems the letter functions rather differently from standard conversation and is an insufficient replacement for it. This explains many of the clumsy or unexpectedly stinging expressions which we encounter here. For example, the mother's letters are frequently characterized by omission of the personal pronoun ('Would like nothing more than to see and speak to you'). Hermine Rosenthal also had to write in standard German, which she did not use in everyday life.

Hiltrud Häntzschel has made important contributions to the study of letter writing in exile, from which this book greatly benefits:

The situation in which the writing is being done is always unnatural, the unforeseen exception: one correspondent has emigrated and is – for the time being – in safety abroad, the other remains in danger at home; one is in danger somewhere in Europe, the other managed to get to safety in America; one is still stuck in Germany, the other has either been imprisoned in a concentration camp or deported; parents hold out in Germany whilst their child has been brought to safety on one of the Kindertransports; old friends or couples are suddenly, dramatically separated for the first time, meaning they are unused to it. Telephone calls or visits are no longer possible.[8]

Almost all these observations are relevant for this collection of documents, and this is also true of the differences between this and 'conventional' letter writing established by Häntzschel. There is almost no gap between the experience and writing about it, as everything is immediately noted down (even if it is only read much later): we 'do not speak for ourselves; instead we turn to someone else,'[9] and it is often very urgent. The great question of freedom (of living, writing, reading) plays an equally important role. Letters can (or sometimes cannot) overcome barriers; they can be censored, seized, read by others. Letters from exile must be written and read between the lines; self-censorship is all-pervasive. We must analyse the sheer materiality of the letters, the paper chosen and ripped off at random, the words hurriedly cobbled together, the newspaper extract attached. And in the letters to be presented and discussed in this book the following observation is particularly noteworthy: 'In every letter sent in response it is clear how much the violently separated correspondents yearned to be sent a letter, and how much joy they took from receiving and reading one.'[10] We will see these observations confirmed (and sometimes questioned) on a case-by-case basis.

Previous studies and conferences concerning emigrant letters – most coming from the nineteenth century – make clear how big the gaps in the research remain.[11] A conference in Gotha in June 2014 discussed several questions, again using examples from the nineteenth century, which are also relevant for this study: what sort of documents are we dealing with? In which historical moments do they become more relevant? What characteristics in particular do emigrant letters possess? Where are the differences between these and other personal letters? How are we to analyse their 'Janus-faced character' ('between the extremes of the private/public sphere, writing/speech, the momentary/semi-permanent nature of the content, authenticity/fiction'[12])? What narrative strategies do they contain?

As far as possible, then, I examine the letters chronologically, and I have inserted explanations or digressions by way of context when I feel they are necessary. My aim is to reconstruct a story of emigration *from the letters*, whilst at the same time asking, and if possible showing, how we as historically interested students of culture working empirically can engage with such resources. What do we learn from the letters themselves? How and where can we find further information about named characters, places, journeys and events? Migration research has experienced an upsurge of interest in recent years. In an article for the edited volume *'To America!' Jewish Migration to the Americas in the 19th and 20th Century* I attempted to present and discuss new approaches to the topic of migration within cultural studies.[13] This treats emigration and immigration as cultural practice and performance and gives an interdisciplinary view of the transitions and distances inherent in migration processes. It also examines objects and their meaning (i.e. the material objects of migration) as well as the phenomenon linguists call code switching, the use of different languages in a variety of situations. In this way research into gender, families and memory culture can be brought into dialogue with migration research.

When I apply these considerations to the specific case of the emigration of Liesel Rosenthal and her family, the most important task is to strike a balance between reconstructing personal experiences and embedding them in the historical context. Ideas drawn from the biographical research of Andreas Gestrich and Gabriele Rosenthal, amongst others, demand a perspective 'which views individuals in a permanent relationship with their environment'.[14] Neither are individuals puppets depending on others nor are they completely free and autonomous; they are actors in what Bourdieu calls a 'social space'[15] constructed through relationships between individual actors and in a constant state of flux. This is particularly true of emigration situations, which relocate the actors' space, physically separate them from each other and oblige the communication which forms the basis of their relationship to be expressed in letters rather than in face-to-face conversation. The shared horizons of meaning and experience are lost when a member of the family – Liesel – leaves their home city to begin a new life elsewhere, in this case in England. For her, however, this opens up a new social space, shaped by communication with new actors (employers, acquaintances who become friends, work colleagues). In both areas private written sources – the letters – are our main resource. They tell of how correspondents process their respective experiences and how they tell each other about them, often over large physical distances and with long periods of waiting. Not originally meant for our eyes, today the letters are an important source for those investigating the fate of German-Jewish emigrants after 1933. On 5 June 2015 a workshop 'Making the Private Public', organized in collaboration with the Parkes Institute of the University of Southampton, was held in London's Wiener Library, during which historical and ethical questions relating to the issue of analysing and publishing private family correspondence were discussed. Esther Saraga has published a book on her parents' correspondence; Shirli Gilbert discusses a huge collection of private letters exchanged between South Africa and Germany in her study.[16] Such collections are still to be found in the cellars and attics of houses all over the world. Many will have been lost when moving house or after a death, some will have been passed on to archives where they can be studied, others will have been kept for particular reasons, such as a noteworthy correspondence partner, the mention of historic events or even an interesting stamp. All these collections tell the story of families who, after 1933, left Germany and moved to one or more other countries to escape Nazi persecution. These processes helped create new ways to perceive and analyse experiences; the pressure of circumstances and the effect emigration had on the 'displacement of subjective means of determining identity'[17] even led to the development of new forms of communication. 'Every family is an archive', writes Caroline Fetscher.[18] This means the voices of all its members should be audible in their writing, and their personalities, their various styles, their anger and their despair should shine through.

The geographical starting point, and principal point of reference, is Heilbronn. The mention of the city in a speech given by Baroness Julia Neuberger (first in Dresden in 2005,[19] on the occasion of the first ordination of reform rabbis in Germany since 1938, and then some years later in Southampton) provided the spark for this project. Julia spoke of how her mother, Alice Schwab, née Rosenthal, the Liesel of this book, forgot all the English she had learned and spoke only in Swabian dialect on the last day of her life. When the daughter responded to her 'I want to go home' ('I will hoim') with 'But Mommy, you are home', she named her *other* 'home': 'No, no, Heilbronn.' I was born in the same (although hardly recognizable) city in 1960 and like many of my generation did all I could to leave. Now, through my research, I have 'returned', in the archives, in conversation with contemporary witnesses and in the letters, and this is not without effect on the text I have written. The dialect of my parents and grandparents echoes still, when I make enquiries on the telephone or when I visit the Götzenturmstraße and ask the current residents about their former neighbours. Something similar had already happened to me when in 2000 Andreas Meyer, Armin Wallas and I visited Fritz Wolf, born in Heilbronn and frequently mentioned in these letters, in the city of Nahariya in Israel to read through his (never published) manuscripts. Of course I was interested in *what* stories he had to tell, but I was much more affected by the dialect he spoke and *how* he told them. I had understood (or perhaps misunderstood) this in different ways as stories told in standard German.

The city can point to a significant mediaeval Jewish presence. Just like in the cities of Speyer and Worms, by the eleventh century a prestigious and comparatively large Jewish community had been established – the common Jewish surname Halperin or Galperin is derived from the name of the city.[20] Even here, however, the history of the community is one of numerous waves of persecution: a particularly terrible outbreak in 1298 was marked by expulsions and resettlement, and in 1476 both city councils took the decision to refuse to tolerate the presence of Jews in the city 'for eternity'.[21] A new community was established only in the second half of the nineteenth century.

In 1933, 790 Jews were living in Heilbronn, forming 1.3 per cent of the city's 60,308 residents. The Swabian-Jewish community was mostly middle class, composed primarily of small- and medium-scale traders and members of the liberal professions. From the very beginning of the Nazi dictatorship it was subjected to harassment, which was possibly even more extreme than elsewhere because the city, with its liberal, social democratic tradition, had long been barren ground for Nazi propaganda and politics.²² A Nazi publication from 1938 criticized the relatively weak 'resistance' of the population to 'the Jews'. The founding of a local group of the Union to Fight Anti-Semitism (Verein zur Abwehr des Antisemitismus) had been controversial amongst the local Jews some of whom thought that this 'manufactured a danger which does not exist in a place where Jews and Christians live together quite happily'.²³ Beginning in March 1933, this trust placed by the Jews of Heilbronn in the democratic tradition of their home was to be completely, and bitterly, shattered.

1

'Liesel, it's time for you to leave.'
Departure

The boxes have been opened, the bundles freed from their strings and the letters arranged in chronological order. I write the story from the first letter down to the last; this seems the only sensible thing to do if I don't want to impose a different order or system on the collection. It means, though, that at some points we will encounter some people just floatingly (the first one is a case in point) and that gaps remain; this is the result of the order Liesel gave to the letters she received (and those she kept). On 10 May 1936, Liesel's 21st birthday, a postcard arrived from Els Hirsch in Frankfurt. She said: 'Prove yourself worthy of your new age; at 21 people expect a person who knows exactly what she wants and can stand on her own two feet. So then: to your health! And: become someone you are satisfied with!' These were friendly, if also rather demanding, wishes, and Liesel would not find it easy to fulfil them in the coming years. Perhaps she thought back to this postcard from time to time. The second letter in the collection was addressed to 'dear Miss Rosenthal' and was sent on 15 May 1936 from Herrlingen, near Ulm. Mrs Kati Hamburg asked if Liesel would be interested in a household position – 'it's independent work in which you would be responsible for keeping the house clean and tidy,' including looking after the children every now and then, for which she offered '15 RM [Reichsmark] + board.'

The third letter, too, with its illegible signature, creates the impression of a world which, if not ideal, is at least normal. The young woman, 'dear Miss Alice', had been on holiday in Zandvoort on the Dutch North Sea Coast and had got to know someone there. He – or more likely *she* – apologized for the Dutch weather in slightly uncertain German and lamented that they had not been able to meet up on the beach. The two had exchanged books, and the correspondent recommended Vicki Baum's *The Career of Doris Hart*[1], which she liked more than Marfa Coray's recently published novel *The Hesitant Heart* (*Das zögernde Herz*). She asked what Alice thought of the book and added: 'This curiosity is rather strange, as I know you [*Ihnen*] only superficially and don't understand why your opinion is so important to me.' Alice (Liesel) and books will be a running theme in this story.

The fourth letter, however, is somewhat different and requires closer attention. Handwritten in German, it was sent on 20 September 1936 from Jerusalem [in

Hebrew יְרוּשָׁלַיִם, Jerushalajim], addressed to 'dear Liesel' and signed 'best wishes from Heinz'. (David) Heinz Gumbel was a childhood friend who was born in 1906 in Sinsheim. In 1918 his family moved to Heilbronn and became the city's leading silversmiths. Heinz did an apprenticeship at the firm Bruckmann und Söhne and became a master steel engraver. In the 1920s he studied at the Berlin School of Arts and Crafts and he subsequently worked in Düsseldorf and Stockholm as well as in his parents' factory. There he manufactured both modern silverware and Jewish ritual objects like candlesticks or menorahs for Hanukkah, using a range of materials, including ivory, alongside silver. In 1936 Gumbel left Germany and after a spell in a workshop – which he will go on to describe in more detail below – began to work as a teacher and senior figure in the metalwork department of the Bezalel School in Jerusalem. He worked with Ludwig Yehuda Wolpert, under whose influence he began to use typography in his creations.[2] We will hear more from Heinz Gumbel but for now here is an excerpt from his letter, which brought news from a different world:

> *I have been sitting in my attic apartment for a few days and when I go to the window or go out the front door I have a view over Jerusalem at night, with its illuminated windows and deathly quiet streets (we have a "curfew"), beneath a deep, southern, starlit sky. I am still working on my apartment, but it now has a face, my face, and I am incredibly happy and proud to be the master of my own home. A living room, a kitchen, a bedroom, this is where I live, alone, at the highest point in the city (and don't forget, that means in the centre of the new Jewish Jerusalem).*

This was an act heavy in symbolism: someone building a home for himself and telling people about it. But who was he telling? People at home? Even if his apartment were 'more like a monk's cell' despite the pictures on the walls, the work gave this German Jew scope to undertake what was in these new circumstances a difficult process of integration, 'Einordnung' as the Zionist shibboleth ran. He assumed that Liesel had already heard of his work 'from my parents, or from Victor's': 'After just a few days I joined Mrs Roth's [Emmy] workshop. She is the boss, and as she spends practically the whole day doing sales I run the workshop and you could say that I am the master.' He wrote that the political situation was not favourable for his industry, but he remained positive and intended to keep his job for as long as he can, and 'afterwards I'll find something else'.

> *I am happy that I have come here, although large parts of the Yishuv are still strange to me and I find it difficult to relate to Eastern Jews or Middle Eastern workers. The path to understanding is through language. It is not enough to simply be able to talk about everyday things – only when you truly understand the language, its nuances and its sounds, can you make yourself understood at a human level. My most immediate priority is to learn Hebrew. There are new courses beginning in October which I will sign up for. The skills I brought with me from Germany have been of great benefit to me and I would advise anybody thinking of moving here to*

learn as much Hebrew as possible beforehand. You won't get very far with German, unfortunately, as you will be restricting yourself to German-Jewish groups. […]

I feel quite at home here in Jerusalem. Of course, that is largely because I immediately found a circle of old acquaintances and friends, but there are other, deeper reasons too. Despite everything that happens here, despite the terror, the tensions and unfamiliar administration, I feel that we belong here. In Europe Jews must produce arguments to defend their right to exist: "We have the right to live here too, even though we're different, we are people too", etc.

This defensive attitude we drag around with us has completely disappeared here. The Arab attacks don't affect us too much. "We are here and we belong here. We have our big problems, but they are a matter purely for ourselves" is our internal logic. Of course this is not always a conscious attitude, most people don't think about it at all, but this logic explains our completely different reaction to anti-Jewish terror, as we were used to in non-Jewish countries. We stay at our posts. We go to work, even when it's dangerous […], without being scared and without making a fuss.

There are of course many people here who feel desperately unhappy and dream day and night of a return to beautiful, noble, cultured Europe, and many of their reasons make a lot of sense. The Yishuv here lacks organization, tradition and culture, there's so much improvisation, bluff and making-do, but it's a start, and in the end it's our people, with all our strengths and weaknesses. No-one can choose their own destiny, and we have to make of it what we can. […] If you earn money without being part of this greater project you will not be happy. But if you do feel part of it you will, despite everything, feel that your life has a purpose. […] For Rosh Hashanah [Hebrew again] I went to a Hasidic and a Yemenite synagogue – the difference between the Hasidic (Polish) Jews and the Yemenites is enormous.

He found the Yemenites particularly impressive:

Their street salesmen and craftsmen looked like princes. It sounds clichéd and corny, like in [the Heinrich Heine poem] "Prinzessin Sabbat", but they do. The men have remarkably lithe bodies and their services, though without the "order" we are familiar with, are full of reverence and awe. It was beautiful to witness and I will go there again at Yom Kippur.

A Yemenite service, a life in danger, an all-encompassing learning process, a way of speaking which contains both religious and Jewish-national keywords – for everyone interested in the lives of Jews who emigrated from Germany and Central Europe to the British Mandate of Palestine, this letter is extraordinarily rich source material.

How did the recipient of these letters react to all this news? What did Liesel – Miss Alice Rosenthal – know about Zionism? Had she learnt Hebrew too and attended services according to the German 'order'? Had she perhaps considered travelling to

Figure 2 Liesel Rosenthal, *c.* 1937 © Baroness Julia Neuberger, Private Collection

Palestine to 'earn money' or for any other reason? Sadly, no letters from her to Heinz remain. This is, in fact, true for the whole of this collection of letters, so we must construct an image of Liesel from the letters she received and kept. She was, however, trusted by her friend Heinz, who shared his experiences with her.[3] Liesel was still in Germany when this letter was written, but she was by then seriously considering emigration herself. It is impossible to reconstruct the stages of her departure from Germany using just the letters. In the interview with the National Life Story collection project (a typescript of thirty-seven pages) she introduces herself:

> My name is Alice Schwab, usually known as Liesel. I was born on the 10th of May, 1915 in Heilbronn-am-Neckar which is in South Germany. My father was Ludwig Rosenthal; my mother was Hermine Rosenthal, née Rothschild, from Cannstadt [Cannstatt] near Stuttgart. There were many Rosenthals in our town; my father was a wine merchant, as was his eldest brother and his father's youngest brother. So there were three firms of Rosenthal wine merchants in the town. My father bought wine from the vineyards, mostly in Wurtemberg [Württemberg] and Baden. It was then stored in our cellars in the Götzenturmstrasse before being sold to restaurants, hotels and pubs all over the area.

From England, and informed by her English experiences, Liesel looked back at her former life in Germany. She remembered her grandmother, her father's mother, Babette (Betty) Rosenthal, who played an important role in her life; reading between the lines, her role was perhaps even more important, or more formative, than that of Liesel's mother and father. Liesel spent her holidays with her grandparents in Cannstatt, which also gave her occasional escape from Heilbronn.

She says that they led 'a wonderful and comfortable life' in the Stauffenbergstraße[4] in a city of around 60,000 inhabitants. Her best friend was the daughter of a brewer (we will encounter her in letters at the very end of this book), and many of the children with whom she went to nursery and primary school came from poor families who had suffered from the deprivations of the First World War, inflation and the high unemployment of the 1920s. She wrote that 'there was a lot of hardship among them'.

Liesel's mother was a granddaughter of Dr Moses Engelbert:

> Engelbert, Dr Moses (b. 1830 Gudensberg, Schwalm-Eder district, d. 1891 Heilbronn): initially religious teacher and preacher in various places, 1860 rabbi in Kolberg (today: Kolobrzeg, Poland), 1862–1864 rabbi in Lehrensteinsfeld, thereafter moved rabbinate to Heilbronn, where he was rabbi 1864–1889/91.[5]

Thus reads the entry in the register of rabbis in Jewish communities in what is now the state of Baden-Württemberg. An obituary appeared in the *Allgemeine Zeitung des Judentums* on 29 January 1891:

> Heilbronn, 18 January. Yesterday the highly-respected rabbi Dr Moses Engelbert passed away at the age of 60 after much suffering. He was born in Gutenberg, near Kassel, and was previously rabbi in Kolberg, Waren and since 1863 in our own district. He had suffered for many years, and Dr B. Einstein from Ulm acted as his spiritual comforter. May his memory be a blessing, both here and throughout our community.

Figure 3 Rabbi Dr Moses Engelbert © Baroness Julia Neuberger, Private Collection

Hermine and Ludwig Rosenthal married in 1914 and two years later Ludwig was conscripted. In 1920 he returned to Heilbronn after spending two years as a prisoner of war in Marseille. Julia Neuberger remembers that he often spoke of his time as a prisoner: 'he also made friends for life in the camp'.

It must have been difficult for him to readjust after such a long time: 'suddenly you find that you have a wife whom you haven't seen for four years and a child you hardly knew', as Alice Schwab says in her 'memoirs'. Ludwig Rosenthal concentrated

Figure 4 Hermine Rothschild before her marriage to Ludwig Rosenthal

on his work, difficult as a result of inflation, although it was made somewhat easier by knowing his winemakers and many of his customers personally. On 14 November 1924 Liesel's brother Helmut was born at home, 12 Staufenbergstraße.

After this look back at her family history, Alice Schwab speaks about herself and the political situation, which saw the Nazis in power in a city traditionally social democratic and liberal in nature:

> I left school in thirty-two and wanted to become an artist. There was an art college in Stuttgart and I already had a cousin who had studied there. I had intended to enroll there, but things were difficult at home because my father's business was not doing very well, as a result of the boycott started by the Nazis. So it was decided that I should not go to art school, but should train as a book-seller instead. I joined the firm of Dr Determann who dealt in antique and modern books, and I learnt a great deal there.

Dr Julius Determann taught her Latin and introduced her to the business of antiquarian books. However, he also sold anti-Semitic publications and was angry that he was not allowed to sell Hitler's *Mein Kampf* (this could only be sold at the Nazi-run kiosks); 'everybody was selling it and he was losing the trade'. This made things 'uncomfortable' in the bookshop. In 1934 Liesel passed her exam to become a bookseller, but she then decided to learn another trade, 'something which would stand me in good stead in later life'. She enrolled in a cooking school and became active in various Jewish youth groups. After a short time at an art gallery in Mannheim – 'which was a lovely gallery with books, pictures, sculptures and so on' – she returned to bookselling at the Strauss'schen bookshop in Frankfurt. It was run by Leopold Lichtenstern, 'who now lives near me in London'. He sold *fine literature*, and here was where the educated Jewish public bought their books. 'If a new book by Thomas Mann appeared, we would order five hundred copies at a go.'

In better circumstances this would have been the ideal place for Liesel. She lived with the Fink family: he was a psychoanalyst, while she, Lotte, was a doctor and a niece of celebrated publisher Samuel Fischer.[6] But Ludwig Rosenthal's business back home was beginning to struggle. Word reached Liesel that arrests were being made, and like many young people in her situation she became increasingly interested in 'the Jewish world'. She attended lectures by Martin Buber ('which gave me a lot of comfort') and met friends of the Finks, whose son had decided to emigrate to Birmingham in England, where the Newth family would take him in. They advised her to get out of Germany: 'Liesel, it's time for you to leave.' She discussed her options with her parents. Even in Heilbronn it was 'no longer possible to feel at ease', as many people she knew had been sent to concentration camps and others had left for America 'or wherever they could'.[7] Many young people became aware of their own Jewishness and joined a *Hakhshara* (an agricultural or technical training school) to prepare themselves for emigration to Palestine. Even the world of literature, hitherto a safe haven, became increasingly hostile to the Jews. The Gestapo seized books by Freud, Heinrich Mann and other authors who were either left wing or had emigrated: this represented about a third of the Strauss'schen book-shop's trade. 'It was a good thing that I had found somewhere to go, just at the right time. I discussed it all with my parents and, seeing how difficult life had become in all ways, I left Germany on the 17th May 1937.'

Liesel travelled back home and bade farewell to her friends, relatives and, most importantly, her grandmother. Her father Ludwig accompanied her on the train to Heidelberg and she stopped off in Cologne to say 'goodbye' to the cathedral. 'Then I embarked for Dover.' The coronation of George VI made it difficult to arrange her passage to England. The perspective from which she wrote this was already an

English one; the life she now began formed the framework for how she looked back at Heilbronn. In Germany matters were becoming more and more complicated. Gregor Sprißler (about whom I have not been able to find more information) wrote from Nuremberg on 3 May 1937 that he was in negotiations with Leopold Lichtenstern and that he was confident 'that I will take over his company in the near future'. He asked if Liesel would be prepared to return to Germany and spend the next three months working in the bookshop again, 'provided that it is approved by the authorities, of course'. She turned down the offer. Instead, with the help of friends of the Finks, she had made contact with a family in Birmingham. On 6 May 1937 Patrick Dobbs (208 Corisande Road, southwest Birmingham) wrote:

> *Dear Miss Rosenthal, I believe Mrs Newth has already written to tell you that my wife and I would be very glad to offer you hospitality whilst you are in England in return for you giving us some assistance with the children and general housework. If you care to accept this invitation I can assure you you will be most welcome and that we shall do all we can to make you feel at home.*

This invitation opened the way for Liesel's emigration to Britain through the domestic service route. Jennifer Craig-Norton in Southampton has been researching what she terms 'he untold stories of the Jewish women who became domestic servants in Britain to escape the Nazis'.[8]

The Dobbs family[9] had four children, three girls who were at school and an eighteen-month-old baby boy, and they lived 'in the outskirts of Birmingham'. Patrick Dobbs gave Liesel tips for the journey, repeating them in a letter on 10 May after he received her reply that she would indeed be coming. The day she planned to travel was a Bank Holiday so there would be many people travelling on the trains, 'but I don't think you're likely to have any trouble'.[10] Shortly before her departure another letter arrived from Heinz in Jerusalem, who offered belated birthday congratulations (she turned twenty-two on 10 May). He had 'the feeling that some kind of change has got into you', and she had clearly told him about her plans:

> *If you can find a good job in England, go for it! I certainly wouldn't advise you against going to Palestine. I very much enjoy living here and everyone who joins our community is a gain for our country. But since you want to continue working in your profession, and given that it's your only qualification, your chances here aren't great at the moment. […] The odds of you finding a job in a bookshop under the current circumstances are about 100 to 1.*

Heinz waxed lyrical about the wonderful view you get from Mount Scopus over the city and its surrounding countryside, all the way to the Dead Sea, and asked her to write to him, 'particularly if any of your projects come to fruition'.

Time to pause and consider the many questions arising from these first letters and memories. First, the city of Heilbronn. What do we know about the city of Heinrich von Kleist's 'Käthchen von Heilbronn' (apart from the fact that there was never a real 'Katie'[11])? What do we know about its Jewish community? Certainly it was in Heilbronn

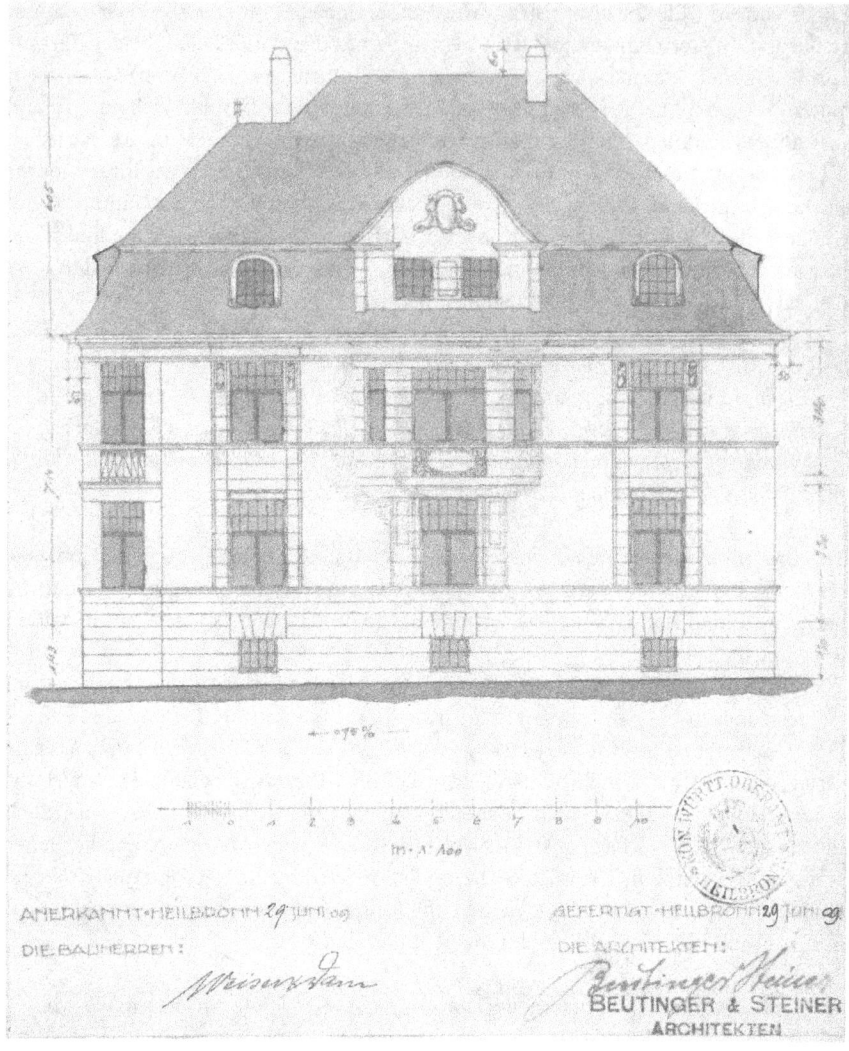

Figure 5 The house on Staufenbergstraße 12, building plan from 1909 © Stadtarchiv Heilbronn, Archivalien, A034-3685, Bauakte

that in 1963, much earlier than in other German cities, a large-scale study was carried out called *History and Destiny of the Jews of Heilbronn*, published by journalist Hans Franke. Unusually, and to his credit, he focused more on the Nazi era than on the city's proud mediaeval Jewish history. Another question concerns the local wine trade. What was the relationship between Jewish wine merchants and the Swabian, Christian winegrowers? Were they a community or in competition with each other? Do locals have memories of this former collaboration? Members of the Rosenthal family and other Heilbronners can be found all over the world. Is it possible to reconstruct their story, their cultural position in the transition period from the Weimar Republic to the Third Reich, as family members and acquaintances gradually settled in various far-flung corners of the globe? Their friends and neighbours play an important role. What happened to them?

And there is Liesel. A young woman who grew up in this family and in this community, who, as these first letters have already shown, had her own 'projects' and her own mind. She was interested in art and literature and was looking to expand her horizons. Under the increasing Nazi terror she felt forced to examine her own Jewishness. She planned her emigration independently of her parents and asked her friends for potential destinations. Who were these friends? Why did Heinz Gumbel emigrate to Jerusalem and did she really consider following him? How would her English life develop in the coming years? And how could she even try to help her parents and her little brother Helmut to escape from Germany in the same way she did?

Through the contacts she made in Frankfurt with Lichtenstern, the Finks and their friends, England became an option. She had contacts from Heilbronn too. On 4 January 1937 Hans Schloss (26 Spring Road, Edgbaston, Birmingham) thanked her in English 'for the trouble you have gone to help me'. I have been able to find out little about Hans Schloss – one of many gaps which make this reconstruction of Liesel and her family's life, and of her journey to Birmingham (and later London), significantly harder. On 18 May 1937 her mother Hermine wrote the first of many, many postcards to her daughter in England, beginning in English but switching between English and German (in italics):

> My dear child!
> Hope that you had a good journey! I think the whole [time] on you and therefore I write you at once with this post. Father is today in Stuttgart and Heller speaks today often from his sister. Many aquain have called on today and (said) told me that they would given you a present, so Mrs Eugen Kirchheimer & Mrs Metzger. Lise Victor has also phoned on yesterday evening. *Now in German, I had worried so much about you, dear Liesel, whether your journey had gone well, whether you had left anything behind, and above all I was scared that your paper bag had split and that forgot to give you the cognac. So tell me about it in detail as soon as possible.* […] Many regards to Mr and Mrs Dobbs & you, many kisses, your truly mother, father and brother. *Dear Liesel, take my advice to heart!*

This is a fascinating document, and not just for linguists. Liesel's mother, a Jewish housewife from Swabia, was forty-five years old. She was learning English and her writing was uncertain, possibly done with the help of a dictionary. This was perhaps a sign that she had accepted her daughter's decision, although she still felt the need to express her worries, fears and admonishments in German. Liesel received the postcard in Birmingham, where a further letter from 21 May arrived, signed 'Your F'. She must have known him well – presumably it is a man – as he gave his own advice along with a request to 'do him proud' in her new surroundings. 'Don't be dim-witted, forgetful, sloppy, obstinate, inattentive, silly or selfish. Instead, be watchful, sensible and considerate of how lucky you have been, etc. etc.' He added two more things: 'hopefully the business with L is done and dusted' and 'a tender press on the most beautiful part of you'. A friend, a lover?

As I am attempting to depict the process of my research as much as the results (and the questions it throws up), I am obliged to consider my role in interpreting such passages. In a different case, Julia Neuberger answered my question with the nice little aside 'I guess he was just another of my mother's lovers' and assured me that I could write about these affairs and lovers; after all, none of them are alive now, so no-one could feel offended. This goes for Leopold Lichtenstern, the bookseller, too, to whom 'the business with L' probably refers. My discomfort is based on the fact that some of the lovers this young woman of twenty-two had had were using a tone similar to her mother's. We will encounter an extreme example of this later. What did she make of this, at the start of her new life?

Her mother wrote another, longer, letter on 25 May (with the additional question 'Did you receive my postcard?'). She knew that Liesel had arrived, but wanted to know more. Who was at the station in Frankfurt? Who was with her on the train? Who was on the train with her in London? How was her work going and how was the family? She was aware that Liesel was still unfamiliar with many English words and corrected her: 'Charwoman is their word for Putzfrau.' She wrote that Helmut was learning English from her as it was cheaper than having classes with Miss Kraft. She talked a lot about him, and clearly by then they were planning to send him to America. 'Dear Liesel, I am so terribly anxious that I am sending him so far away as I don't know where he will end up or if we will ever see him again. I can't sleep any more, but I know of no other way, as he has to get out.' The boy was kind, understanding and considerate, 'but Am[erica] is so vast and I won't know where he's going until just before he leaves'. Liesel had sent books from Frankfurt – 'You have so many modern books, should I open a lending library?' – and left behind washing which her mother now had to sort out. Ludwig was away and relatives were complaining that they hadn't heard anything.

Hermine Rosenthal was trying to create some semblance of order out of the chaos. She demanded regular, ideally weekly, reports from her daughter and was looking for ways to preserve at least some of the old family order. 'Do you have a prayer book? Have you given Walter B. his things?'[12] Ludwig, too, asked after Liesel's wellbeing on 1 June and emphasized that it was out of the question to send her money more often, 'as your food and accommodation are free'. If she 'scrimped and saved' she would manage just fine. His letter was included alongside her mother's, which thanked Liesel for a 'detailed' report but which also did not fail to repeat the question 'Have you got a prayer book now or do you think it is not necessary? D. Liesel, this is a pressing matter, as it is through prayer that you find your inner peace & you can also be thankful.'

She found her daughter's emerging independence unnerving. 'I am truly astounded that you already want to travel to London, you have only just arrived in Birmingham. You scarcely have enough time with your work permit. This is unnecessary spending when you should now be saving and saving some more.' Somewhat euphemistically she refers to personal matters. 'Dear Liesel, you could perh. find more happiness if you dressed modestly and didn't make yourself so well known among the men. We only mean well and we would be very happy if you could say you were spoken for.'

She should have nothing to do with 'the men', but ideally she should have something to do with one man, whoever he might be. Could a young woman discuss such things with her mother? Perhaps she could with a friend, and she had one in Hilde – her surname is unknown, possibly she was a colleague from the bookshop – who wrote from Frankfurt on 2 June. She talked about her own love life, but also seemed to know Liesel's very well, saying: 'It must be a load off your mind that the F.W. business has sorted itself out, or are you very sad about it???' But admonishment came from her side too, and the following excerpt is worth quoting as it reveals something about Liesel's personality:

You mustn't go on like this and let your depressive nature take hold. Be happy that you have found something, even if it isn't the most ideal of circumstances. You have already got used to the instability & you seem to be involved with decent people & relatively nice children. At the moment the most important thing is that you learn to speak English properly. [...] And your homesickness will disappear the moment you meet a nice man; he won't just drop from the sky! Be patient!! Are you at least being treated decently and not being exploited? After all, Englishmen are well known for being particularly bad in that regard. [...] A residence permit can definitely be extended; don't get so worked up about it. [...] You'll find your way back to bookselling.

We can picture the scene: Liesel was living in Birmingham with the Dobbs family, her daily work was done, the relatively nice children were asleep and she had time to read these letters.[13] Be patient! Don't get so worked up about it! Do this and not that! What did she do in response to these commands? (And why did she keep these letters?) Lotte Fink wrote on 8 June from Frankfurt to Liesel, her 'absent foster daughter': 'I hope by now you have become the model domestic servant, which shouldn't be such a huge change for you given how wonderfully ordered everything is over there. Have you registered? Got your work permit? You know I always think practically, so make sure you get all the necessary things done.' Liesel's 'Vice-Mama and benefactor' meant well.

More agreeable post came from New York in a letter sent by Kurt Jeselson on 16 June 1937. It introduces a new theme: the transnational connections between Jewish emigrants from Germany. When we read Liesel's story as an individual one, the knowledge of the fate of hundreds of thousands of others remains in the background, and these were people who had similar – or indeed very different – tales to tell.

In January 1936 Artur Prinz published an article called 'Conditions of the Jewish Emigration Debate' in *Der Morgen* magazine. Prinz, a leading member of the *Hilfsverein der Deutschen Juden* and publisher of the *Jewish Emigration* bulletin, discussed the existential crisis of the *little people*[14] looking to find a new home somewhere else. He wrote that since April 1933 thoughts of emigration had entered even those families who felt deeply bound to Germany, and it became a topic of discussion within the increasingly marginalized Jewish community. By the end of 1935 around 100,000 people had already left Germany despite its restrictive foreign exchange laws and the difficulties imposed by the immigration laws in other countries.

> *At most, barely a third of these 100,000 emigrants are still to be found in Europe today; another third live in Palestine and at least a third are in countries beyond the seas. As far as is known, Jewish emigration has spread to around 40 countries. These 100,000 people are, however, most likely just the vanguard of further large-scale emigration.*[15]

Author Hans Sahl was forced to leave Berlin in 1933. In his memoirs looking back at that moment, he provided a vivid depiction of what awaited the members of the Rosenthal family who had remained in Heilbronn:

> *I returned to the Romanisches Café, where those who the wind had "blown in" sat, wondering how they were still sitting there, reading newspapers and playing chess. They sat, their poses ones of frozen beings, waiting to be blown away, to be taken away. It was as if they had lost their identity and were awaiting a new one which would save their lives. Some were leafing through railway timetables, others were poring over maps, others were writing letters to a relative who had emigrated to America and made a success of it. The lucky ones were those who had an uncle in Amsterdam, or a nephew in Shanghai, or a cousin in Valparaiso. I had no relatives abroad. My family had stayed in the country and were trying to make the best of it.*[16]

In many cases the members of a family or circle of friends began their emigration journeys separately, and those journeys often went in very different directions. The emigrants were forced to reconnect with each other through laborious, unfamiliar forms of transnational communication. How did they communicate with one another? What experiences have they detailed in their letters? What kind of network were they forced to build up? How did their various experiences – of both the journey and living in such different places[17] – affect family relations? What impact on self-perception and identity, on language and religious orientation, on hopes and disappointments did these experiences have? Did the members of family ever meet again? In many instances individual descendants have gone to great lengths to piece together the various separated threads of their family history, but there is as yet no international archive to collect such private documents and make them available for research.[18]

This is another reason why the discovery of all these letters to Liesel Rosenthal represents such a stroke of luck for a researcher of the history of this post–1933 German-Jewish emigration. There are, however, research problems here as well.[19] I have been able to find out little about Kurt Jeselson, who wrote to Liesel: 'When I read your letter I could scarcely believe how brave you are being in travelling to Great Britain.' Then he discussed the topic of language and her ability to create a new home for herself; for his part he felt completely at home in this new, captivating language, some of which he used in the following excerpt:

I hope you have settled in well and that you like it there. The English Gentlemen are indeed rather dull, but they are good sports and you should not be bashful. It can only be an advantage that you are learning the language in England and perhaps from there it is easier to travel here than from G. Nonetheless it is still [un?]necessary that you have a relative there who will vouch for you, but I can't imagine anyone without one. You definitely haven't dug deep enough [...] I am not surprised that you have made so many acquaintances in Erez, but the fact that emigration away from there has already begun will soon reduce the number of your (and my) acquaintance[s] considerably. It is sad, but true, and it confirms what the sceptics were saying 4 years ago. Only out in the countryside do people feel a connection with the soil. The towns are not Palestine (or rather – not Erez), but Europe – or perhaps that should be America. [...] I only hope you will write me soon about your new environment and experiences with England and the boys. If you want, we can switch for the exercise's sake into English. At least part of our correspondence. I myself feel perfectly at home in this new and gorgeous language.[20]

This was a private letter in which he also wished her a belated happy birthday. But at that time political matters penetrated deep into the private sphere. The atmosphere within the Jewish community in Palestine ('in Eretz', the land of Israel) was economically tense too, so this was not just abstract news for Liesel. Rather, it played a big role in her deliberations as to whether she should move there or to New York. Heinz was in Jerusalem, Kurt in New York, and both represented a small part of the network of communication and information she had built up, for herself but above all for her parents and brother. Heilbronn made sure that she did not forget that:

My d. Liesel, your letter finally arrived. It was so short it can't have been worth the postage, it would have fitted on a postcard. But we enjoyed reading what you wrote, and we saw that things are going well for you & that you like it there. Always be thankful for everything. You will have to work wherever you end up, even your mother works from morn until night. D. grandmother and Aunt Berta have been with us since Sunday [...], I have rearranged the living room. Gretele from Zürich got engaged on Sunday in Berne, she'll write to me soon to tell me more about it. A wonderful silver brooch arrived today from Mrs Gumbel, probab. Heinz's birthday present [for Liesel]. [...] Cecilie Wolf, Fritzle's mother, died of a heart attack on the ship back from Palestine. They were at Fritz's wedding. [...] I must learn English so that I can speak with you, when I will visit you. Yours truly, Mother.

Back in Württemberg, Liesel's mother was also living in an ever-changing network of relationships. Emigration to England, or indeed anywhere, seemed not to be an option for her, and instead she was gathering her own family around her, now without Liesel. Relatives were living together in their flat in Heilbronn, and many of their friends' children had already gone abroad. One name in the letter stands out: 'Fritzle' was Fritz Wolf. As mentioned in the introduction, I met him in the city of Nahariya, in the north of Israel, not far from the Lebanese border. Together with a colleague and a friend of Wolf I visited him in 2000 in the small house in which he had lived since emigrating, where we wanted to examine the manuscripts of this poet, whose works had gone almost entirely unpublished and who had earned what little money he had working for the local postal service. I well remember how disappointed he was that his autobiographical stories were of greater interest to us than his literary works. He spoke with the accent of his and my home city, even after more than sixty years. Of his rich body of work it is the musical *Nahariyade* which has been best remembered. Premiered in 1942, it was a musical comedy about the development of the cities and lives of the German-speaking Jews ('Yekkes') in what was then Palestine.[21] There are also two volumes of remembrances published by his former home city in 1986 and 1993, one of which he presented to me with the thought-provoking dedication 'Best wishes – from Heilbronn? From Nahariya?'.[22] In the City Archives I have found many letters to and from Fritz Wolf, which will be discussed towards the end of this book. He is one of the figures whose name crops up again and again in the piles of letters, an integral part of this transnational network Liesel created around herself.

Amsterdam is another important reference point. Hermine's sister, Luise Loeb née Rosenthal, lived there with her husband Richard, whilst Leopold Lichtenstern's family spent the initial period after emigration in the city and would return there after their years in Westerbork and Theresienstadt. Liesel Victor, a family friend, wrote 'Amsterdam' over 'Heilbronn, Bismarckstraße 27' on the letter paper belonging to her husband Otto (Ottl) when she told Liesel of their family's plans on 24 June 1937:

> Ottl landed here unscathed at the start of June and I travelled here with [daughter] Gaga to meet him, as I didn't want him to go back to G, that would be completely unnecessary. You never know what can happen, in any case I definitely prefer it this way. […] Over the past few days Ottl has been doing lots of negotiating and now it will probably work out in South Africa. If it does work out, as we hope it will, Ottl will become the manager of a large English firm which has branches all over the world. The owner wants Ottl to take over the technical side of things there and to oversee the fur sorting in Cape Town, Durban, East London and Johannesburg. […] Ottl deserves this bit of luck – though it could of course very quickly come to an end. […]

> As for you, I am sure that things aren't easy for you, but I nonetheless advise you to hold out and not to return to your fatherland, beautiful as it may seem. We hear so many silly things, and I don't imagine that living in England your love for this beautiful country will grow much – I heard today that in the "Basel" and Dutch newspapers they were saying that Aryan doctors aren't allowed to treat Jew. patients. If this is true, which I do not doubt, you can see how it's time to move on – you will already have heard the news that Aunt Cecilie died on the way back from Palestine of a heart attack (on the ship), and that Paul Scheuer's mother has finally died, after a horribly long period of suffering. This is the sad news, unfortunately there is nothing happy to report.

There were other members of their family in Amsterdam: 'Eugen Victors', who were doing well for themselves financially, as well as Trude and Max Victor, who were soon to follow Maxen's parents to the United States. Like Zürich, Paris and Prague, Amsterdam was one of the first focal points of the exile, still within Europe, where those remained who still believed that the Nazi dictatorship would fall and that they would soon be able to return to Germany.[23] The letter illustrates how they came to lose this belief, and with its reference to South Africa it is an example of how those going into exile had to develop a whole new image of the world – a new 'geographical imagination', as Derek Gregory put it.[24] If at first they pored over railway timetables for trains to the capital cities of neighbouring countries, now they were investigating how to travel to distant countries by ship. The challenge was made doubly difficult as they were simultaneously working in two different directions: as can be seen in the letter, in addition to planning a way out they were attempting to get, and pass on, news from their own circle of friends and family. Germany, however, was never far from the thoughts of those who were already 'out'.

'Inside', in 'G', the world was getting smaller. Jacob Boas showed in his article 'The Shrinking World of German Jewry' how, post-1933, German Jews' freedom was increasingly restricted in the towns and cities they still called home, not just by Nazi laws and measures but also by changing attitudes amongst their non-Jewish neighbours.[25] In her letters, Liesel's mother showed how this played out in everyday life in Heilbronn:

> *Otherwise I don't know what to tell you, I don't get out of the house much now. Dr Gumbel has sold his villa for a pittance and is moving to Stuttg. The Scheuers are moving to Erez in the coming weeks, and last week we had a big farewell do as Eisen-Dreifus is moving to Stuttg. & so many are going away, […] Aunt Sofie Kahn has already left to go to her children in America, first she's going to Königstein im Taunus for 14 days & going on from there.*

Dr Siegfried Gumbel, whose move away to Stuttgart was mentioned here, was a key figure in the Jewish community in Württemberg in the years before and after 1933. A lawyer who specialized in civil litigations, for many years he was chairman of the Heilbronn lawyers' society, presided over the local chapter of the Central Association of German Citizens of Jewish Faith and was also a leading figure in the German Democratic Party. 'In dozens of assemblies of all kinds,' wrote Hans Franke, 'Dr Gumbel fought for the democratic cause and proved himself a devotee of pacifism and humanity.'[26] On 5 August 1932 he succeeded Dr Ludwig Heuss in the Heilbronn district council.

> *As the Nazi party already had members in the town hall at this time, there were unedifying scenes at his swearing-in ceremony. The three Nazi party members left the assembly room and subsequently gave an anti-Semitic explanation, upon which Mayor Beutinger rebuked them with a call to order. […] On 16 March 1933 there were shameful scenes at a sitting of the town council when the Nazi party formally called for the council to be reappointed following the election results of 5 March 1933, demanding as points 5 and 6 that "the Jew Max Rosengart" have his freedom of the city revoked and that "the Jewish councillor Gumbel be stripped of his mandate with immediate effect".*[27]

Figure 6 Siegfried Gumbel visiting his son Erich in Jerusalem © Stadtarchiv Heilbronn, Fotosammlung, private photographer

Gumbel resigned shortly afterwards, and in 1935 the Reich Citizenship Law took away his right to practise as a lawyer. Hans Franke wrote that, in his activities with the Israelite Council in Stuttgart, 'he made sure that emigration became the basic principle behind all its decisions'. Gumbel also told Dr Julius Hirsch, head of the council, of his conviction that 'over the course of the coming years the situation of the Jews in Germany will become intolerable'.[28]

After the pogrom of 1938 Gumbel was taken to Welzheim concentration camp. After his release he returned to work for the Israelite Council and the 'Welfare Office', until he was arrested again in autumn 1941 and taken to Dachau, where he was murdered on 27 January 1942. His speech on the occasion of the 50th anniversary of the consecration of the Heilbronn Synagogue in 1927 is testament to his importance within the community:

> *That was the feeling in 1877 [...] In our circles we were convinced that the time was finally at an end when the Jew was abused and treated as if he had no rights, or was less worthy. It was written in the constitution that the rights of the citizen were not dependent on his faith, and we were confident that the equality founded in law, which no administration had hitherto granted us, would gradually establish itself. We lived in hope that the prejudices which still existed against us would slowly disappear and that the social disadvantages we suffered would no longer hold. But not all our dreams have been realised. Ice and thunder have poisoned the atmosphere, and we*

have had to fight hard to defend our rights and our worth. [...] It is an awful destiny to be the scapegoat for the guilt of others. It is a terrible fate to be the victim of racial darkness and madness.[29]

This bleak foretelling was to prove accurate, as we can see from the details of the Rosenthal family's letters. On the one hand Nazi laws forcibly limited the freedoms of Germany's Jews. But it was not just that: the neighbourhood they knew, its streets, its shops, its places of entertainment like theatres and cinemas, became threatening spaces they preferred to avoid. And many friends were going 'away', including Hermine and Ludwig's own daughter. As much as possible they tried to preserve a sense of normality – they sent parcels of chocolate to the Dobbs children as well as a skirt for Liesel's 'summer holiday'. But the tone in Hermine's (and sometimes Ludwig's) letters was becoming noticeably more urgent, as a pair of letters from 2 July 1937 makes clear:

> So I have again written a letter to you without receiving an answer. [...] We are extremely agitated, as it must be 10 days now since we last heard from you. Hopefully you are well. Uncle Sigmund celebrated his 85th birthday on Thursday. Aunt Therese was there too, and she complained that you haven't written to her.

When a letter did arrive from Liesel its receipt was confirmed, but with an added 'we had waited a long time to hear from you'. Slowly, the relationship between parents and child was changing.[30] The difficult circumstances contributed to the undermining of the father's absolute authority. 'Papa can't travel, everything is much more difficult', reported Liesel's mother on 15 July in a postcard. He was staying at home and could do nothing, whilst Hermine was very busy, mostly with dealing with relatives, but she was still worried that her child would go off the rails. On 7 July, for the first time, she made her feelings clear on a topic which would dominate – and overshadow – Liesel's correspondence for the next few years:

> Now for some big news. Hannele Meyer has got engaged to Dr jur. Sternfeld, who is always writing for C.V. Newspapers. A fine, intelligent man from Berlin, he is right now travelling to San Francisco & Hanne will follow him there & get married. Mäxle is going there in a couple of weeks too. Hanne is a very beautiful girl & they are the perfect couple. So things in England are up in the air. Dear Liesel, I would much prefer it if you didn't have so many male friends, but had just one who you would marry. A girl with that many suitors won't get married. [...] All 3 Scheuers are leaving today.

The plan to send Helmut to America had come to nothing. So Hermine asked Liesel – 'You with all your connections' – to speak to the Dobbs and ask if there was another (Quaker) family who could perhaps take the boy in. 'There's certainly no rush & I'm happy for him to stay here for a year or more, but it's worth looking around as early as possible.' Liesel had probably told her not just about her 'many male friends' – for her a sign that she had truly arrived, for her mother a worrying development – but also that she would rather live in London and work in a bookshop. 'Dear Liesel, I strongly advise you, under no circumstances should you think about your bookselling again. Stay where you are & be thankful & work cheerfully.' She did not take Liesel's complaint that her life was 'merely doing the washing up' seriously. 'But you have so much variety.'[31] She told Liesel to be 'a fine, decent girl' towards Hans (probably the aforementioned Hans Schloss), who she clearly had in mind as a potential husband. 'Is he still with someone else or do you have a chance?'

What Hermine didn't know, 'Vice-Mama' Lotte Fink probably did: in Frankfurt Liesel had had a relationship with Leopold Lichtenstern, a married man. In a postcard on 26 July Mrs Fink demanded that the 'girl' end it:

Dear stepdaughter. I believe full honesty is the best medicine. End it <u>now</u>. Like all married men he is […] a fraudster. He would never get into material need for you – everything is already rosy for him. He is going <u>with</u> his family to [?]. The place the family has arranged is perfect. He still feigns a little sadness. She is happy, as father, mother and child are now truly together, and all mistresses will be forgotten and buried – perhaps underneath a tasteful flowerbed. C'est la vie. And now please put an end to these silly affairs once and for all. […] <u>Under no circumstances are you to meet him again</u>.

In Heilbronn Helmut had 'a hideous amount of schoolwork', was preparing for his Bar Mitzvah and was 'very grown-up', meaning that he was another child who would soon be going his own way, and that he presented another problem to be solved. Ludwig had had his last remaining teeth pulled out, and it is probably not an exaggeration to see this (or at least the mention of it) as symbolic of his increasing loss of authority; it meant Hermine had to be even more resilient. More relatives were coming to visit and Aunt Berta (Ludwig's sister) had also hired a 'young woman', who was 'so strictly religious that the whole household has to adapt'. Willy and Irma Rosenthal (for some reason their surname was crossed out on the letter from 6 August in thick pen) were going to America, with their own business and a house which was already furnished. Hermine's comment – 'how happy we would be if we could be so lucky!' – was the first time she had spoken of the possibility of her own emigration.

Luise and Richard Loeb wrote on 8 August 1937 from Amsterdam: 'Dear Liesel, do you have to cook as well, and what does it taste like? South German or English?' According to Luise, both had 'settled in nicely', with the children and an uncle nearby, and Uncle Richard was 'enjoying his private life'. The flat was lovely, 'more homely than the one in Stuttgart', and there was even a bathtub, 'and as I have never had it so good I am enjoying these luxuries to my heart's content!' She also sent news from relatives, maintaining family communication, although 'I don't hear very much from Zürich.'

Letter writing during the emigration process had various functions. For Hermine it was more than anything else an urgent task to be done regularly, as she showed in a letter from 13 August:

It is very wrong of you to write so little to your parents, once a week at least should be enough for you to write a postcard or a letter with something "interesting", & like all the children who are away, here or abroad, you should set aside one particular day, so that you can have a routine. You'll find the time, in 2 minutes a postcard is done &

in 5 minutes a letter with something "interesting". [...] Have you written to Therese & Hilde? Do keep on good terms with people who might be useful to you.

Just three days later another admonishment followed. News of a very different kind, however, came from Kurt Jeselson in New York, who put her to rights (she had clearly been complaining about her lot):

I am glad that you now live amongst decent (if also somewhat scrawny and unfriendly) people and not amongst Germans who have lost all sense of civilisation, and that the mild sun of freedom and the (admittedly a little stuffy) traditions of an honourable people are showing you something of the noble goals of humankind on this most beautiful of worlds. I hope – to be serious for a moment – you realise how great the difference is between a free nation and an oppressed people and you really shouldn't – given how enormous this freedom is – be petty in criticising what to us might seem a little square and unfamiliar. [...]

England is the last remnant of that old European ideal of humanism, which helped liberate the world from the darkness of the Middle Ages. [...] A sort of waistcoat pocket economy. But as I say, Englishmen are damned decent chaps and you can learn a lot from them. So study them a little more closely.

This is another one of those moments when it would be good to know what Liesel's reply was. These letters do, however, hint at how in the context of emigration – and exile – the bigger and the smaller things affect the lives of those involved in different ways. It is impossible to tell – and Liesel certainly couldn't in her situation – whether everyday trivialities would suddenly obtain great significance, and perhaps that is why she focused on them more than on global politics.

Another point arises from these letters. Each person thinks and acts from the standpoint of his or her 'business'. In normal circumstances this is scarcely noticed, but, when the ground which has always been beneath your feet becomes shaky, clinging to old habits appears almost tragicomic.

Ludwig wrote a long letter – Hermine was visiting relatives in Zürich – on 20 August. First it dealt with Helmut's future: Ludwig said he was 'not in a position' to pay the boy's school fees. Liesel's efforts to find a school for Helmut, he explained, were therefore 'completely futile'. He didn't want to rely on his relatives for help with this either; Liesel had tried to get their well-off Uncle Jakob (sometimes Jacob, but I have used the former spelling throughout) involved, but apart from a 'four-page letter' nothing concrete became of it. Ludwig dedicates the second part of the letter to one of his own ideas. The firm for whom he worked as a travelling salesman, Ludwig Mayer, Vineyard owner in Bingen am Rhein, wanted Liesel's address so they could send her price lists for selling Rüdesheim wine in England. In great detail he explained to her how the pricing was done,

per 12 bottles, not as we do per 100 litres = so when the Rüdesheim is on the list for 48 sh [shillings] that means a ¾ litre bottle – 4 sh; the prices are for London, so

English import duty and freight to London are included; my firm has a large wine store with a hauliers in London and can always supply customers immediately from London.

He added: 'I assume that when you have the lists you will do all you can to help your father [...] it depends entirely on your diligence in spreading the word.' Nothing came of it, of course, which was as obvious as the disappointment it would cause Ludwig. Hermine wrote from a rainy summer holiday in Switzerland, worried about the upheaval at home and about her son, who their Zürich relatives were unwilling to help: 'Uncle Jakob is of the opinion that we should leave Helmut at home as long as possible.' She herself wanted her children 'out as soon as possible', which meant that England was the best option – 'so explore every possibility'. Liesel was to stop writing begging letters to Zürich, as it would be better if Jakob and Hede supported those still in Heilbronn rather than her. 'You waste everything on frippery and the cinema!' and 'Instead, write letters where you're happy!'

But Liesel was not happy at this time. Trude Victor visited Liesel's 'people' – [Leute] as Swabians often call their relatives – in Amsterdam and wrote on 25 August: 'I completely understand that it's not ideal for you to stay in domestic service for so long. Do you really think you will find something in your profession over the course of time?' Trude said that her husband Max thought it very difficult 'to get something from your people' without a clear plan. Liesel was in contact with various acquaintances, including namesake Liesel Victor, who wrote with the friendly greeting 'My dear old thing!' telling her to write more often and in more detail. But what actual plans could she make in Birmingham? In a postcard from 30 August 1937 Ludwig said he was sorry 'that you have no chance with the wine, but try anyway'. He was at home and soon it would be High Holy Days. 'Yom Kippur on 15 September', and he added 'I hope you make time to go to church!' The word 'church' was even underlined.

The next letter in this chronology marks the start of a very long storyline. To go into it in better detail I will for the most part discuss it in a separate section of this book, but for now I will say that it would keep Liesel on tenterhooks for the coming year. It was about plans, and in particular it was about hopes and disappointments. And it was about a man, known for the time being only as 'Gerhard'. The undated letter (only 'September' could be made out on the postmark) ended, unsigned, 'with best wishes', sent by 'Gabriel, Offenbach am Main, Buchrainweg 9'. Despite the formality – 'Dear Miss Rosenthal' – the tone was as if this were a close relationship. The sender expressed thanks for the good wishes for the 'New Year' (5697/98), so this clearly involved a Jewish family. The man worked 'usually in schools and on the land' and was very busy: 'we both have no time to enjoy the good weather'. Then the son's name was mentioned. 'You will have heard from Gerhard that my husband and I spent three weeks at Bad Kissingen this year.' After further news of family relations who had emigrated to the United States he appeared again. 'The whole time we had nothing but good news from Bombay.' The sender concluded by wishing 'that the worries in your life become less' for Liesel. Gerhard Gabriel, then, and Bombay – we will soon hear about this story in great detail.[32]

During the festival (on 3 September) Hermine had time to write Liesel 'a long letter from home'. She described her stay with their wealthy relatives in Zürich – 'it's a hotel, daily visits, everything provided, at enormous cost. Dear Papa doesn't earn in a month what they spend in a day.' Great hopes were placed in their relationship with Aunt Hede and her husband, Uncle Jakob (Wertheimer), and Liesel too had asked for financial help. How was I to find out about them? Julia Neuberger wrote: 'The aunt in Switzerland was Hede, my grandmother Hermine Rosenthal's sister who married Jakob Wertheimer of Zurich. Their grandson Roman Rosenstein is still alive and lives in Zurich, but won't know much. But we could ask.' Julia got in touch with him, and Roman Rosenstein replied on 27 December 2013:

> Liesl [...] was a regular visitor at my grandparents' home: Tödistr 1 in Zürich, a well known address for Jewish refugees and Schnorrers [scroungers]! Hede, my grandmother, and Liesl I believe to remember, got along with each other very close, both were descendants of the Rothschild family, unfortunately not the banker! I am aware that my grandfarther Jakob Wertheimer has undertaken some risky trips to Germany to bring relatives and friends to Switzerland. I think he did one or two trips with his famous Cadillac even after gasoline supply was not anymore guaranteed, only a short time before [...] WW2 broke out. There is one story that he returned to the Swiss border late at night with a german family member or friend of similar age in his car. At the border station my grandfather showed his Swiss passport, got it back, while the border police agent walked around the car my grandfather passed his passport to his passenger who showed it at the other side to the border police agent and off they were.[33]

This is one of the few pieces of evidence from the close family circle which deals with the memories of Jakob Wertheimer and his role within the family legacy. We learn little about Liesel. I have left the following two examples as I received them, to make clear the difficulty of this research. The information they contain is extremely valuable, but it is coloured by the respective memories. Joachim Hahn, rector in Plochingen in Württemberg, is an expert in both Swabian and Alemannic Jewish family history, and he sent me the following on Hermine's (née Rothschild) family:

> In Cannstatt there were several Rothschild families. The Rothschild family to which Hermine belonged came from Gemmingen. Hermine's mother was a daughter of Dr Moses Engelbert, later rabbi in Heilbronn, which is not without interest. The register also states that daughter Hede/Hedwig married Jakob Wertheimer in Zürich.[34]

Active online family genealogy yields the following additional information on Jakob Wertheimer's background:

> Simon Wertheimer [Parents] was born in 1850. He died in 1932. He married Jeanette (Hannchen) Wertheimer. Other marriages: Wertheimer, Mina. [...] Jeanette (Hannchen) Wertheimer [Parents] was born in 1859 in Emmendingen. She died in

Figure 7 The Wertheimer family

1883 in Kehl. She married Simon Wertheimer. They had the following children: M i Jakob Wertheimer, F ii Jula Wertheimer, F iii Sophie Wertheimer. Jakob Wertheimer [Parents] was born in 1879 in Bodersweier. He died in 1963 in Zurich. He married Hede Rothschild. Hede Rothschild was born in 1889 in Canstatt. She died in 1964 in Zurich. She married Jakob Wertheimer. They had the following children: M i Hans Wertheimer, F ii Gretel Wertheimer, F iii Lotte Wertheimer.[35]

This gives us a degree of framework which can help put what little we know from the letters into some sort of order. Hermine was a born Rothschild from Cannstatt, whilst her sister Hede was a good match with Jakob Wertheimer, and they moved to Zürich together. But this information reads like entries in a large book belonging to the past, a register of life but also, and almost more so, a register of death – no wonder Joachim Hahn points to memorial books and 'stumbling blocks',[36] and to forms of memory research in the places where those involved once lived. Evidence of life is instead to be found in the letters: 'Aunt Hede gave me a fabulously beautiful green dress with a loose ¾ length jacket, and I intend to give it to you.'

Hermine added that Determann had 'moved his shop to the Allee', Heilbronn's main street. He had been 'very kind' to her when she had shopped there. The social conventions of a happier period are, partly, still existing: Mrs Rosenthal was a customer and her daughter Liesel had done her apprenticeship there, but she felt it necessary to emphasize that he had been kind to a Jewish customer. 'God willing, you will be just as lucky!'

Aunt Lina thanked Liesel for her good wishes at New Year on 17 September, but did not neglect to warn her: 'When will you start interacting with people, and not just live in your books?' Neither she nor Hermine knows how Liesel's new life was going. Shortly beforehand, on 13 September, a letter from the Jewish Refugees Committee arrived, addressed to 'Miss Liesel Rosenthal, c/o Mr. Dobbs, 208 Corisande Road, Birmingham 29' (Weoley Park):

> *Dear Miss Rosenthal, I do not know why you are so terribly excited, if the people offer you a proper salary, if the Ministry of Labour form is filled up and if they prove that they need somebody for the foreign department, I do not see why they should not get the permit. But you must see that these three items are mentioned.*

The sender, Anna Schwab, would go on to have a large role in Liesel's life in England and become one of the important (and few) constants in this life. Anna Schwab was described by Julia Neuberger as 'from Frankfurt, arrived London 1906, chaired the Welfare Committee of the Refugee Committee at Bloomsbury House'.[37]

Another key figure in aiding refugees was Otto M Schiff, who had a 'unique leading role on behalf of Jewish refugees in both world wars'.[38] After his death in November 1952 the Jewish Telegraphic Agency (JTA) wrote:

> *Mr. Schiff was instrumental in rescuing some 12 000 Jews from Germany during the first World War and helped Jewish refugees from the Nazis from 1933 until recently. He was chairman of one of the first committees in Britain to aid Jewish victims of Nazism.*[39]

Information on the specifics of the work done by the Refugee Committee can be found through the Association of Jewish Refugees (AJR) and in the memoirs of emigrants such as Jerry Springer:

> *The Jewish Refugee Committee (also known as the German Jewish Aid Committee during the war) was an organization in London with which Jewish people fleeing Germany could register to find help upon their arrival in the UK. New arrivals would register at Woburn House in Bloomsbury and receive advice about subsistence and accommodation. The surviving records show refugees' addresses, arrival dates and any other help they might have received.*[40]

Ernst Lowenthal (Löwenthal by his German name) also recorded his memories of arriving in the UK. Not only did he have to 'report immediately to the aliens' police in Bow Street, near Covent Garden', but he was also advised '[to] register as soon as possible with the German Jewish Aid Committee (GJAC) at Bloomsbury House'.[41] Bloomsbury House, he continued,

> *was at least 70 years old at the time, a dilapidated, four-storey hotel building where the most important British refugee aid centre had been located since the spring of*

1939. The rooms used by the largest committee, the GJAC/JRC, in nearby Woburn House were no longer big enough. [...] A "card" was provided, which consisted of a sturdy cardboard file into which all correspondence was to be placed, a similarly large blue file for personal information and, later, "refugee stories", and an equally large red file for logging all support payments.[42]

Lowenthal described vividly and in great detail the interior of the house, all its floors 'and the different atmosphere each one had', as well as the various help centres, from the Germany Emergency Committee of the Society of Friends (Quaker) or the Church of England Committee for non-Aryan Christians to the Emergency Committee for German Scientists Abroad. He mentioned the names of many people who will appear throughout this book: Mrs Rueff, Maud Karpeles, Miss Tomlinson, Mrs Weiner, Lily Schiff, Anna Schwab, Augustus Kahn, together with the individual activities undertaken there, including accommodating refugees ('hospitality'), household service (the 'domestic bureau'), language courses (the 'Education Department'), investigation into further emigration ('Emigration Research'), statistics and the central register (in the 'Central Office'). He also discussed the luggage department, headed at first by Mr Makower and later by Selma Metzger, which was tasked with 'looking after the luggage of those who had planned to emigrate further but who were now unable to'.[43]

Liesel Rosenthal, then, was looking for a new job. She had begun the process of leaving the Dobbs family, without asking her parents what they thought of it. 'As for you, dear Liesel,' wrote her mother on 18 September 1937,

I am truly astonished & taken aback that you are taking this step, I do not approve of it. In domestic service you have a home and food, and you receive pocket money & a salary because you're good at it. [...] I would forget about the bookshop and try to earn enough to survive, you are at the age, 22 ½ years old, when you need to put something away for later. Don't rely on our relatives, Uncle Jakob won't send you anything at the moment, with good reason. If you leave domestic service I am sure nobody would benefit.

Others, such as Hannele Eckert or Alfred Lindner, were getting engaged. And her brother Helmut was preparing for his Bar Mitzvah, which would be expensive. 'The tallit and tefillin cost so much money! So save what you can, we have to make plenty of sacrifices for your sakes!'

Hermine had to buy the tallit and tefillin for the celebration – only now, and in passing, do these sources speak of the Rosenthal family as a Jewish one. It is, however, clear from reading these letters that the misery which dominated the family and tore it apart, a result of the Nazi rise to power in 1933 and the laws they had passed in Germany, was becoming more and more unavoidable in Heilbronn – the city's democratic tradition was now history.

Ludwig Rosenthal was a local wine merchant, whilst Hermine was a housewife who felt a deep connection to her hometown and her local community. Although she was buying the necessary items for a Bar Mitzvah, she was doing this as if she were one of her Protestant or Catholic neighbours for a confirmation, and Ludwig told his daughter

Figure 8 The street with the Heilbronn synagogue and the new post office, c. 1930

to go to 'church' at Yom Kippur (soon afterwards another letter would come from him, undated and written in pencil, in which he expressed his hope that Liesel would 'get out a little more and visit the local synagogue' in Birmingham). When Hermine sent a picture postcard on 24 September 1937 – 'love from back home' – showing the 'new post office and synagogue' on the aforementioned street,[44] I read it today, retrospectively, as a sort of statement: Here we are, and our 'church' (the synagogue which would only survive for another year) is part of this city! I cannot be sure, though, if that was her intention.

Before we return to the chronology of the family letters, it is worth discussing the wine trade in Heilbronn. In his book *How Wine in Central Europe Became Jewish*, Kevin Goldberg has shown that 'Jewry, Jews and wine [have] a complicated common history'.

> *While historiography of the wine trade in the 19th century has tended to ignore the Jewish contribution to it, it similarly overlooks how newer wines and the discourse surrounding them reflected contemporary societal fears. In particular, these focused on the commercialisation of the wine trade and the role of Jewish merchants in traditional countryside winegrowing moving away from its roots.*[45]

Like his father and two of his brothers, Ludwig was one of these wine merchants. Goldberg writes:

> [It] *turned out that in the decades between 1860 and the First World War nothing dogged the Central European wine trade more than the debate surrounding synthetic wine. These never-ending debates filled the pages of trade journals, dominated the*

discussions at trade conferences, provided a constant supply of gossip fodder for winegrowers and encouraged the meteoric rise in the science of oenology, which sought to determine once and for all what was permissible in natural winemaking and to weaken the threat of the German and Austrian market. [...] Arguments over additives, de-acidification, branding policies and labelling ignited a decades-long debate between producers, merchants and consumers from all regions and social classes. Any historian who studies Central European Jewry – even if he was previously unaware of the significance of wine in Jewish history – will quickly recognise the tactics and rhetoric employed in these seemingly unrelated debates over wine. [...] [M]odern wine was produced in the exact same social context and using the same language which was used to exclude the Jews from participating in national cultures, particularly in Europe.[46]

So there were wine debates within the wider German-Jewish history, and it is safe to assume that they were of great significance in Heilbronn, where the wine trade played such a large role in the local economy. No less a figure than Theodor Heuss had earned his doctorate in the city's 'Viticulture and vine dressers' in 1905 (we will encounter him, too, in our letters).[47] 'Raising the "Jewish question" became a central part of the criticism by the winegrowers and politicians in winegrowing regions of the techniques and practices of labelling and marketing, which they regarded as spurious, lacking in credibility and misleading', continues Goldberg, who points out that the 'Jewish question' was often discussed within the context of the 'synthetic wine debate'.[48]

Goldberg's research primarily focuses on the Burgenland border region of Austria-Hungary, but in Germany, too, anti-Semitic organizations such as Theodor Fritsch and Max Liebermann von Sonneberg's German Social Party linked 'the *Jewish* and the *synthetic wine* questions'. 'Price-fixing through monopolies' was one accusation, 'producing low-quality goods' was another.[49] Julius Kahn, a Jewish merchant from Bingen, was accused of an array of misdemeanours, including adding water and sugar to his grape must.[50] Ludwig Rosenthal had business connections with Bingen – had he experienced such accusations?

Unfortunately, there is no study of the wine trade comparable to the one carried out by Stefanie Fischer on the history of Jewish cattle traders in Rothenburg and its surrounding area.[51] Neither did Klaus Fischer's research in Bad Wimpfen yield any further information 'on the relationship between local, long-established winegrowers and Jewish wine merchants in the city of Heilbronn'.[52] Fischer writes that 'some' of the Heilbronners he asked 'still [remembered] the "Wine merchant Rosenthal" ... in some cases it was seen as competition, as winegrowers fought for their own patch', and he continues:

As the wine merchant was able to offer a wide variety of products, he was without question a serious competitor in the wine market. Between 1935 and 1940 there were around 320 full-time winegrowers in Heilbronn, and in the Böckingen, Neckargartach and Sontheim areas there were a further 54. By comparison, the 1938/39 Heilbronn directory (the last before the war – wartime secrecy meant that no directories were published thereafter) listed 20 wine merchants (by then without the Rosenthals). The Heilbronn wine exchange and the Heilbronn Winegrowers' Association were major marketing opportunities for these producers. [It was] *an extremely hard job, and always a struggle against the vicissitudes of nature, to get a good, fruitful vintage into the cellar. The producers felt that it was rather easier for the merchants, who did not have to go to such lengths to make their profits.*[53]

In the February 1965 edition of the *AJR Information* journal Ernst Lowenthal wrote a short report to mark the publication of Otto Anhaus's *100 Years of German Wine Trade – 100 Years of the German Wine Journal. A Contribution to the History of Wine* (Mainz: J. Diemer Verlag 1964). This festschrift praised – repeatedly – the important role Jewish figures played in founding this trade journal and in the development of the wine trade as a whole. With regard to the successful wine merchants, particularly in the Rhine-Hesse region, Anhaus wrote: 'The liberal attitude of these internationally-minded and art-loving Jewish merchants did much to keep the German wine trade from second-rate provincialism.' He also, however, noted that Max Adler and Willy Rosenthal had been forced out from their position in the Württemberg Wine Merchants' Association in 1933.[54]

By the end of September 1937 Liesel had left the Dobbs family (though her post continued to be sent to their address at Corisande Road). 'I would very much like to know more, and in more detail,' wrote Hermine in an undated letter,

> *why you left the Dobbs family so quickly, are you going back to them*[?] *It's embarrassing to me really that you don't have a job now and are staying with the Sußmann family, have the decency to make a real effort to help them out as much as you can. I'm giving you the address of the Dreyfus family in London, tell them that you are my daughter & that you would like to get to know their daughter Marta, who was a friend of mine. Tell her that I have kept all her Engl. letters from Trinidad & that I would very much like to resume our correspondence in English.*

Ludwig added: 'Write and give me a clear description of what you are doing, as I am worried because you are without a job & alone & living with the sole hope of finding something in a bookshop or not is utterly pointless.' In a letter from Hermine on 7 October 1937 the talk was again of Gerhard Gabriel.

> *Now I come to the main purpose of my letter. Last week I spoke to Mrs Wilh. Schloß & she said to me that Mrs Rosenfeld from Bombay told her that Mr Gabriel was seriously interested in you & would like to be with you. Mrs Schloß said to me that Mrs Rosenfeld had told her that Mr Gabriel has a business which is going very well & is a fine man. [...] You know, dear Liesel, my opinion of him, I have always thought him an excellent man, a frugal, focused, good man his parents can be proud of. His parents, too, make the best possible impression on me. This cd. also be a future for your brother.*

Helmut had also been impressed by the 'young man', 'the parents too, who you and I visited together that one time' – probably from Frankfurt. Liesel would be well provided for with Gabriel, she would be landing on her feet with him – 'so if I were you I would go for it'. I can imagine how nice it must have been for Liesel to hear that her father would 'go for it'. What did she want for herself? She kept a newspaper cutting which contained information that Walter Schatzki from Frankfurt was transferring control of his bookshop to his longstanding colleagues Richard Schumann and Gerhard Dross. Was he forced to give it up? Walter Schatzki, bookseller and antiquarian, owned the Children's Book Shop on the Theaterplatz, where he began to 'build up a comprehensive collection of old children's books, 690 of which he sold to the New York Public Library in 1931. He was one of the first to recognise the antiquarian value of children's books and act on it.' This information comes from Wikipedia (little could be found anywhere else), where it goes on: 'In December [1937] Schatzki opened a new shop in New York, initially in shared rooms with Hellmuth Wallach.'[55]

This must have been important to Liesel, and perhaps when reading this cutting she thought of her mother's letter from 7 July: 'I strongly advise you, under no circumstances should you think about your bookselling again.' She did try though, as shown by the copy (or draft) of a typed letter, which begins with only 'Dear Sir' and ends with only 'Yours faithfully'. I cannot be certain who wrote it (though it may well have been Hudson, a bookseller in Birmingham) and who it was addressed to (probably the British Home Office). But the content is interesting:

> *Miss Rosenthal came to England five months ago to learn English and whilst she was trying very hard she found that she was physically not fit to adapt herself to the duties she was requested to do. Miss Rosenthal is a typically academic type of girl and when we were asked to interest ourselves in her we did so because we actually needed somebody on our foreign department. We require somebody who is especially acquainted with German books on technical and general subjects and she has had five years experience in bookshops in Frankfurt and Heilbronn. Through various channels we have tried to get an assistant suitable to do that work, but have not been successful. We are the only bookshop in Birmingham who sells these types of books and the requests for the same are definitely increasing. It is therefore essential that we should have somebody well versed in these particular lines in our bookshop. We shall feel greatly obliged if you will reconsider your decision conveyed to us in your letter. We are prepared to give Miss Rosenthal every opportunity to increase her knowledge of English so that she will not only find a post with us, but prepare for a future career which unfortunately has been denied to her in her home country.*

This introduces a new part of the story: the UK government's policy towards refugees from Germany. Since the Aliens Act of 1905 immigration to Great Britain had been heavily restricted, and potential immigrants were required to disembark at specific ports where the authorities could monitor them and if necessary send undesirables back.[56] Recent research has cast doubt on how effective this legislation actually was and has emphasized the significance of the Aliens Restriction (Amendment) Act of 1919, which almost completely prevented Jewish immigration after the First World

War.⁵⁷ Even after the Nazis came to power in Germany in 1933 this position was scarcely relaxed, as shown by the urgent letters addressed to Frank Foley in the British embassy in Berlin. Foley, the man later celebrated as 'the spy who saved ten thousand Jews',⁵⁸ was unremitting in his reports to the Foreign Office in London of the increasing anti-Jewish persecution in Germany and demanded that the authorities accept more refugees and that they improve the legal status of the emigrés already in the country.⁵⁹

Above all – how little refugee policy has changed since then! – this was a question of work permits. Whilst recognized experts, academics, technicians and engineers, with their renowned German education in business and universities, were gladly welcomed (and quickly found English support committees willing to help them), and while young women were allowed in relatively hassle-free as domestic workers, the situation was rather more complicated for many other professions.⁶⁰ Even though the document is incomplete it is clear what had happened. Either Liesel or acquaintances in Birmingham acting on her behalf had contacted Hudson's bookshop in Birmingham, which in turn had applied for a work permit for her. Rejections of applications were normally justified on the grounds that refugees were not allowed to work in jobs English citizens could do instead. This explains the argument of the author of this letter – probably the bookseller himself, Mr Hudson – that he had tried without success to find 'an assistant suitable to do the work'. It is possible that Liesel's still insufficient knowledge of English was another reason for the application being rejected.

On the same day her brother Helmut, who had previously only added his scribbled name to his parents' letters, wrote a short letter of his own for the first time. In autumn 1937 he was thirteen years old, and in further letters over the coming years we will trace – in his writing style and the language he used – how he grew from a child to an adolescent, and then to a young man, and eventually to become a soldier. In childish calligraphy (Roman – he found German easier), he wrote that he had 'very little time to write'. He thanked her for the books he had received and was 'keen to read them' (a potential ally?), and he was looking forward to his Bar Mitzvah, having already received some presents. Hermine added a report of the preparations for the occasion: 'There will be 9 of us at the table & 10 or 15 for coffee, as I had to invite the rabbi, both teachers, the Löwengardts, Adolf Meyer & Ev & Helmut's friends.' She then scribbled another line: 'What do you think of the opportunity with Mr G?'

Mr G was in touch on 18 October, 'with best wishes and kisses' and with a cheque 'No. 89867 for £20 (twenty) from National Bank of India Ltd. London and I request that you confirm receipt'. Such bureaucratic language makes me wince a little. Gerhard Gabriel certainly seemed to be fulfilling the role Liesel's parents wanted him to fulfil, asking her 'not to be stingy with the money, but to use it'. In my imagination, however, she was probably wondering what the real price of accepting this gift would be.

Her namesake Liesel Victor wrote one last time from Amsterdam on 22 October 1937. She had also heard about Liesel's unsuccessful work permit application and comforted her: 'You'll find something, so things will turn out well in the end.' She and her husband Ottl were to travel from Southampton aboard the *Pretoria* to Cape Town, arriving on 10 November, and by the end of the year she would be in Durban. Liesel was a close friend – 'well, either it will go well or you will get married as soon as he can support 2 families', she wrote, referring to Leopold Lichtenstern – and she signed the letter with best wishes from an 'unhappy, happy old friend'. This was probably an accurate description of Liesel's own state of mind at this point. She could be happy that she was 'out', but unhappy that she had not been able to make her life work out quite as well as she would have hoped.

The Bar Mitzvah celebrations in Heilbronn had gone well:

Your brother did what he had to do marvellously, like no other boy, he wasn't scared, he was so brave, everybody was so thrilled, particularly about his wonderful voice. He gave a speech & sang the prayer wonderfully. He got presents, some beautiful, truly valuable things.

This was all that could fit on the postcard. On 11 November a more detailed letter followed:

On Friday evening Uncle Julius & Aunt Mile came & we went to the synagogue, afterwards we had dinner, soup, chicken with broad noodles & salad. Next morning we had a leisurely stroll for breakfast at the synagogue. Helmut looked truly wonderful, he received the yarmulke from Bella Flegenheimer, who dressed him expertly, his beautiful outfit with tie & I bought him a luxury men's coat in grey, which he looks so good in. He said his blessings more wonderfully than any boy before him, everyone was so thrilled & moved & afterwards we had so many visits from people who had never been to us before & who we had never been to either & despite that everyone gave presents. […] all of them high-quality. As all our close acquaintances have left recently I said to Papa, Helmut will hardly get any presents & what a surprise, there were so many of them. He got money from almost all the relatives, from Ede R he got a wonderful wool travel blanket, f. Uncle Sigm. an umbrella, lots of books, including the bible from the congregation, the prayer book from his school friends, he even got the book "How the world is governed". 2 suitcases, 5 fountain pens, various silverware, including something from Gumbel (Silver), a splendid piece with colouring pencils from Willy Victor. Various wallets, including a very nice one from Mrs Lene Kahn, and from Mrs Josef Kahn (Grete's parents) he got a very eleg[ant] gift of fountain pens, signet & letter opener in silver.

The relationship between Swabians and their 'things', their possessions, is a cliché which is nice to discuss in times of peace, when a person's belongings can be kept and presented properly.[61] But the peace had been disturbed, and the many acquaintances who had 'left' had not done so by coincidence. Even if Hermine did not mention it, the threat was there between the lines. Listing all the presents showed the respect accorded to the Rosenthals and the feeling that in the eyes of their neighbours and relatives they were 'worth something'. In this way a kind of normality still reigned, with Helmut's celebration, and they were about to travel to the wedding of Gretel (Hede and Jakob Wertheimer's daughter) in Zürich. Hermine had had a beautiful dress made, and 'even Papa had dressed up smartly & we looked as lovely as everyone else'. And yet it is noticeable that their relatives in Switzerland could celebrate differently, not just because they were better off, but because they were freer, 'in Grande Taill[e]' and in the Grand Hotel, with the festivities and dancing lasting into the small hours, and without having to worry about their neighbours.[62] This long letter ended, inevitably, with 'And what's happening with Gabriel?'

Even Anna Schwab was becoming impatient with Liesel. 'Dear Miss Rosenthal', she wrote on 27 October,

> you can be sure that people will do all they can to help you, but you are simply annoying the home office if you keep badgering them. I have spoken with Mr Powell and really will try my best. If you can't stay with the Dobbs any longer then you must hand in your notice "for health reasons".

This was probably what she wanted to do, to the alarm of Hermine: 'What a life you want to have!' The celebrations were over and she had plenty of work to do. 'I'm doing without the cleaning lady, washing, sewing and ironing everything myself', she wrote on 18 November, and she made even clearer her wish to see Liesel marry. 'Dear Liesel be honest and tell us if you have somebody you want to marry or if we should sort something out, it is our biggest wish to provide for you. I would immediately stop hassling you about it & be heartily thankful.'[63] In a letter on 16 November Ludwig showed that his thoughts had turned to something else. 'Imagine, I'm learning English too now and I'm really trying to make progress, all that's missing is our uncle and aunt in America! But it's serious, if only [we] had the chance!' He makes reference to the 'business with Gabriel' too, but in this case it was not just about providing for Liesel. 'We and Helmut would have somewhere to go, think about it again!'

In the meantime Liesel had left Birmingham and the Dobbs. 'Now I see', Uncle Paul dictated to his wife from his sickbed in a letter to Liesel (from where is unknown),

> that you have chosen London to be your battlefield. It can't be too difficult to find somewhere to live there, for as you can see from the attached cutting more than 10,000 Austrian women a year are coming to England who can cook nothing more than a simple apple strudel. You can do this too, I'm sure, so why shouldn't you be able to find something in London, after all apart from strudel you can cook a whole load of other things English people like.

For once I can imagine Liesel laughing when reading this excerpt. Such a casual viewpoint was unheard of from her parents. 'You can imagine how worried we are', wrote Hermine on 28 November. She was writing 'long English letters' to other acquaintances – 'I made some mistakes in the letter, but I was so *in hurry* when I was writing it, the one *great mistake* was "your truly" instead of "yours" and so on'. She was attempting to get hold of clothes and to get daily chores done, but the fear was growing. 'Soon the Ottenheimers, Rypinskis, Oppenheimers are leaving for America & the Leopolds for Sao Paolo. Lisel Leopold is a splendid girl, she is a cook with Strauß at the Adler. The Adlers in the Wilhelmstr. are going to England.' Helmut added that he had lit his first Hanukkah candle. 'At the synagogue the rabbi gave a sermon to the young people [...] on Sunday we have the Hanukkah service at the Jewish school and

I'm taking part in it.' He had left the 'Club' [it is impossible to know which] so he could play table tennis. And Ludwig thought that Liesel's silence – she had not answered their questions about 'G' – was increasing 'our inner worry we have about you'.

Life in Heilbronn, then, at the end of November 1937, involved a household in chaos, an ever-decreasing circle of friends and a Jewish boy who had no future in the city. Meanwhile in England, E F Hudson had decided 'not to engage Miss Rosenthal' as the restrictions imposed by the Home Office could not be overcome. At this time Liesel was living with the family of Siegmund Sußmann in Hampstead, the focal point of German-Jewish immigration, meaning she was in close proximity to people who shared her story and institutions specifically aimed at helping them. What we would today call networking was becoming more important, making news from friends and relatives from all corners of the globe was vital in the exchange of information about how German Jews could rebuild their lives. Liesel Victor had arrived in South Africa and wrote from Port Elizabeth on 5 December. 'My sister-in-law, her sisters and Robert were standing on the pier [in Cape Town] to pick us up. It's very nice here (I compare it with social life in Heilbronn and there's not much more going on).' The weather was lovely and fruit season had begun, with plums, oranges, passion fruit and paw-paws ('a kind of melon'), but living was expensive and took some getting used to. Emigration is a constant learning curve and in many respects represents a broadening of horizons, which children, in this case Liesel Victor's daughter Marga, often cope with best:

> She took everything in her stride and never had a minute's fear of the natives. [...] this was Africa and was all part of it. I am delighted she thinks this way and is sensible in this respect, as obeying is not yet a word which appears in her dictionary. She never obeys anything, you have no idea how disobedient she is. But I have to say that it is much more important to me that she is healthy.

Emigration is no abstract process. It has an everyday dimension, and a part of it is a change in family relationships.[64] Carlos Sluzki has written a very important essay on this issue, and his findings are of great significance for our story: Initially, each individual migration represents a kind of family drama, and as such becomes part of the family's story, which as time goes by can even become an anecdote in some cases. Migrations always have a pre-history. They often begin with a family member taking the first steps to prepare for their emigration. Letters, whether to relatives or to authorities, visa applications and similar documents give substance to this intention. How long this initial phase lasts depends not just on the political circumstances but also on the nature of the affected family and the relationships between its members. As part of this, Sluzki writes, there are 'up and down curves', short periods of euphoria mixed with moments of stress, disappointment and failure.[65] New rules must be negotiated within the family discourse, during which confrontations that the family has never experienced before can arise. In some cases – particularly if it involves fleeing extreme hardship or if one of those who 'stay behind' dies – it is possible that the first person who leaves is seen as a traitor: 'the member of the family who breaks away first from the collective family mourning is frequently scapegoated as a traitor'.[66]

It is this person, however, who experiences the new reality of both the loss of their homeland and their encounters with strangers, and they must pass this information on to their family. This experience of transition, which emigration and immigration represent, cannot be conveyed or negotiated within the framework of pre-existing family rituals. Acting as a scout, they meet people in their new surroundings who have comparable experiences and use this circle to create a network of contacts and exchange, which those who 'stay behind' cannot understand as they cannot know what is going on 'outside'. For many emigrants the journey by ship, either to Palestine or to the United States, is especially symbolic of this experience of transition, not least because during the passage they can strike up important social relationships. Sluzki therefore speaks of 'Ship brothers and ship sisters' (he uses the German notions 'Schiffsbrüder und Schiffsschwestern')[67] who become a replacement family, to the chagrin of their real family.

Whilst the pioneers 'share' the subsequent processes of acculturation and of beginning to integrate with those in the same position as them, they can only 'communicate' these experiences to the members of their family. Consequently, family rules and values which were taken for granted back home are no longer considered to apply or be useful to them. But it is not easy for the family to change its framework of rules. New rules for coping with this new situation and the acceptance of new forms of communication, and indeed new hierarchies, must be chosen and discussed. As the old rules were often symbolic for the essence of the family's understanding of itself, perhaps with regard to its national or ethnic identity, this renegotiation of the family structure alters its members' perception of the world. 'The specific styles, modes, values, and myths that constitute an ad hoc, family-specific view of the world and of their own history'[68] are challenged, and in many cases it is only the members of the next generation, or even the one after that, who find an acceptable *modus vivendi*.

Many of these findings refer to migration in the 1970s and are based on the perspective of a family therapist. They are, however, of great interest for students of German-Jewish emigration in the 1930s and for our Rosenthal family. Emigration from the familiar surroundings of Heilbronn, where the family roots stretched back for generations, represents a dramatic event. As a pioneer, Liesel had taken on a new role. She had acquired a new group of friends, independent of the family, and in her communication with like-minded people had learnt new rules which clashed with the traditional rules in her parents' household. Preparations for Helmut's, and then Ludwig and Hermine's, emigration were extremely time-consuming and required numerous specific steps to be taken, whilst at the same time the atmosphere was laden with tension and characterized by unfamiliar emotions (in Sluzki's terms 'euphoria' and 'dismay'). None of those involved had studied emigration, and the former rituals of understanding and exchanging were no longer adequate for describing the new reality. Global history was experienced as family history and understood from this perspective. Only Liesel, as the first to go, expanded her horizons to any considerable degree. Although no-one would put it quite so bluntly she was to some extent considered a 'traitor' (to the formerly accepted family rules), she was also, or at least would go on to be, the family's saviour. On 8 December 1937 Ludwig tried to reassert his authority.

> *Lina Kahn told everyone that you were staying with the Sußmanns & I wouldn't have spoken out about G, otherwise it would be* public *here. Such things should first and foremost be discussed with your parents & not with strangers. I definitely think it is advisable from your point of view to go for it. You are now at an age where you should know what you are doing & not be a little bird flitting from one twig to another, in other words you should take this one thing & not all the other things you have around you & the main thing is you have thought about it properly and know where you can settle down.* [...] [It would be possible] *to play the role of an employee for a few more years, but then your youth will be over & it will get harder and harder to find a husband. So as I say, what your parents want most of all is to know that you are happy & spoken for. It would be a great relief for us & would show that you have a future.*

'To *play* the role of an employee'. These words must have been hard to her to swallow. A day later Hermine wrote and repeated her urgent wish to know that Liesel was 'spoken for'. She did, however, add a line which this Heilbronn housewife would never have uttered five years before: 'India is not out of the question'. Mrs Kaufmann's daughter was there and found it to her liking: 'we must all go a long way to find out happiness'. Hermine knew this, but found it difficult to accept it in the specific case of her daughter.

Liesel continued to look for a job as a bookseller and had agreed to meet with Lola Mayer (Bookseller, 34 Lanhill Road, London W9). Gladys Skelton, secretary of the Save the Children Fund as well as the Inter-Aid Committee for Children from Germany, also intervened on Liesel's behalf in a letter to 'The Publisher's Circular' on 14 December 1937. 'She is seeking work in a book-shop or in some post connected with the books trade.'[69] Liesel told her relatives in Amsterdam about her efforts to obtain a work permit, and in a lengthy letter on 14 December Lore (Mevrouw Ludwig Kahn, Courbetstraße 13, Amsterdam) expressed her hope that Mrs Schwab – 'whose name we hear a lot' – could be of assistance to her (her being 'dear Liesele'). She was working on building up networks. 'Ludwig has a second cousin in London, a charming, hard-working woman, who emigrated from Berlin about four years ago, and she knows a whole load of people, perhaps she could help you out? In any case give her a call and send her our best wishes [...].'

This was nice and friendly to read. Heilbronn, however, was unrelenting. Hermine wanted to speak 'sensibly' with Liesel, woman to woman (and she had probably thrown away a postcard an enraged Ludwig had written in the heat of the moment), but she was very clear in her idea of what sensible meant.

> *Dear child, have you really not thought about your parents' "future"? Do you not know that nowadays parents rely on their children & follow them? Have you ever considered where <u>we</u> will have to live? It doesn't help us if you find Helmut a school as he can still stay here with us. It only helps you & us if you marry, & indeed marry a man who can support himself & is a respectable citizen. G is both of those things and moreover is a fine, warm-hearted man. We & you can only speak of happiness if he wants you as his wife & we think that is the starting point!*

Other children, including Ruth Lindner, Helle Bauchwitz 'and Rabbi Dr H's sister' had found places in London and were earning good money. Ludwig was away again on business, but 'he makes very little, we are running out of money'. So she was looking for a 'profession' for herself. Perhaps as a hairdresser? Or in manicure and pedicure?

In the midst of the chaos a letter from Bombay, written on 23 December 1937, arrived for Liesel. Gerhard's sister Lisbeth was awaiting 'dear Liesel's' imminent visit – 'I assume I am allowed to address my brother's bride in this way?' – and offered advice on clothing on behalf of her pragmatic brother, who was looking forward to being married. 'Before I do that I want to tell you how desperately I hope that you will be happy with our Gerhard, he with you and you with him.' Lisbeth had always wanted a sister and was looking forward to the moment when she could greet this new member of the family as she disembarked from the ship. 'In our circle' she would feel 'quite at home', even though she would be in an unfamiliar city. She meant well, but what did Liesel make of it? Was there too much about the family, perhaps, or too much about her new home? She went on to discuss shoes, tights and socks, underwear and bras, nightshirts, clothes for daytime and evening, coats, hats and 'fashionable extras' like 'neckwarmers' or corsages which 'all Europeans' should wear. Gerhard didn't particularly care for this 'modern jewellery', though. This was all the information 'which a lady in Bombay needs'. What this special lady was actually looking for in Bombay was a different matter.

In London she was still unemployed, 'so without earnings', as Aunt Luise Loeb in Amsterdam noted pointedly in a letter on 26 December 1937. As had happened so many times before, Liesel was reproached for not writing often enough, and how was Luise supposed to understand the 'incidental mention' that Liesel would 'probably get married'? 'Probably'? And to whom? Marrying would be a life-changing decision! Hermine, too, was 'almost on the edge of despair' because Liesel did not reply to urgent letters, as she showed on 27 December.

> I absolutely must know if you are going to Bombay & if I should come, we will discuss everything in London. You should know that it is uncertain if I will be able to travel at New Year & see you and I would so dearly love to speak to you.

Again and again Hermine Rosenthal expressed her wish to 'speak' with her daughter as she was used to, before the usual means of communication were severed. They had to make do with letters 'to continue the significant conversations over a spatial separation'.[70] Liesel's grandmother wished nothing more than to hear that Liesel was 'happy' on her 95th birthday. The postcard was addressed to Miss Liesel Rosenthal, c/o Paynton, 33 Westbourne Gardens, London W2 – new friends at any rate (Jack and Olive). Someone called Margaret got in touch (in an undated letter) wanting to meet Liesel in the bookshop, 'either to rejoice with you, or to discover with you some way of defying a damnable future'.

As these English letters show, Liesel was extremely active in trying to stand on her own two feet, as she had to be. Messages from Heilbronn were meanwhile becoming increasingly urgent. Hermine wrote again on 29 December: 'We have to know what's going on!' This pressure can admittedly be explained to some extent by the uncertainty created by new laws passed in the Third Reich – would Hermine even get permission to leave Heilbronn and travel to Amsterdam or London? – though it is highly questionable whether Liesel's parents were using the right tone. 'Our last message is this: marry Gerhard! […] We are doing our very best for you, do your very best for us as well.' Ludwig wrote: 'If you still want to have parents, then listen to what they say and obey it!' And on an attached sheet of paper, which was undated, he added:

> *Your actions towards us make us less inclined to support you, after you have been & remain deaf to all sensible advice; as for Gerhard I demand of you now that you finally take a position – yes or no – your sad game won't go on for ever, don't forget that the post from here goes to B & we can arrange what is necessary; I also think that he himself will soon have had enough of you […] you won't get away with it for ever. It is just a shame that we can't speak to you, perhaps we could talk you out of this nonsense.*

And what was happening to Helmut? He was learning English, and 'he wants to be with his Liesel, he is quite in love with you & constantly waits for the post'. Liesel was told to put out feelers, as there could be the chance for him to receive a technical or agricultural education; 'he's gone off learning'. With this news from her mother and father the year 1937 drew to a close amid great uncertainty, with scarcely a moment to breathe. A young woman, just twenty-two years old, had left Germany as she saw no future for herself there under the Nazi dictatorship. Her parents and her brother remained in the city of Heilbronn, but the time had come for them to plan their own emigration. Liesel Rosenthal had built up a network of friends in England, was in regular contact with friends and relatives, and a marriage to a man in Bombay whom she had only met briefly was in the offing. However, as Aunt Luise wrote, she was probably experiencing 'the same old fear of making a decision'.

2

Digression: 'Dear Liesel, there are still so many questions.'
A trip to Bombay

As mentioned earlier, I wish to interrupt the letter-by-letter chronology for a moment in order to tell the story of Liesel's trip to Bombay in one go (however fragmented it may be). On 8 July 1937 Gerhard Gabriel wrote a letter in reply to Liesel, using his firm's headed paper (GERHARD GABRIEL, EXPORT IMPORT, BOMBAY KARACHI & AHMEDABAD, Ahmedabad House, Wittet Road, Ballard Estate, Post Box No. 534, Telegrams 'Mainqila', Telephone 22446). Unfortunately none of her letters to him have survived, and it was difficult to find out anything about him or his business. For the German version of this book, I could use only two leads, in the first of which Gerhard Gabriel is named as the founder of a metallurgical manufacturer: *The History of Translloy group goes way back to the pre-independence period of India. The first ever metallurgical company in INDIA was set up by Mr. Gerhard L. Gabriel in the name of Bombay Metal & Alloys Manufacturing Co. (Private) Ltd. in the year 1945.*[1]

Gerhard Gabriel is identified in another source as a founding member of ORT India.[2] On the World ORT website there is the following reference to him:

Rabbi [Hugo] Gryn was keen to see ORT set up in India, primarily to provide vocational training for local Jews who were, by and large, as affected by poverty as their non-Jewish neighbours.

In the 1950s he wrote about the Indian Jewish community: The outstanding problems are education and employment, the two going hand-in-hand. The finest thing for India's Jewry would be a technical training school of the sort ORT runs in many parts of the world. World Jewry would perform a great service if it saw to the realization of such a project. Technical skill is at a premium in India and well-trained Jews could easily form small-scale cooperative industries.

Such a school started operating in 1962 with Rabbi Gryn's close friend, industrialist Gerhard Gabriel, as the inaugural Chairman of ORT India. Ms Gryn thinks her father would have been happy to see how ORT was pursuing its mission.[3]

All my enquiries about both Translloy and ORT India, the latter still in existence, went unanswered. However, I believe it highly likely that it was this Gerhard Gabriel, the founder of the Indian branch of an international Jewish organization which today is 'the world's largest Jewish education and vocational training non-governmental organisation', who was writing a letter to 'My dear Liesel' whilst suffering from lumbago. He had a great deal to do, he wrote, and had no time 'to write you a nice, amusing letter'. The 'main purpose' of the letter was to send her a cheque for twenty British pounds so that she had something to fall back on 'if at any point something should happen'. If she wanted to travel to Germany she could pay the money into his English account and withdraw it again at a later date. Liesel must have asked about his 'way of working', and he answered that he would 'rather work very hard now to make things somewhat easier for me further down the line'.

The tone of the letter was friendly and caring. I am unsure if he had already expressed his wish to marry Liesel, or if he had even invited her to Bombay by then. 'I can well believe that you feel at home in England, as for one thing it isn't difficult for you to settle in anywhere and for another you have got out of a kind of prison.'

After the publication of the German edition, Rabbi Hugo Gryn's daughter, writer and filmmaker Naomi Gryn, gave me access to some letters from Gerhard Gabriel, written in the 1960s and 1970s. And her mother surprisingly provided me with the email address of his children, David and Miriam. They added the following information:

Gerhard Gabriel was sent out to India in April 1929 to open up scrap metal operations on behalf of a Frankfurt based Company called J. Adler Junior. At the time J. Adler Junior was one of the largest scrap dealing companies in the whole world. It was a partnership firm owned by four Jewish brothers who had Rothschild as their family name – but as far as I know these Rothschilds were not related to the Banking Family having the same surname. Gerhard started working with the firm as a young 16 year old back in 1923. He rapidly made a name for himself and when only 21 years of age was selected by the Partners to go out to India where he was required to trade under his own name GERHARD GABRIEL because only employees over the age of 25 could sign Letters of Credit on behalf of the Company. To get round this 'problem' the Partners didn't change their company rules, instead they provided a Banking Facility to 21 year old Gerhard Gabriel, in his own personal name.

On his first trip back to Germany, in the summer of 1932 having travelled by Trans Siberian Railway from Vladivostok to Berlin he was met at Berlin's Railway Station by the son of one of the Partners who said "Ah young Gabriel, the youngest employee, based the furthest away from Head Office, making the largest amount of profits for the Company." He felt very proud to hear that. However on the train from Berlin to Offenbach he heard Hitler Youth singing "When the blood of Jews runs from our knife blades, we can be happy again". Clearly things were no longer bright and rosy for Jews in Germany bla so he resolved that he would have to leave Germany. He left Adler Junior in April 1933 and returned to India setting up his own business. In late 1933 he brought his sister and her husband (a leading Dentist in Frankfurt at the time) out to India. In 1935 he visited Germany on a holiday. This must have been when he met Liesel Rosenthal.[4]

In any case, Gerhard Gabriel and Liesel Rosenthal met when he came back from Bombay to Offenbach for a second visit in the summer or autumn of 1935. There is no trace of a correspondence before the letter of 8 July 1937, in which Gerhard expresses his hope that '[you have] left your lazy writing habits behind in Germany' and that she would now better understand

> *why those of us living abroad are particularly sensitive to this – sometimes I really didn't know what to make of it and, by the way, you know full well not to take such parts of my letters to heart. But really from our correspondence I learn very little about you.*

He hoped that her parents and brother were doing well, and this would have been a pleasant end to the letter – from Liesel's point of view – had he not added the following:

> *You still haven't told me what your job is, or how you got into it. How is it that you have friends in Birmingham, are they Jewish emigrés? Dear Liesel, I must bring this letter to an end, but I would ask you to be extremely careful in your dealings with emigrés and people you get to know in a foreign land. I know that you aren't a little girl, but it wouldn't be the first time someone in a foreign land has fallen in with friends who seem like good ones.*

Mr G was no emigré himself as he had moved to India for business reasons before 1933.[5] But he was aware that Germany was 'a prison', so he knew exactly why so many Jews, including Liesel, had emigrated. Where, then, did his critical attitude and mistrust towards them come from?

This letter marked the start of a regular series of letters to Liesel in England. On 19 June 1937 he sent a short missive telling of a lawsuit he had to deal with and on 2 July he wrote another longer letter in which he thanked her for a book, which 'arrived by mail steamer'. He did not know if he would be able to read it any time soon, but he realized that saying this might annoy Liesel a little: 'You will be startled and astonished to read that there are people who have to force themselves to read a book. India is a funny country, and for me it is very tough, as the amount I have to work at the moment is quite enough for this climate.'

He sent her a jacket with cashmere embroidery – 'please confirm that you have received it' – and thanked her for telling him about her living arrangements in Birmingham. 'It's good that you have the chance to get in with a decent English family, which rarely happens to continental Jews.' He somehow failed to strike the right tone; he described Liesel's suggestion that they number their letters as a 'big mistake', as she was 'a long way behind' and, moreover, because his letters, being single-spaced and without paragraphs, contained rather more information than hers. The following handwritten letter from 23 August 1937 was an example of this tight spacing, and he again complained about the lack of letters from her:

> *You can see that I am very demanding, but you already knew that. I would dearly love to spend a day with you by a lake or in the mountains, but that's not possible*

when we're so far apart and so we must be sensible, and you will laugh at this because you will say that every other word from me is something to do with being sensible, but people can never be completely changed, particularly once they have reached a particular age, like me (don't laugh).

A week later things got serious. It is not necessary to be an expert in declarations of love or marriage proposals to find the following – if it even is a proposal – difficult to swallow. In a lengthy introduction he wrote that he had been joined by a young man from Offenbach, who as a 'Half-Jew' had had difficulties in Germany and was happy to have escaped, and he listed the rest of his employees ('three German-Jewish gentlemen, two typists and about fifteen Indians') to emphasize the 'considerable responsibility' he bore. He then went on to say:

It will soon be two years ago that we met at Flesch's. Probably up until the last few weeks of my stay in Europe back then I meant very little to you, thus we had little opportunity to get to know each other properly, so up to now we have only been able to write letters to each other. That was until you left Germany and were treated poorly and, particularly from your point of view, neither with any urgency nor with particular interest. This is no accusation, but after all we are mature adults and it is right that we should be as clear as possible. What other reason could there be for you changing so much since you have been in England and writing more often, even regularly, to me? Do you believe that in the course of a correspondence such as this we can get to know and treasure each other sufficiently to lead a life together in the not-too-distant future? Do you believe that you know me well enough and do you think that you could live happily here with me?

Dear Liesel, there are still so many questions I would like to ask, and must ask, but I have no more time today and so I want to compose myself and tell you about just a few more things you need to know before you can consider my questions properly. – From my (at least apparent) dry and business-like tone you must have noticed that I am by nature a very serious man, even to the extent that I rarely laugh. I am, at least for now, an absolute materialist and so I have to be like this if my business is to succeed.

He then went on to talk, or rather write, about his company! As an independent businessman he needed working capital (i.e. assets), and he regarded this as the basis of a marriage. His professional success was to some degree dependent on political circumstances; he had for instance lost his customers in Italy due to the Italian-Abyssinian war, a difficult situation which 'completely dominates my thinking'. Liesel, by contrast, had been trained in a profession 'in which you can more or less go where your spirit takes you'. She was very well-read, 'while this is completely not the case for me', and although she was used to having good friends around her 'I have hardly any experience of that'. Could a life in India, where there was 'practically nothing to nourish the soul' and where 'nobody trusts anybody else with a single rupee', ever be conceivable for her? Would she feel at home there?

After that, radio silence reigned (unless there were other letters which did not survive). 'I haven't had any post from you for weeks, why not?' he wrote on 11 October. 'What is the reason for your silence?' She had probably written on 3 October, but the post took a long time to arrive. He was planning some big trips, particularly to Japan, and feared, as he wrote on 28 October, that her letters would always be 'trundling behind after me'. As ever, the letter concluded 'with best wishes and kisses'.

It was at this time that Liesel was planning her departure from the Dobbs family and applying for a work permit for the position with Hudson's bookshop. Mr G was sceptical. 'There is no point in dreaming of things which are impossible and by that I only mean that I can't imagine any reason at all why the Home Office would give approval for such a job.' This was in a letter written on 13 November on board the SS *Conte Rosso*, 'outside Colombo'. He described life on board in graphic detail, including the dancing, the cinema, the swimming and the rowing, and then answered her question about 'when I am coming to Europe'. At the moment he was away for almost three months, meaning that any journey to Europe could only happen next year at the earliest. Or was there another option?

> *There is no point running into a brick wall, so be sensible, as there is no other way to do this than if you pack your suitcase and come to me, but the journey via Siberia is long and gruelling and at the moment it's very cold there, I know this from personal experience as I travelled from Japan via Siberia to Europe in 1932. What would your parents and friends say if you took such a step? I eagerly await your reply and remain, wishing you well, with best wishes and kisses, your Gerhard.*

This was, in mid-November 1937, the first mention of this idea. It soon gained traction. Just three days later, from just outside Singapore, he had time to write again:

> *There is another way via the USA or even better via Canada, so Liverpool – Quebec – Vancouver – Japan [and] I would put together an itinerary for you. [...] You could then consider if you want to make this journey and I would meet you in Yokohama or Kobe, wherever we agree later, and in both places there are English consulates where you can be processed officially (at least that's what I assume, but in Kobe there's a synagogue too, I don't know if there's one in Tokyo). Now you will probably be worried and scared and you won't know what to do, but you can take your time to think about it and send me a telegram in Kobe.*

He would order the tickets for her and have them left for her at Thomas Cook in London. But then he backtracked. Liesel would not have the time to see her parents and discuss everything with them. As it was not yet clear if Liesel was happy with the plan, it had to be 'kept secret' at all costs from her parents, from his parents and from his sister. It was therefore

> *completely up to you to decide if you want to make this journey and consequently to marry this man who perhaps you still don't know well enough. [...] Dear Liesel, there is absolutely no point saying "yes" based on the situation or your mood right now and*

> *so I ask you to take your time to consider it properly before you decide, as it would be wrong to let others think about this and decide for you. […] A "no" would in no way change my thoughts and feelings towards you, you can be certain of that.*

Liesel was therefore not to tell anybody about their plans. However, as he added in a postscript on the reverse of the letter, he had told an old friend, Betty Meyer, (Charlottenstraße 12, Zoppot, on the Baltic Coast) the whole story. He told Liesel that she could confide in Betty, who had once taken in his sister and who could 'tell you a few things worth knowing about me'. I can imagine that another mother or sister figure was the last thing Liesel needed in this situation. On 17 November Gerhard found no post from her in Singapore, and he hoped to receive a cable 'and a yes' when he arrived in Kobe thirteen days later. This did not happen either, so his plans had all been in vain. 'It is a shame for many reasons,' he wrote on 17 December from Tokyo, 'that you couldn't bring yourself to travel here, but there's nothing to be done about it.' She had presumably written to him that she would prefer if he first came to London so that they could make the journey together. He could not agree to that as he was already away. Therefore

> *I wonder what caused you to cancel. I could almost think that it was to do with the dowry and things like that and to that I would only say that it has never been in any doubt for me that I do not look at financial matters when it comes to marriage, only at the person.*

So he could 'afford' to get married! And to 'create a nice and comfortable home' for her! Ideally he would like to get married in Japan 'with just the two of us there' as in Bombay he would have to put on a large celebration and take his business into account. But Liesel, it seems, wanted to go to India.

He began to plan her journey and to arrange first-class tickets, as 'there are so many people who would think it odd if my bride didn't travel first class'. He suggested she take the Lloyd Triestino steamer *Victoria* on 20 January 1938 from Genoa, which would arrive in Bombay on 31 January. He was waiting 'eagerly' and wished that it would not be long 'until you are with me'. Travelling by rail through Siberia was out of the question, as confirmed by travel agent Cohen in London in a cable on 18 December: '[we] are told Siberian trains are terrible'. In response Gerhard telegraphed to Cohen 'I agree, please book passage "Victoria" 3rd week of January' and he told Liesel of this in a letter on 21 December. He had also written to his sister Lisbeth 'that she should take care of all the necessaries for the banns etc.' and asked Liesel to send her passport number, date of birth and all other important information to Lisbeth Feibusch c/o G.G., Post Box 534, Bombay. As a German citizen – which Liesel still was – she needed a visa for India, and Cohen could take care of that.

Gerhard assumed that Liesel was coming to Bombay to marry him. I have the impression that she travelled to assess the whole situation – and him – properly. She did not tell him that, making the distress which was coming almost inevitable. Gerhard dreamt:

My dear Liesel, I don't know what your and your parents' position is with regard to a religious marriage ceremony, but I have in any case asked my sister to make the necessary enquiries with the congregation in Bombay and would ask you to write to Lisbeth immediately with your view so that the necessaries can be arranged. You would probably have to have a wedding dress made for you in London and I also ask that you find some nice evening dresses, as in India we always go out in our dinner jacket [...].

She would also need evening dresses on the ship, particularly in first class, and she should enjoy herself whilst on board: 'I take it for granted that you will be careful who you spend time with.' Lisbeth would let her know about what clothes she would need for Bombay – we have already seen this letter from 23 December 1937. Gerhard gave more advice for the journey and preparations for it, as he was very experienced in these matters. 'Don't kick up a stink if the price is rather high and make sure the boys work hard.' He did not recommend that she travel to Germany to see his parents, as they 'probably don't have passports so won't be able to sort anything out'. It could also be the case that the letters Liesel's future mother-in-law would soon send to her 'won't exactly make you 100% happy', and she would need some time 'to get used to the different circumstances'. She still saw 'the child' in him. Then he mentioned another cousin in London who Liesel should definitely not try and contact; there was a story there which he did not yet want to go into in detail. 'I am sure that you trust me not to keep anything secret from you, even if I do not yet put it on paper or if I do not mention it in the first hour we are together.'

Thomas Cook & Son were arranging the journey in correspondence with Messrs. A Cohen & Co. (Great Dover Street, London). A single first-class cabin 'with private bathroom and toilet' had been booked. Gerhard had left £250 in Kobe, and, including taxes and the sleeper from Calais to Genoa, the journey would cost £69. On 28 December he sent a short letter 'to the ship to Genoa' in the firm hope that she would board it on 20 January. He wished her a pleasant journey and that the weather would be favourable, but for some reason he felt obliged to give her another few burdens to worry about on the journey. How else are we to understand the following?

But why must I always go on about business, even in this letter, when I will be able to burden you with it soon enough. Yes, dear Liesel, sometimes they are real burdens, and I don't know if you can imagine how much I am looking forward to having someone with me soon to help me with them, just one person, who will make it possible for me to talk about them and not have to carry every issue around with me and deal with it alone. In my business there are new things every day which take time to be considered and resolved, and I would very much like to talk about them with another person, but up until now that has rarely been possible. [...] Dear Liesel, it is difficult to put all this down on paper and I hope you understand what I mean.

Did he love her?[6] Did he think she was beautiful and desirable? Was he looking forward to discussing her artistic and literary interests with her? Did he want to start

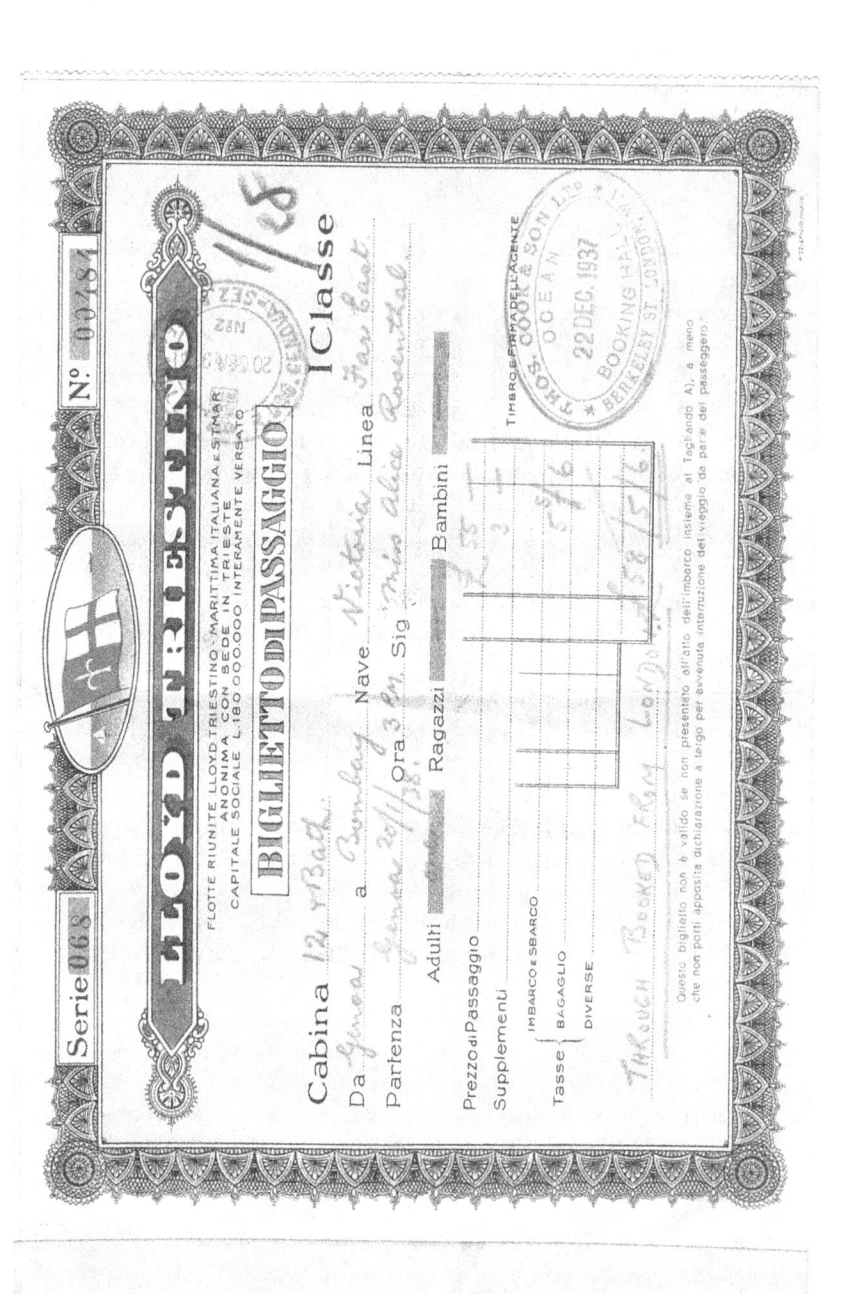

Figure 9 The ticket to Bombay © Baroness Julia Neuberger, Private Collection

a family? She would have already asked herself these questions and she had tried to discuss her uncertainty with friends and family members. On 6 January a telegram arrived for 'Rosenthal c/o Mottek, 83 Greencroft Gardens, London W6' containing the short message 'Marry Bombay, Friedel'. Marry the whole of Bombay – the scale of what she was getting into may indeed have seemed that big. The telegram was found together with a fancy 'Biglieto di Passagio' for Miss Alice Rosenthal, printed by Lloyd Triestino, 'da Genoa a Bombay'. Liesel had probably written to her Aunt Luise in Amsterdam that Bombay seemed very far away to her. 'In terms of distance', replied Luise Loeb to her on 6 January 1938,

> this no longer matters, on the contrary, only going abroad is the right thing to do for today's youth. And just think, others are going abroad aimless a[nd] without a plan, a German is there waiting for you with love and desire, a good, decent man & character. Tell me, what more could a girl want?

Liesel's argument that she did not want to leave her friends in England was dismissed. 'Well tell me how much you get from friendships with young people? [...] Only a husband will become a true, genuine friend for life, he will lead and direct you with a strong hand & with loyal, unselfish love you can be a friend to him.'

Under the pressure of the circumstances in Germany, the older generation was prepared to send their children away, and indeed in some cases far away, but they could not let go of their traditional views on marriage and family (and on the respective role of husband and wife within them). Liesel had an unconventional, financially precarious independence and with her interest in art, books and enjoying life with friends she ran counter to these expectations,[7] which did not find favour with Luise.

> You never write about Mr G in a loving, thankful tone, "the man" or "he", those are your names for him. Not one single loving word about Mr G in your letters. I could almost think that you are not worthy of such a decent, honourable man. You write of having regrets & I think that flirting around in your friendship circle appeals to you more than finding a stable, decent life. Am I right? [...] You might not be this lucky again.

In this letter (undated, but written after receiving Liesel's reply) Aunt Luise demanded that her niece begin her great journey 'with confidence' and that she become 'a loyal wife'. Lore Kahn took the same line on 7 January:

> I have to say it amazes me that you, as a bride-to-be, do not have one single loving word to say about your future husband. [...] And I must tell you that it is unpleasant for me to see that you only ever call him "He". You write that you have such regret and cry a lot. Well, dear Liesele, do you not like Mr G – not enough to become his wife? You mustn't think that I am trying to influence you when I write to you that you don't know how lucky you have been. Everywhere we only hear the best of Mr G & he has been waiting two years for you and wants to make you happy. Tell me, do you really know what you want?

No, she did not know what she wanted. How could she? Perhaps to Liesel's surprise, Aunt Hede in Zürich expressed understanding in a letter from 10 January. Liesel had told her and Uncle Jakob of the great journey she was about to take.

> *We cannot advise you as we do not know the man. You will know yourself what you have to do in such a serious situation. I also wrote to your dear parents that you should go to Heilbronn to see all your loved ones again before you go, if it really does happen. […] I think a lot about you and would like to wish you a bit of luck, don't rush, you will know what you have to do, being abroad makes people more mature and more rounded, nothing can be forced.*

Liesel was being given all this advice from her own relatives, some more understanding than others. She then received a two-sided letter from Offenbach, as Gerhard had told her she would, sent on 18 January 1938 and signed 'Your mother-in-law' on one side and 'Your father-in-law' on the other.

> *You will certainly have had "plenty" flooding in for you to deal with recently, and you will still have to say goodbye to your parents, and yet you have an advantage over many others – you are not going to be completely on your own in unfamiliar surroundings. Gerhard will welcome you with all his love and do everything in his power to make you happy. Moving away in these circumstances, you have no reason to be gloomy about the future and I call on you to "Look up!" Everyone who receives has a duty to give back, become a good wife to my boy, from now on his happiness is in your hands.*

This section of the letter concluded with blessings and good wishes, and Gerhard's father added:

> *From now on your happiness means my dear boy's happiness. Our dear Lisbeth, who depends on her brother so much, is also happy to get a sister. All the conditions are there for you to get a lovely new homeland and a happy home. We have already been in contact with your dear parents, and we hope to get together with them in person soon to chat about our dear children.*

On 15 January Gerhard wrote a handwritten letter and confirmed receipt of her telegram. She would indeed arrive on the *Victoria* on 31 January 1938 in Bombay. But things were still not clear.

> *Your telegram from 9 [January] is and remains a puzzle for me, particularly after I read your letters here in Hong Kong. It is difficult to describe how I felt when I received your cable on the "Empress". In any case I hope that you arrive safely in B. and then we will speak in more detail. If you arrive in the morning I plan to go somewhere quiet for the rest of the day so that we can speak without being disturbed.*
>
> *I also intend to take a room for you at the same hotel I'm staying in, as if you live with my sister or somewhere else privately we will never be able to talk without being*

disturbed. It is incomprehensible to me that you want to come incognito, but you'll have an explanation for it. Bombay is still essentially a village and something like this can't be kept secret there, and after all we don't want to create difficulties or malicious gossip for ourselves to deal with.

On the day of her arrival a telegram from Liesel's future sister-in-law Lisbeth, her husband Ernst and Gerhard came for 'Rosenthal, Passenger Victoria': HERZLICH WILLKOMMEN LISBETH ERNST – BATGEMACHEN GILTNICHT KUSH GERHARD.[8] After that there is a lengthy gap in the letters lasting until 12 March, or perhaps even longer than that. It is as difficult to reconstruct what happened during her stay in Bombay as it is to decipher what Gerhard was implying about Liesel's telegram from 9 January. In the end, all we can be sure of is that the story did not end well – in the family memory Bombay is a small episode, and Liesel will have kept her feelings to herself.

Our job here is not that of a detective, but it would be nice to know more about what happened over the following weeks. All we can do is look at the letters again and try and find fragments which might reveal what happened in India. The first clue comes from a letter from Hermine in which she asked the 'dear children' for them to send just one letter, as neither she nor Gerhard's family in Offenbach had heard any news for a while. Best wishes were coming from all corners of the world, 'but no news from the main characters'. Had Liesel and Gerhard 'forgotten [everybody else] in their happiness'? In that case at least Lisbeth Feibusch (Gerhard's sister) should have written by now! Hermine wanted a letter every week and emphasized: 'Marry soon, as on your wedding day we are expecting his parents and your dear grandmother wants to celebrate your wedding with us before her 95th birthday.' This was followed by a letter written by Ludwig's trembling hand.

Heilbronn, 3 January 1938. Dear Liesel, on behalf of your dear grandmother I am to thank you for the telegram, you would have given us much more joy if you had told us that you were finally married by now. The grace of God has determined a noble partner for you, strive to be worthy of him. Take him as your example and don't play around with him, as patience wears thin and everything has a limit. You are trampling over your happiness, making you and your parents unhappy. All the visitors who come to us cannot understand why the wedding has not yet taken place. We have a destiny and fate, you have yours in your own hands, if you do not marry this noble, selfless man you will suffer the fate you have created for yourself. Why did you really go to Bombay? It's not just a simple day out to Stuttgart. You have enjoyed the hospitality of Mrs Dr F for almost two months, so put an end to it and go and lie in the bed you have made for yourself.

It makes sense to focus on this episode without a happy ending because Ludwig was to a certain extent right. His despair, if not his tone, is understandable and his and Hermine's urgent pleas that Liesel marry Gerhard were based on the uncertainty the Rosenthals felt about their own situation at least as much as their worries about Liesel. These worries would grow in the coming weeks as Liesel – finally! – suffered the fate she had 'created for [her]self'.

Surprisingly, a few fragments of drafts of letters in which we hear Liesel's own voice have survived from the last days of her stay in Bombay. She wrote to Georg and Suse (Schwarzenberger, presumably) that she had decided to get in touch with friends 'when I know for certain what I am doing'. She planned to send the following letter to her friend Joan (Joan Hamlyn, 'a Scottish teacher who was a close neighbour in Antrim Mansions'), written in astoundingly unsure English:

> *I have not written you for a long long time and I feel very sorry about it. Please do excuse myself. You have sent me always such very nice letters and I did not reply and had so much time, but you know there are only one excuse, I could not write, because I was never shure about all my private things. I wrote Olive* [Paynton] *two days ago that I am coming back, and I think she has told you it. I wrote her that I am still engaged with Gerhard and that we decide to get married if he is coming to London in August.* [...] *He is the honest and besthearted man I ever met.* [...] *Joan, life is terrible, since I left Germany, but I try to live as long as possible and if it does not go—-* [...] *I know if I coming back to England now I loose all my relations, but I do hope that my friends will stay with me.*

A few letters followed after this, but they would not change the outcome of this Indian episode. Gerhard was, as he wrote on 8 April 1938, the day of her departure, 'deeply distressed and very lonely'. He had bought her a return ticket to ensure that she would have no problems getting back to England. He took her to the ship and watched it leave, and now he wished that she would 'find complete clarity and strength for your future decisions from the difficult hours, days and weeks you now have to fight through'. His sister was looking after him and he said she believed that the many clever and intelligent friends Liesel had were perhaps 'not the right ones after all' and that they had too strong an influence on her: 'she mentioned the names of Dr Fink and his wife'. However, he expressed his hope that Liesel was fully aware 'that I am there for you, hold nothing against you and still love you, even if I do not agree with the step you have chosen to take'. He still hoped that what had happened was just a trial run and that everything was still open. He could even amuse himself at the people who behaved towards him 'as if I were in mourning'. On 11 April he sent copies of his letters to Liesel's friend Olive Paynton and to her parents.

His letter to Olive shows that Liesel's decision to leave was made late and at short notice: 'she had finally decided on this step only on the day previous to sailing'. He repeated his suspicion to Olive that Liesel had false friends who in his opinion were no good for her: 'numerous friends and other influences which in my opinion were not at all good'. By contrast he thought Olive to be someone 'who take[s] life more as it is'.

Whilst in India Liesel had given the still ongoing affair with Leopold Lichtenstern as a reason for her hesitation. This was the first Gerhard had heard about it, and to then learn that his competitor had continued to send telegrams to India must have been rather humiliating for him. 'I do not wish her to be unhappy but I also have the right to happiness.' Fair enough, you might say.

The letter to the 'Rosenthal parents' was even more difficult. Gerhard had met Liesel in Offenbach in November 1935 and between then and the end of May 1936 had 'spent a lot of time with her'. He had the impression that they were 'agreed', and it was him who was not yet ready for marriage as he wanted to focus on building up his business first. From England she wrote more regularly and affectionately, but never answered his question about whether there might be another man in her life. 'It was only several weeks after her arrival that I learnt of the existence of this "Mr" Lichtenstern.' But Liesel was in constant contact with 'him' and it was thanks to his influence – Gerhard assumed – that she had let their (or his) nice little plans fall through. He wrote all this to her parents and sent Liesel a copy. He also let her see his letter to confidante Betty Mayer – Liesel kept this one too – in which he expressed his suspicion that she regretted leaving at the very last minute, on the ship, 'but by then it was too late and it wouldn't have worked to get all her things off the ship'. He no longer concealed his anger. 'I would never have thought that Liesel could be so devious and malicious.' She also left a short love letter from Lichtenstern behind in Bombay, as he told Liesel on 15 April 1938.

By all measures of morals and politeness, which were as important to her almost-husband as to her parents, our hero had not behaved properly. You could even say she had been 'false and dishonourable', as Gerhard wrote to Betty Mayer on 6 May (once again Liesel received a copy and kept it). She had found six letters from him when she returned to London and replied with just one, which in his opinion contained only trivialities. His response contains some interesting details for us, however.

> What did you put in your letter? That you had a long conversation with the immigration officer, that you are staying with a lady from Australia and her daughter in a hotel, that you have opened an account for yourself with Lloyds Bank, want to give me six kisses, one for every letter. That you are of the opinion you had written rather a lot to me from the ship, with which I cannot quite agree. At the end you also write what you did with your luggage and suchlike, that you spoke personally to Dr Reiter on the telephone and on Saturday and that I would have enjoyed his sermon and that there was more to come – Dear Liesel, do you really intend to continue this kind of correspondence with me in the future or what are your thoughts?

He wrote that she was spending too much time with acquaintances and friends, and that she should focus on him and the question of their future together. Again he counted exactly how many letters he had written, and how few she had, in the next letter on 14 May. He had fallen out with his family because he still wanted to 'stand by her side', and it seemed to him that she was looking for a way out 'which enables you to live for yourself in London and to pursue your dreams with regard to work'. She would have to be 'wholeheartedly and completely' willing to live with him and be ready 'to make every sacrifice'.

It is clear that sexuality and physicality, often ignored as so many seemingly more important issues need to be negotiated (politics, economics etc.), play a large role in understanding the actors and their relationship to each other in this case. Remarkably, Gerhard mentioned this. It might still have been possible for him to come to England despite the problems with his business, but, as he wrote in the letter on 14 May, she would have to be clear, *that it will not do if you want this to be a matter of physical pleasure for a few weeks, the hangover which follows is not worth it and a woman's body is not there to live for a few weeks with one and then with another, that only leads to an abyss and to being used, and that, dear Liesel, would be shameful for you. The idea that a woman should only have physical relations with the man she will spend her life with has a lot to commend it.*

We hear her own voice briefly in an excerpt from her letter ('from 9 to 11 May') which Gabriel answered on 17 May. He quoted her: 'I feel sick. I am miserable, sad and could cry. 23 years old and here I am, a completely messed up life, do you not think?' He could only understand this in reference to himself and thought that she would have found marriage to him a 'botched solution'. He made hardly any attempt to understand her. Another quote from Liesel's letter:

I am indescribably tired, I am not living properly here at all. Sometimes there are hours which I dread more than others, when I have a terrible fear of living. Then there are hours when I am happy, when I am glad to be with my friends.

Again he only read this excerpt as her 'dreading' a life with him. She had never taken any interest in his business, although it was such an important part of his life, and life in India had not agreed with her. In a handwritten letter from 24 May 1938 he told of his acute problems (which should really have been hers too); he had had to 'have his teeth out' – like Ludwig the year before – and again this news feels symbolic. The monsoon was coming, boats with goods had to make a dash for a safe harbour (and the goods could not be sold) and the terrible global events, in the context of which this private tragedy was played out, came to the fore again:

The newspapers look worse every day and when I think about it, dear Liesel, you have caused more problems by leaving than I had thought possible. I am constantly sad and ask myself every single day what will happen and why it was necessary to act the way you did.

The website *Chronologie des Holocaust* (a timeline of the Holocaust) contains amongst others the following entries for the weeks in which Gerhard and Liesel were exchanging these letters:

13 May 1938: Reich Minister for Economics issues a decree on the taking of emigrants' personal belongings. A detailed list must be given of items emigrants wish to take with them. New purchases must be justified by need. The exchange office decides which items may be taken with them.

19 May 1938: First decree for the implementation of the Civil Status Law. Anyone who was a member of a Jewish organisation should have this noted in the civil status register.

20 May 1938: Decree for the implementation of the Nuremberg Race Laws in Austria. The German Reich Citizenship Law from 15 September 1935 and the Law for the Protection of German Blood and German Honour from 15 September 1935 now apply in Austria. "The exclusion of Jews from public office, embodied by this decree, was particularly strictly implemented."

(RGBl I, p594-595).

24 May 1938: Reich Finance Minister issues a decree. As there are no difficulties to be feared as a consequence of the transfer of numerous businesses from Jewish to Aryan hands, all sales outlets, both those to be authorised and those already authorised, are now required to buy their goods from Aryan suppliers.[9]

Each one of these measures had the potential to affect Liesel's parents in Heilbronn and Gerhard's family in Offenbach. 'From my parents', he wrote on 14 July 1938 after a long break and in reply to a warmer, more detailed letter from her,

> *I have had final confirmation that they are seriously preparing for emigration and I assume that they will come here at the end of this year and that I should be able to see them in Europe before then, i.e. they are completely ready to go now, as they can then never come back to Germany. […] I have heard nothing from your parents for a very long time but I think I owe them a letter, only I don't know what I should write to them.*

One last letter from Bombay survived. She had written not once but twice, on 4 and 13 August 1938, from London to Bombay and tried to keep everything open. He wrote on 23 August:

> *If today you believe that you have changed and that you are indeed willing to marry me, then this is certainly for you a subconscious result of the current state of things, but unfortunately I cannot help but think that you would immediately regret this step, when your external circumstances in a marriage with me have changed you will again feel that India and the marriage with me are oppressing you, you will toy with the idea of divorce like before and want to go back to London alone and I will sit here and wait […].*

Instead he recommended that she give her return ticket back to the travel agent. 'That way you will get at least £30 back, perhaps rather more.'

3

'This morning I got a letter from Jack.'
A way out for Helmut

On 30 January 1938, five years to the day since the Nazis came to power, Hermine Rosenthal wrote a letter to her daughter in Bombay, once again awash with accusations and admonishments. 'Received your letter from Port Said early today, your worry for Helmut at Uncle Jakob's is laughable, as you are the main problem now & when you're married Helmut can then be sorted out.' Equally laughable for her was that Liesel still addressed her 'dear stepparents' with the formal *Sie* form. In this chapter I will no longer focus on the issue of her marriage; instead, the main question will be what would happen to Hermine, Ludwig and, most urgently, Helmut.

The situation in Europe, and in particular the imminent Anschluss with Austria, was worrying Liesel's friend Olive Paynton, with whom she had stayed before leaving for Bombay. 'Clare is very worried about all this Austrian business – I wonder where her family are – and what is happening to them. Oh Liesel, the world is in such a bloody mess – what the devil can we do? – and where are we all going to?'

In February 1938 public opinion in Great Britain was split over how the government should react to Hitler's expansionist claims to Austria, which would soon extend to the Sudetenland and Czechoslovakia. Proponents and opponents of appeasement were trying to find an appropriate response, and people like Olive and Jack Paynton (33 Westbourne Gardens) were particularly committed to the issue. They were friends with a number of refugees from continental Europe and were familiar with their reports of life in Germany under the Nazis, although they knew refugees from other countries too. Olive wrote on 16 February that she and a friend had joined the Paddington Spanish Aid Committee and had taken part in the events it held, where films from the Spanish Republic such as *Defence of Madrid* were shown and 'some singing and dancing by Basque children' was laid on.

In British society there was considerable interest in the fate of the victims of fascist injustice, but a significant amount of the population did not want to get drawn in to the conflicts on the continent either.[1] Liesel was very lucky to meet the Payntons, and their friendship would last for the rest of her life (Jack was a photographer and took a great many portraits of Liesel). They were amongst the 'friends' Gerhard Gabriel so mistrusted, even though he regarded Olive herself as someone with a sensible head on her shoulders. In a further letter from 10 March Olive gave some good advice: 'In the meantime you must make as many friends as you can, treat them well and appreciate them, enjoy everything there is to enjoy, write articles about life in India, study Indian law and the customs of the Indian people, and in your learning and knowledge maybe you will find peace.' Despite everything, Liesel could still travel to such a far-off land! This sounds sensible, encouraging even. Lola Mayer, the bookseller, also wrote a very friendly letter on 1 March asking after Liesel's wellbeing and wishing 'that things there turn out as well as you hoped.'

Olive wrote regularly. This was from 18 March:

Here in England we are all very nervous, the war tension becomes stronger. You are I think better off in India. Look at Vienna, look at Rumania, and I fear before long it will be England. [...] Oh how hateful all this talk of war is. All we want to do is to be left to enjoy living our life as we wish, to read and enjoy beautiful things. [...] Everybody is frightened and there is only one question on everybody's lips – is it war or not? What is Chamberlain going to do? He sits and bites his nails and behind our backs gives a free hand to Italy and Germany to rape whoever they like – thinking that in so doing they will not rape us. But will Italy and Germany be satisfied – I think not.

Even though she and other friends, among them Paula Bernhardt and Renate Banhall, sent letters of encouragement to Bombay ('After all, you are not the first girl to get married [...], cheer up, because something much worse could have happened to you and don't feel so gloomy,' wrote Renate on 21 March), her own fears focused on the possible fate of England.

In Heilbronn things were becoming increasingly difficult too. Helmut had exams, but his school was under threat of closure. Ludwig wrote on 28 February: 'Both the big cigar factories have been sold now, it's getting bleaker for us.' In a letter from 31 March Hermine threatened that Liesel would 'hear & see nothing more from us', as 'you would be damned from all sides & no hair will grow on your head' if she did not put an end to her 'pig-headedness' and marry the 'honourable Gerhard'. Ludwig wrote that 'I prostrate myself before you to beg that you stay there & marry him' ('It would melt the hardest of hearts', added Hermine, 'to see a father "prostrate himself" before his daughter to ask for something'), but both of them knew that their own position was becoming increasingly untenable. 'Dear child, we will soon have to follow you, it is impossible to wait any longer.' Helmut was learning English, even sending her a joke written in English doing the rounds in London emigré circles. He had received high marks for his exam, not just in 'Phisics', English and Geometry but also in Ivrit (Modern Hebrew), Chumash (Torah), Prayer (Tefillah), Jewish and Bible Studies, which he was presumably taught at the Heilbronn Israelite Religious Society at the 'Adlerkeller' public house. In a postcard from 15 April Hermine went into more detail:

Uruguay will be the goal. Believe me, it is extremely difficult for us. Dear Papa is 58 & I have bad feet, but after you were so inconsiderate others have to consider everything, as your brother has to worry about us. Can't find a place to live. [...] All three of us are learning Spanish.

Ludwig sent another angry letter afterwards:

> Your behaviour in B. to leave 1 day before the wedding is so shocking & heartless to dear Gerhard & Lisbeth & family & also to us that we are completely mentally broken & out of sheer shame are embarrassed to leave the house – if I had you here I would beat you every day as no other child in the world is so stupid, short-sighted & heartless & so selfish, what do you care about the fate of your parents & your brother?

Mrs Schwab from 'Woppernhaus' (Woburn House) had told them that she could do nothing for Liesel, and Ludwig felt that she should not intrude on the 'S. Family': 'do you have no shame at all?' He did not know, and nor could he, that it would be this Anna Schwab who would help Liesel arrange her parents' escape from Germany.[2] Instead he demanded 'within 48 hours' an explanation for her behaviour towards 'L.' [Lichtenstern] and, if he did not approve of it, would find out where he was staying from the police and, 'accompanied by a very energetic man', would bring to account the man who in his opinion had prevented his daughter's happiness with his 'scheming'. In the same letter Hermine added that Liesel should return to Gerhard 'as a penitent woman', work hard and assure him of her eternal love, though by now this was a losing battle. She knew that the dream was over, as did Ludwig: 'Now we have to make a decision.' He still thought, as he wrote in a letter from 29 April 1938, that 'we will look after our future ourselves & you do not need to worry about it'. Hermine added: 'I was in Stuttgart at a big important lecture given by Max Warburg & he advised us to go abroad. […] You will notice that we want to leave.'

For Liesel that meant she had to find a new job. Eduard Rosenbaum from the London School of Economics and Political Science (LSE) wrote to her on 18 May 1938 that a position as an unpaid intern ('with future remuneration') was out of the question as there were so many English applicants. 'In the light of your language skills' would she perhaps consider a secretarial position? Gertrud Bing from the Warburg Institute wrote a few days later on 23 May:

> I fear it will be a serious blow for you when I tell you that it is exactly the same for the Warburg Library. I would very much have liked to help you, and I believe that you would have done very good work for us whilst at the same time receiving training. But the important factor against it is that we urgently need English staff for the library, for dealing with our readers, and that what I had hoped to achieve, namely employing you alongside an English librarian, is financially beyond our reach.

Mrs Bing, too, advised her to apply as a secretary, as perhaps there was a job for her which would offer 'a certain intellectual satisfaction'. So we find Liesel on the fringes of two academic institutions which were in fact closely connected with German-Jewish emigration to London.

> LSE was founded in 1895. The decision to create the School was made by four Fabians at a breakfast party at Borough Farm, near Milford, Surrey, on 4 August 1894. The four were Beatrice and Sidney Webb, Graham Wallas and George

Bernard Shaw. [...] The aim of the School was the betterment of society. By studying poverty issues and analysing inequalities, the Webbs sought to improve society in general.[3]

Today the LSE is the world's most international university and back then it opened its doors to many refugees, not least of whom was economist Friedrich Hayek, who had emigrated from Austria and in 1974 would be awarded the Nobel Memorial Prize in Economics, along with Swedish economist Gunnar Myrdal.

The Warburg Institute was named after its founder, art historian Aby Warburg (1866-1929).[4] His successor Fritz Saxl (1890-1948) brought the renowned research library to London, where from 1934 it was accommodated in Thames House and from 1937 in the Imperial Institute Buildings, Kensington. In 1944 the Institute was incorporated into the University of London. Gertrud Bing (born 7 June 1892 in Hamburg, died 3 July 1964 in London), who told Liesel the bad news, was herself an art historian and philosopher who had received her doctorate from Ernst Cassirer in 1921 and had edited his *Collected Works* (*Gesammelte Werke*, 1932). She played a role in saving the Warburg Library from Nazi attacks in 1933 and in relocating it to London. In 1955 she became the director of the Warburg Institute.[5]

Liesel was still unable to find a job which would pay her enough to get by, as Hermine was demanding ever more urgently. 'On Friday I was in Stuttgart,' she wrote on 18 May,

> *at the important offices regarding Helmut's future as he can leave school in Nov. or March at the latest & there's absolutely no more time to lose; everywhere we were asked if you would be able to look after your brother & us. [...] I wish that you had had to sit in the interview room at the office, you would not know what hit you* [Dir würde Hören und Sehen vergehen] *& all your arrogance would disappear! I well believe that you have such a good friendship with the important Mrs Schwab, but it's nothing new or surprising to me that wherever you were & are you make friends with these kinds of people, like in Heilbronn, like in Stuttg., like in Mannheim w/Mrs Neter,[6] in Frankfurt Mr & Mrs Hirsch & Mrs Epstein, who by the way have all gone now. All know you well enough & regret that you are so helpless & without a stable job. Otherwise nobody incl. Mrs Schwab has brought you any happiness.*

This was without doubt written out of desperation. Invoking religion and the prayer book, which Hermine had 'laid on my bedside table ever since all those hours of worry', reinforced her traditional view of the distribution of roles between parents and children: 'Well brought-up children,' she wrote for Liesel, 'are the fruit of your grace, my God, but woe betide them if they should become wayward!' And she added: 'Much has changed here, our friends have gone.' Ludwig continued the letter, writing that all their friends found Liesel's return to England 'a puzzle in such times as today, where children, as is the case in every other family, should be the pioneers for their parents & siblings'. This is quite understandable. Why, though, did Ludwig feel the need to add the following? 'They're right, those people who say that young girls who work in bookshops have a screw loose, look at Peiser and your little old self.'[7]

This must have provoked Liesel, more than any comment on Gerhard Gabriel and the chance she had missed. It seems she had told her friends the Sußmanns about how she had never 'got on' with her mother, and this had inevitably been passed on to Ludwig in Heilbronn. She was expected to simply ignore these provocations and be a sensible child – 'after all we have to stick together'.

Hermine's next postcard, on 24 May, was written from the waiting room 'at the aid organisation' for German Jews [the *Hilfsverein der deutschen Juden*] in Stuttgart. For her what was now important was that Liesel be married, whether 'to G. or Li., we don't care who'. This was the first postcard to be sent to Miss Liesel Rosenthal, 25a Thurlow Road, London NW3. Hermine was still sitting on the dowry for her daughter, and was sewing and stitching various things. On 2 June 1938 she formulated her thoughts on marriage.

Now you have the perfect opportunity to marry Lich[tenstern] after the mourning has begun, father Lich has completely disinherited his son & his brother has taken him in, weakened, in Schlepptau, but without you. What you write about the other man is only provisional & how unhappy you are when there is no mammon there for you. [...] Oh I could tell you of so many cases where what started out as loving marriages became hyena marriages. Sensible marriages are the ones that last. When an honourable, hard-working man loves you then you have all the luck. Dear Liesel, the reasons you gave for not marrying Gerhard show your silliness and moreover your stupidity. As a woman you do not need to play tennis & go swimming with a boyfriend, as there you can darn his tights and clothes, look after the household & keep it in order & cook. Your husband is happy when his wife has cooked. You write that Gerhard would be right for an older girl, well tell me, aren't you already an older girl at 23?!! Most girls are engaged & married at 19 & 20, the older ones find it difficult. Almost everyone from your year is married. No parents have experienced as much tetchiness and agitation as we have.

Such conflicts are common in many families, and those involved will tell each other about them. The world of Heilbronn emigrés was small and their network was clearly close-knit, as the following letter from Hermine on 7 June shows:

You must have told the ladies at Woburn House all your tales of woe & they pass them on to visitors from Heilbronn & that's how we know everything. For on Saturday Dr H with his bride Gretel St. visited Uncle Sigm. & [I] asked Gretel if she had seen you, Dr said they had got wind that 1 lady from the committee had invited you round.

In the political circumstances such conversations transcend private or family nature. They were discussions on each individual's future and the demands of a potential emigration.

Dr then said you can't judge a city & a country's customs if you are there for 10 weeks, what really matters is willpower. In every lecture we are warned of drawing comparisons somehow – most would thank our creator if they were given what you scorn!

Hermine went to a number of lectures. Jewish aid organizations made efforts to provide information on possible emigration destinations, and at these talks, based on reports from emigrés all over the world, the attendees were indeed warned against comparing conditions in the new countries – often unfavourably – with life in Germany. In Israel, amongst the Yekkes (the Jews who had emigrated – not always willingly – from Germany) the 'Beiunsnik' who maintained thought that 'amongst ourselves' ('bei uns') everything had been better was a common feature of stories.[8] Hermine's letter finished with the admonishment: 'I've said my piece enough by now: marry soon, then you will be a happy, joyful & satisfied person again & everything will be easier for you & your standing in the family & with all friends will be made good again!' Ludwig repeated the warnings and right at the end Hermine added: 'Helmut's friends are all going away this month, he's alone now. Rosel Ucko is going with family to Colombia, Eugen Kirchheimers to America & Rosenthal-Majors to Genua for now and then further.'

On 29 June Jakob Wertheimer wrote a stern uncle-letter to Liesel from Zürich. She had visited her relatives there on her way to Bombay, leaving them with the impression that she was on her way to the 'haven of marriage' to become 'a nice little wife'. Shortly afterwards, however, she had sent 'a crazy telegram' asking if Jakob would help her if she did not marry. Both times he answered her 'like I was answering someone whom I mean well', but no response had been forthcoming from her. 'This fits your nature, your way of trying to avoid being thrust into reality at all.' For this reason he was not in favour of giving Helmut over to her care (implying thereby that that was what she was trying to do!); it would be better for him to 'first learn a trade and then come'. And as Jakob was someone who never sugar-coated things, he added a few lines about Heilbronn:

> For your parents it is a constant hither and thither with America, Montevideo etc. Every week your mother hears of another country where you can live cheaply, but she doesn't grasp that wages there will match. Of course it's not nice for Jews in Germany, but despite everything your parents can live there for a long time yet with our support, they won't get it as nice anywhere else. – Simply leaving isn't enough, we see it all too often at our meetings where these things are always coming up.

This was written at the end of June 1938. We cannot use hindsight to judge such remarks, but Liesel, through her contacts with Woburn House (which by now had become the most important centre in London for those fleeing Germany), *could* assess the situation in Germany. This letter disqualified him as an appropriate advisor in her eyes: 'They won't get it as nice anywhere else.' Thankfully she knew better.

I will pause for a moment here, having just read an excerpt from a letter Gerhard Gabriel sent to Liesel on 19 July 1938 from Bombay. The question of what I am really doing in this book, looking at each individual letter from the collection and attempting to reconstruct a story from them, is clear by now, but it keeps cropping up whilst I am writing. I cannot shake off the strange thought that this is an unwritten novel. I am of course trying to *reconstruct* events which actually happened – as far as possible – but I am aware that I am also *constructing*. A different author may perhaps have selected other excerpts from the letters and may, for instance, have treated Hermine (who still held on to the dowry for a marriage which would never take place) more sympathetically, or given the wisdom accumulated over the years by sixty-year-old Jakob Wertheimer more respect. This would make the story read differently. This is not a physical experiment, which in the best case scenario would always give the same result whoever carried it out.[9] Gerhard Gabriel wrote:

> *Everything has become so dissatisfactory and difficult thanks to your ill-considered actions that I sometimes wonder if all this has really happened or if it's just a bad dream, but unfortunately it is reality and perhaps you, dear Liesel, are the stuff of novels. I think of the short story you have left behind for me and perhaps I will see everything that happened in book form again. After all you are not without talent and are also selfish enough to use it as material for stories or a book. Afterwards you will probably be delighted by the success of your book and forget everything else.*

Now it is not Liesel who is ordering 'everything that happened' into a book, but in my imagination I see Gerhard looking over my shoulder as I write. I could not ask him if he would agree to become part of a story and it unnerves me that he perceived this problem. A writing strategy that takes such considerations seriously might involve treating Hermine Rosenthal with more understanding, particularly when she wrote (in an undated letter which was not kept in its entirety, as these sources so often are): 'I always cry when a yg. girl gets engaged. All this unpleasantness would have been spared if [you] had not gone to B. & had not trumpeted it to the world & had not led those so well-respected parents in Offenbach up the garden path.' She was writing this story too, from her own perspective, and it is unfair of me to expect her to do so in any other way.

And even the facts themselves do not always want to be put into an order. Hermine was still asking on 18 July 1938 'do you have a stable job that earns you money & means you can save something? Now you must worry about the future, you are getting older & suitors are getting fewer. I am anxious you have missed your opportunity.' She sent this postcard to 25a Thurlow Road. The sequence of events in Alice Schwab's recollection was rather different, however. After telling of how she left Germany and how she arrived England during the coronation celebrations she says in the interview:

> *I left Birmingham after six months and came to London, where I stayed with friends. To earn some money, I looked after children and did that sort of thing. I also worked in Woburn House, the centre for the care of refugees, later Bloomsbury House, with my future mother-in-law, Anna Schwab, helping to interview people and things of that sort. I found this very difficult, since their problems were so like my own. Luckily, at the beginning of 1938 I had an interview with Marks and Spencer with a view to a job as a trainee staff manager. At that time I managed to get my young brother out of Germany. At first I arranged for him to stay with a very nice family in Dulwich, who sort of mothered him, since he was only thirteen years old. Then I got him into a school, a small private school in Brighton. This was arranged through Woburn*

House, but I managed to help a bit financially. Woburn House was an organisation that was started in 1933 when refugees first stated to come over. They did a fantastic job. When I was helping there, pleasure boats were still coming from Germany in connection with the "Kraft-durch-Freude" scheme. Some people made use of the scheme to get out of Germany, arriving as so-called "tourists" in England and simply not going back. And my future mother-in-law had to go to the Foreign Office to explain why they couldn't go back, because things were so difficult in Germany and that was the only way they had of getting out. At that time, through friends, I got myself a little attic room, at 25a Thurlow Road. It was a wonderful place. I was the only refugee living there among a group of young people.

Alice Schwab, too, was writing her own story, looking back at her life and addressed primarily to her daughter and grandchildren. Does it matter that what she said in the interview does not tally with the letters? If I have understood it correctly, the interview with Marks & Spencer (the firm, founded by East European Jews, employed many refugees) came first, then the room in Thurlow Road, then the new job – 'I joined Marks and Spencer in September 1938 in their Hammersmith branch' – but Helmut was not to arrive in England until much later. The 23-year-old Liesel did not yet have the confidence with which Alice Schwab presents herself to us at the age of seventy-five. She was, however, on the way towards leading an independent life.[10]

The next document in the chronology should be included here, although it is incomplete: unfortunately, of all things it is the first page of this seven-page letter which is missing, meaning that the date is unknown. It is scarcely reliable as a historical source. However, in one section the writer speaks of an event 'just over two weeks, on Friday, June 10th'. The only year in which 10 June was a Friday was 1938. The letter was signed 'Sam' and we can identify him easily enough. Julia Neuberger wrote: 'Sam Barron was an old friend of my mother's who I knew quite well. He died in the late 1970s, early 80s. He was a very assimilated and left wing Jew – and rather socially awkward. I think he did marry eventually, if briefly, but not sure.'[11]

This letter, too, dealt with marriage, and it was a sort of personality profile of Liesel and of 'the man with whom you have been dealing during the last four weeks'. Liesel translated words she did not understand for herself and added some comments. This is therefore a sort of ego-document, and what Sam had to say about her and her relationship with her family is of interest to us. While he had already announced his marriage to Liesel to his whole family, she was not ready to do so:

You, on the other hand, have not the slightest interest in all this. You've attempted to cut yourself off completely from your family, and doubtless have built up a sentiment of contempt for family relationships in general. You take great pride in looking upon yourself as the black sheep of the family.

Whether this was true or not, it was clearly the impression she had given some of her friends in London since returning from Bombay. Sam described himself as 'a typical Englishman', which first and foremost meant showing great restraint in personal emotions:

> I've carefully taught myself to restrain my outward expression of my emotions. My face and eyes and my general demeanour never show my real, strong emotions. [...] My work as a barrister merely strengthens this ability to hide my emotions.

She, however, was easy to read:

> You exhibit all the symptoms of narcissism. Your conflict with your mother – cause, the birth of your brother when you were a spoilt, pampered lone child of nine. The conflict between you in recent years has been due to a rationalization of this earlier basis of dislike. Hatred of your mother as a youngster – over-intensive love of your father as a compensation.

In contrast with many refugees he knew, she had no political awareness:

> You are déraciné, Liesel, and everyone over here realises that you must quickly take new roots in England to save you from the utter demoralisation that has been the fate of so many German refugees.

'For family reasons' it was impossible for him to see her as a lover, or to live with her, unless they got married. 'But this, for you, isn't a reason at all. Your attitude is, I did it, why can't you?' In his view the best thing for her would have been 'to have married someone with your own German middleclass Rhineland [!] background' – for example, the man in Bombay. 'I admired your return from Bombay as a display of independence; I now look upon it, in view of what I know of you now, as a piece of lamentable recklessness.' He was still prepared to marry her, but did admit that after reading this letter she was unlikely to come running to him.

This was amateur psychology, but it does show why Liesel (in his opinion of course) had problems not just with her relatives and her German inheritance, but also with the 'adaption' to English society. In both systems there were similarly clear expectations of morality and decency, and both were an uneasy fit for a young woman striving for independence and autonomy, as unsure and foolish as she was. At the time she received this letter Liesel was experiencing *emigration as emancipation*. This was difficult for her, and the imminent role reversal was difficult for her parents, and indeed some of her friends who only wanted the best for her, to accept.

The course of events had broadened her horizons, without her necessarily being aware of it. Her life plan – which she could only explain to her parents piecemeal and with some awkwardness – now extended beyond the restrictive image of marriages of convenience and dutifully having children. All those writing here realized this, and it was painful for each of them in different ways. Worse, however, was that these private family conflicts were being played out under the shadow of an ever-increasing threat. This was clear to see in a letter from Ludwig and Hermine from 2 August: 'The man,' wrote Hermine – who he was is almost immaterial, though it was better not 'Lich.' – 'could act as guarantor to go abroad & we could go wherever with your brother. Our relatives explained that they can't do anything & this chance has fallen to you but you didn't want it.'

No, she did not want it. She wanted to sort things out herself, which had only become a possibility as a result of her emigration. The interview at Marks & Spencer was without question a promising sign. Meanwhile, Uncle Sigmund had died in Heilbronn. The postcard (from 12 July) with the news was sent from Oststraße 112. Luise Loeb wrote from Amsterdam that 'we are glad to hear that you have a job at the moment', and she also said that Hede from Zürich and Julius were there with Therese to find a solution 'for Eugenie regarding her husband, who unfortunately was caught again'. On 31 July Hermine wrote again and – after the familiar litany of accusations – went into more detail on her own situation:

> We are deeply, deeply unhappy! First because of you, second dear Papa has no work any more, third we have to move out on 1 October & fourth we don't know where to turn to get away from here. Everyone says you have a great daughter, she should do something for her parents and brother. You probably could have let Helmut come, but our relatives would have had to pay for it & would not be a positive thing where he could have learnt a trade.

The family conflict in which Liesel was so deeply involved – 'You write in a letter that Rosenfeld is a pig, your father said immediately and rightly what you then are' – was only ostensibly about Gerhard Gabriel.

> Dr Heymann [Dr Heimann, then rabbi of Heilbronn] & Gretel Steigerwald have their wedding in August, they are so happy and cheerful, like Margot Schwarzwälder, just turned 18, marrying in August. They are all going away & into uncertainty. You dear Liesel have certainty & were envied by all your friends & by us & now we are in a terrible position.

Hermine had begun to sell the clothes which had been intended for Liesel's dowry, 'as perhaps we will only find a room to live in'. From her perspective 'your many problems you always have are nothing'.

Her perspective was, in terms of life in Heilbronn, completely understandable. Journalist Hans Frank's work *History and Fate of the Jews in Heilbronn* documents in detail the increasingly restrictive measures imposed by the Nazis and their impact on the local situation for the Jews:

> On 25 April 1936 a decree from the Württemberg Political Police forbade them from using the Hebrew language at their meetings etc. and the Jews began to be placed under special supervision. More and more frequently the sign "Jews not wanted" was visible on restaurants and "Aryan businesses", and the Jews of Heilbronn were forced to retreat to the "Adlerbrauerei" and later the "Adlerkeller", which were designated as their drinking, social and meeting spaces. Alfred Würzburger even received an "accolade" from the […] Stuttgart periodical "Flammenzeichen" when he hung up a sign saying "In this establishment only Jews are allowed."

There were still a large number of individual businesses, but the evidence suggests that the remaining customers only dared enter the shop by the side or back door and that they brought, or were forced to bring, plain shopping bags with them to avoid being identified as someone who shopped at such places.

Dealings with Jewish citizens became harder and spying was the order of the day. Telephones were monitored. Many were too scared to keep in contact with former friends. Leaders at all levels were incessant in their speeches inciting hatred of the Jews. […]

Much worse than anything which had gone before for the Jews, however, was the "Decree on the Registration of Jewish Property" (German Reich Law Gazette I p414 from 26 April 1938). All Jews were required to register their possessions and if there were any changes to their property, regardless of their economic activity or anything else they did. The Nazi party initially justified the move on the grounds that an overview of the size and proportion of Jewish property within the wider economy was needed. In accordance with this decree property was considered to be everything they owned; the only exceptions were items designated for personal use and as luxuries, as long as their worth did not exceed 5000 Marks.[12]

It was the restrictions in dealings with customers which hit Ludwig, who in addition to working in a wine store frequently used to travel as a wine salesman, particularly hard. School regulations affected Helmut and the everyday repression, notably in terms of where Jews could and could not shop, made life difficult for Hermine. But her view that Liesel's problems were by contrast 'nothing' cannot be supported. On 26 July Liesel wrote to Mrs (Flora) Solomon[13] (who presumably worked at the aid organization for German-Jewish refugees in England):

I have just received a notice from the Passport Authorities that my permission to stay in this country expires on the 31st August 1938, unless I can make some arrangements for the future; and in these circumstances it is vitally important that I get something arranged immediately.

We must read both stories alongside each other, particularly because neither mother nor daughter was able, despite all their communication, to fully understand the life each other was leading. The anti-Jewish measures listed by Hans Franke make no mention of forced evictions or seizures of property yet; more than anything it was the economic pressure – the removal of Ludwig's ability to earn money – which forced the Rosenthal family to give up their flat at 10 Mozartstraße. On 6 August Hermine wrote: 'We are so unspeakably restricted, we have taken a 2 ½ room flat in a rear building without bath or WC.' Liesel had told her she was ill. 'Probably from bathing in the sea', replied Hermine. In the meantime Liesel needed to sort out her own residence permit in England.

As Uncle Jakob had noted, Hermine was always coming up with new plans. 'I had already considered,' she wrote in a letter on 9 August 1938, 'whether in South

Figure 10 The house on Mozartstraße 10 (around 1910) where the family lived from January 1933 on © Stadtarchiv Heilbronn, Archivalien, D079-95 Nachlass Beutinger

Am[erica] I should open a library, I would need your books for that.' On 15 August she gave more detail about their living arrangements:

> We are renting & in the rear building at Hanauer's place on Cäcilienstr., it's terribly small, 3 tiny rooms, no bath, a bucket as WC, kitchen a tiny corner, but we are happy to finally have something, no matter what it's like. Terribly run-down & despite that nothing can be done. You're working with Mrs Schwab, did you not get the warehouse job? Helmut helped out with Schiffer the butcher for a few days, the boy was happy to bring his self-earned money home with him. Dear Liesel I tell you, Helmut is a good, considerate boy, always happy, never in a bad mood, even when I beat him or shout at him. [...] Our departure will have to wait.

Should she travel to England? Or send Helmut after all? 'Now we are wondering if it wouldn't be better for him & us if you could get him an apprenticeship.' The boy had become lazy and had 'forgotten lots and lots'. Hermine seems at last to have understood and indeed accepted that her daughter would now have to look after Helmut. The reproachful tone of the previous few months has almost disappeared – 'we thank you for your lovely letter & your concern for Heller [...], has Gerhard written again?' – and this created a space for new forms of communication. Their relatives in Zürich appeared to see things the same way. Uncle Jakob had already written on 7 August: 'most importantly we must forget this idea that you must get married to look after yourself and make you unhappy for the rest of your life'. Aunt Hede wrote on 25 August in a similar vein:

> I, too, was delighted to receive your last two letters and I have the feeling that you are now on the right track and that love and understanding for your family have resurfaced. As you see it does not take much to win the sympathy of your family back. [...] I was for example never angry with you at your marriage story, because, as I told your parents, it is your ultra-personal business, it was only the trip to Bombay that shouldn't have been made. [...] I believe I am not wrong when I say that everything you have experienced has made you a different person, which would make us all very happy.

She even wanted to go with Jakob to visit London, which neither of them had visited before, and hoped 'to be together in love and family harmony'. Jakob sent her his best wishes and kisses.

What had happened? A lot at the same time. What to Hermine and Hede seemed to be the return of the prodigal daughter into the family bosom was undoubtedly part of a growing maturity – not to take the notion of emancipation too far – in which the trip to Bombay played an important role. But there was still the matter of her calling off her marriage to Gerhard, which to everyone else was inexplicable. After it, and perhaps even as a result of it, Liesel had been reminded (again) of her responsibilities towards her family. But she had summoned up the strength to do this herself.

'Now on to Helmut!' Ludwig wrote a letter on 27 August. Hermine did the same and there was another postcard from her on the same day. The contents of the three missives do not quite match up; possibly one of the dates was wrong. Ludwig wrote:

I am gobsmacked that it should go so quickly & it is terribly difficult for me to believe that something will come of it; how long would he go to school for? What opportunities might he have after leaving school? Our opinion & intention is still to have Helm. learn a trade & not an acad. profession & later he can go anywhere as a capable tradesman & be his own man & also support us, as life nowadays demands that children, when they are grown up, must also look after their parents.

Hermine wrote in her letter: 'Regarding Heller I have always thought that he should go to a school where he can learn practical things & start earning money quickly so that he can look after us outside.' Helmut was currently in Munich staying with relatives, but Hermine sensed that things would now move much faster.

What kind of school is it in Brighton? Dear Lisel, don't forget that Helmut has not been at a proper school for almost 2 years & has become very lazy and careless. [...] He has nice clothes & [I] can always send anything else he needs, the only important thing to me is that the boy needs his mother & his mother needs him & could never see him again?

Should she not rather come with him and look after her daughter, who kept falling ill?

On 30 August Hermine reported that Helmut had returned from Munich 'looking absolutely splendid and cheerful'. The relatives he had stayed with were to go 'to USA [...], they have to go on the 14th'. On 11 September a school transport was going 'there' (to England), but would everything be ready by then? Which initials should she sew on his clothes, would HR be enough? Should Helmut take his bike with him? As she wrote on 2 September:

We want to go to Ur[uguay] but don't know how long it will take & so we wouldn't mind if he could learn a professional trade there, by which I mean with you. If we have to leave he absolutely must come with us.

This phrase, 'there, by which I mean with you' [*dorten, also bei Dir*], is fascinating. It stood for the Other, which Liesel, not Hermine, controlled. Similarly, 'Uruguay', for which (as far as we can tell from the letters) no firm preparations or contacts had been made, stood above all for her access to the 'boy'. The notion of geographical fantasies, which emigrants must develop when planning their journey, can only begin to be meaningfully – and that means individually – understood in connection with the specific ideas and experiences of each person affected.

The chronology of the letters from Hermine and Ludwig was interrupted by a long, handwritten letter from another Sam, sent from 238 Crawford Street, Toronto, Ontario, Canada, on 6 September 1938. The sea crossing – the time in between, not here and not yet 'there' – was the focus.

> *My dear Lisel, well, here I am in Toronto, a little bewildered by the strangeness of this vast country, but living on the veritable fat of the land with my relatives. The crossing was incredibly bad. We had stormy weather each day, and as the boat – the "Duchess of Richmond" – was carrying little or no cargo, the ship rolled and rocked in a dreadful way. In my part of the vessel, nearly all the passengers were ill almost until we reached the entrance to the Gulf of the River St. Laurence. […] I thoroughly disliked what I saw of the province of Quebec. All one could see were priests and nuns, and poverty and churches by the hundred. I hate that sort of environment. […] The Jewish community here in Toronto is almost entirely [crossed out: first and second generation] ostjüdisch [Eastern Jews], but that's the type I get on with best, I think. There is much more entertaining here than in London, & everybody seems to know everybody else. […] The newspapers here are full of information about European events (and, my God, how the atmosphere in Europe has degenerated even since I left England a bare three weeks ago!), nevertheless, because they are over 3,000 miles away from the nearest scene of trouble, people are less afflicted with pessimism and the fear of war. It is, for me, a very welcome change. […] What is happening to you? Has your labour permit come through, & is Marks & Spencer now your employer, as you had hoped? […] Please give my regards to the whole crowd at 25a.*

Sam was another of the 'friends' Gerhard Gabriel had warned Liesel about. Gerhard Gabriel – that seems such a long time ago now. Liesel had gained friends and she had made an impression. Hannah Arendt drew attention to the 'praise of friendship', which is constituted in discussions about the world,[14] and its particular significance in times of emigration. In Sam, Liesel had a friend in Canada and at this time other countries, above all those three thousand miles away, always represented possible alternatives.

The 'cases' Liesel heard about in her work with Anna Schwab at the Council for German Jewry at Woburn House show how the situation for Jews on the continent was becoming ever more desperate. On 10 September 1938 Hilde Stekel wrote, telling of how Mr Feuermann, a violinist from Vienna, was now prepared to come 'with or without his parents'. The same was true of a (nameless) female pianist. Hilde feared that their applications were rejected 'because they originally wanted to come with their relatives'.

'Today the schoolchildren travelled back to England again,' wrote Hermine on 7 September, '& Mr Wißmann accompanied them, he said to Helmut he would gladly have taken him.'[15] Mrs Anna Schwab had also written 'and we will reply to her tomorrow'. Liesel's networking was beginning to have an effect. 'Dear Liesel,' Ludwig added, 'it is very difficult for us to give Helmut up, but hopefully he will study diligently & a useful person will become of him. Is the school in your area?' Two days later Hermine wrote again. Once again the mix of everyday issues and politics, of apparent triviality and clear necessity, is of considerable interest:

> *Rushed about in Stuttgart today & tried to get suits as instructed & shirts etc. & everywhere, including at Bamberger & Hertz, I was told to get a flannel suit, whether dark grey or light grey! Still unsure with the 3 grey flannel shirts. I ask you dear Liesel*

now to try and arrange for an invitation to a school visit for Helmut to be sent from there, it's probably also a question of a ticket. We now have to go and get a child travel pass & it would of course be very important for me to know when Helmut should leave by, we would very much like to have him here still for the holidays. When we have his pass & know when Helm. will go there, then we can send the copy from Mrs Schwab to Berlin.

The Kindertransports had not yet begun at this stage, but clearly the aforementioned school transport had also taken Jewish children from Heilbronn to England, including Gerhard Rothschild, Siegfried's son, and Mäxle Flegenheimer, 'Bella's boy'. The flannel suit and matching shirts stood for England and English school uniform. Hermine informed Liesel on 13 September that the letter, or rather the guarantee, which Anna Schwab had provided for Helmut had been sent to the British Consulate in Berlin, and now they were awaiting the exact date of Helmut's departure. 'If it all works,' Hermine wrote on 19 September,

Heller will travel early on Thursday with Willy & Ida, unfortunately we still don't have his papers, Papa is going to Frankfurt on Tuesday to sort this out, even here he still doesn't have what he absolutely needs. If he can travel he will arrive 6.15 early on Friday in Harwich and 8.38 in London. I thank Mrs Schwab from the bottom of our hearts, if I have time I'll make her a nice laundry bag.

As for Hermine and Ludwig themselves, they were to move into the smaller flat on 22 September.

A small sheet of paper, 'to be filled out in block letters', shows that Liesel carried out the first task she was asked to do:

Name of applicant: *Helmut Rosenthal*
Last resident in Germany (Austria [crossed out]*) until (Month and year:*
   20 September 1938
In *Heilbronn a/Neckar*
Street and house number *Mozartstrasse 10*
Address in England *Beaconsfield College, Brighton-Hove, 71 The Drive (Sussex)*

On 'Thursday, 27.9.38' Helmut wrote:

Dear sister! How are you? I like it here very much. Please send me the rest of my things. I have not heard any news from our parents yet. Have they not written to you either? Please send me my Marks a[nd] *my football boots with the next package.* […] *Hopefully you won't forget me. Helmut.*

This was the start of a new, English life for him. He had his Bar Mitzvah behind him, which in Jewish terms meant he was considered a man and a full member of the community, albeit one which he did not yet have. Good, then, that he had football.[16]

Figure 11 Liesel's brother Helmut, who now called himself Jack Rosen © Baroness Julia Neuberger, Private Collection

On 30 September 1938 Liesel paid back the 22 pounds the German Jewish Aid Committee at Woburn House had 'advanced to you on behalf of your brother'.[17] Having been considered by her relatives to be 'silly' and 'impossible' just a few months ago, Liesel was now regarded as an expert at saving people. Aunt Ev requested urgently that Liesel look after her daughter Lilo, who would turn eighteen on 18 December and needed a 'permit'.

Now another postcard appears which was dated 27 August, but which most likely was written on 27 September. In it Hermine wrote to Liesel: 'On Sunday wrote you & your brother a long, long letter & sent you a large sausage'. Ludwig added that he was 'quite astonished at how quickly you arranged everything'. They accidentally sent the postcard to 'Mrs' and not 'Miss' Rosenthal at Thurlow Road, but this was probably only a distant echo of their great hopes earlier in the year. Now it was October, and the worst news from Heilbronn was yet to come.

4

'Dear Liesel, Urug. is no longer an option.'
What happened to the parents?

Dear Helmut, we were very happy with the first letter you sent us, we had to read it to grandmother five times. We are glad to hear that you are doing well, and hopefully you like it, soon you will be settled in and feel at home. […] Eat healthily, but don't be ashamed if you feel homesick.

Aunt Bertha and Aunt Emma wrote a joint letter to Helmut in England on 1 October 1938. Ludwig Rosenthal added: 'Your English letter arrived too, I see from it that you already speak more English than me […]. So all the best, you are always in my thoughts.' A new parent-child drama was developing. Hermine Rosenthal, who the day before had been in Munich, wrote her first letter to Helmut (and Liesel) on 2 October. Their relatives 'were desperate to know how you are doing, dear Helmut, they are angry with you dear Liesel because you never wrote to them'. She wrote part of the letter in English:

[P]erhaps I will answer You in English, I will send you soon an English dictionary. Your sister is very busy and I hope she will be always well. On Thursday I sent you a great parcel, have You received it? Please give soon answer! Give your dear sister also some goods. [In German] *I ask one more thing of you, see to it that you always do things properly & cleanly.*

Liesel's role was changing, and not just within her own family. Lilla Eisig, a friend of her parents, wrote the following letter from Schaffhausen, Switzerland, on 3 October:

Of course you'll be wondering why you've received a letter from me from here, but it's easier to write from here. We heard from your dear mother that you are doing well a[nd]. that you've found a satisfactory position. Now Helmut is with you too, which you'll certainly be happy about. I wish we were at that stage with Hans. I don't know if Ida Rosenthal talked about it with you during her stay there. You know the situation in Germany, you can't teach the boys anything. And after you dear Liesel have made yourself known at all the important offices I would very much like to ask you if you could perhaps give us some advice or be of help to us in any way. […] How do you make it possible, a. how do you pay for it all?

Liesel was to take over from her mother in overseeing Helmut's education. Hermine wrote a quick postcard on 18 October 1938 saying 'we received a letter yesterday from Helmut as well, he wants be known as Jack Rosen'. Migration research has established that name changes like these were particularly common in Palestine, where German first and last names were hebraecized according to the Zionist ideal, but we also find it in Britain, especially among the younger generation. For Helmut, his 'will' to now be known as Jack Rosen was symbolic of his new start at his new school.

Liesel's contacts – who until recently had been the 'too many friends' – were now beginning to be of use. The aforementioned Lilo, Gertrud Eva Mayer's daughter from Stuttgart, got in touch from Sierre, Switzerland, on 27 October. She attached her CV and hoped that Liesel could sort something out for her, ideally with children, if need be in domestic service. Ruth Richter, also from Stuttgart, wrote on 29 October that she had managed to get a visa for herself for the United States and so would not be applying for a job (which 'dear Miss Rosenthal' had arranged) with Mrs Manson in London. She had a replacement however:

> Now my friend Lotte Gumberich, from Stuttgart Süd, 18 Tübinger Straße, has no chance whatsoever of emigrating. The family circumstances are such that it would be a great relief for them if their daughter could emigrate. My friend has already worked in domestic service and I definitely believe that she can fulfil the role. I would really be very happy if I could help my friend out through your recommendation.

Hans Schloss wrote from Birmingham on 31 October: 'I come begging. Friedel has been in England since Saturday.' She was due to begin a job in domestic service, but the lady 'of all things seems to have had a nervous breakdown on Friday' and so nothing came of it.

> Now I remember that you once said to me that you, if it came to it, could find something suitable, and I would be very grateful to you for your advice and help. [...] I am awfully sorry to have to resume our correspondence with a request of you – the reason I turn to you now is that I set more store by your experience than by anyone else's, as you know Friedel personally and know what she's like.

In addition, more and more letters from Liesel's growing circle of English friends began to appear amongst the letters from Germany (and Switzerland). Harry S. [Jacques Schupbach, known in the family as 'Harry-Darling'] thanked her on 19 October for meeting up with him, hoped for a repeat, and that it 'has started a good friendship'. Liesel could always use friends. Margaret was one of them, and she sent greetings from a holiday in Paris on 1 November: 'tonight we go to the Casino de Paris to hear Maurice Chevalier'.

On 2 November 1938 a letter arrived from Max and Frieda Fink in Memel. They thanked Liesel for her willingness to help their son Helmut. They had waited before replying to Liesel's questions, 'because we wanted to wait and see how the situation develops here. Now the tension has eased somewhat so that we can't really speak of any acute danger [and] Helmut, we have been told, can stay here for a while longer.'

Two days later Ludwig wrote a postcard from Frankfurt. He talked about everyday incidents and a package which had gone missing in the post, as well as bringing the news from the family that Liesel's grandmother was not in the best of health. It also contained a surprise, which he left without further comment: 'Gerh. is now married to a woman from Berlin.' That was quick. After this there would be no further mention of the Bombay episode.

Hermine wrote on the same day, saying that she was happy that her children had spent a lovely Sunday with each other and that 'our fantastic daughter is developing as a cook'. Heller's imminent 14th birthday would be celebrated without him in Heilbronn. The following section contained no surprises: 'Dear Lisel, you aren't getting any younger & I am so, so worried that you should be married & provided for soon. God willing we will yet experience this joy & my most intimate wish will come true.' What came after that, however, is astonishing to read: 'What's really going on with Licht.? Do write honestly, I'm your mother & am constantly by your side.'

Margaret wrote another letter on 11 November, again using the headed paper from the Hotel de Calais on the Rue des Capucines. She had spent a pleasant evening with Dr Freudenthal 'and another Jewish girl and a Mr Rosenthal'. The letter is indeed dated 11 November 1938, the day after the November pogroms in Germany, and news must have reached Paris of what had happened – but here there was no mention of it.[1] The only trace of it comes from Helmut (albeit undated):

Dear Liesel! Received your letter a. wrote straight away in your flat. Dear Liesel do you know that the Nazis are intercepting every letter the Jews write. Our parents wrote to me about 2 letters I haven't received yet. Only received this postcard [not included]. *The liberal synagogue in Heilbronn is destroyed*[,] *the orthodox is still there. Lido Kino* [?] *wished me happy birthday, greetings Jack.*

Jack, formerly Helmut, was now writing to his sister from Brighton and so could explicitly mention the pogrom, whereas Ludwig and Hermine could only hint at it. What happened on the night of 9/10 November 1938 was commendably described by journalist Uwe Jacobi on 7 November 2008 in the article 'Citizens Were Perpetrators and Victims' in the *Heilbronner Stimme* newspaper:

One of the 267 synagogues set ablaze and destroyed in Germany 70 years ago was the temple on the Allee in Heilbronn. The instigators of this arson came from within the upper echelons of the Nazi regime. At a local level fanaticised Germans, stirred up by Nazi slogans to hate their fellow Jewish citizens, carried out this shameful act during the night of 10 November 1938. 'The night that I helped set fire to the synagogue was when I first began to doubt that what we were doing was right', reported Elise Joos (1904–1993), who later became a city councillor in Heilbronn, in 1943. 'Whenever I struck a match to fan the flames the wind blew it out.' In 1988 Paula Hoyler (1905–2002) spoke of another arsonist. 'He boasted openly that he had seen there was finally enough wind.'

Figure 12 The Heilbronn synagogue on the day of the fire, 10 November 1938 © Stadtarchiv Heilbronn, Fotosammlung, photographer: Ludwig Ruff, Heilbronn

It was forbidden to take photographs. One of the few historical records shows the Heilbronn synagogue looking south. By morning the main dome had been gutted down to the metal framework. Fire and smoke rose from inside.

It was impossible to find out any more about this testimony from Elise Joos, so we must (and can) rely on Jacobi's reconstruction of the events.

The call came at 23.30 in Heilbronn. Gynaecologist Wilhelm Kahleyss, whose clinic was next to the synagogue, heard noises at around 1 in the morning "like the clanking of petrol cans". Speaking in 1983, his wife said that when they saw a light inside the synagogue he called the fire brigade, who at first did not come. He said "They want the synagogue to burn." At around 5 in the morning neighbours heard two explosions. Estimates of when the fire in the dome could first be seen from the street varied between 6 and 7 o'clock. At the latest the dome had burned out by 8.42. We can tell the exact time thanks to a photo which shows curious onlookers on the Allee and the clock on the main post office building. The Nazi newspaper "Heilbronner Tagblatt" said the next day that the fire was seen by many as "a just punishment". Rolf Palm's recollections in 1988 were different: "Everywhere the mood was gloomy. Many said: God will not be pleased that a temple was set alight."[2]

Hans Franke also goes into great detail on the destruction of the synagogue, the role of perpetrators and onlookers, and the aftermath of the 'Reichskristallnacht', and this raises issues which directly affected the Rosenthal family. Franke first depicts the destruction within the neighbourhood:

> Jewish shop windows were smashed. Terrified residents were driven into one room of their house or flat while the rest was ransacked; furniture was broken to pieces, cupboards were overturned and emptied, and people raided the larders to help themselves to food supplies. Of all these criminal acts, only two cases went to court. They were the incidents which affected master tailor Henle and merchant Max Rosenthal at 6 Klarastraße and factory owner Fritz Landauer at 5 Klettstraße. In Henle's case, the commander of the troop stated at the trial that he and five men he did not know had obeyed orders and entered the house to wreck the shop and throw rolls of fabric onto the ground to make them unusable. They had gone further, up to Rosenthal's flat on the second floor, to cause similar damage. It was established that they had obtained entry to the flat violently and told other residents of the building who were coming home late to keep quiet. In Landauer's case the commander said he had been assigned to the troop to prevent acts of violence. Incredible devastation was wrought at 5 Klettstraße, a sign of pure destructive rage. Within around half an hour the furniture in the house had been hacked to pieces with various kinds of iron bars. Even "harmless objects like medicine bottles or a row of coat hooks were smashed and destroyed; 33 window panes were smashed, as well as trophies, glasses, vases, bowls, crockery, furniture, a sewing machine, a typewriter, the radio and even a fireplace made from Italian marble". Here, too, the residents confined to a room were threatened and intimidated.[3]

Max Rosenthal's flat at 6 Klarastraße was part of the topography of the Jewish wine trade in Heilbronn. It first appeared in the local directory in 1901, and at the same time Max Rosenthal's name appeared in connection with Max Rosenthal and Josef Dornacher's wine store, alongside Ludwig Rosenthal, at 43 Götzenturmstraße. Later in his work Franke details the ruins of the destroyed synagogue – where Helmut had celebrated his Bar Mitzvah the year before – and discusses what happened to its cult objects.

> The ruins of the synagogue lay untouched for a long time and were a thorn in the side of the authorities in their prosecution of the perpetrators. On 16 February 1940 demolition was begun, and it was completed on 16 March 1940.
>
> The question of what happened to the synagogue's cult objects occupied minds both at the time and post-1945. Very different versions of events have emerged. On the one hand some said they saw them being taken away in good time to the district office. On the other, a witness stated in one of the trials against the perpetrators of the

Figure 13 The burned-out synagogue, 1939 © Stadtarchiv Heilbronn, Fotosammlung, photographer: Fritz Walderich, Stetten

> *Kristallnacht that on that evening (i.e. one day later, 10 November 1938) he had seen how "at certain intervals Jewish cult objects were taken to the hall (the Turnerzimmer of the Harmonie Concert Hall), including Torah scrolls and tefillin, Hebrew banners, but also Jewish trade books etc." This contradicted the view of police commissioner W, who said that he thought he remembered that these objects were stored with all the files in the attic of the Gestapo offices (at 4 Wilhelmstraße); in any case they remained there for some time.*[4]

Friends of the family were arrested and taken to concentration camps, among them district rabbi Heimann, who was released after seventeen days in Dachau as he had already begun to plan his emigration. He was later rabbi in New Jersey and California, where, by then known as Dr Harry Hyman, he was rabbi at Huntington Park from 1957 to 1977.[5]

I would like to make reference to two further aspects discussed in Hans Franke's work, as they posed an existential threat to Hermine and Ludwig Rosenthal. One was the ban on further economic activity, and the accompanying 'Aryanization', and the other was Nazi policy on emigration. The 'Decree on the Exclusion of Jews from German Economic Life' (RGBl. I p1580), passed on 12 November 1938, forbade Jews from running retail businesses, mail-order businesses or ordering offices, as well as being independent tradesmen. 'As at this time most Jews who were able to do so were planning their emigration, they sold their property or gave it up, losing so much of what they owned to pay for emigration and save some of their possessions, all in the name of aryanisation.'⁶ Further decrees restricted the 'Appearance of Jews in Public' (28 November 1938, RGBl I p1676). These measures had a direct influence on Hermine and Ludwig's decision to accelerate their own emigration. Franke writes:

> 151 Jews had left Heilbronn in 1938, in 1939 another 156 followed. This emigration of 1938 and early 1939 can be described as a mass exodus. Even those Jewish citizens who saw themselves as deeply rooted in Germanness and who had believed they knew how to survive realised their mistake. Consequently it was almost entirely older people who remained, as they did not think they could survive the rigours of emigration, or the destitute. Whilst in the early years of the regime they were still officially allowed to transfer property abroad after paying the relevant levy, these numerous barriers now made it impossible for emigrants or those who stayed behind to sell their property or belongings in an orderly fashion. Similarly, at first personal belongings could be taken with them in considerable amounts. Now, when sales were transacted, they were doing little more than giving their things away. Anything the Jews had left had to be paid into a blocked account, and this included all further income; if emigrating Jews wanted to unblock their account they faced high charges.⁷

All these events are only dimly reflected in the preserved letters, almost certainly as a result of the dreaded censor. Shortly before completing this book I received an extremely moving account from Dr Ruth Latukefu in Newport Beach, Australia. The daughter of Friedel and Lotte Fink was seven years old at the time and described her experience of the family's frantic departure in the night of 10 November 1938:

> On that winter's day, Muttie helped me to dress and insisted that I wear two flannel dresses, one on top of the other, with two woollen cardigans as well, under a thick winter coat. She explained that we were only allowed to bring one suitcase on the train and we must therefore wear as much as possible. She put on all her rings and jewellery and wore her warmest dress under a long camel-hair coat. I looked around the empty apartment, now so bare that it no longer felt like home, as all our furnishings had been packed into crates to be sent to Australia, via Rotterdam. Oma Freund, my small white-haired grandmother, whom I loved so dearly, was there with Onkel Hans, and as she hugged me "goodbye," she whispered, "I'm coming to Australia very soon." I was almost seven years old and though I knew we were going on a long journey to Australia, I did not understand why we were leaving or that this was to be the last time I would see Oma Freund, Onkel Hans and the apartment in Garten-Strasse where I had spent my early childhood. Papa was waiting for us at the Frankfurt Railway Station. I was very excited at the thought of going for a long trip on the steam locomotive to places which I had never seen. I had heard of the castles along the river Rhine and of the far distant sea, but only knew about them from picture books. The train had comfortable seats and wide windows and I sat with my face pressed to the glass, taking in all the new sights and listening to the rhythmic clacking of the wheels. It was so enjoyable that I hardly noticed how silent and serious

my parents were, nor did I realize how anxious they must have felt throughout this journey. As the train came to Emmerich, a station near the Dutch border, it halted and uniformed S.S. entered the carriages ordering all Jews off the train.[8]

Lotte Fink herself gave an account of this stopover:

At long last my husband and I had received the papers which allowed us to leave Nazi Germany and we anticipated glorious freedom. However, a few miles from the Dutch border the train suddenly pulled up and uniformed Nazi S.S. officers boarded, ordering all Jewish passengers out. Then in pitch darkness we were marched over a field, not knowing what lay ahead. We came into a brightly lit street lined with people who jeered and swore at us. Some spat from their windows, as we filed below to the prison centre. There we were searched and stripped of all our luggage, even my doctor's bag with medicines. Fortunately, after a night and day we were freed, our belongings returned and told to catch the next train across the border. A few hours later we were free at last![9]

Unfortunately, Ruth Latukefu was unable to find any letters from Liesel to her mother, and I do not know when Liesel learned of the Finks' successful emigration. Lots of news was coming her way. Aunt Luise, Uncle Richard and their daughter Lore wrote from Amsterdam on 13 November 1938:

Dear Liesel, we heard from your parents that we should turn to you, if it would be possible to take steps at the relevant offices (Home Office or Woburn House) immediately, so that your parents can get accommodation as quickly as possible in order to travel from there to Montevideo. Please let us know immediately how high the guarantee must be for temporary accommodation. Hope you and Heller are doing well, which is the case with us so far, we worry greatly about everyone.

Uncle Jakob wrote on 14 November from Zürich that he – like Liesel – had received no news from Heilbronn for a while and that he had tried in vain to send her parents money, only to be 'told' (perhaps on the phone, or maybe from friends who were able to travel to Switzerland?) that 'we are not allowed to send anything'. So he sent Liesel a cheque for 100 francs,

so that you can deal with the matter, your parents will probably leave any time now, if nothing else comes up, for Montevideo. – In any case they are in good health and weren't directly affected by the criminal progroms [!].[10]

It was not until 17 November that Jack Rosen, Beaconsfield College, Brighton Hove, 71 The Drive, Sussex/England, received a note from his mother. 'Today you're just getting a postcard greeting telling you that we're in good health. We would like to come to see you children, speak with Mr Headmaster to see if this is possible. […] Many, many loves & regards, your mother.' A day later Aunt Luise and Uncle Richard wrote, with added greetings from Uncle Julius, who was staying with them in Amsterdam. They told Liesel *that we have applied for your parents to stay here temporarily. We have also now paid the fees for Uruguay, meaning the application with the form you sent in is now invalid. We hope that this business works out, as we're doing everything to get your parents out – to the best of our ability – which is currently severely restricted for us all here & means a great sacrifice for us.*

Hermine wrote a long letter, partly in English, on 21 November 1938 to both children – more exactly, to 'my golden treasure' ['Goldschatz'] and to 'my dear Lisel'. She had not taken any language classes for a long time, as 'all the friends who have taken part, are away and I have no money to take lessons in languages, I have finished also with the Spanish lesson, because it was so dear for father and me'. Liesel's grandmother was in good health ('she is always asking after her little scallywag') and the letter ended with: 'Your classmates can't all keep going, so we're even happier that you two are together. Dear Liesel see to it that there's a chance.' The fear of interception and censorship colours the language, and the most important issues were hardly discussed. They found it difficult to come to terms with Liesel and Helmut's English life, particularly Helmut's in his new school: 'If you are cold you must take the feather bed, don't need to feel embarrassed, all German children do it,' she wrote, and Ludwig added: 'Playing football is fine, my boy, but be careful.'

Hans Schloss got in touch from Birmingham, hoping that Liesel would soon come and visit him. He wrote on 23 November:

I fear you are exactly as worried as we are about the fate of your people, after your father was interned together with mine in Dachau. – I know that the word "Dachau" means concentration camp and unspeakable horror, but as I don't know how much Heilbronn has told you about what happened to your father I would like to tell you that they were put in a special camp, so not a concentration camp, where they had some personal freedoms and could even buy food etc. – no hard labour and life was quite bearable. You will know that the people, as soon as they get an entry permit for another country – are immediately released, you are also I'm sure happy to be in such a good position with Mrs Schwab, who I'm sure has set in motion all the necessary things for you all. Woburn House is the only way to do it these days and we went through it to apply for my parents. [...] You can certainly get a permit for England for a certain amount of time, and then you have to see. You had already been told about all this anyway, and if not, then it will perhaps contribute to improving your mood somewhat.

This is another point when Alice Schwab's recollections, taped in 1990, do not quite match up with the letters. It could also be the other way round – I do not wish to cast doubt on her memories, rather I am highlighting the problematic nature of the sources. In this case, Hans Schloss had misunderstood quite badly. Julia Neuberger reacted promptly to my question about her grandfather's internment after 10 November 1938: 'My mother says in her "Thank you for everything" that he was not interned because he had been a POW in WW1.'[11]

In fact, the story is told in a very matter-of-fact way in her 1990 interview, and I am including this excerpt first before I go into the more complex (at least to me) version from the sources. Alice Schwab started by describing her job at Marks & Spencer as 'the fifth girl on the second hosiery counter'. The shifts were long, from 9 o'clock in the morning through to 10 or half past 10 in the evening, and it was often cold in the shop.

> *Still, I was employed! I earned three pounds which helped me to pay for my brother. On my half day I also taught German. I remember giving German lessons in Putney which wasn't very far from Hammersmith, and coming back to Thurlow Road on the 30 or 74 bus, and reading the Evening Standard about the start of the pogroms in Germany. Suddenly I realised how bad things had become since I had left. […] I had already noticed that my parents couldn't say very much on the telephone and I learnt that more and more people from our part of the world had left. Some of my relations, cousins, came here and then went on to America. The people I had stayed with in Frankfurt, the Finks, emigrated to Australia and warned me that things had become very difficult. I got worried about my parents. Luckily, my grandmother died at that time, at the age of ninety eight, and there was nothing more to keep my parents in Germany. So I tried to get them out. My Birmingham connections were very helpful, and Anna Schwab from Woburn House. I also had a friend whose father was a bank director* [possibly Nathalie Gurney. The Gurney's were Quakers.] *and he lent me the two hundred pounds I needed as a guarantee for my parents, since the authorities would only grant an entry permit if you could produce a guarantee. So I got permission for my parents to come.*

At a 'get-together for refugees' organized by Nathalie Gurney on Monday evenings Liesel met Professor Wolpe, whom she told of her worries about her parents. Above all she feared that the visa they were hoping for to go to Uruguay would arrive too late. Wolpe introduced her to Mrs Winifred Rathbone, who suggested a hostel run by a Mr and Mrs Seligmann in Wimbledon as initial accommodation and contact point.[12] Liesel's biggest worry concerned her father:

> *I was determined to get my father out as quickly as possible, because it was more important to help the men, since they were under a greater threat of being thrown into concentration camps. The camps had already been set up! I had an uncle who had already been in a camp, but they let him out again. However, he was re-arrested, taken back to camp and killed. After the camps were set up, things changed completely. We knew about Sachsenhausen which was probably one of the earliest camps, but there were also local camps, although we didn't know exactly where they were. There was certainly one in the Schwäbische Alp [recte: Alb] to which people were taken. Of the people taken, some were returned to their families, broken and frightened. I had an uncle in the Palatinate who was taken; a few months later his ashes were returned to his family, plus his watch and personal possessions. In good German fashion, these were returned. It was therefore a great relief to my brother and myself that we managed to get our father out. When he arrived, we took him to that lovely hostel in Wimbledon Parkside, where he was very well received by the other refugees who had been brought over by Mrs Rathbone and were living there.*

I assume that the uncle she refers to here was Ludwig's brother Max Rosenthal, whose address in Heilbronn is given by Hans Franke as Weinhandel, Fa. Rosenthal u. Dornacher, 6 Klarastr.; 27 Moltkestr.; 32 Allerheiligenstr.; 10 Badstr., from 14 January 1941.[13] According to Franke he was taken to Haigerloch on 23 March 1942, from there to Theresienstadt on 22 August 1942, and finally deported to Maly Trostenets on 29 September 1942, where he was murdered. Clementine and Hermann Rosenthal, who were related to Ludwig and Hermine (though I am not sure how exactly), died in April and December 1943 in Theresienstadt, respectively.[14] Emma Dornacher, born in Heilbronn on 17 August 1870, Ludwig's sister, was deported from Frankfurt and threw herself off the train, according to family memory.

All these deaths were part of the deportations of the last remaining Jews in Heilbronn, not of the pogrom of November 1938. The way that Alice Schwab tells the story – or, perhaps we should be careful to say, the way that her story was recorded – comes across as rather impersonal. Many phrases sound more like lines from a TV documentary than family stories and recollections, of which there were not in fact very many. Helmut Rosenthal, for example, who became Jack Rosen at this time, 'never spoke at all about anything from Germany', as Julia Neuberger told me.[15] It seems unlikely that Liesel would be unaware of the existence of the early concentration camps, in the south of Germany primarily at Dachau as well as the 'Heuberg', near Stetten am kalten Markt in the Schwäbische Alb. However, it could be that Ludwig and Hermine wanted to shield their children from knowing about such things.

> *The Jewish residents arrested during the night of the pogrom were held at the Gestapo headquarters, 4 Wilhelmstraße, until they were taken to the concentration camp at Dachau. At the outbreak of war in 1939 the Jews still living in Heilbronn were forced to move into "Jewish houses" controlled by the Gestapo. These were, until 1941/1942: 32 Allerheiligenstraße, 10 and 22 Badstraße, 2 Bergstraße, 3a Bismarckstraße, 26 Dammstraße, 46 Frankfurter Straße, 25 Herweghstraße, 14 Innere Rosenbergstraße, 5 Klettstraße, 6 Schillerstraße, 7 Urbanstraße, 53 Weststraße. [...] The Wollhausplatz was the assembly point for deportation via Stuttgart to Riga on 21 November 1941. Of the people living in Heilbronn in 1933 at least 235 died as a result of deportations during the Third Reich.[16]*

Returning to the chronology of events, we encounter a letter from Uncle Richard from Amsterdam on 24 November 1938. 'To get your parents out of Germany as quickly as possible we have decided to submit an application for temporary residence in Holland. At the same time we have sent the guarantee money for Montevideo by air mail.' Uncle Jakob was agreed, and the best thing would be if he travelled with Ludwig to Hamburg as soon as possible and apply for a visa at the Uruguayan consulate.

> *So we've done everything we can do from here. We still cannot say how long it will take here to receive our entry permit, given the huge number of tens of thousands of different applications.*

Uncle Richard, too, pointed out that the guarantee money for Liesel's parents had meant 'an extraordinarily large sacrifice given our means' and that they now had to cut back financially. He therefore thought that applying for a entry permit for England was no longer necessary.

'Lilla' Eisig wrote on 30 November, still hoping that Liesel would be able to do something for her son Hans. He was staying with her mother-in-law in Stuttgart, 'busily typing up CVs' so that he could apply for a job in England. She briefly hinted at how her husband 'H' had been taken to a concentration camp after the pogrom:

> *Finally yesterday I had a short letter with H's greetings. You can imagine how much I had longed to receive one after the others got news a few days ago. Now I'm in the process of writing to Woburnhouse, as we've been told that through them the men might, when they come back, get a residence permit in England until they can emigrate to America if they need to. Have you heard anything about this, a. do you think that it could succeed? We'll try everything. I bumped into your dear mother a few days ago at the post office, she's always on the go a. very busy.*[17]

With this, I hold in my hand a letter from a woman from Heilbronn who became a victim of the Nazi extermination policy. The address on the letter is 16 Moltkestraße in Heilbronn. Hans Franke states that from there Melitta Eisig (born 26 October 1895 in Tauberbischofsheim) and Hermann Eisig (born 23 December 1888 in Heilbronn) were deported 'to the East' on 26 November 1941 and murdered in Riga on an unknown date in December.[18] The mother-in-law she mentions, Helene Eisig (née Rosenthal, born 18 June 1865 in Heilbronn), was taken to the so-called Jewish home for the elderly in Eschenau and from there deported to Theresienstadt on 22 August 1942, where she died on 4 September 1942.[19] The archives show that Hans was unable to escape Germany either. He was born on 8 April 1923 in Heilbronn, and at the age of twenty, on 8 November 1943, he was deported from Berlin-Charlottenburg to Auschwitz.

At this time Liesel was still receiving tip-offs from friends of possible job vacancies she could recommend to 'refugees looking for jobs', but families were almost always looking for a 'girl help'; the chances for a young man like Hans Eisig were slim. Hans Schloss (whose typewritten letter from 8 December 1938 was unsigned, but the address 42 Richmond Hill Road, Edgbaston, Birmingham is identical to the ones he wrote on his otherwise handwritten letters) had 'found a position for him as a trainee in one of our factories producing bicycle components'. However, he added that it would require further financial support: 'you will appreciate, of course, that as much as I would like to do so, I personally cannot accept any responsibility whatsoever in this respect in view of my own commitments'. In another letter on 20 December he confirmed that the firm Walton & Brown Limited was prepared to employ the young Eisig, but could pay him no more than the normal wage for boys of his age of 14 shillings. Schloss hoped that Woburn House 'will undertake to pay the difference'.

Liesel's friend Minni Stern from Bad Nauheim was looking for a 'residence permit in England' for her husband Alfred, as she wrote on 2 December 1938.

I didn't want to bother you, but now dear Liesel I have to, as I know of nowhere else to go for advice. The matter is extremely urgent in my (Alf's) case – I can't explain in any more detail, hopef[ully] you understand me correctly. So I'm asking you now, can you get me a guarantee from acquaintances, friends or whoever else (it's more or less a formality) & as quickly as poss. – We are in a great hurry. […] I place great hopes in you, you surely have many friends there.

On 7 December she repeated her urgent request ('You have so many contacts & one of your friends is surely in the position to put up a guarantee') in a postcard. Hans Schloss, in his above letter, did not think there was anything he could do for Stern, 'a much older man'. He added: 'Heilbronn: I have received the following petitions as the result of my enquiries as to young people still left there', but the second page of his letter was unfortunately not kept. These desperate pleas from Germany do not appear in Alice Schwab's recollections.

Ludwig Rosenthal, who Liesel most urgently needed to rescue, wrote on 7 December. He planned to accept Uncle Richard's support in Amsterdam, 'and once we're at Aunt Luise's we'll visit you both'. Hermine had travelled to Hamburg: 'we'll see what she can sort out'. It is impossible to find out why Uruguay represented such a prize destination for them. Holland would be a good starting point as relatives lived there, and England would probably be good too as their children were there, but even here he still wrote:

As a matter of fact that is our intention & assume that you are in the picture to take Heller to Monte with us – but it would be very nice for me to finally hear your opinion on our project & if you might come to us in Monte later?

'Monte' was perhaps code for the idea of finding their own way out of Germany. But progress was slow, as he wrote in pen in a postcard from 7 December. Aunt Bertha added: 'Sending best wishes again, perhaps the Sussmanns or Halevy where Werner is will take pity.' Three days later a letter arrived from Ludwig by air mail:

So far I have absolutely no papers for Monte, dear mother is in Hamburg & hopes to get them by Monday evening & you must wait for these to be returned, I'm waiting for them on tenterhooks, as here there's still so much to sort out & I'm busy morning till night. There's little point sending a telegram to Hamburg as the consulate is so busy with work and people that it probably won't answer, so wait until mother comes back, might call you Tuesday evening between 8–9 on the phone, stay at home in case.

He definitely wanted to take Heller with him 'to Monte', as 'it would be hard for us there without our children'. In stark contrast to just a year before, Ludwig gave the impression that he was speaking to his daughter as an equal and that he appreciated her efforts. In a review of Sonja Wegner's book *Refuge in a Foreign Land. Exile in Uruguay 1933–1945* (*Zuflucht in einem fremden Land. Exil in Uruguay 1933–1945*) Till Schmidt writes:

In Uruguay, too, opinions on Jewish immigration were that it should be rejected. From the mid-1930s anti-Semitic articles were regularly published, particularly in the conservative newspaper La Tribuna Popular, which voiced opposition to the growing number of Jewish immigrants. Whilst no anti-Jewish immigration law or decree was passed in Uruguay, as was the case in Brazil and Paraguay, both Uruguay and Argentina sent a similar secret memo from their foreign offices to their consulates. It was directed against Jewish immigration at a time when it had reached its peak in terms of numbers as a result of the November pogrom. Circulated on 17 December 1938, it read: "Under no circumstances is approval to be given for persons of whom it is to expect that, for clear political or religious reasons, they will not return home". Many of the Uruguayan consulates did, however, continue to supply visas – and many accepted large payments for them.[20]

At the centre of this investigation into emigration to Uruguay are the refugees themselves, who were driven by events but who also wrote history through their own actions. This observation is only true of those who survived, and comes with a degree of hindsight. At the time, restless activity and forced inactivity combined to produce an almost paralysing feeling, as is clear to see in Ludwig's letter. Aunt Helene contributed a few lines to the letter from 10 December, writing that Dr Ludwig Farnbacher (London W1, 72 Wardon Street, c/of Mr M Wronker) would 'liaise [with Liesel] regarding Alfred'. As Alfred – her son-in-law – was a farmer by profession it should not be too difficult to find work. 'As long as he has no visa to leave immediately he won't get out of there, don't you understand that?' 'There', I assume, meant Dachau.

Minni Stern wrote again on 10 December 1938 from Bad Nauheim. She had obtained a surety for Alfred, a waiting list number and even a 'ship ticket', but

as delighted as we are to have a surety, at the moment it is of no use to me. Please dear Liesel, don't forget me & don't tire if it doesn't work immediately. I'm placing so much hope in you. If I only had a guarantee f. Alfred, I want nothing more, the rest will sort itself out. […] So I think you've understood me correctly, I only need a guarantee for a transit residence. We all want to go to America. […] Now it's over 4 weeks that A's been there. On 8.12, the day before yesterday, I got a letter from him, quite short of course. – Dear Liesel, on 8th we had our birthday, we were born on the same day – a nice birthday, don't you think? I myself don't know where I will get the strength from to hold out for so long. – Often I think it won't go on & then it does go on because I have to. – Oh Liesel, how difficult life is – I have never found it easy, but now it is almost unbearable. Please, please dear Liesel, do what you can, it is so desperately needed.

On 17 December she let Liesel know that the police had called, saying that her husband was to be 'picked up' (from imprisonment) as he was not able to be released.

In fact, he came home under his own steam by car. He had contracted pneumonia, was very weak and mentally ravaged: 'people were dying around him daily'. This made it ever more urgent to intensify the attempts to rescue him – his waiting list number for America was 20386. On 23 December she wrote again, now asking for a work permit for herself as well, 'as I don't think I can send my husband alone to England now, as I initially imagined'. The unsaid was there to read between the lines. Could Farnbacher help? Or Rosy Mayer (22 Lordship Park, London N16)? German consultant lawyer A. Horovitz was actively pursuing the case of Alfred Stern. Liesel had found in Jack Paynton someone who was ready to provide a guarantee, and as Stern was a farmer it might be possible to find him a position 'in one of the Hacksharoth', as Horovitz wrote on 10 February 1939. This was an institution which prepared young people for emigration to Palestine by training them in agriculture and craftsmanship.

A genealogical website on the Loeb family gives information on Alfred and Minni, as well as on the 'Florsheim family'. '*Minnie Florsheim* married Alfred Stern from Heilbronn, Am-Neckar. She perished in the Holocaust. Alfred was arrested by the British, sent to the Isle of Man, then to Australia. See his book *The Dunera Scandal* published in Australia.'[21] The central documentation centre of the Israeli memorial site *Yad Vashem* contains the following entry:

> *Minni Stern, née Flörsheim, was born in 1905 in Bad Nauheim, Germany. She was the daughter of Hermann and Helene. She was married to Alfred. Before the Second World War she lived in Bad Nauheim, Germany. During the war she was in Bad Nauheim, Germany. Minni was murdered at Auschwitz, Poland, in 1942. Source of this information: memorial page sent in by: nephew* [Alfred Oppenheimer].[22]

So they did succeed in getting Alfred Stern out of Germany. However, his wife Minni, Liesel's letter-writing partner, was deported and murdered at Auschwitz. Aunt Bertha, née Rosenthal, Stern by marriage, lived at 43 Götzenturmstraße at this time. She scribbled on the letter 'Greetings to Heller from everyone and from me'. Hans Franke's work states: 'Stern, Berta, née Rosenthal *14 May 1874 in Heilbronn, housewife, widow, 43 Götzenturmstr.; Frankfurt/M., 7 Sandweg, 18 August 1942 Theresienstadt, [date of death] unknown.'

These events have only partially survived in the family memory. Not all news made it to England, and particularly during the war contact was almost completely severed. The family 'archive' is heavily fragmented.

At the centre of this book stands the story of a successful emigration. Whilst writing it, however, more and more information on the fate of friends and family members murdered in the Holocaust came to light. At the same time I worked together with James Jordan from the University of Southampton and Lisa Leff from the American University in Washington to produce a special edition of our journal *Jewish Culture and History* on the subject of 'Jewish Migration and the Archive'. Our introduction ended with a sentence summarizing the results of our research, which often dealt with very personal, private, family 'archives' from suitcases and boxes:

> *Studying archives in the context of migration history can make us aware of the fact that these repositories on which we rely for our research don't provide us with "complete" narratives – much rather, they tell stories about absence, fragmentation, and loss, challenging researchers from all fields to develop new and creative ways to write history.*[23]

A story of rescue (of both people and historical records) can only be written if it includes the memory of those who were not saved.

Margaret Freudenthal got in touch from Paris. Most likely she dictated this to a friend who then translated it into German:

> *Sadly the situation in Europe and that of the Jews in particular is currently so bad that a way out may have to be found. I was able to see this again today as I was on the boat-train to Cherbourg, which left Paris full of German refugees. Almost all were travelling to America and it was a very sad sight.*

She filled the rest of her letter, in her familiar handwriting and in English, with reports of a happy-go-lucky life in the restaurants and theatres of Paris. If I have understood correctly, her personal sangfroid and her somewhat distanced view of 'Europe' was down to her possessing an Australian passport; she was in any case eager to be of use to friends, including Dr Freudenthal, who were emigrating to Australia. Liesel's acquaintance with Margaret is most likely the reason that strangers contacted Liesel, like a Mr Artur Okonski. He wrote on 21 December 1938, asking if she would 'make efforts so that I can move to Australia, Sydney or another city'. Okonski came from West Prussia, while his wife Betty came from Upper Silesia. He had 'learned the scrap and metal industries', was also 'experienced in the shoe trade' and hoped that she could make use of her 'good connections to Australia' for him and his wife.

Hermine Rosenthal wrote to her 'golden child' and 'little treasure' on 13 December – Helmut was spared bad news. Once again she added 'You Liesel may be very thankful, my dear' to the many greetings and kisses (and the warning to 'keep your nose clean'). Liesel was in fact very active at this time. She received a letter with an illegible signature, sent from Valence Lodge, Westerham, Kent, on 14 December. The author's apology for the communication problems which had arisen was long-winded, but the letter also contained this key message:

> *If it would help at all & you could put the suggestion to Mrs Schwab, I would willingly let her have & give to you as a deposit to the German Jewish Aid Committee, one hundred and fifty pounds of my own & the fifty pounds of yours, making L 200 as a deposit.*

An attached draft of a letter to Rev Michelson, 52 Bedford Way, London W.C., gives more detail. The sender was F[red] Schupbach and he would fill out 'a blue form of application',

> *giving particulars for a guarantee which I wish to sign. I have approached my bank asking them to give me some letter showing that I should be in a position to carry out the obligations under the guarantee. The bank tell me that they will be very pleased to give me a reference if the German Jewish Aid Commitee will write in to them for it.*

The process required close cooperation between the 'guarantors', the Jewish and non-Jewish aid organizations and the British authorities. Clearly it was Liesel who held the threads together and established contacts; one was German Consulate Lawyer A

Horovitz (34 Coleman Street, London EC2), who contacted Liesel on 20 December 'regarding the case Stern Floersheim as well as of your parents'. Anna Schwab wrote for a similar reason on 30 December, now addressed to 'dear Alice', that 'without a guarantee from an Englishman it's impossible to get the man out'.

Aunt Emmy and her daughter Eugenie, known as Gina, requested Liesel's help just as urgently. Gina was looking for a job in England, either 'room service or kitchen'. She wrote 'in an extreme predicament', and she returned to the old Bombay story: 'I [...] defended you to everyone during & after your engagement, while almost the whole of Heilbronn without exception poured scorn on you.' This seems like news from another life (and also reveals so much about her specific view of the city – 'almost the whole of Heilbronn' here meant the few remaining Jewish families), as so much had happened in the meantime. 'A is back,' wrote Aunt Bertha, 'but went straight to bed, has a heavy cold, no wonder'. A day later Minni confirmed the return of her husband from the concentration camp. Ludwig Rosenthal wrote quickly to report that he had obtained the entry permit for Uruguay. Hermine wrote in more detail:

I am in such an unspeakable hurry, dashing from place to place, Saturday was in Stuttgart, thank God got what I wanted, today here & in the evening travel to Hamburg, this time it's not for us but for Eugenien's husband, we want to travel together and she is so helpless. Mezger family are all gone now, to Montevideo, the boys met them in Le Havre & went with them. [...] Don't run yourself into the ground for others, not one single person helps us apart from my siblings, Aunt Luise, Hede & Mile are wonderful, if I, rather Papa & I, didn't have them we'd be completely alone. They are so very worried about us. If Urug. was blocked off, then you would have to see if Australia would be poss. for us. I'll find out tomorrow in Hamburg & let you know then. [...] Did the sausage arrive? Do you need any documents? Warm kisses, dear Mother.

On 21 December an old friend, Kurt Jeselson, got in touch again after a long gap. He had heard that Liesel had 'tumbled into marriage', but was unable to reach her and had received no news from other friends: 'a saga was woven for me concerning you'. Now she had written to him and he rushed to answer her.

I myself am on the march. I.e. my sister is here. My parents will, I hope, be here soon, we will have a home again and everything won't look so desolate. It is difficult to talk about Germany. Unfortunately everyone speaks too much and too little changes. What will come of it, only the gods will know. A flood would be best, but the rainbow prevents that. But maybe the Lord God will make a new miracle happen after all. I hope that the news at home with you is bearable. Because for many it isn't, unfortunately. [...] Write, please![24]

The whole family arrived in the United States – a hopeful sign. Herta Catsell (Kern) was in contact with former Heilbronners, just like Jeselson: 'You will probably be quite interested to hear about the many Heilbronner friends Hermann has met again in the USA. His letters to us are full of them,' she wrote in an undated letter.

Max Samuel, who I assume was a friend Liesel had made on holiday in the Netherlands, wrote a letter from Blackburn telling of his success. 'The machines have been running for three weeks and this is music to my ears, I think it will work out, a start has been made and my old customers are sending in orders.' He had set up a small home for himself and had been waiting for his furniture from Germany to arrive for some time: 'but now that I know that the pigs are destroying everything I'll buy myself some new furniture'. He added that he had 'great interest in you' and would 'welcome you like a queen' if she came to visit. Max Samuel, born 9 January 1883 in Argenau, died 2 September 1942 in Blackburn, was a businessman and leader of the Jewish community in Rostock. In 1930 he became chair of the Israelite Council of Mecklenburg-Schwerin, but after 1933 he was unable to continue in this role. His son Herbert emigrated in 1934 to Blackburn, northwest England, 'to found a branch of *EMSA Works*. His daughter, Käthe, followed in 1936. In 1937 his wife Berta died. After his firm was seized, Max followed his children into exile in England in 1938, although he had stated often that he did not want to leave Germany.'[25]

Today, the Max Samuel-Haus in Rostock serves as a memorial to him and as the home for the foundation for Jewish history and culture in Rostock. Herbert Samuel made it available to the foundation in order to preserve the memory of Max Samuel and of Jewish life in Rostock. I was unfortunately unable to find out when he and Liesel met. With his letter, the correspondence from 1938 came to an end.

But none of the many 'cases' had yet been resolved. Minni Stern wrote from Bad Nauheim that Alfred was slowly getting better; the doctor had told him that 'the main thing is that he must be fed well' and that he should stay in bed for a while longer. She had no rest. 'You don't know what consequences might befall the men. Do you understand what I mean? We don't yet have a firm date, but many others do & so we don't know if it'll still work out.' This careful phrasing refers to the fear that the men might be taken to a concentration camp again if their families were unable to supply the necessary documents for emigration in time. In Frankfurt Minni had met Rabbi Friedmann, whose wife was a sister of Anna Schwab:

> *Perhaps Mrs Schwab will warm to us when she knows that her people know us well. Perhaps she even knows us Flörsheims herself. Just tell her about the "Hotel Flörsheim", Jonas Loeb from the old promenade hotel is my uncle. [...] Perhaps this way we can do something for our father, who I really can't leave here on his own & who is on our surety.*

She added that she would love to 'have a natter' with Liesel one day about 'you and your love life', and would like to come to London for that reason alone. 'One thing I can tell you, a woman must – "if she is in love" – be able to give up a lot of her "self". This is necessary, even if you are such a good match for each other.'

Trude Victor wrote on 2 January 1939 from Aerdenhout, expressing her hope that Liesel might want to spend her holidays with them in Holland at some point. Everyday life went on; there were holidays, love life problems, friends who wanted to meet up with her. Everything, however, was overshadowed by the uncertainty over the last remaining ways of getting out of Germany. Hermine wrote a postcard on 4 January, talking about possible presents for Liesel's English friends and parcels for the children which had been 'messed up' by the delivery firm. In the middle of the text stood this: 'Dear Liesel, Urug. is no longer an option. We are inconsol.[able], what are we to do?'

On 5 January a letter arrived from Ruth Leser in Bombay. She described life as an emigrant there, and in Switzerland where her son was at boarding school:

> We sometimes had visits from emigrants, which means no work but does take up time, travelling round the city, paying visits to things etc. We're glad to do all this and we're happy to be as helpful as we can to some people. We're unhappy not to be able to do anything. And I find the recognition that we are so helpless dreadful. That's how it is for me, it makes me so confused. Yes, my time in Europe was not a pleasant one. Of course I do not wish to be ungrateful, I was together with the boy, was happy and satisfied that I could have my child. But otherwise I felt very lonely and miserable in Europe. I.e. I had the good fortune to be in very nice hotels, I was well looked after etc. But it became very clear to me that there was no home for me there, that we didn't belong anywhere any more, and sometimes I was so scared and worried about the boy and for the young as a whole. [...] Then the misery of emigrants in Switzerland, those days of crisis when more and more refugees came to Switzerland. [...] Now more and more people are coming [to Bombay], many Viennese, and in the baths you hear more and more German being spoken. And what do they talk about, always about the same thing, what you can do for whom, and everyone talks about what they've heard and read.

Ruth Leser and her husband belonged to a 'little organization', as she called it [David Gabriel thinks that it was called the Jewish Relief Union (JRU) or Jewish Relief Association (JRA)][26], which supported refugees. All the men were very busy with 'aid work', in addition to their jobs. Society life in Bombay, of which Liesel had been on the fringes when she visited Gerhard Gabriel, had almost disappeared, and it was with regard to this that Ruth, who clearly missed Liesel, spoke about the 'story': 'I don't get together with your former in-laws at all. Lisbeth works with her husband, Gabriel's parents are here now, his father works with him in the office, I only know his young wife in passing.' And even for the seemingly successful Levy family, things had not been in order for quite some time:

> My mother and sister, still unmarried, are still in Berlin. Could you possibly tell me of a good way to get them to England? We have already put in an application for France for them, but don't yet know how it'll go, and it's all very uncertain. If it doesn't work out, how could we get the two women to England? I can't bring my mother here on account of her heart condition, I would like to spare her that.

She and her husband were still British subjects and could guarantee living accommodation for both women.

Mrs Leser added one more sentence which accurately summed up the situation, as her description of the emigrant scene in Bombay had done: 'This is how it is, you of course don't receive any private letters any more, people always want to know something. Well, that's how it is for us too.' In the first few years of the Nazi dictatorship the political situation had been something akin to disruptive background noise for her, as someone who had considerable financial means, who could travel, and who could even acquire British citizenship. Now, it was penetrating directly into her private life ('then came 10.11., which makes everything so much more urgent').

Liesel's role in this process had changed fundamentally. The somewhat odd and unsure Miss Rosenthal, who had spent some time in Bombay and got to know nice people like the Lesers, had become the 'hard-working girl' who was always available to turn to, not least thanks to her good connections at Woburn House. The hopes of many people depended on this, and on Liesel as a person.

This, in turn, worried Ludwig. He wrote on 8 January 1939:

I am firmly of the opinion that you should now first and foremost worry about us & Heller & forget about other people's wishes, as the latter are bedevilling you, you're being exploited, unnecessarily wasting your time & still have unnecessary things to do. Just make sure that you stay healthy & under all circumstances do something positive for us.

He had written down an announcement from the British consulate which summarized the travel possibilities to England from 1 January 1939, and he attached it to this letter. Above all this – and his plans – focused on people who possessed 'proof of the possibility of further emigration', and this also had to be approved by the German-Jewish Aid Committee at Woburn House, Upper Woburn Place. They were required to state the exact country they were to emigrate to, 'and the certified documents which are supplied for this'. 'A deposit for living accommodation' had to be provided, with the address of the depositor, who had to be 'a relative or an acquaintance'. This was the £200 which F Schupbach and Liesel had gathered together. Hermine added some sad news: 'Dear grandmother has died, it is indeed hard, but now she has been spared the great agitation that the children have gone. She had reached a great age & died peacefully without illness. She still talked a lot about you and Helmut.' Hermine emphasized Ludwig's plea that Liesel should not 'burn yourself out for all the other people', as no-one 'is looking out for us apart from my siblings'.

Now the news from Heilbronn became ever more urgent. On 14 January Hermine wrote, 'We would be almost ready here, but we have no idea where we would go, Urug. isn't an option.' She asked Liesel to go to the Uruguayan consulate in London, to visit Sol Dreyfus ('make sure you look good!') and to remind her friends 'that you are my daughter, née Rothschild from Cannstatt'. From Ludwig's and Hermine's perspective of the ever-narrowing world they still lived in in Germany – 'Uncle Max is moving into his parents' house [at 43 Götzenturmstraße] next week'; 'Aunt Böhm […] is moving to her sister's'; 'Aunt Ev and Uncle Mayer are going to America soon, Grandma Kallmann will go to the retirement home in Stuttgart' – the outside world seemed like a haven, but they found it difficult to accept that they could not control its rules from Heilbronn.

In amongst all these pieces of family news lies a letter from Kurt (Maschler), which was clearly intended to be private – although as Ruth Leser had noted, nothing was really private any more. On his English headed paper (41 The Highlands, Burnt Oak, Edgware) he wrote that Liesel should come to terms with the fact

> *that it is wholly impossible for me to force myself back to the opinion I once had of you. Our natures are so very different that there are no stable bridges, at most a weak emergency structure which will collapse in the first storm or floods.*

She should immediately and abruptly bring herself back down to earth; she would 'find life much more agreeable than you think'. This, too, was part of her story of emancipation: to not get overly attached to certain things (any more) and to learn to rely on herself. I asked Julia Neuberger about her mother's connection to Kurt Maschler, a well-known publicist and cofounder of the German PEN Club, and she answered: 'Sometime lovers, I suspect, and very old friends.'

In 1929 Kurt Maschler published Erich Kästner's *Emil and the Detectives* in Berlin. In 1935 he founded the Atrium publishing house in Basel, through which Kästner, whose books had by then been banned in Germany, was able to have his work published. He transferred the rights of the Williams publishing house, which he had acquired in 1933, to Atrium, where Stefan Zweig, Kurt Tucholsky, and later Erich Fried and Norman Mailer published their work.[27] Maschler was forced to leave Germany in 1937 and ended up in London. While he was still alive, the Kurt Maschler Award was established in 1982 as a literary prize for authors of children's books whose work stood out for a successful balance between text and illustration. The winners received '£1000 and an "Emil", a bronze figurine'.[28] In this way Kurt Maschler represented an important connection between Liesel's interest in literature and the cultural activity of the German-Jewish emigrants in London.

Ludwig sent the postcard I cited right at the start of this book on 17 January:

> *Dear Liesel! First of all you must ask the Uruguay*[an] *consulate* immediately *if it is possible for us to travel from Engl*[and] *to Urug*[uay]. *We will of course take our own furniture with us, just as* [we] *would sort out our boat tickets here. If not then you must next try to arrange Australia for us, but I fear that this project is dragging on so long, and we urgently need a tangible, quick solution. There is no need to telegraph us, save your money, but please try to do more for us. Let us know as soon as you can about Uruguay, as d*[ear] *Mother may have to go to Berlin on that account next week. W*[ith] *love and kisses for you and Heller. Father.*

At this time it was still possible for emigrants to take household furniture with them when they left Germany, although the requirements (provision of detailed lists) and charges (taxes) to do so were becoming ever more stringent.[29] Just two days later he sent another letter in which he repeated this urgent plea – 'so that we might finally find a definite way out'. From his perspective in Heilbronn, where the measures implemented by the Nazi regime were having more and more of an impact, it was important that they could identify 'a positive country to emigrate to', be it Uruguay, Australia or even the United States, as without 'a definitive country to go to [we will get] no luggage allowance'. Here, though, for the first time he stated that 'I would of course prefer it if we could be taken in together with our children in England, then Heller could finish his school & we wouldn't have to take him with us'. This new attitude – with which Ludwig and Hermine were almost infringing on Liesel's responsibilities – was a result of the news which Hermine included on the reverse of the same letter:

> *Today we received word from Mrs Schwab that a visa has been granted for us. It's wonderful & we will thank Mrs Schwab & send her our best wishes, as well as the man I mentioned, my best thanks to you as well.*

The noticeable reticence owed itself to the fact that the visa was not enough on its own. Would they be able to stay in London?

> *Then we'll get our lift and tickets etc. all sorted out & it can all go quickly. If we don't stay in England then things will be difficult, we can only apply for luggage allowance if we know exactly to Urug. or Australia or America. Because we want to pay for the journey & all freight with German money. We need a lift in any case, we must have a home & see if we can master the situation with that.*

I had the chance to get to know the author Hans Sahl, cited earlier on in this book, after he returned from exile. In our conversation on everything he had experienced in his life he asked the curious question: 'Have you ever emigrated?' Although this sounded (in German: *Haben Sie schon einmal emigriert?*) a little eccentric and awkward, it was phrased intentionally so, in order to recall the feelings of uncertainty over the conditions in Germany shortly before emigrating. Within the framework of cultural approaches to the topic of migration this short question opens up a very important perspective: *How* did the people whose lives we are researching emigrate? How did they prepare for and plan their journey? Which forms did they have to fill out? Which taxes did they have to pay? Which offices did they have to visit? What did they pack in their suitcases?[30] Where did they get their train and ship tickets from? Which places did they have to go through before they reached their destination? How did they experience the passage? For many emigrants the journey by ship (a week to Palestine, almost two weeks to the United States) constituted a real opportunity to think about their own life, their origins and their future.[31]

Emigration as cultural practice has scarcely been approached systematically until now. Israeli cultural geographer Gur Alroey is one of the few researchers to have attempted to answer these questions through archive research (though his focus is on the large wave of Jewish emigration from Eastern Europe after 1881).[32] Discussions with travel agents, enquiries with emigration agencies as to whether particular professions were needed in particular regions, investigation into places to live in ports of transmigration and much more were all part of this process. In this respect the repositories available to researchers, such as the YIVO Institute for Jewish Research or the Leo Baeck Institute, have not been fully exploited. In emigrants' memoirs there are numerous examples of the preparation and realization of emigration, as well as its effects of everyday life. There are also hints as to how dependant individuals were on decisions made by state bodies, which came in its most extreme form under the Nazi regime. It is only when we collate personal recollections and combine them with an analysis of measures taken by the authorities that we can get a clear picture of the cultural practice of emigration.

Emigrants were driven by need to get hold of atlases and maps. They studied the emigrants' handbook *Philo-Atlas* and the pamphlets and newsletters from the Aid Organisation for German Jews.[33] They looked for ways out of Germany. They applied for visas and tried to get invitations to other countries. They attempted to make use of pre-existing contact and information networks or to build new ones. They studied life in other parts of the world, from climate to living and working conditions. For example, while Ludwig and Hermine were filling out forms for Australia and visiting the consulate in Hamburg and Berlin, they were simultaneously trying to sell their furniture in Heilbronn. Hermine wrote on 22 January 1939:

> *Everything is dragging on so terribly, as we always have visitors or something else on; the worst thing however is the flood of people wanting to buy furniture who then don't buy anything because they have no money & we have to sit and wait at home all the time. Sold nothing apart from giving away.*

Emigrants packed suitcases and weighed up which items were worth taking with them, asking friends and relatives for help.[34] They learned languages. They ordered tickets and discussed which methods of transport were the most suitable. They were forced to do all this under pressure from the regime, which on the one hand 'wanted to get rid' of them and so initially (between 1933 and 1938) forced their emigration, but which on the other hand made life increasingly difficult with new rules, additional taxes and further restrictions.

Without this pressure they would probably not have left. Now that they were leaving, however, they acted as if they were travelling. The emigrants, amongst whom were many well-off and well-educated people, educated tourists so to speak, made use of their knowledge during this journey and described the experience with words we are familiar with from travel and tourism in times of peace. In some cases the journey they were forced to undertake even became a positive, liberating experience, as the ship carried them from a land of desperation and persecution into a – mostly unknown – freedom.[35]

A dissertation, locked away in the archives, written by Walter Hirche in 1939 discussed 'Jewish migration and its difficulties, under particular consideration of the conditions in Germany from 1933 to 1939 […] as a result of Jewish journalism in Germany', as he put it. This was the language of the new 'people's community', the *Volksgemeinschaft*:

> *What follows assumes the situation which arose after Hitler came to power as a starting point and as well-known. The steady growth in anti-Semitism and the increased pressure exerted on the Jews by the German people, the Anschluss with*

Austria, the annexation of the Sudetenland and the creation of the Protectorate of Bohemia and Moravia, which necessarily increased Jewish efforts to emigrate, are assumed to be factors.[36]

The *Volksgemeinschaft* created a new normality of exclusion. With this in mind the 'migration' between 1933 and 1938 was 'comparatively normal', as the immigration requirements in the countries they left for were 'not yet so strict' and as 'these immigrating Jews', Hirche wrote, 'presented no special difficulties when being taken in.'[37]

A coolly calculated, slick operation was being carried out, and Hirche, a Nazi academic, was able to cite Jewish sources in his dissertation, using an excerpt from the *Jüdische Nachrichtenblatt* from 17 March 1939 to describe what had happened since 1938. 'In the last year this movement has taken on the unmistakeable characteristics of an Exodus.'[38] Jews 'of all classes and age groups, who had begun to reintegrate themselves' (after the 1936 Berlin Olympic Games) felt forced to emigrate, but after the failed Evian Conference of July 1938 they were faced with an ever more restrictive immigration policy in potential reception countries.[39] Hirche wrote:

It is necessary to emphasise at this point that until the start of this new wave the majority of Jews living in Germany [...] only toyed with the idea of emigration, and did not seriously consider emigration. A determining factor in this position taken by German Jewry was the illusory hope that, as in former times, its capacity for adaptation could outlast national socialist Germany, which, whilst it restricted the legal and existential basis of the Jews, did not destroy them. Integration into the situation created post 1933 is therefore unmistakeable.[40]

The German Jews who had stayed, because they were Germans and considered themselves to be Germans, had adapted to the new 'situation', according to Hirche. In fact, German-Jewish artists and intellectuals, most notably within the framework of the Jewish Cultural Federation (*Jüdischer Kulturbund*), had developed new forms of Jewish cultural work in the ghetto situation created by the Nazis for this time – though they did not yet know it – of transition.[41] And moreover, outside of this utterly artificial opportunity controlled by the regime they tried to continue living in Germany as Germans. 'Only in November 1938', wrote Hirche, did it become clear to the readers of Jewish newspapers, even the Zionist *Jüdische Rundschau*, 'that Germany's desire to solve the Jewish problem is irrevocable'. Perhaps I am wrong to quote Nazi sources like this one – I do not need Hirche to reconstruct the historical events – but the cynicism with which he commented on the status of German Jews was the same which those hoping to emigrate (including Hermine Rosenthal) encountered in the offices they were required to visit.

Jewish emigration from Germany post 1933 can be understood in Wolfgang Benz's terms 'as a reflex'[42] to the Nazi takeover of power and can thereby, correctly, be read as an inseparable and moving chapter in *German* history. From this German perspective the numbers reflect, as Benz states, 'Nazi policy in their intensity'. Of the half a million people excluded from the *Volksgemeinschaft*, 38,000 Jews left Germany in 1933, in

1934 it was 23,000, and in 1935 it was 20,000. After the Nuremberg Laws were passed[43] the figure rose to 25,000 in 1936 before reducing slightly to 23,000 the following year. In 1938, the Year of Terror, it rose again to 40,000 before shooting up to between 75,000 and 80,000 in the year war broke out. After that the gates to the outside world were practically sealed.

Emigration from Germany is presented as the main subject in many studies, which conceals the other side of the coin: *immigration* to Palestine, Great Britain, the United States, Argentina and other places can be read as a chapter of a *Jewish* history. It can be understood as an attempt by both groups and individuals to prove their worth and – as far as possible under the circumstances – to find their own ways out, and even to discover new horizons for themselves in the process. It is only in this context that a letter like the following can be fully understood, written by Alfred Stern from Bad Nauheim after he had survived the consequences of imprisonment in a concentration camp and sent to Liesel:

> *The "Where" & "When" are all that's worrying me. Dear Liesel, you have to understand this & must not be angry about it. When I say that I would like to leave soon, that has its reasons. Older people have time, it's good when they get away but there is still no acute need just yet. […] Don't think that we're being idle here & are just waiting. I am immersed in discussions with every country on earth & will go where 1) it's quickest & 2) a visa can be granted under relatively favourable circumstances. Unfortunately I'm not quite ready to travel right now, so I have had to send my secretary (Minni). She's somewhere different every week, on Friday 8 days ago she was in Cologne where after much trial & tribulation she managed to speak to the Canadian commissioner at half 11 at night. All in vain. Do you understand why it's so urgent for me to have respectable & above all documentation that will give me a chance, particularly as here the rumour will not go away that people who have to wait longer than 2 years (which includes us unfortunately) will be rejected from England. And one final plea to finish: don't tell Heilbronn of everything concerning me, neither in a letter nor on the telephone. It leads to misunderstandings & completely useless talk.*

The letters from Ludwig and Hermine should be read in the same context. On 20 January 1939 Ludwig asked again if it was possible for all of them to stay in England. At the same time he was filling out 'the form for Australia […], it could be that I soon go there [England], whilst dear mother can only come after making sure everything is done'. Hermine had an appointment on 24 January with the Uruguayan consulate in Berlin, but was waiting for news from Liesel before going. In the meantime she wrote to 'Miss Lawson', one of Liesel's friends who would vouch for her as a guarantor, thanking her

> *for your great love & attentiveness to stand by us for our future. This is wonderful of you & we will forever be grateful to you. […] Yours sincerely, thankfully, Hermine Rosenthal. My husband also thanks you from the bottom of his heart.*

She did then travel to Berlin, as Ludwig reported on 25 January, 'for Monte'.

We have now got to know a family going there by ship on 4.2.39 via Boulogne s/ Mer; the family's son-in-law lives in Berlin & will help us to get the same result for Hermine; hopefully it will work, but people only get an entry visa for one year.

Uncle Jakob agreed that Liesel should continue to try 'for Australia':

I have sent you a 2nd form to fill out & have since heard that in the south of Australia in the area of Adelhaide [Adelaide] there is a large vineyard, so please put in the list that I am an experienced wine expert with unrivalled knowledge of cellars and distribution; perhaps that'll improve my chances & you can leave no stone unturned. [...] Mother is travelling back to Frankfurt to get her English visa, how long it will take I don't yet know. [...] Don't leave it so long until you next write, & what you are doing for us is child's play, we have truly done everything we possibly can for you!

A package with Hutzelbrot, a kind of spiced currant bread, came with the letter: 'It tastes wonderful!' Hermine wrote a postcard from Berlin on 26 January saying that she had as yet been unable to do anything as the consul general was 'not there any more'. She added: 'I am so happy if father comes to you, he is always so worried & so he always wants me to do everything. I don't like being here at all.' In a detailed letter written from Stuttgart railway station she gave more information on her experience in Berlin and her restless activity.

After much exertion I succeeded in being allowed to see the urug. ambassador & he, as we knew each other from Hamburg, was very nice & talked with me for over an hour & the end result was to go for England and forget about Urug. as there is an indefinite ban there. But for England there's no chance there unless from Hamburg. Then he told me that Helmut should absolutely get an English school education, that way it will be easier for him to support his parents. So I was almost in despair, I wanted Engl. but only [as] a starting point! Last resort – Shanghai. Set off, gathered all courage, ran to the travel bureau – waited for hrs – with the final result: wait for eternity. Quick friendship & a chance to go via London a bit earlier. Happy and yet miserable I wandered back to my guesthouse without food or having anything else. [...] In the afternoon had a discussion with the director about Shanghai. He told me not to take Helmut out of his Engl. school & thought that of course the best thing would be to go to you. In the evening travelled from Berlin to Frankf., from the train to the Engl. consulate & quickly got everything.

In this confusing situation, which demanded not only great physical effort but also the considerable mental exertion of having to re-orientate oneself to the world, Hermine Rosenthal – wife, mother, German Jew and Swabian housewife – concentrated on her 'things'.

Now we would have got so far in one part, but the other is difficult. Now listen dear Liesel, so far I haven't been able to get rid of any of our furniture. I'm giving a lot away, but dear Papa thinks we should keep bookcase & desk. Tell me dear Liesel, could you poss. have some of the splen[did] furniture at your place? I intend to take our bedroom with us, the sideboard which we've split up into two commodes, table & chairs, then the small lounge cupboard & the nice fittings. Now the tricky issue is the piano. Everyone is advising me to keep this magnificent piece & dear Papa cannot bring himself to give this splendid item away so cheaply, and the piano tuner he paid for last week supported him. [...] Now I've had the wash basin made into a commode & as we don't want to buy couch or bedstead the bed bits would be there if you lived with us, particularly as [I] have your beds and mattresses. [...] Let me know asap, would you like to keep that charming gaming table? Have suitors for it for 4 RM: it was in the dining room & is very nice. Today was in Stuttgart for a discussion abt lifts. Everything could still take some time.[44]

What in hindsight may seem incidental was, at the moment when Hermine Rosenthal was planning and carrying out these tasks, a way of clinging on to what still seemed solid and certain. Exile research has begun to consider the subject of things, of material objects, in emigration more and more in recent years. Together with my colleague Doerte Bischoff I organized the annual conference of the German Society for Exile Research in March 2013 and put together the following ideas, which might help understand Hermine's actions a little better. After giving up his business, and before his own emigration to the United States in 1940, Julius Kirchhausen, also from Heilbronn,[45] worked for a few months at the Israelite Welfare Office in Stuttgart. His job there was to

be responsible for the Jews in the Württemberg Lowlands and the neighbouring Baden region, provide them with the documents necessary for emigration and assist as much as possible to ensure that everything went quickly and smoothly.

In addition to negotiations with consulates from possible destination countries and with the various German authorities, his job also involved making lists of items which emigrants wanted to take with them, or (as in most cases) send ahead of them.

To make a list of moving goods I had to go to the house of the people involved, record what furniture etc. they had as well as when they acquired it and the value of the individual items. This was very time-consuming, particularly when dealing with people living out in Künzelsau, Öhringen, Talheim, Freudental, Sontheim, Bonfeld etc. In general the moving goods were furniture, clothing, linen of all kinds, carpets, curtains, beds, house and kitchen appliances etc. After 9 November 1938 (Kristallnacht) furniture, paintings etc. damaged by the Nazis could no longer be taken with them, so it could not be put on the lists. Clean copies of the lists were compiled at night in my house with a typewriter [...].[46]

Documents like these memoirs (or like Hermine Rosenthal's letters) tell us much about the significance of objects and household furniture (and how that significance changed) in the process of letting go of roots and the search for a new home.[47]

Objects are manufactured; they consist of particular materials; they are used as part of everyday cultural practices in the context of work or home life; they are repaired (as part of a 'makeshift economy'); they are inherited, rededicated, dug out again, forgotten and remembered again.[48] However, cultural anthropology has long tended to focus on the objects that stayed where they were and not on those that went 'on a journey'.[49]

Object research, such as the seminal work by Eugene Halton and Mihaly Csikszentmihalyi, *The Meanings of Things: Domestic Symbols and the Self*, has mostly focused on the question of how people 'carve meaning out of their domestic environment'.[50] But what happens when the 'domestic environment', the home, is threatened, taken away, destroyed? What happens to belongings and their significance? The excerpt from Julius Kirchhausen illustrates this situation: Jewish families, who in the light of Nazi persecution decided to emigrate, had to re-examine their belongings, assess whether they could be used in another place, itemize them for the purpose of taxation, pack them and ship them. British legal theorist Jeremy Bentham highlighted the importance of the *relationship* between an object and its owner as early as the end of the eighteenth century: ownership is the basis of hope. Only the law can ensure that the relationship can be continued into the future for the next generation – 'an assurance of future ownership'. If this security is attacked or threatened, more is on the line than just the object itself: 'Every attack upon this sentiment produces a distinct and special evil, which may be called a *pain of disappointment*.'[51]

Jean Améry, too, later described 'feeling at home' as a relationship with the objects we possess. In his essay 'How Much Home Does a Person Need?' (1966) he wrote:

> *We are accustomed to living with things that tell us stories. We need a house of which we know who lived in it before us, a piece of furniture in whose small irregularities we recognise the craftsman who worked on it.*[52]

Objects, as Doerte Bischoff puts it,

> *make the world comfortable and homely by creating relationships between people who pass them on to each other and who leave personal traces on them which later owners can come to know and love. Exile as a (violent) expulsion from familiar living environments destroys this familiarity with objects and the communicative and mediatory function they possess within a close-knit world of owners of the same house – in a literal and figurative sense. Scenes like these are described again and again in the literature created by experiences of exile. Judith Kerr's children's book "When Hitler Stole Pink Rabbit" makes clear in the title that the experience of exile was primarily seen as, and reflected in, the loss of a privileged object (here, a nine-year-old girl's favourite cuddly toy). As an object of transition it reflects closeness and separation, not just in terms of the wider process of individualisation, but also in reference to the experience of losing familiarity and security, which had until then defined the child's world.*[53]

Saying farewell to this familiar world primarily meant saying farewell to places and objects:

> *They went from one room to another and called out: "Goodbye Dad's bedroom ... goodbye hall ... goodbye stairs [...] Goodbye piano ... goodbye sofa [...] ... goodbye dinner table ... goodbye serving hatch!"*[54]

In the Rosenthal family many things were happening at the same time. Ludwig was clinging to his plan to go Australia and had convinced Uncle Jakob in Zürich and Uncle Richard in Amsterdam of its merits. Everyone would now have to row in the same direction, but communication within the family was difficult and the tone was tense. 'As we can't stop worrying, despite our "horrified" letter (your words), that we have heard nothing about the Australia business, I'm writing to you about this today.' Writing on behalf of both of them, Richard told Liesel that they were prepared to put up the 'required' guarantee money for Australia, but they would need more information, which Liesel was asked to get. 'As your letters mostly talk about things other than what we need to know, it should not be a surprise that we are indignant.'

The family in Amsterdam (and presumably Uncle Jakob in Zürich) had already supplied 10,000 Swiss francs for Montevideo, and now they wanted to know how much the required sum would be for Australia. Both uncles also demanded that Ludwig and Hermine pay the entire travel costs, from Heilbronn to Australia, in Reichsmarks – 'what can be paid in marks must be paid in marks!' – and that they take 'only the bare necessities' in terms of furniture with them. 'If tickets and shipping were only bought to London, then from London new tickets and freight would be paid in £, and we want nothing to do with that.'

Liesel was required to answer all the questions connected to this – but how? Like her parents she was dependant on financial support from her relatives, but was it even possible for her to acquiesce to their wishes? She had, after all, already acquired the entry visa for her parents to come to England, was that now useless? Her friend Hans Mayer confirmed to her in a letter from Paris on 27 February that she had been 'very lucky', as requirements for entry were getting more and more stringent in almost all potential emigration destinations:

> *My parents are giving me great cause for concern, as they still have not got their papers for the USA, even after such a long time. It's unbelievable what the consulate demands. My father is in hospital to have a fracture operated on, though he's never had problems before. The consulate is very strict with fractures and won't give a visa unless an old fracture is completely healed. […] The German Jews have the greatest difficulties in getting a transit visa through France for even a short time. My relatives, with whom I've been living for over a year now, have put in an application for my grandmother. Even for elderly people the process is the same, the applications take as long as they do for younger people, and there is scarcely any more chance of them being approved.*

This must have strengthened Liesel's determination to get her parents out of Germany to England, and Tante Luise at least appreciated it. She wrote on 28 February:

> *Looking at your letters from 24th & 22nd of this month I wish to tell you that we have already written to your dear parents that they should prepare as quickly as possible to emigrate to England. As there is currently no chance of emigrating to a different country & you have thought that they could perhaps stay there, we don't want to leave this option unexplored. […] The main thing now is that your parents can leave Germany as quickly as possible.*

Figure 14 Letter from Hermine Rosenthal to her daughter Liesel, early 1939 © Baroness Julia Neuberger, Private Collection

The same day, Hermine confirmed that she had received the letter from Amsterdam.

The main message is that they think we should stay in England & not let our permit expire & everyone thinks that with your help we can work to get us through. Dear Lisel that would be my deepest desire if I could find a job, can I still get a work permit over there? […] I think dear Papa will poss. travel to you alone without me in 8 to 14 days. I'll stay here for the time being. […] I've finally given the piano away for a song.

Now it was becoming real, and Ludwig seemed to see it too. He wrote: 'I took my first English lesson today & it isn't easy for me!' Jack (Helmut) wrote on 7 March:

How you surprised me when you wrote that father is coming. Why isn't mother coming then. Write to me when he comes a. answer straight away. Today the Scouts Commissioner came and made us Scouts. […] Add my greetings to the letter to mother and father a. give me an answer on Sunday.

Jack was becoming an Englishman; English terms and phrasing were interfering with his German writing. Liesel, too, was becoming more of a local, if that is the right expression. On 2 March 1939 she received an invitation from Anna Schwab to lunch for 'midday Sunday'. Their work together at Woburn House had brought the two women closer – on 2 March Mrs Schwab wrote again to 'dear Liesel, […] with best wishes'.

On 7 March Ludwig got in touch again:

Tomorrow dear Hede [from Zürich] is coming & we want to discuss the whole affair in detail & we hope then that there will at long last be a solution for us. We were & still are of the opinion that we can get there & that we can settle maybe in Hove or in another small place, where we can perhaps earn money by renting; it's out of the question to not take any furniture with us as we've registered them as moving goods & consequently can't change anything now. Anyway, our own home is always nicer than if we have to camp with strangers.

Their arrival was already sorted out. Winifred Rathbone – using the headed paper of the Refugee Committee Wimbledon, Merton and Morden – wrote that she had shown Liesel's letter to the Hostel Committee,

and they felt they would greatly like to receive your parents as guests in this Hostel for Refugees once we have a new opening. Lincoln House has been lent to us by Dr and Mrs Seligmann who have left many books and games for the entertainment of our visitors; there is also a lovely garden.

Rathbone added, however, that 'visitors shall have some payment guaranteed […] by their relatives'. The house was dependant on guests helping out, 'and for this reason I assume your mother being an excellent cook should be very helpful'. On 15 March 1939, after a long and expensive telephone conversation ('RM 34.20, more than we still have left'), Hermine announced that Ludwig would arrive 'next week'. But there were still a few uncertainties to deal with. On 18 March Ludwig wrote that it

> would be for us of course the ideal time to know if there is a chance of getting to Monte, as our shipper has to provide information about this; this never-ending hither and thither – one moment England and then something else – is very unpleasant for us.

As if Liesel had caused this 'hither and thither'! It was her parents who were still clinging on to 'Monte', even though, as Hermine confirmed in the same letter, they

> still have no visa for Urug. in our passport & Papa can't travel until we do. Otherwise he could go in ten days & I once I've packed. Aunt Hede was with me in the travel office, now we have to wait for an answer, which I will pass on to you immediately. In any case if we go to England Papa will come soon. Keep the hostel open for us!

I do not fully understand their hesitation. At the same time that the Rosenthals were preparing for their emigration, the drama in the Stern-Flörsheim family in Bad Nauheim was being played out, and the two stories briefly collided with each other. On 19 March Alfred Stern thanked Liesel for her letter,

> which we are only answering today as in the meantime we were in Heilbronn & the surrounding area to get my mother out of here. We spoke to your parents too, they're doing well, they're ready to go. We also spoke to your Aunt Hede who happened to be there. You'll know that Eugenie, Willi & Selma are shortly coming to be near you. After I heard about a week ago via the USA that my brother-in-law's brother had corresponded with Mr Paynton & assured him that he will guarantee everything, I hope that my business can also be sorted out. Dr Horov. wrote on 10.3 that all the documentation has been ready since 20 February. Where they are I did not quite understand however. But he meant in Bloomsbury Street, which it seems will organise everything from now on. Should I go straight to them to complain or will you do that. It seems high time to me to finally sort this matter out. As soon as I have the permit, which has barely any limits on it, in my hands, Minni will look for a job so that we can travel together.

We already know that this last point at least, Minni Stern's emigration, would not be realized. Jakob Wertheimer in Zürich was slowly losing patience. He was kept 'up to date' by Richard in Amsterdam about 'what's happening in terms of your parents' emigration. Aunt Hede went out there in the meantime, but without achieving anything positive.' Uncle Jakob, on whose financial support the success of all the plans depended, made things clear (not long after he had still been trying to force through the Australia 'solution'):

> In the same post I wrote to Heilbronn, finally it's only the immediate departure to London that's being discussed, I've found out exactly how to get the tickets, how

luggage is to be shipped & I hope that your mother's hither & thither will finally cease, otherwise there's no helping things & then they should do what they want. I have written so many times to you dear Liesel, you shouldn't make the same mistake your mother unfortunately has; if you were to read the letters I have here in front of me, your various letters to Richard, you wouldn't have got out, everyone of your letters wants something else. – We do of course want to help & you can be sure that nothing is too much for us but you & they shouldn't make it so difficult for us. You only ever write about yourself, how hard you have to work, how ill you are & everything you're doing. Forget this, but do as is proper by saying to yourself, I have the duty to look after my parents & you should be happy to do it.

It was perhaps easier to write this from the safety of Zürich. Happily, it is at this stage in the chronology of the letters that we find a document – short and incomplete though it is – in which we hear Liesel's voice. It is a draft of a letter (London, 20 March 1939) to 'My dears', presumably Jakob and Hede Wertheimer in Zürich and Richard and Luise Loeb in Amsterdam. The typed text is partially covered in pen, so I cannot tell if and in what form the letter was actually sent. But she defended herself against their accusations:

I received your letter, dear Uncle, many thanks for that. I am [quite of your opinion] *that we would probably understand each other* [much] *better if we could speak to each other rather than write. I have already sent an overview of my "money situation" to Uncle Richard. As you know, I am still working here as a sales assistant* [shop girl] *and you can imagine* [you know only too well] *what that pays. I have given Helmut 10 sh. every week, so £2. – a month, as well as personal things* [and pocket money] *when I was still doing tutoring in addition to my job. I can* [gladly] *make this money available for my parents. I don't know if you view doing tutoring in addition to a shift in the shop of 9–10 hours as a "sacrifice". I absolutely don't know what more I could do* [deleted]. *Father is apparently coming next week. After a long search I have found a home for him outside London which my parents will take for a short* [time] *and where they will have to pay around 15 sh. a week per person for food and board, which by English standards is incredibly cheap and only for* [here the draft ends].

Hermine and Ludwig wanted to start packing. 'As soon as we have approval for our luggage we'll send our lift to London,' wrote Ludwig Rosenthal on 20 March. They would let Liesel know so that she could find an appropriate 'and not too expensive' room to put their furniture: 'for us it is in any case an advantage to have our things with us & for later, when perhaps [we'll] move from England to another country'.

Aunt Emma wrote to Helmut on 22 March to let him know that there would be big changes after the death of his dear grandmother. 'We're giving up the flat, we're selling the furniture and have to clear everything out, which means a lot of work. The city is interested in the house.' I will return to this subject in the last section of this book when examining the question of remembering this story and when dealing with the subject of processing Heilbronn's Nazi past, as well as the discourse between the city and the emigrants who became 'foreign Heilbronners'. For now all that needs to be said is that the house was sold for a pittance to the city, and it was only in the 1960s that the family received small compensation for it.

Aunt Emma, still writing to Helmut, added that she was trying to find accommodation in a hostel,

> *but this is very difficult. [...] For me the worst is when you have no children as you are on your own, if only I could come to England, perhaps the Halevys you were with before will take pity on me, speak to them. I was delighted to hear from your father that you are doing well, and they will go over to you soon, God willing, which you will be very happy about, even your father can hardly wait, he depends on you so much and loves you very much, just be good to him and help him, as recently there has been a lot of stress with your M[other], but don't let that show.*

This was probably an attempt to get the fourteen-year-old Helmut – who in happier times would have had a right to inherit the family home – to take over some joint responsibility for the family, but it was also a sign that the family as a unit was breaking up. The 'stress' which Emma Dornacher talked about referred to Hermine's continuing vacillation between clinging on and letting go, specifically in terms of their 'things' but in a more general sense in terms of their former life. Hermine wrote on 25 March 1939 to Liesel 'that dear Papa will definitely travel on Thursday 30 of this month', although she herself wanted to stay a little longer:

> *I'm hurtling about everywhere, you can scarcely imagine. Now there's the old house, we're getting not a p[enny] for it & now I'm paying the price, for my hair is going grey; yesterday I handed in in Stuttg., now have to wait week after week until I get something. My junk gets me nowhere & I can't leave anything as it is. Everything now depends on me & am so ill that I cry with pain. There's no help. So Papa is definitely coming this week. Concerning ticket to Montev. have tried everything & found a possibility, but that would take a long time.*

There was another delay. On 29 March Ludwig wrote: 'I am sorry that I can't come to you as promised, the rules mean I have to take care of a few diff. things for another few days & you'll just have to be patient.' In Stuttgart, explained Hermine, 'he was told he should wait'; 'Stuttgart' here may refer to the aforementioned Israelite Welfare Office, although it is hard to imagine its staff advising against emigrating as soon as possible at this time. In London Winifred Rathbone asked Liesel why 'your parents' arrival is delayed', as she would not be able to keep the accommodation set aside for them free for much longer. Jakob Wertheimer wrote on 2 April 1939 – the letter was torn lengthways, although that does not necessarily mean anything – asking Liesel to tell him exactly how much money she needed from him to support her parents. 'Perhaps you don't know that in Switzerland we also have thousands of emigrants, more or less everyone is helping look after them.' Then he added:

Figure 15 Postcard from Hermine to her daughter Liesel from 25 March 1939 © Baroness Julia Neuberger, Private Collection

I will probably have to go to Heilbronn in the next few days & at least put your father on the train to London, otherwise he simply won't leave & then won't get out, if your mother doesn't want to go with him I will allow her to enjoy waking up with her furniture.[55]

Ludwig's next letter came on 8 April from Amsterdam. He was 'out' and with Richard Loeb at 52 Michelangelostraat. Their relatives wanted him to stay a week with them to get the financial affairs in order, but all the preparations were already being made in London for his imminent arrival, as Liesel wrote in an undated letter to Mrs Rathbone: 'I am very sorry that you should be put to so much inconvenience on account of my parents.' Ludwig wrote that he would

definitely leave here on Tuesday evening and arrive 8.38 early on Wednesday & hope to be able to greet you both at the station, have addressed my large suitcase to London Liverpoolstation. I am very much looking forward to seeing you again, & you??

Hermine now had to address her despairing news from 13 April to 'Dear Ludwig, dear children':

Due to pack on Monday, no-one is here to help, they only came to stop by and chat. Tell me now: should the bicycle come to London with me? What are the important things to take? Should the trunk go in the lift? […] Write the important things, not the unnecessary ones!

Gina Rosenthal (at 43 Götzenturmstraße) had heard that she could take a job in Birmingham. She wrote on 16 April that she would arrive at Liverpool Street Station on 'Friday morning' and asked Liesel to pick her up, 'as I don't know my way around there at all'. For reasons unknown, at one point of her journey she turned back and never arrived in England. For the next eight days there was a pause in the family correspondence while other letters – including one from Heinz Gumbel in Jerusalem – arrived. I will focus on these in the next chapter. On 24 April Ludwig wrote from Wimbledon:

> *I hope you have asked Helmut to be at the station at half 8 Wednesday [27 April] & to poss. wait for a later train, as I could poss. be late due to delays at Harwich.*

The next day a new letter arrived.

> *Helmut visited me yesterday & will pick mother up early on Wednesday at the station & have lunch with us. I spoke to Mrs Maier today about your staying from Wednesday to Thursday & she turned this down on account of "lack of space". Be so good & don't come on Wednesday evening then, but when you're free on Thursday, you can call mother on Wednesday evening.*

Richard Seligmann, owner of Lincoln House, which had been rebuilt to be a hostel for refugees, wrote on 26 April that

> *we are very grateful for the opportunity to have helped people like your father, and are indeed glad to know that in his case at any rate we have been somewhat successful. I hope that the future will soon appear in a somewhat rosier light for him and others than it has heretofore.*

Although there was no written confirmation of it, Hermine arrived in London on 27 April 1939, and news of her successful emigration soon got back to Heilbronn. On 1 May Minni Stern wrote from Nauheim that Liesel surely was happy 'to have your dear parents there'.

In later life the family often talked about the help they received when they were packing their things back home, and in the story Ludwig's friends from the First World War and subsequent imprisonment in a POW camp played an important role. Julia Neuberger wrote to me:

> *In a way, it actually saved his life when he emigrated, because a number of these former prisoners were people from our area. […] When my parents were packing up to leave – it was already pretty late in 1939 – a man came to supervise the packing officially, to see that they took nothing forbidden with them. But he was an old wartime friend of my father and said to him, "Come on, Ludwig, you take it all with you, I'll sign it".*[56]

Figure 16 German POWs in Marseille, photographed in August 1919. Ludwig Rosenthal sits front right © Baroness Julia Neuberger, Private Collection

This is a good example of the overall ambivalence of history, when we consider it from such a close, personal standpoint. The 'old war-time friend' treated Ludwig generously and humanely, as the family remembers, but of course he was a member of the Gestapo, or the police at least, and in other cases must have acted differently. The dates in the following excerpt do not quite match up with what I have deduced from the letters, but in this speech broadcast by the BBC on 26 January 2012 to mark Holocaust Memorial Day Julia Neuberger succeeded in conveying the symbolic importance of the Rosenthal family's possessions and of rescuing them to England (where, as we have seen, Ludwig and Hermine had finally arrived), as well as placing what happened in a larger, and important, context:

> It's Holocaust Memorial Day tomorrow, so I want to tell you a story. My mother was a refugee from Nazi Germany who arrived in 1937 and worked as a domestic servant for the wonderful Dobbs family in Birmingham. She got her parents out of Germany in 1939, three days before the outbreak of war. They came with nothing, and settled in a single room of a hostel for refugees.
>
> Five weeks after the war began, great containers started arriving, full of their possessions, from valuables to everyday china. My grandparents stacked it up and lived on top of it for years. The men who had been Prisoners of War with my grandfather in France during the First World War had gone into my grandparents' apartment,

packed everything up, instead of looting it, which is what usually happened, loaded it on to horse-drawn wagons, and taken it into France. It then travelled up to the Channel, and arrived in London unscathed.

These stories are very uncommon. Fortunately, though shattered by the fact that they both lost most of their families in extermination camps, my grandparents were able to thank the men who sent their stuff, after the war. But the question we have to ask ourselves, as we think about other genocides, Rwanda, the Congo, Darfur, Bosnia, is what would we have done? No-one forbade people from sending stuff after those people who left Nazi Germany terrified for their lives. But very few people did it. Would we have helped, if it had been us? Would we do such acts of kindness, go against the crowd, if we were in that situation? Would our voices, or actions, make a difference? That's the message of Holocaust Memorial Day. I still have the evidence of what those men did – my grandparents' china, glass, linen, and ornaments. They brought my grandparents some comfort, and a belief in humanity. Would we, could we, do the same?[57]

5

'An alien of a most excellent type.'
The war years in London

With the help of Betsy Emanuel, an old family friend of the Schwab family, deeply involved with refugees in Brighton, Liesel got Jack into a grammar school in Hove. In her 1990 interview she says that the headmaster acted with particular 'kindness and helpfulness' towards them; he looked after four refugee boys who remained friends for life. Liesel herself continued to work for Marks & Spencer and was promoted to store supervisor in the Marble Arch branch. Many refugees shopped there, and one day Liesel bumped into a friend from Frankfurt who she previously believed had been deported to Poland in 1938.

Very soon afterwards Liesel was transferred to Wood Green 'as a staff manageress trainee [...] to replace the men, if they were called up'. This reflected the British perspective of the immediate pre-war period. For those persecuted by the Nazi regime the most important thing for the time being was that they had escaped Germany, although many still lived with the fear of what might happen to their relatives who had stayed. These differing perspectives become clear when examining the research carried out in this area: while British historians traditionally focused on the policy of the British government, primarily Neville Chamberlain's appeasement policy towards the Third Reich and the crises which can be summarized with 'Munich', it was only in the 1980s that a new line of research emerged which foregrounded the lives of refugees, investigating events from their point of view.[1]

Despite the restrictive immigration policy at this time, London became one of the most significant centres of German-Jewish emigration and the religious, cultural and political activity associated with it. The synagogue at Belsize Park was one of the most important meeting places:

> *The first service held by what was to become Belsize Square Synagogue took place on 24 March 1939 in the continental liberale manner, organised by a group of refugees mainly from Berlin and Frankfurt-on-Main. Initially there was no formal congregational organisation, and each service was conducted by a different rabbi and cantor recently arrived in the UK. The group was supported by Lily Montagu, one of the founders of the English Liberal Movement and a lay minister in the Liberal Jewish Synagogue, who enabled them to use the Montefiore Hall for Friday evening services. However, despite her help, the founders of Belsize Square Synagogue could not*

simply integrate into an existing synagogue like their orthodox and reform refugee counterparts. Coming from the continental liberal movement, English liberalism was too radical for them. In June 1939 this ad hoc state of affairs was formalised by the foundation of the New Liberal Jewish Association, which became Belsize Square Synagogue in 1971. Lily Montagu was its first chairman and Rabbi Dr Georg Salzberger (formerly Frankfurt-on-Main) and Cantor Magnus Davidsohn (formerly Berlin) its first permanent ministers.[2]

Through her work at Woburn House and her relationship with Anna Schwab, Liesel was part of the inner circle of this culture in exile, in which the German language initially played an important role.[3] In May 1963 *AJR Information* published Walter Schwab's obituary to his mother:

In 1909 my mother, who was born in Frankfurt/Main, came to England to marry. My father who also came from the same town, had arrived in England a few years previously to join his uncle's banking firm. They set up house in 180 Goldhurst Terrace, Hampstead, and lived there happily ever after. [...] Hardly had my mother settled down in London, when the First World War broke out, bringing with it a mass of problems, including a swarm of refugees from Belgium and other countries over-run by the advancing German armies. My mother's best bed was immediately given away to a newly arrived Belgian family in grave distress. This incident may well have been my mother's first practical effort at social work in England. [...] Later on in the twenties, she joined the First Women's Lodge of the B'nai B'rith, my father already being an active member of the Order, and it was in and through the Lodge that most of her future activities were conducted. [...] But then came 1933, and it was as if all her previous work, all the contacts and reputation she had acquired in the community before then, had been a preparation for the tragic struggle that lay ahead. One of her very first activities on behalf of refugees may illustrate her methods of operation. The evil news had come from Germany. It was clear that rapid action was called for. "We must have a centre to which refugees can turn on their arrival", said mother. What better use could be made of the B'nai B'rith room which the Women's Lodge then occupied in Woburn House? [...] As the refugee work developed and the organisation grew, my mother's own activities broadened. Officially she was Chairman of the Hospitality Committee of the Refugee Committee but this was a carefully ill-defined position. Everybody who needed help came to her. [...] She was interested in people. Each person who came to seek her advice was an individual. [...] Her home was always open and rapidly became an unofficial extension of her place of work. At one time the Post Office asked my father to install a second line at home because the telephone was always engaged.[4]

Anna Schwab (Anna Hindel Schwab, née Ellern) died 'peacefully in her home', as her son wrote, in London on 16 April 1963. At the time she was active – the time of Liesel's arrival and first few years in England – she was a key figure, not just in aid work but also for German-Jewish émigrés and their increasingly English culture as a whole. Various aspects of this culture have been examined in detail in a range of different publications, so we do not need to go into it here. What is worth mentioning, however, is the important role played by the circles (clubs, religious communities or political societies, some private and some official) in accelerating the integration of thousands of refugees from Germany and Austria.[5] Although in a specifically British context, they were similar to those established in New York, Tel Aviv and Jerusalem.

A dissertation by Traude Bollauf, 'Servant Emigration. How Jewish Women Were Able to Escape from Austria and Germany to England', investigates this story in detail and details the work of both Woburn House and Bloomsbury House. It describes Woburn House as 'the headquarters of the German-Jewish Aid Committee and the place to go for Jewish refugees prior to the creation of the Central Office for Refugees at Bloomsbury House in January 1939':

As a result of the Anschluss with Austria in early 1938 an increasing number of refugees came to Britain. By then, however, the situation had become increasingly unclear in terms of both the number and the responsibilities of British refugee aid organisations, which were now supplemented by self-aid organisations such as Austrian Self Aid and Deutsche Selbsthilfe. Therefore, in accordance with Home Office wishes, the Co-ordinating Committee was founded, in which the individual refugee organisations were represented. In January 1939 a Central Bureau of Information was set up in a former hotel in the Bloomsbury area of London. Bloomsbury House became the "headquarters of the principal organisations concerned with the welfare of refugees from Germany and Austria". Neither the work done by the refugee aid organisations nor its relocation to Bloomsbury House went completely smoothly. In January 1939 Otto M Schiff, Chairman of the German-Jewish Aid Committee, accused the Committee of being "in many cases a hindrance rather than a help" in the Jewish Chronicle. [...] His opinion was that Miss Schwarz [recte: Schwab], head of the Committee, herself of either German or Austrian origin, spent too much time minutely studying every letter that arrived and giving guidance on how to write replies, which she also checked over herself before they were sent off. Although in terms of efficiency this way of working was without question excessively time-consuming, the recipients of these letters, impatiently and anxiously waiting for a chance to leave Nazi Germany, would have been extremely grateful for these personal letters.[6]

Heinz Gumbel, whom Liesel had told of her work with Anna Schwab, wrote from Jerusalem on 23 April 1939.

You really are a hard-working girl, I must say. Looking after your brother and now getting your parents to come. I've been working to try and get my people a certificate for half a year now. So far without success.

His career was going well. He was no longer working in the workshop but as a freelancer, and he was doing some teaching work, which forced him 'to really think about the problems of design craftsmanship'. An art magazine yielded a portrait, and the Keren Kayemet (the National Fund of the Jewish Agency) ordered some pieces for the Palestine Pavilion at the World Exhibition in New York. At the same time

Figure 17 David (Heinz) Gumbel in Jerusalem, 1963 © Stadtarchiv Heilbronn, Fotosammlung, photographer: private

he volunteered as a policeman and was required to report for drill, field exercises ('commanded by Jewish corporals') and roll call with British officers.

Both worlds, as different as they may have seemed, were in fact closely tied to each other. Palestine was governed by the British Mandate on behalf of the League of Nations, and it was at exactly this time, 17 May 1939, that the White Paper on the future limitations to be imposed on Jewish immigration to Palestine was published. Under pressure from Arabian states and the Colonial Office, the number of Jewish immigrants was to be reduced to 75,000 for the following five years and regulations on the purchase of land by Zionist organizations were to be tightened.

At the same time the Jewish community in Palestine was developing its own underground army, the *Haganah*. Nevertheless, as Heinz wrote, the endless *Schmirah* (watch) gave him the opportunity to look at the stars in the Palestinian sky and Jerusalem at first light ('the romance of Schmirah is when you have to go on patrol through a mixed Jewish-Arabic area. And the prose, when you feel weary in the morning and dirt gets under your skin'). He had also met a girl, 'simple and naturally clever', although he did not yet have enough money to get married. He sent best wishes to Erwin (Rosenthal), Georg and Suse (Schwarzenberger).

Ludwig and Hermine's 25th wedding anniversary was approaching, and Ludwig asked Liesel and Helmut to get him an English pipe with fine-cut tobacco, something we might call an 'object of integration'.[7] While Heinz was becoming a (Jewish) Palestinian, the Rosenthal family was attempting to adjust to life in England. Jack wrote his letters to Liesel in English, still a little unsteady but with increasing confidence:

> *I just want to tell you that you cannot see me at the 18th, because we have there school. Therefore I suggest that you should better [come] at the 21st. Write me a card a tone to say that you agree and then write to the headmaster and tell him that you will come.*

The news from Germany was despondent. 'I assume you have by now become the complete Englishwoman,' wrote Minni Stern from Bad Nauheim on 1 May 1939 to Liesel. 'Purely in terms of appearance you certainly look no different from the *Ladies*. Is your English perfect yet?' Minni's only wish was that she and Alfred 'could be with you soon, even if we would have a very hard life there. But being here is almost impossible for young people.' Liesel would be able to imagine this, although the pressure seemed to be getting on top of her; Max and Trude Victor wrote on 4 May that they could 'feel your despair. Take refuge with us, we're always delighted to see you!'

It would be no surprise if Liesel's despair had something to do with the sudden presence of her mother, which she had both hoped for and dreaded at the same time. Hermine missed 'a great deal' of her things, as she wrote on 8 May, and wanted to replace them. She had asked Woburn House for money to get her suitcase repaired, which was turned down, and she urgently needed a hatbox. She demanded an accurate list of all the money Liesel had 'paid for us' recently, just as she had listed in minute detail what Liesel had received from her and Ludwig – she owed this to her own siblings, 'who did & are doing so very much for us'. And no sooner had she arrived and begun to 'settle' than the motherly nagging resumed: 'Save & don't invite anyone round, it always costs you money.' A day later she invited Liesel to a 'cosy little evening of performances and music' at Lincoln House. She had already organized a place to stay for the night, and she did not neglect to add: 'So if you want to come then let me know asap & make sure you dress well.' It was an illusion to believe that pre-existing conflicts would resolve themselves after a dramatic event such as emigration, or even that they would become less of a problem; on the contrary, they all emigrated with them. On 9 May Aunt Emma congratulated Liesel on her upcoming birthday and made a point of mentioning how nice it was that she could 'spend it with your parents' this year.

Now Ludwig and Hermine joined in with the attempts to find ways for relatives still in Germany to emigrate – but Liesel had to do much of the donkey work. 'Dear Mother promised Eugenie [May] before she left that she would ensure that cousin Siegfried gets the permit for England as soon as possible.' Liesel therefore needed to speak to Bloomsbury House about the matter, 'as Siegfried must be out of Germany by the end of May at the latest, otherwise he runs the risk of being caught again'. Although there were more and more successes to chalk up in this field – on 11 May Ida Stern wrote from Stuttgart, expressing her thanks for all their help and saying that she, like her sister, had obtained a permit, meaning she could now start a job in domestic service in Putney – it was rather unwise to make such promises. Hans Schloss turned to Liesel for help with an urgent matter on 14 May:

> *It is about our former travelling salesman Ernst Selz and his wife from Affaltrach and my parents tell me that it's high time to get him out, as there is the risk that he could end up in Dachau again. Now I know that you yourself have enough on your plate already, but perhaps you have an idea of how to help the man. He is around 44 years old, healthy and his America number is in the 20,000s. Selz wrote to me about if he perhaps could come over with his wife as a servant couple and if you could use your contacts at Woburn House or wherever to find anything out I would be very grateful to you!*

Hans Schloss's own 'people' had already been in England for five weeks and were going to 'ship out to Australia'. As soon as someone had got themselves out of Germany they became a resource for those still looking for help. Family members often went in very different directions, ending up in all corners of the globe.[8]

Extensive correspondence documents the case of Hans Eisig. Letters were exchanged between the Movement for the Care of Children from Germany (British Inter-Aid Committee) at Bloomsbury House, the Israelite Welfare Office in Stuttgart (36 Hospitalstraße) and the Federation of Israelite Charitable Organisations between 9 and 15 May 1939. All of them are characterized by utter helplessness in the face of the bureaucratic restrictions imposed on both sides. 'We will do everything we can to accommodate the boy here, but unfortunately we can't promise anything.'

> *The person you ask about in your letter was sent by us to Berlin for child transport. As he has since turned 16 we are afraid that he will no longer be dealt with by your department. An uncle of Hans Eisig had arranged a job for him, but so far no money guarantee has been provided.*

Hans's mother Melitta wrote about their futile efforts:

> *Those who want to help often can't, a. people who could often don't want to. And yet it is so urgent. I often think it is like when someone is drowning a. calls for help a. the people on the bank don't help as they are afraid of getting wet.*

Hans himself wrote his CV by hand:

> *My name is Hans-Eduard Eisig and I was born on 8 April 1923 in Heilbronn a/Neckar. My father is businessman Hermann Eisig, my mother is Melitta Eisig née Vogel. At the age of 6 I started at the local primary school which I attended until the age of 11; I then attended the Oberrealschule, now called the Robert-Mayer-Oberschule. As of Easter 1939 I am receiving my certificate of secondary-level education.*
>
> *I would now like to prepare myself for a profession. In terms of foreign languages, I have learnt French for 5 years, Latin for 3 years, and for 1 ½ years I have been*

privately tutored in English. I have played violin for 4 ½ years and have played in many concerts for the local orchestra. I would like to learn a technical trade such as electrical engineering, radio manufacturing, motor production [...]. If I should be unable to find anything in these professions I would also enjoy learning photography [...].

It is my wish to go to England to improve my knowledge of the language in the country and to develop into a hard-working adult.

The notion 'victim of the Holocaust' is very abstract, and the figure of 6 million who were murdered is difficult to imagine. This was the voice of one of them. The attempts to rescue Hans and get him to England failed and, as already mentioned, he was deported from Berlin to Auschwitz in 1943. How petty and pathetic, in contrast, seem the arguments amongst those who got out! And yet the fact that tragedy and farce, large-scale politics and small-scale everyday issues, were being played out at the same time has a part to play if a complete history is to be written. Someone had complained about the behaviour of the Rosenthals at Lincoln House, and on 25 May Ludwig had to

protest quite vigorously, we're not running around after the English, rather the other occupants follow the ladies wherever they go; we have no need whatsoever to run around after anybody, not even the supposed "Lord of the manor" who's told you of the complaint about us & whom you've gone crazy about [...]. By the way, I must confess, we have more important things on our minds than these silly rivalries and fights for prestige in this house, perhaps on Whitsunday you'll have time for a serious conversation with your parents, as this home here is no long-term place for us.

In addition to her day-to-day job Liesel (who, I guess, ignored this) translated begging letters from potential emigrants, like for R H Morgan (Hamilton House, Mabledon Place, London WC1), who asked in a letter from 7 June: 'Is it the girl's father she desires to get over here and do you think the Jewish Agency would help?' She worked for the London Union of Girls' Clubs, as shown by a letter from its 'organizing secretary' A H Ross from 22 June, and was training for a badge so that she could lead activities with girls under sixteen once a week (even if she had to interrupt this for her 'training as a manageress' at Marks & Spencer). She took part in events organized by the Bernhard Baron St. George's Jewish Settlement Organisation 'under the auspices of the West London and Liberal Synagogues'.[9] And she even went on holiday to the Victor family in Amsterdam, where Ludwig sent his best wishes on 8 July, reporting that now Max Rosenthal had to 'move out' of Heilbronn too. The holiday was relaxing, but the return was not. Liesel herself wrote to 'dear Mr Igersheimer' on 20 July 1939:

It has now been a week since I bade farewell to you. Everything seems to me like a dream, I feel like it [was] months since I was in Holland. No-one took into account that I was on holiday and that I should be treated leniently, in a whole year I have not shed so many tears as I did on Sunday and Monday. I truly was delighted to meet you and I think a lot about you. I would love to sit with you by the sea and bury my feet in the sand, but that is one of the things that are over now. I still think a lot about *the Victors and Elizabeth too, and then above all about little Hanna. <u>When I was there I could be myself again</u> for once. Have you been working hard? How do you spend your days? I am being transferred to a new shop from next Monday and am looking forward to it, following your motto: always have something to look forward to, that way life is much easier. Do you hold it against me that I am writing this on a typewriter? Firstly I am in love with my typewriter, secondly my handwriting is very messy, and thirdly I just never write with a pen.*

Hermann Igersheimer replied on 24 July that he was glad to hear from her but saddened 'that the first few days after your return were so difficult for you'. It seemed to him 'that you are a little to blame for this yourself: you came back from your holiday with the feeling that it would be unpleasant there'. He wrote further that there were some days when you get up full of confidence and then everything goes well, and there were some days when you have the feeling that they will be bad days and then everything goes wrong. He therefore advised her to establish in her mind exactly why she was bickering with the people around her (and perhaps why she was 'angry' with herself). In the rest of Igersheimer's letter he addresses a problem which is significant in terms of understanding not just Liesel's behaviour, but also, in a much more general sense, the attitude of the emigrants who had escaped Germany:

Establish the reasons and you will find that in comparison to the unspeakable suffering around us they are not so bad. But even if you don't want to make comparisons and say to yourself: "In the end it's my own life with my own suffering, no matter that others have it worse in so many respects than me", then I would counter: be happy that you have bad days. If you do not know disappointment and pain then you also do not know real joy and real happiness. If you don't know what it is to be cold then you cannot value warmth. […] How do I spend my days? […] Well, reading, late of course, when Amsterdam sleeps.

This neatly described her situation. She had problems, no matter that they were small, while she was constantly being reminded of the problems of 'others' and confronted with them. She was living her own life, but the lives of others, of her superiors, her colleagues and not least her parents, interfered again and again in her life. I think she had plenty of experience of what it meant 'to be cold'.

I was only able to find two snippets of information on Hermann Igersheimer. In 1940, when he was again in touch, he was a 'Wholesaler of books, 231 West 96th St., NY'. According to a genealogical website he was 'a cousin of Max Horkheimer', and he had emigrated to Amsterdam as early as 1924, from where he moved to New York. There he became a 'member of the board of directors of the Hermann Weill foundation, supporter of the Institute of Social Research'. The Houghton Library at Harvard University holds a letter Friedrich Pollock wrote to him from 1948 (in the Leo Lowenthal Papers, MS Ger 185).

The mention of Max Horkheimer's name made me curious. In a later letter (12 February 1940) Igersheimer told Liesel that 'a part of New Year's Eve I spent with people of the institute of my cousin [Horkheimer] and I have met the Wiesengrunds

[Theodor W. Adorno and his wife Margarete (Gretel) Karplus]'.[10] Unfortunately, despite the generous support of staff and archivists at the Institute for Social Research and the New School of Social Research, I was unable to find out any more information about him[11] – in the meantime Lars Fischer, in his review of the German version of this book, wrote that 'extensive correspondence between Horkheimer and Igersheimer is in fact held by the Horkheimer Archive in Frankfurt'.[12]

Hermann may have been a nephew of Otto Igersheimer, bank director and senior member of the Jewish congregation, whose fate is described by Hans Franke:

> On many occasions the victims were dragged through the streets and mocked (such as pastor Dr Stegmann), harassed, jostled and beaten. In some cases threats and abuse lead to suicide. Concerted efforts were made to maintain the "people's anger", the well-organised, regular stirring up of the masses. One such was the gathering outside the "Heilbronn Bank Union", where a chanting crowd demanded that bank director Otto Igersheimer be handed over. He, however, had been warned and had already left. Another was the attacks on the Landauer brothers' warehouse on the Kaiserstraße and the zur Brücke textile warehouse.[13]

> Otto Igersheimer, banker, 1936. He was listed as a community and institutional curator. After David Vollweiler was deported he ran the "Advice centre for provision and support for the Jewish congregation in Heilbronn a. N.", which was officially tasked with carrying out the last measures within the congregation. Born 14 March 1879 in Heilbronn, he was taken to Oberdorf on 20 May 1942 and from there to the extermination camp at Auschwitz.[14]

On 8 August 1939, just a few weeks before war broke out, Ruth Leser, Liesel's friend from Bombay, whose son was still at school in Switzerland, wrote from Bad Schuls:

> We are back in Europe again, this time all three of us are together. We're enjoying our holiday with our boy, just a shame it's coming to an end so soon. If things remain peaceful he can stay at school in Switzerland. [...] We intend to travel back to Bombay at the beginning of November from Marseille with P&G. In the middle of this month we'll travel to Zürich, my husband will probably go to America for 3-4 weeks at the start of September. Will I come to London this time? It depends on what happens with my mother and sister who are still in Berlin. Both have the English permit, but are still waiting to see if they'll get the French visa. We and they would prefer the latter, as mother would feel better in Menton, where she could go and stay with a friend of my husband's, than in London. Now we have decided that my mother and sister have to have left Germany before we return to India.

The subject of transnational migration has already been discussed. Emigrants do, inevitably, become transnational actors: they cross borders, familiarize themselves with foreign languages and the customs of other countries and broaden the narrow horizons of their former life, particularly when, as in this case, they have the financial means to do so. It is therefore sensible to bring the questions and methodology of transnational historical research into a positive dialog with migration research, and to ask questions such as the following:

> *How, without choosing to, do individuals forced to flee a country become transnational actors? To what extent can transnational approaches enhance investigations into the relationships forged between migrants through diaspora research? How can the experience of migrants be considered alongside that of the "reception countries", and (how) can we succeed in opening a "third perspective" within which both experiences can be brought into dialog with each other?*[15]

First we must ask if the experiences of German-Jewish emigrants can be compared with those of non-Jewish Germans since the mid-nineteenth century. A conference organized by Stefan Rinke and H. Glenn Plenny in 2013, held at the Institute for Latin American Studies of the Freie Universität Berlin, had as its goal 'to examine Germans living beyond the national borders and to discuss new ways of telling German history [i.e. outside of Germany]'.[16] This was an interesting approach, but scarcely applicable to the topic of German-Jewish emigration. The question of how 'German' the Jews in London, New York, Tel Aviv or Buenos Aires who came from, and who were driven out of, Germany has a hackneyed feel to it; the much more interesting question is how their relationship to Germany, to its language and culture, interacted with the British, American, Israeli or Argentinian identities offered to them. 'Classical socioeconomic and historical research, from investigations into international relationships amongst German businessmen, industrialists and settlers to depictions of German communities in cities such as Mexico City and Buenos Aires',[17] only seems to end with questions such as whether there were enough German *Gesangvereine* for them to sing in.

In contrast, the question we are interested in here is how many voices there now are in the choir and how the German voice in all its variety can be understood alongside other voices. Can what arose from the various experiences be adequately investigated by the tools used by research into transnationalism? Terms like 'Germanness Across Borders' or even 'Visions of Germanness' ('*Deutschtumsvorstellungen*') only partially apply to the world of Ludwig Rosenthal and his family. Germany was indeed present in their letters: in the language, in their clinging to familiar habits, in their conflict above all with the country they were forced to leave. Yet they are also just as marked by their attempts to integrate and grow into British, English-speaking culture and society. The experiences of the journey, and of being *on* a journey, as exemplified in Ruth Leser's letter, speak of Switzerland, 'America', India, England (and, in the background, Palestine, though it was not explicitly mentioned) as *places* 'irgendwo auf der Welt', somewhere in the world. In the context of emigration and immigration these places gained new significance and had to be viewed differently: namely in terms of whether or not they were suitable as a new home.

It was the act of leaving itself, the cultural practice of making a journey, which tells us something about this. The new 'geographical imagination' they suddenly had to develop – just consider Uruguay and Australia in the letters from Heilbronn – demanded new cultural practices, the study of atlases and maps, negotiations with consulates, the acquisition of papers and tickets. An observation made by Jan Robert van Pelt and Deborah Dwork is particularly important here, as it can help us make a connection between the news from Heilbronn of persecution and deportations on the one hand and the experiences of the refugees on the other: 'Fleeing does not write refugees out of the story [of the Holocaust]; it simply takes the story elsewhere. Indeed: it takes it everywhere.'[18]

Address books would seem to be a possible source for the networks formed during these processes. Indeed, Christine Fischer-Defoy has shown in her study of the address books belonging to Walter Benjamin and Hannah Arendt how historical research can make use of such sources.[19] But the course of events makes even these sources fragmented and incomplete; as Bertha Zuckerkandl wrote in her memoirs, many of the old contacts soon become useless and address books must be rewritten:

> *When you flee somewhere, you mostly forget the important things and take the most unimportant things with you; that was what I did. When I left Vienna I left many valuable things behind. But when I was unpacking the few manuscripts and books I had brought with me in Paris, the first thing I saw was my Vienna telephone book. Who had had the stupid idea to pack the dullest of all books? [...] When you lose your home your memory wanders back to it. Here, it was entwined around these names and numbers.*[20]

The places of origin played an important role in deciding where to flee to: while only ten per cent of all visa applications for the United States came from Berlin, this figure was much higher in many of the rural regions from where emigrants had left for America in the nineteenth century. This indicates an important connection between the various eras of emigration from Germany and the specific German-Jewish emigration post-1933. Patricia Clavin writes in her seminal work 'Defining Transnationalism' that the concept, 'despite its early identification with the transfer or movement of money and goods, is first and foremost about people: the social space that they inhabit, the networks they form and the ideas they exchange'.[21]

In the last few weeks before war broke out things were hectic at Bloomsbury House. Ernst G Lowenthal wrote about the 'guarantee problems' in the department where he worked:

> *Sometimes I had up to 50 people come to me a day, one after another. But we still had to "process" them as quickly as possible. [...] How many of them had in their eyes the spectre of the last ship which would take them abroad! And how right these people were to think that. Despite the fact that the British embassies on the continent had been granting visas more quickly than before, the committees had not reckoned with such a massive surge of new arrivals as came in the weeks immediately before the outbreak of war. Waiting rooms and corridors in Bloomsbury House were chock-a-block without interruption for days on end and people were swarming around like bees everywhere. Patience was required – on both sides. This was because every "case" needed a proper hearing and attention paid to it, even if work went on long into the night. Until the last possible moment work feverishly continued at both Bloomsbury House and Woburn House (Immigration Department).*

In no other period of my life have I met so many people from so many social classes of a society as I did in those frantic, frenetic weeks before the war. Back then [...] the "need" began with the guarantees. Either they had been given on a more pro forma basis to get people out, or the guarantor had assumed that his responsibility would not last very long as the applicant possessed a comparatively low registration number for further emigration to the USA. In some cases he was no longer in the financial position to comply with the guarantee as he thought he could owing to his being called up. This resulted in a large number of new demands on the committee, but it was this which meant that the guarantee department had to be kept running. For the duration of the war those "guaranteed" to migrate further often became semi-permanent immigrants in need of support.[22]

These observations form the basic framework for the 'cases' being played out in our letters. As good as Ruth Leser's 'international contacts' were, she still needed to ask Liesel for help getting her mother and sister out of Berlin:

Without putting yourself to too much trouble could you advise me how & where the both of them could stay? [...] I thought perhaps they could have two rooms furnished/half-furnished with a family, with board, poss. even with emigrants who would surely know what they're going through? Could you advise me on this and tell me something about costs. I am asking you urgently.

By then it was very late to be asking such things. On 1 September 1939, the day the German invasion of Poland began, Anna Schwab wrote on the notepaper of the Welfare Department of the German Jewish Aid Committee at Bloomsbury House: 'I confirm with thanks the cheque for 1.10 and completely understand your position. Unfortunately world affairs otherwise look less positive.'

The work done by Bloomsbury House provoked considerable controversy among the emigrants. David Herzog (1869–1946), the former rabbi of Graz, was very critical: he was able to emigrate to London at the beginning of January 1939, initially living for a few days 'in the home for refugees, which was at the time located in the house of the Jewish College (Woburn House) but which then moved to Bloomsbury House'. While there he asked for help for the people 'in my congregation', that is, Graz, but also for those in other places desperately waiting for an opportunity to leave.

But I had little success as the whole organisation was flawed. Neither Otto Schiff nor Anna Schwab was suitable for this great cause and the task they had been given. I would have a lot to say about this Bloomsburyhouse [sic]. But today, for reasons of delicacy, I will hold my tongue.[23]

The outbreak of war had an impact on both the work of the Refugee Committee and Liesel's private correspondence from then on. According to Ernst Lowenthal,

An abrupt, sometimes far-reaching change entered into the refugee work. Both immigration to England and further emigration to other countries came immediately to a standstill. White as a sheet and with great emotion, Otto Schiff spoke in the tuck

hall at Woburn House to his hundreds of members of staff, the English and those from abroad, the volunteers and the paid. Schiff told of the restrictions in continuing the work which would arise as a result of the new situation.[24]

Hermann Igersheimer wrote in English from the RMS *Nieuw Amsterdam* of the Holland-America Line while on the journey to his new life. His letter illustrates the mixing of holiday and migration experiences we have been discussing:

> We had a big storm on sea – during one day and one night. 90% of the passengers were seasick, but not me. As an old sailor I like high waves. There are about 1200 passengers on board, chiefly Americans, going home now. Although we have music, dance, sports and movies every day, people made no real fun this time and anybody feels a depression owing to the awful circumstances in the world. Standing on the deck I sometimes think of the pleasant hours we have had together at Zandvoort and I ask the waves to send you my best greetings from the ocean.

Igersheimer gave 428 West 177th Street in New York City as his first address. This is right by Morningside Park, where the statue of German revolutionary of 1848 Carl Schurz (1829–1906) is located, and nor is it far from Riverside Drive, where Hannah Arendt lived.

Max Samuel got in touch again from Blackburn on 10 September, saying that he would like to go to the 'Schoe and Leather fair' in London and then meet Liesel. 'This war' was causing problems for his newly founded business, 'but this destroyer of world peace Hitler must be dealt with eventually, as no country and no man can live in peace thanks to this one man'. In a handwritten letter on her personal letter paper (180 Goldhurst Terrace, London NW6) Anna Schwab thanked Liesel for a bouquet of flowers and sent 'meanwhile once more all good wishes for a peaceful, brighter future'.

On 22 September 1939 more news, only some of it good, came from Leeds. Alfred Stern had managed to emigrate, but his wife had not. He was already writing in English:

> Dear cousin Liesel, [...] Three weeks ago I arrived in Leeds with one of the last trains from Germ. Unfortunately I am without Minnie, but I learned via Holland she is very well. I am very busy and I know most streets, synagogues, reverends & chasonim. Just so I have seen an enormous quantity of houses because my friends & myself too took an interest in renting. I send you greetings for the New Year [...]. Please write soon to me by return & I will do the same.

Inevitably, the German refugees viewed the situation differently from their British friends and colleagues. On 12 October one of Liesel's colleagues from work wrote from the St Mark Ward in Westminster Hospital that 'The world is certainly very interesting just now. I find it rather too exciting, trying to follow all the news.' British society was preparing itself for life under wartime conditions, and memories of the First World War – and the German enemy – were strong. The emigrants could not share this experience, even if, as Max Samuel wrote, they hoped just as desperately for Nazi Germany's defeat. Liesel (and Poldi, Leopold Lichtenstern, who she was with at this time) had English friends from 25a Thurlow Road who were in regular contact. This included people like Frances, who had found a position in domestic service with a family in Bath and who was worried about her boyfriend Bernard, serving in the Royal Navy, and Barbara, who had already had enough of the war, 'even after a month and without any air raids'.

But politics had other ideas. The term 'Enemy Aliens' came from the First World War, when in both Britain and the United States there were demonstrations against Germans and all signs of a German presence (in many cases places called 'Berlin' were renamed). After the outbreak of war in September 1939 and particularly after May 1940 citizens of enemy states, including Jewish and antifascist refugees, were subjected to severe restrictions in Great Britain. They were not allowed beyond a zone of three miles from their place of residence and were forbidden from owning vehicles, radio receivers, cameras or maps. As lawyer A Horovitz wrote on behalf of Alfred Stern at the end of November, they could only write to 'addresses in this country', meaning that their contact with relatives still in Germany (in Stern's case, his wife Minni) was broken. In mid-September tribunals were set up to determine the 'degree of loyalty' of non-British citizens.

Once again, world history intervened in the life of the Rosenthal family. Liesel's friend Joan Le Mesurier used the letter paper of 'The Vicarage, East Molesey, Surrey' to draft a letter 'To whom it may concern':

> *Mr Ludwig Rosenthal & his wife have been known to me since they came to this country & they are the parents of Miss Alice (Liesel) Rosenthal who is one of my best friends. Mr & Mrs Rosenthal are loyal and trustworthy people* [crossed out]. *From my knowledge of Mr & Mrs Rosenthal I am certain that the authorities in England can safely relax the restrictions on them as enemy aliens. They have an admiration for English life and & ways, & are not sympathetic to Germany in this present struggle. From my knowledge of Mr & Mrs Rosenthal I can highly recommend them. I am prepared to answer any questions that may be put to me about Mr & Mrs Rosenthal.*

The Rosenthals themselves received a version of this letter (without the name of the sender). On 26 October Hermine asked Liesel:

> *Today we received a very nice letter & we would be so grateful to you if you would let us know <u>immediately</u> who it is who wrote us such a charming letter, at the top it says "The Vicarage, East Molesey".*

Barbara wrote from Edgbaston, Birmingham, on 31 October:

> *My dear Liesel, I have been wondering how this nightmare has affected you, if you are still at Hampstead and remain at your job of work. I do sincerely hope all goes well with you and that you are as happy as these dismal circumstances will permit us to be. In any case please do remember the services of a friend are always available, and I shall be happy to do anything I can at any time. [...] How is your brother, Liesel? And your parents? I hope comfortable. Do write to me. It's so nice to hear from everyone.*

Figure 18 Liesel Rosenthal, photographed by Jack Paynton, London 1939 © Baroness Julia Neuberger, Private Collection

Joan and Barbara were two of the 'many friends' who Hermine and Ludwig (and also Gerhard Gabriel) had once warned Liesel about. They, too, had had to either move or look for new jobs, as their employer had been evacuated or had closed down. Jack Paynton had been moved to Wimbledon, and Olive, who wrote on 16 November 1939, was 'frenetically busy with Tribunals'. What would become of Helmut (Jack)? Hermine was making plans. He could learn to be a cook or a baker, or perhaps he could work in a bank; she had met someone who worked for Australia Bank 'in London & here'. And how were Hermine and Ludwig going to manage financially? Uncle Jakob wrote from Zürich 'that he can't help any more & now it's your responsibility', which was very bad timing as Liesel herself did not know if she would be able to keep her job. Meanwhile, Liesel's 'degree of loyalty' was being tested. R H Morgan wrote a letter of recommendation for her:

> *To Chairman, Alien Tribunal. Miss Alice Rosenthal of 25a Thurlow Road London N.W.3 has been well known to me for the last three or four years. I am glad to be able to say without any reserve that she has proved to be an alien of a most excellent type. Well educated, of good character, she has worked in business firms of high standing with marked success. Banned from her own country, she is working patriotically and strenuously in her newly adopted country. She can be trusted in every way. Signed, R.H. Morgan.*

'An alien of a most excellent type' – this commendation was a result of Liesel's dedication to both her work and her support for other refugees. Her relatives had advised her against the latter often enough, but her determination had won through.

With this, 1939 came to an end. In England the weather was, unsurprisingly, very cold. Hermine and Ludwig had by then found a flat at 56 Worple Road, Wimbledon SW19, and Hermine continued to worry about her things. She wrote to Liesel on 12 January 1940:

> The suitcase belongs to me, I got it as a silv. wedding & birthday present from Uncle Jakob & Aunt Hede, it only cost 65M[arks], I only gave it to Papa so that he could take it to London with him as I wanted him out of Germany, but no-one ever said that you should take it!

Joan wrote ten days later, using the letter paper of the London School of Economics and Political Science (LSE) (which had been evacuated like everything else and was now based in Cambridge): 'We had time to think of you & the misery you must have undergone these last two weeks in the cold.' She recommended that Liesel go to the lectures being held by the LSE ('Profs Twany, Laski, Robbins & Dr Jennings') and asked her to send more of the cake Hermine had baked.

Those who were further away probably had it better. At least, this was the message of a short letter with a completely illegible signature from 24 January 1940 sent to Liesel from New York:

> Well, here I am, almost an American, although I don't sing my English through the nose. It is a wonderful city, beautifully planned and built. Life is at a terrific speed & I wonder how Americans survive it. […] I like the Americans, they are simple & very hospitable. […] I am doing interesting work & have at my old age become a public speaker. I am addressing meetings & shall soon start on a long tour through the U.S. on my own […]. I've forgotten completely that there is a war in Europe & begun to understand a little the American mentality of isolationism. They are determined to keep out of war although convinced that sooner or later they will have to fight.

A lot was happening at the same time. Lots of people who were together one minute – perhaps in London, at 25a Thurlow Road – were suddenly spread across the world the next.

Around about this time Liesel had to go to hospital, which Hermine was very agitated about. The hints were that it was rheumatism and that there were 'pains', but perhaps she simply wanted to be beyond people's control for a few days. Her friend Barbara from Birmingham wanted to see her, as she wrote on 5 February, if only just to come to London again and to sound out the feeling in the city at the time. 'Most of my London friends are now evacuated, and it is quite a problem to keep a note of all the changes of address!' She added, with what can best be described as the spirit of the Empire: 'P.S. It's a great life, Liesel, if you can take it, don't you think?'

Researchers have written about the relationship between British society – individuals and institutions – and the refugees, and for a German working at an English university it is interesting to see how this can be interpreted differently. Those, like Anthony Grenville, who document what happened to the emigrants from the perspective and experience of their descendants will emphasize their gratitude for the support and hospitality they received. Others, like my British colleague Tony Kushner at Southampton, who critically examine their own society and shine a light on British immigration policy will question the mistakes that were made and why more support was not provided.[25]

Jack had had 'enough of Brighton', he wrote on 8 February 1940. He was living with a Dr Sohn (more precisely: 'our old, miserable Dr Sohn') and his family in an old house which 'threatens to collapse at any minute'. He was still having trouble adjusting to the English school system and would not be able to take his exams that year. The headmaster of the County School for Boys, Holmes Avenue, Hove, confirmed this on 20 February:

There is no hope whatever of his passing the School Certificate of Matriculation in Mathematics this year, and it is therefore a waste of time to put him in for it. Mr Baxter informs me that he has improved enormously but that there is no doubt that he has little grounding in the subject.

With hard work he would be able to improve his French, and things were looking good in every other subject. He therefore had every chance of taking his exams the following year. F L Norden finished with the dry comment: 'I should have been pleased to have helped him myself, but unfortunately, I do not know any Mathematics. I have only taught it.'

On top of the worries about Jack, who was ill at the time (though he did not tell his mother what was wrong), wanted to leave school and – like other 'boys' – find a job in London, there were money problems. The Jewish Refugee Committee asked Liesel on 5 April if she could help '[to] increase our contribution to your parents' maintenance as cost of living is rapidly getting higher'. Raschela (Roschele) Rubinstein had succeeded Anna Schwab at Woburn House, and she urgently demanded to speak to Liesel, asking if she could come and visit on one of her free afternoons.

As if this were not enough, the refugees were under threat of being interned. Of all people it was Alfred Stern, imprisoned at Dachau for weeks, who was interned by the British as an Enemy Alien. Although his lawyer Horovitz wrote on 10 April 'I have been informed by the home office that instructions have been given for the release of Mr Stern', in July he was still writing from a camp on the Isle of Man.

Lotte Fink, who had already recommended that Liesel should 'learn a page of idioms every day' and use *Langenscheidts neues Konversationsbuch* to improve her English, wrote on 30 March 1940 from Australia: 'We are only speaking English, even at home, and have only English speaking friends, Yes, my darling, such is life.' Her daughter Ruth had already won two prizes at school; for the time being, the war was yet to reach Australia.

Hermann Igersheimer got in touch again on 14 April with a lovely, very personal letter in which he ruminated on his homesickness from Europe:

Looking through my windows: the big Broadway traffic, and millions of lights in all colours. But my thoughts are – in Europe. They go back, to small towns, with rivers and bridges, churches and trees. To the mountains and to the sea. To all the beautiful countries I saw since my childhood, France, England, Scotland, Italy, Germany, Poland, Austria, Switzerland, Belgium and my dear Holland. They stay there and are very sad. Sad, because it is apparently impossible to live in peace as along as "human beings" do exist. Life goes on. New generations are coming, and they will not live in peace, either. […]

Read "Grapes of Wrath" by John Steinbeck, then you will become familiar with [the] life of American peasants. Do you intend to come to the States too in the near future? Please remember me to the Victors and to Mr Maschler when you'll see him. And write again.

The constant flow of letters hither and thither also produced a sea of fluctuating emotions. Post from Lotte Fink or Hermann Igersheimer was intimate and friendly, and reassured Liesel that she had a reliable circle of friends around her – this is particularly evident in the discussion about books. By contrast, post from her family almost inevitably involved crises and criticism. Ludwig wrote on 7 May that Liesel should send her brother more money. That she had not yet done so

reinforces my conviction that you do not much care for your younger brother & your parents, and instead care only for "one" who is not worthy of you. Now you are turning 25, get some sense into you for once, let go of this man so that he can go back to where he belongs – as a married man – by his wife & son's side and don't ruin your future for ever. Listen to me for once & let him go, or do you want your father to die of pure worry & grief. Best wishes! Father. – Best wishes too for your birthday. Berthel Walther was here on Saturday with Mäxle Feigenheimer, Mäxle said farewell to us & is going to America alone.

What a lovely birthday greeting! Even Hermine noticed, and she added on the reverse: 'I thought dear Papa was just writing your birthday letter, but he was writing you his criticism letter'. Still, she shared her husband's views and asked Liesel for the chance to have a talk 'with Lichtenstern, you & us'. Her birthday wishes were if anything even nicer: 'I wish you all the best for your birthday, above all that you develop some sense & that you will give us something to be joyful about.'

Uncle Jakob was furious. Hermine, his sister-in-law, had painted a picture of financial hardship, but he was not willing to give them any more money, as he informed her in a letter on the same day, 7 May:

I have written to you so often that you get much further with honesty than with concealing the truth, you reflect this when you don't tell us what people expect of you in the future. But this plays no role in my answer, as the committee ladies who you dear Hermine put forward can only reinforce what I have preached again and again: to finally stand on your own two feet & to not have to say merci to anyone. Your Liesel is so extraordinarily hard-working, you dear Hermine mention that in every letter & I also think she has great character, so it seems to me that the way out is if everyone sees her looking after the family, that's much more reliable than the parents continuing to rely on charity.

He even demanded that Liesel look for a flat:

you all move in together, you dear Hermine look after the domestic side of things etc., Liesel & the boy live with you, Ludwig should have found some kind of work by 1.6. (it doesn't matter what), as he's had enough rest & it's no shame whatever you do. […] Your boy should go to work too where he can earn something, if it's not much it'll be more soon, but you won't get anywhere with diplomas in your situation. […] Now I don't want an answer about what the committee l[adies] say, rather about how you have acted exactly in accordance with what I say above, otherwise from my point of view you are on your own two feet & can do what you like.

He might as well have saved himself the bother of writing the 'best wishes' at the end. Jack, though, was in agreement with his uncle in that he wanted to earn his own money: 'I don't want to be paid for any longer and I want to earn my own money,' he wrote on 9 May 1940. His letter was the only truly warm greeting sent to his sister for her 25th birthday the next day that she kept: 'Take this little present from your brother and be happy with it. Many happy returns, Jack.' His English was getting better and better. Ludwig sent her a copy of the 'coarse' letter from Zürich and asked for her opinion 'as you are so heavily involved with this'. His view was that Jakob

is completely right in terms of living together & it's always been your fault that we haven't been able to live together. You know full well that we are financially dependent on Jakob, and if he won't keep it up what then?

Hermine told Liesel to 'steel herself' and answer Uncle Jakob, adding that she should be 'decent and polite'. Moreover, she was (once again) of the opinion that Liesel should be 'more careful and considered': 'You never cared a jot for us, always selfish.' And: 'Invite Schupbach on Sunday, but you must be there 2 hrs beforehand!'

As it had been in the initial period after Liesel's emigration, it was the bigger picture which was troubling Hermine and Ludwig and making them act in this way. 'I have terrible thoughts,' wrote Ludwig on 31 May,

about what will become of Helmut if we are all interned, after all we can't leave him on his own in Brighton, we must always bear in mind the fact that we could be interned & advise you to pack your suitcase ready to go, which we'll also do now. […] Every day brings new hardships.

Perhaps they could send Heller to a farm to work 'for the interests of England'. Would that save him from being interned? The family was also greatly worried about Richard and Luise Loeb in Amsterdam, as on 10 May 1940 units of German Army Group B had attacked the neutral Netherlands and advanced as far as Ijsselmeer, not far from the city. The only way of maintaining contact with family members in Holland was now the Red Cross. But did this justify the extraordinarily authoritarian tone with which Hermine and Ludwig continued to upbraid Liesel? It did not stop; Ludwig wrote on 9 July:

> *Dear Liesel, I refer to the telephone conversation we had early this morning & am terribly disappointed with your behaviour towards us. We have told you repeatedly, in person & on the telephone, that we must now pay £5 rather than £4 per month from tomorrow & you agreed when we spoke on the telephone this week to send us 10sh*[illings] *a week, now you're going back on your word again, that really is no way to behave towards your parents, your hiding behind Helmut is completely invalid if you send him 1sh or 1sh 6d now & then & the bulk of Bloomsbury House is paid for him. We have already made so many sacrifices over the years for you that, if you had only a small flicker of our love for you, your actions towards us would be quite different; here we have very many elderly parents like Weissenbeck & Simon from Munich whose daughters and sons are helping make their parents' lives easier – but with you unfortunately it's the opposite.* […] *Mother has already given you every bit of clothing and furniture you need without it costing you anything & despite this you keep buying more things without considering if your parents can continue to pay for your living arrangements – after all our chances of working to earn money are gone. On top of this is the most unholy rate we have to pay, which gives me no rest day or night.* […] *You have promised so often to solve the price & like with the money you have never kept your word. I am so agitated because of you & demand that you be truthful & upright & although I am not a rich man, I don't let my good name be dragged through the mud as a result of your actions, your grandmother, if she were still alive, would despair with worry at your behaviour. Your father.*

She had agreed to give her parents more money. Perhaps, afterwards, she had recalculated and worked out that she could not manage it – no-one can know. And she still had not ended her affair with Poldi Lichtenstern. This may all be true, but how was she supposed to reply to this? Unfortunately I cannot say if she sent him a reply, but she did write to Uncle Jakob in Zürich on the same day, giving us a glimpse of her anger in her letter:

> *Dear Uncle Jakob, my parents gave me your last letter to answer. This is no easy task; as this letter shows such ignorance of the situation here that it is necessary to refute each individual sentence.*

And that was what she did, sentence by sentence. The sum of money he had been sending Hermine and Ludwig was no longer enough as prices in Britain had risen dramatically. The amount they had to pay for their accommodation was relatively small, and that should have been clear to him when converting it into Swiss francs. That they 'had asked you to send more was only to cover the increased cost of living'. With regard to the changes he demanded: Ludwig and Hermine were living in Wimbledon, far from the centre of London. Liesel had a job which involved being sent to a different branch every few months, so she could not live 'in one of these far-out places'. Getting a flat together in Hampstead would in any case be more expensive than their relatively cheap living costs now. 'These are no fantasy rents.' It was also 'very easy' to say that Ludwig had to find a job by 1 June:

> *At the moment it is completely out of the question for a German 1) to find a job and 2) to get a work permit. Even people who had a job have lost them in recent weeks. You must believe me, as I can judge this better from here than you can from Zürich. Foreigners who work without a work permit are put in prison and then interned.*

Yes, she was worried about Helmut and was doing everything she could to find a job for him, and yes she had made enquiries at her firm.

> *I have the impression that you have a preconceived opinion and don't want to understand me. I have done everything in my power for my parents and Helmut, and will continue to do so. But there must be some common sense. By moving in together as you want we will save nothing and help nobody. If on account of this you want to withdraw your support for my parents, you will have to come to terms with your own conscience.*

This inevitably makes me think back to Gerhard Gabriel's comment that this whole story could also have been a novel. If so, we would now have reached a decisive point in the plot. The young heroine who had learned to stand on her own two feet (this cliché was used rather a lot in the letters) had had enough of the never-ending criticisms and harsh judgements from her relatives and was at last standing up for herself. *I know better than you.* What would happen next in the novel? Although I am only writing a family history I would wish for the knight in shining armour to appear (he would indeed come soon, but not just yet).

Hermine had anticipated the impending problems and told Mrs Lloyd of the Wimbledon Committee that her guarantor could no longer send money, as Raschela Rubinstein of the Jewish Refugees Committee at Bloomsbury House told Liesel in an anxious letter on 11 June. Mrs Rubinstein asked Liesel again for a meeting the following Thursday afternoon, but was friendly enough to add: 'If you are wise, you will pop in at tea-time.'

Money was tight and the Rosenthals' landlords were 'anxious that we might not be able to keep paying', as Hermine wrote to Liesel on 13 June. At the same time she reported that she was doing not just Alfred Stern's washing, but also Poldi Lichtenstern's! 'Three mother-of-pearl buttons are missing from Lichtenstern's pyjamas, should I buy them and sew them on?' Hermine Rosenthal, from the good, conservative Jewish Rothschild family, was darning a man's pyjamas – a man married to someone else, who was sleeping with her daughter, not only against Mrs Rosenthal's will, but to her disgust. You could not write that script.

I have already alluded to the materiality of the letters, and this became more striking in wartime. In a letter written on 17 June, in landscape format on very thin, almost 40-cm long paper, someone called Richard (it seems) in Coventry complained about the lack of cooperation between the various aid organizations for refugees, saying that it was a case of one hand (in Coventry) not knowing what the other was doing (in London). He wanted to join the 'Auxly. Pioneer Corps' and needed signatures from both refugee committees. He ended his letter:

> *Lieserl, do not be downhearted. Even if the poor French had to give up. The higher he climbs the bigger the bang will be when finally, for the sake of universal satisfaction, he will be falling down.*

This 'he' was Hitler. When immersed in the everyday life of the family you could almost forget about him. Hermine was darning and ironing clothes to save a few pennies, and – as I quoted earlier in this story –

> *I am so cross with myself that I did not go straight from here to Uruguay, where I had all my papers ready, where I had sent my money and where my two lifts in Montevideo were paid for. We could have lived there quite nicely from the interest and I could have found a job. Now I live in a constant state of worry and I am using up all my money. […] Only speak English on the telephone, or we'll lose our telephone! Best, Mama.*

We had not had 'Mama' before. She also wrote in English, her own idiosyncratic English, to Liesel when talking about Helmut: 'This morning I got a letter from Jack, he will be in our house to morrow-morning. He wrote me today, he says goodby to his school & to-morrow he is here.'

Alfred Stern was the next to write, on 1 July 1940, from Onchan Internment Camp, House 53, Isle of Man. The policy of internment remains controversial to this day amongst historians; the measures taken by the British government were considered necessary in the name of security, even though this meant considerable hardship for those affected by them.[26] The letter was addressed to 'Dear Selma [Lowenthal]', but he also spoke to Liesel directly in the last section. Stern asked the two addressees to tell everybody they knew that they could end up in the same situation at any time – 'do the people outside not know that the reason they have not been arrested is fluke, and nothing at all to do what each of them has done?' He was held at Warth Mills for six weeks without news from the outside world and without his belongings, and since his arrest he had worn the same suit and shoes. 'On my writing pad was a draft of a letter to Minni, hopefully you can send it to me.'

The camp at Onchan where Stern was writing from has largely been ignored by historians, who have tended to focus on the largest and best-known internment camp on the Isle of Man, at Hutchinson in Douglas, *particularly noted as "the artists' camp" due to the thriving artistic and intellectual life of its internees [...], Hutchinson Camp opened in the second week of July 1940. It initially had only 415 internees but by the end of July this figure had risen to 1,205 internees, almost all of whom were German and Austrian. Numbers fell from September 1940 when the internees who posed no threat to Britain began to be released. This was particularly marked in Hutchinson Camp, where there was an unusually high proportion of Jewish and anti-Nazi internees.*[27]

There was great unrest at Worple Road, too. On 4 July Hermine wrote that the police had been inside the house, and the women were scared 'that we would end up with the men'. An undated letter ('July 40' was all that was written at the top) brought further news:

Mrs Löwenheim & Singer had letters from their husbands today, they only got away last Tuesday & father has been away for 14 days now & still no letter. [...] The men are asking for parcels. [...] Today & tomorrow we all have to go to the police with identity card, don't forget!

This shows that Ludwig was interned. Again, however, the few bits of information we can glean from the letters do not quite match Alice Schwab's later recollections. There she said:

All the refugees were classed as enemy aliens and the men, including my father, were put into camps, mostly on the Isle of Man. My father had to go to a camp near Liverpool where he joined lots of other men over sixty years of age from all walks of life. [...] The police knew where to find the refugees because they all had had to register at the local police station. I had to register too, because I was a refugee. I remember being summoned to the police while I was waiting for my permit for Marks and Spencer to come through. I was absolutely terrified when they said, "You've got another fortnight, otherwise we'll have to send you back to Germany." [...]

My father, as already mentioned, had been taken to a camp at Huyton near Liverpool together with one or two other gentlemen who were living at the hostel. But Mrs Rathbone, whose husband had formerly been Lord Mayor of Liverpool, went to the authorities and told them it was ridiculous to detain Mr Rosenthal and managed to have him released. Altogether, the Rathbone family did a fantastic amount of work on behalf of refugees.

She also wrote that, once her parents had been reunited, their friend Rose Verner decided to buy a small house in Wimbledon and make it available to the Rosenthals:

[S]he carried out her proposal and, through her kindness, my parents were able to move to a house in Worple Road, Wimbledon. Their income was, of course, very restricted because they had not been able to bring anything with them from Germany,

> *but my father managed to get a little job sorting waste paper, for which he was paid a pound a week. My mother made net bags which she sold now and then. […]*
>
> *I also helped financially and they had help from my mother's sister and brother-in-law in Holland. But once Holland was invaded and they were put into a camp, there was nothing more coming from that source. There was also a sister in Switzerland, from whom they got something from time to time.*

Judging by the letters, the move to Worple Road had already taken place before Ludwig was interned, and the support from Holland had also stopped by then. It is interesting that she mentions the sister (Hede) in Switzerland but not the oft-cited, often angry Uncle Jakob. In this look back at the family history everything seems very straightforward and uncomplicated: yes, Ludwig had been interned, but thanks to their contacts in the right places he was quickly released, as the British, about whom there is not one word of criticism in her 'memoirs', soon realized their mistake. In the contemporary letters things read rather differently, with a much greater sense of drama. Is it important to draw attention to such differences? Clearly, Alice Schwab – like so many other refugees – was speaking from a position of gratitude towards Britain. In addition, consciously or not, she wanted to pass on to the next generation an image of the family integrating successfully:

> *My father absolutely adored England; he liked the easy life; he liked going to the pub, the small talk – it suited him extremely well. It was probably more difficult for my mother, because it was a hard struggle to make ends meet, produce meals and so on.*

Negotiations with the Jewish Refugees Committee over the accommodation for the Rosenthals stretched right through the correspondence of July. Evelyn Lloyd and Raschele Rubinstein repeatedly asked when (and from whom) the next cheque would arrive. But I would question whether Ludwig indeed 'absolutely adored England', at least in the summer of 1940. 'The main purpose of my letter' was, according to Hermine in a letter to Liesel on 30 July:

> *everyone in the house is working to get the men released, you were with Erich Hirsch, please do everything you can & asap. Your father wants to come home, you have to make an application at the Home Office. Mrs Lloyd is helping all the ladies whose husbands had a job, with father she said there's no use, please just do everything you possibly can.*

She repeated her urgent plea that Liesel and Poldi should not live together:

> *I beg of you Mr Lichtenstern, take another room, as if it comes out there will be an embarrassing story, particularly now, where daily the police can look at it. As I now know that you have Liesel's room together, I can hardly go in if something comes up. In addition the people you are living with are not discreet & the business will become public.*

Ludwig was prisoner number 54504 at B-Comp, Aliens Internment Camp, 38 Belton Road, Huyton (Liverpool). His first (preserved) letter from there to Liesel came on 17 August 1940, having received a letter from her from 2 August along with a 'suitcase with sweets'. He had had to go to the doctor with high blood pressure and headaches, and was very agitated as a 'Miss Alice Rosenthal' had said she would visit the camp but had not turned up. 'Do you really intend to visit me here? Or was that a mistaken address?' The letter had been addressed to an Erwin Ludwig Rosenthal. The letter ended: 'These are indeed terrible times, hopefully the English will soon get the better of the scoundrels.'

Hermine was alone at this time and desperately wished that the family could be closer together. 'Helmutle' now had to spend every night 'in the schelter' and then get up early, without his mother to look after him. Other children 'are put to bed by their mothers & looked after in the shelter so that I hardly have any room to sit down', while he had no-one looking after him.

> Dear Liesel of course I think of you as well, but you want your own destiny. I would strongly advise at least that you live together with Heller, that you two are together, I would like to cook a decent meal for you 1 or 2 times a week. When dear Papa comes back then we'll all move in together, when Lichtenstern comes back he can take his own room. This is definite. [...] Yours and Licht's washing is done and ready to be picked up.

I am not sure where Lichtenstern was 'coming back' from. It is possible that he was interned, but a question from Liesel's friend Dora, who invited her to Welwyn Garden City for the day on 29 August, does not make it sound like that: 'Have you heard yet how Poldi is liking his new life?' By July 1940 the first German bombing raids on English and Welsh cities had begun. Hull was hit on 19 June, Cardiff on 3 July and Plymouth on 6 July, while Birmingham and London were hit for the first time on 9 and 24 August, respectively. Then, on 7 September, began the Blitz, the relentless series of devastating raids which lasted until May 1941, in which around 30,000 people in London were killed. Living and surviving in the shelters was one of the most common, and most lasting, experiences for Britons, and above all for Londoners, during the Second World War. The BBC has collated a wealth of sources and testimonies on people's experiences,[28] and an online documentary asked an important question: 'The view of Britain as a nation that pulled together under the Blitz is a compelling one. But is it based on reality – or are the memories of those who were there a better source of information?'[29]

Living alongside the refugees, frequently suspected of being Enemy Aliens and each with their own stories to tell, was also a thorny issue. On 12 September Ludwig was still in the camp at Huyton. He was 'confident that with God's help England will achieve the final victory over her enemy, so that we can look forward to happier days'. He thanked Liesel for a parcel with 'tins of turkey, salmon, eggs, chocolate, cigars and cigarettes and a load of sweets'. This was almost too much, and he said that Liesel should save her money instead and, like Hermine, should write every day, 'as am very restless'.

By 23 September, however, he had been released from the camp and was able to write from 56 Worple Road, complaining that 'we are very worried that in these difficult times we hear absolutely nothing from you'. This intra-family communication was, I think now, a ritual which Liesel went along with as much as she could. Festivals were coming up again and Ludwig and Hermine wanted to spend them with their children, perhaps going to a service in Hampstead.

The promised 'knight in shining armour' had still not yet made contact, although his brother, Corporal H C Schwab, Anna Schwab's younger son Harry, did on 20 October 1940. He was glad to hear that Liesel was 'still well & keeping going'; where he was posted there was so little to complain about 'that we feel all the more worried about things at home'. The letter was sent from 'Headquarters [S], 12 Reserve M.T. Con., R.A.S.C., c/o A.P.O 500', meaning he was stationed in Iceland. 'We are going to get some Icelandic lessons', so he had been unable to finish the book she had sent him, Vicki Baum's *Nanking Road (Hotel Shanghai)*. 'Iceland itself is growing on me. The only Icelandic people I have met are very charming & well above the average intelligence, and altogether there is nothing backward about the people.'

Hermine had Helmut, or rather Jack, with her and wrote to Liesel in English on 29 October. While of course it is amusing to see the mistakes, it is perhaps more remarkable that this 48-year-old housewife from Heilbronn had risen so well to the challenge of learning the language:

> *Jack is very glad to live with us, he looks splendid. Yesterday he was by Mr Halevy & on Friday he spent with Miss Veden by a very nice lunch. To-day he cant come to you, it is to much trouble for you [...], so I think you can arrange to meet him on Thursday 4 o'clock you will be together by a cup of tea one hour [...]. In love your mother (and father).*

A day later, Ludwig asked Liesel to 'call Helmut in the shop'. Alice Schwab briefly described what had happened:

> *he had to leave the wonderful school he had been at and came to live with my parents. He got a sort of engineering job, because such jobs were easy to come by during the war.*

In terms of content, the difference between the chaotic hither and thither of contemporary letters on the one hand and the later recollections on the other is clear. However, literature experts, linguists and even the untrained reader will also notice differences in tone, word selection and writing habits. Fear and nervousness shine through in the letters, vividly reflecting the state of mind of their author when they were written.

Liesel's friend Frances said farewell from (and to) Bath, as she was to leave for the United States on 7 November, away from the bombs: 'I'll write you when I am on the other side.' Her husband Bernard *is off again, he sailed from the London Docks, Wednesday week, though they were in a mess. They are not unusable – I hope he is not again torpedoed, it doesn't sound a healthy recreation – though he looked quite fit after it.*

Kurt Maschler wrote of his regret that Liesel – 'Fräulein Rosenthal' – had to stay in London, 'where you are exposed to the hail of bombs day and night'. In her interview she spoke of the experience of the bombing raids:

The enemy planes came over in a never-ending stream one Sunday afternoon. I got my staff down into the shelter and told one or two of the noisiest ones: "If you stop singing, I'll kill you, you must carry on singing." From two in the afternoon until six in the evening the planes were coming over. And downstairs they were singing. [...] During this period Marks and Spencer managed a shelter in Spitalfields and the senior staff used to help there one night a week, serving food and so on. This shelter was for people who had become homeless and where they could spend the night. It was safer in the shelter than where they had lived. They came to the shelter every night with all their clothes, luggage and bedding. One night I was there with my invoice clerk and we were very badly hit, I'll never forget it. I can't remember the exact date, but I do know that we were up all night trying to make the best of it. Next morning we thought we could go back to our store, have a wash and sort ourselves out. But when we came out of the shelter, the whole of Liverpool Street was down. [...]

There was such friendship and kindness, and the staff were wonderful. They came to work, even though they had been bombed-out the night before. "We couldn't leave you alone, Miss Rosen." They knew me as "Miss Rosen", cutting the "thal" off the end of my name. Then I helped in communal kitchens. Marks and Spencer had opened a soup kitchen in North Kensington, which had been very badly hit. [...]

Marks and Spencer needed us women after the men had been called up, but it was quite a thing for this to happen because in my time, when I was young, women weren't as important as men – you had to fight for your rights. There were a lot of opportunities for women during the war when the men had gone away, and women showed what they could do in all walks of life. [...] I was directed to go to a factory near Manchester to become a draughtswomen. It needed the intervention of Marks and Spencer's personnel manager to stop them getting me. [...] I was thrilled to know that they thought I might be able to do a job like that. But I didn't get the job and stayed with Marks and Spencer. In any case, it was easier for me to stay in London.

Alfred Horovitz, 'Continental Consultant Lawyer' as he now called himself, was preparing Alfred Stern's emigration, either to the United States or to Australia, as he told Liesel on 14 November 1940. His letter also talked about the luggage that Stern had sent to England, which had been stored in Reading by the Refugee Committee. As Ernst Lowenthal wrote, the luggage department at Bloomsbury House looked after more than just the containers 'which as a consequence of the outbreak of war were stuck in Western European ports'; it also looked after the possessions of those interned in England in 1940. In addition, in cases where the 'things' had been lost, as frequently occurred, it tried 'to get compensation for those affected, who were often left destitute'.[30]

A colleague from Marks & Spencer called Lydia wrote from Exeter asking Liesel: 'What is happening in the wide world? We have no wireless and, imagine it, very seldom read the papers. Is London still where it was?' And even the ever-optimistic Joan was in despair. She wrote from Birmingham on 12 December that if anything should happen to her 'all I have goes to Richard', and that, if both of them were killed in a bombing raid, Liesel was to get everything and look after Richard's mother 'a little'. 'The laws of probability suggest that we'll all survive but it is just as well to make plans in case the worst happens.' And Alfred Stern? He was still interned, and asked for fruit to be sent to him. 'You understand that I want out, after all it's hardly a good feeling to be held together with Nazis.'

This sad bit of news brought the correspondence of 1940 to an end. Some time later, on 10 February 1941, Kurt Jeselson got in touch from New York. Her letter, for which he thanked her, had given him the impression that she had by now learned to accept things as they were. This was recognition of the fact that – and in what way – Liesel had grown up, and of how much she had grown up: 'You all on John Bull's island have a hard turn, I guess, but England does a remarkable stand and fight.' He answered her question on whether he had changed with some interesting remarks on life in a democratic society:

> Of course, it's a different world from Europe and in certain respects one changes completely. [...] America itself is changing from a conservative frontierland to a more refined, modern (in an artistique sense) life. I believe that the immigrants of recent years have had a part in this respect. In other ways, we have learned immensely from here. We never knew what that democratic way of life could really be, within a truly and honestly democratic country. To many of us this was the biggest experience. [...]
>
> I have not much contact with people I knew from over there. [...] The only thing still dear to me from "over there" is the continuation of Eduard Strauss' "Bibel lesen" [Reading the Bible][31] which is as exciting and interesting as ever. It is built into the frame of a new "Lehrhaus" founded a year ago as successor to the one at Ffm. The boys are trying hard to cope with all the problems of combining old German tradition with new American ways. [...] I have cut off my German navel cord.

The first (preserved) letter from Leopold Lichtenstern was sent on 16 February 1941. He had not been interned and was living at 90 Melbourne Street, Derby, with a number of other people and a landlady, although the rumours 'that we shall be billeted in the barracks again' refused to go away. He wrote of how he had been allocated to the fire service on Sunday of all days, although 'this is Army life and you can't grumble'. Poldi, whom Liesel had sent books and sweets, was perhaps the major, ever-present absent figure in this story; as this is not a novel I will not attempt to imagine or find out too much about him, to ensure that his place here is the same as the place he had in Liesel's life: 'Lister could be Poldi-Leopold Lister (formerly Lichtenstern), once my mother's lover,' as Julia Neuberger wrote. We first encountered him in the Strauss'schen bookshop in Frankfurt, then as the writer of secret letters to Bombay and most recently as Hermine's worst nightmare. He called Liesel 'Wibele'. It is perhaps indicative of how close he and Liesel were that in a four-page letter I can find not one single section worth mentioning here. Julia added: 'My mother stayed close to Leopold Lichtenstern (Poldi Lister) till he died three months before she did. I officiated at the funeral.' We can safely leave it there.

The Blitz continued to dominate life. Liesel's first host, Patrick Dobbs, wrote on 15 March 1941: 'Last time I saw you was the night before the blitz began, wasn't it?' The number of preserved letters is noticeably lower than in previous years, and most served to inform their recipient that the author was still alive and that his or her house had not been destroyed. Food rationing was also a cause for increasing concern, and the blackout meant that most stayed at home in the evenings. Lotte Fink wrote from Australia on 26 March that she did not know where her mother was; she had been in Paris when the Germans captured the city. Lotte was glad to have reached Australia with her husband and daughter Ruth, and she risked the rather cheeky question: 'How are your love affairs in those terrific times?'

Remarkable times indeed, when a conversation about someone's love life is simultaneously about a war! Such conversations also dealt with the fate of family members. Horovitz, the lawyer, was writing letter after letter to try and get Alfred Stern released and to get hold of Stern's luggage stored in Reading.

I have now got a communication from the Home Office that Mr. Stern has been reclassified "C" category and that the Home Office has approached the government of the Commonwealth of Australia with a view to facilities being granted to Mr. Stern to complete visa formalities within Australia and on the issue of such visa to effect his release for emigration as soon thereafter as may be found practicable.[32]

Max and Trude Victor wrote from New York on 10 May 1941, praising the city:

It is a fascinating town. Everything here is different from Europe. But if you don't compare, and you take it just like it is, you like it very much. Life is really comfortable and easy here, and New York is sometimes a really beautiful town. If you are a young girl and you have a job in town, you can lead a very pleasant life here. You are inspirited to buy things everywhere and at all times. [...] I saw your cousin Grete once, she is also a salesgirl, and she looked very smart. I can imagine, you have other sorrows than these, but I know you are interested.

Australia and New York were real symbols of other possibilities; these places, which must have seemed well beyond the reach of a young woman in Heilbronn, were now where her friends were living. Friends who asked Liesel repeatedly to come and visit them there, and perhaps even to come 'for good'. How did she reply? Sadly, the estates of the Finks and Victors, which might have contained letters from Liesel, could not be found, and rarely do the letters Liesel received reveal anything about her: 'I am sure we will see us again,' wrote Trude Victor from New York on 25 August, 'anytime, anywhere, and I hope you will come through the hard time now in the spirit your letter was written.'

However, in the City Archives I have found an account written by Max Victor in 1984 about his family. Two Victor brothers came from neighbouring Horkheim to Heilbronn in the 1860s and established a shop selling exotic hides and leathers, which developed into the well-known leather manufacturer Victor Bros. 'The shop and the house were at 8 Bergstraße, exactly opposite the house where my mother, Mathilde Kirchheimer, grew up.'[33] The factory workers were 'mostly good social democrats' and opponents of the Nazis, but after 1933 a small group of Nazi party members took over management and a non-Jewish director was appointed. Eventually the factory was sold to the Knoch leather factory 'for about half its value, paid in Sperrmarks [a devalued currency emigrants were forced to use]' and only transferable abroad in small instalments. Max's parents died in 1934; 'neither would have survived the exertion of emigration and resettling, so their premature death turned out to be a blessing for them'.

Max attended the humanistic Karlsgymnasium grammar school and was 'the only Jew in my class'. Trude grew up in Frankfurt and, like her sister Emmy, received 'her main education in the "Kameraden", a German-Jewish youth movement encompassing the whole country'; it was at a Kameraden meeting that she and Max met in 1929. After studying economics and sociology Max was awarded his PhD ('summa cum laude, no less') at Heidelberg for his thesis on the Social Democratic Party's foreign policy between 1870 and 1914. Between 1928 and 1932 he spent 'the best years of my life' at the Institute for the World Economy in Kiel. Trude and Max married in 1931, but after the Nazis came to power he was unable to find employment and returned to the factory in Heilbronn. Both were active there in the Kameraden, 'in which we tried to help Jewish young people develop their sense of awareness as Jews and to prepare them for emigration, whether to Palestine or to another country.' Paul Scheuer and Heinz Gumbel were both members.

> *We were clear that we had to leave Germany, but we had to sell the company and make preparations for a new start abroad. I am often asked why we did not leave immediately when the Nazis came to power in 1933. Firstly, it was generally expected that Great Britain and France would not let Hitler create a German army or continue infringing on human rights. […] And secondly, it was not so easy to emigrate to another country. […] As a capitalist you could go to Palestine with assets of 1000 pounds or more and at the beginning of 1936 we went there on a trip to investigate (and to visit Trude's parents, who had gone out there to stay with her sister). Trude would have been ready to go to Palestine as well, but I saw no chance to earn a living other than in a Kibbutz. And thirdly, the real persecution of the Jews only began in November 38, […] so you could prepare for emigration without excessive haste. You could get a visa to emigrate and take your things with you if you paid an emigration tax. […] Eugen went to Amsterdam in 1936, where he opened a shop with business associates selling hides, and we went in April 1937.*[34]

After another, less promising reconnaissance mission to the United States the couple decided to stay with their children Ursula and Hannah – Trude kept Liesel regularly updated of their progress – in Aerdenhout, Holland, where Liesel visited them. By August 1939 it was clear to them 'that Holland was no safe haven', and they moved to Chipstead, Surrey, where Trude in particular felt at home. They obtained a visa for the Dominican Republic through a friend acquainted with its dictator Trujillo, and after six weeks' internment Max was 'released straight onto the boat, where I met Trude and the children'. They joined 'a passenger ship, the SS *Orduna*, in August 1940, together with other refugees and 200 English children who were being evacuated to Bermuda', and sailed in a convoy of freighters and a torpedo boat. On just the second day of the journey they were attacked by a German U-boat, but they successfully reached Cuba, where they were detained for two weeks until finally being allowed to travel 'to Domingo'.[35] There they moved into a house with Eugen's family, self-taught their children and waited for an entry permit for the United States, which they had already applied for before leaving Britain. In spring 1941 they got it. 'We sailed in a small boat to Puerto Rico and after a stormy crossing reached New York on 17 April. [...] Now began the "normal time", which I do not need to talk about.'

Liesel stayed in close contact with her friends and work colleagues. Dora, Frances, Margaret and others were regularly in touch and sent letters of encouragement. On 20 June 1941 Kurt Maschler asked what Liesel thought of the idea for Marks & Spencer to considerably increase its 'book department' and to do 'very good business with books'; he wanted to 'put my idea in person to Mr Marks or someone else who makes the decisions' (Liesel did not respond to this proposal, which was in all probability rather absurd anyway, and Maschler complained bitterly about the rebuff).

She had so many different things to deal with, from all sides, that it must have been difficult to maintain her 'calmness', as an (unknown) pen friend from Canberra admiringly put it on 17 July. Hermine wrote on 12 August that she had the impression Liesel was 'always so *in hurry* & excitement' and looked 'miserable'. Her motherly cure remained unchanged: 'The best thing for you would be that you marry, it is not too late. Father still has that wish. Don't laugh, it would be better if you would speak with me honestly and confidentially.' Did she laugh? Hopefully she did. It could also be that the 'spirit' Trude believed she could feel in Liesel's letters, which she valued so highly, was the same spirit of defiance and independence which was too much for her mother. But Hermine's wish was about to come true. A letter, unfortunately undated (only saying 'Saturday'), arrived from Sgt W M Schwab, 38th Div. Amn. Coy, R.A.S.C. for Liesel. Walter, Anna Schwab's son, wrote:

> *My dear, I still don't know how to spell your name, and your signature doesn't give me any help. Is your name really Alice then? I always imagined it to be Elisabeth. [...] Since I have been in London [...] my mind has been numb. [...] I am just trying to tell you that I have not been able to adopt any attitude to my experiences over the week-end. I think about it vaguely all the time, and then push it carefully to the back of my mind and go to gather in a little more dope for the proletariat at the nearest cinema or go and read a detective story. I don't know why it is, that I should have gone all like this.*

If I try to imagine my position to myself I see that I came to London to see somebody, whom as you yourself say I hardly know. When I meet her and have talked with her for an hour or two I go back to Aldershot and am bewildered. […] I hate the word "love" for I don't know what it means. I felt that we were very close to one another, probably closer than I have ever been with anybody before. I think that we are very close to one another, though how it will turn out neither you nor I can say. […]

You are playing for time, you want to get over an emotional experience that has proved a great strain upon you […]. I respect it. It may seem a little hard on me, sitting, waiting for you to overcome your emotions, but I see what you are driving at. […] I want to do so many things and I want you so badly. This is utterly ridiculous and fantastic nonsense that I am writing, but I am determined to write it because I believe that you must know how I feel. […] I am all of a muddle and don't know what to think and I say "Good night and God bless you" in the hopes that you will answer my incoherence soon. In the meantime I shall try to write you a more normal letter.

The knight in shining armour was in sight, and he even had 'a decent nationality', as Liesel's friend Suse Schwarzenberger had demanded of her future husband in an undated letter. Walter's brother, cadet H C (Harry) Schwab, who had already written on multiple occasions about his experiences as a soldier, wrote from Clifton College, Bristol, on 18 November 1941:

My dear Liesl. In a way I owe you an apology for never writing to you, but I was waiting to hear from Walter, & the glad news arrived to-day. So here's all the very best and let's hope that you will soon be able to settle down together very happily. To see me do the real gushing brother-in-law stuff you must wait till I get home next week – Saturday to be precise. Please forgive the shortness and haste, but I have to go off to an exam now – the results of which will determine whether or not I am to become a gentleman or not next Saturday! See you then!

This seems to have been a secret; Dora, for one, sent greetings to Liesel and Poldi on 31 December, and on the same day Kurt Maschler sent thanks for an invitation to 'Miss Rosenthal and Mr Lichtenstern'. We will have to wait a little while longer to see if the new year 1942 would bring a resolution. By then a trip to the United States was out of the question, as on 8 December 1941, the day after the Japanese attack on Pearl Harbour, the United States had entered the war. The year 1942 began with the Declaration of the United Nations of 1 January and the United States joining the Anti-Hitler Coalition alongside Great Britain and the Soviet Union.

On 14 January 1942 Margaret's husband Bernard thanked Liesel for her best wishes, described his army life, expressed his hope that they would see each other again soon and added: 'I'm surprised that you have not yet got married – really, I think it is about time you made up your mind and put those admirers of yours out of their agony.'

This was precisely what was about to happen. Cousin Bertel Walter wrote to the 'dear Rosenthals' on 18 January:

Such good luck for Liesel's wedding. I am so very sorry not to be able to come to the ceremony or the reception, as I received the invitation much too late. I will write to Liesel myself soon. All the best again!

And there was a wonderful letter from Ludwig Rosenthal on a small piece of paper:

Dear Mrs Schwab! I hope you are in the best of health & you are certainly very happy to be together with dear Walter again for a few days. Enclosed is the correspondence we have received as well as a telegram from Zürich. The handbag from Mrs Rose Verner is a splendid piece from India, I hope you have thanked her for it by telephone. You can read the rest of the correspondence that's arrived when you're here. Otherwise everything's 'all right'. Best wishes and kisses for you, dear Walter & the whole Schwab family. Please don't forget to sort out the belt & braces. Mother sends her best wishes, she is very busy.

We need to sort a few things out ourselves. Walter? As I said at the start of this book, Julia Neuberger only gave me the letters her mother left behind, and she wanted to keep a few bundles of letters from her father – this Walter Schwab, who had so inadvertently got married[36] – for herself. Even these letters, however, unfortunately contain no information which could satisfy our curiosity regarding this development. In 1990 Alice Schwab was, as ever, matter-of-fact:

On the 18th of January, 1942 I married Walter Schwab, whom I had known for quite a time. I met him through his mother when I was working at Woburn House and I was often invited to their home for dinner on Friday nights and other occasions. Walter had been in Palestine on a kibbutz and had been sent back to England to help with the agricultural training of refugees who were going to Palestine. When war broke out he joined the ARP [Air Raid Precautions] as a full-time worker and, in December 1939, enlisted in the army. At first he was stationed at various places around England, but in 1942 there was a strong rumour that he was going to be sent overseas. He had three days' leave, during which we got married. We were married at St Johns Wood synagogue. It was quite an extraordinary wedding since it took place during the worst time of the war. People contributed bits and pieces, everybody helping. As I remember, it was very, very nice; my parents were happy and my brother. At the wedding there weren't many relations from my side, apart from my immediate family. […] Walter went right back into the army and I went back to Marks and Spencer.

When we consider how much time and paper had been expended by all those involved with the unrealized marriage in Bombay, this wedding seems a rather sparse affair – of course this was no surprise in wartime, but there is also a noticeable absence of emotion. Nevertheless, Ludwig could now experience the joy of addressing his daughter as 'Dear Mrs Schwab'. Cousin Lisbet found it 'terribly difficult to put my wishes for you into words. Stay the old Liesel, then everything will be alright.' Joan was pregnant and expecting twins. Dora had had a baby, 'a very nice little boy', as she wrote on 10 March, 'just the kind I wanted'. I have heard from many German-Jewish emigrant families that they – like Liesel and Walter were to do – wanted to wait until the end of the war and the Nazi dictatorship before having children.

It may be that Liesel saw in her friends further proof of the British wartime spirit. It was mentioned again and again: on 10 March her friend Richard, stationed with a fighter squadron, hoped that she was 'happy and beautiful as usual' and that she would face all problems as well as he had survived the 'acrobatics' of his pilot. 'This, my dear, is the spirit which in due course, and in GOD's own time, will win the war.' He looked forward to meeting Walter soon. Paula Bernhardt wrote on 5 April that she was glad to see Liesel 'with or without spouse'. Anna Schwab and her husband lived at 180 Goldhurst Terrace, and letters and greetings were sometimes sent there too.

Only one person was strangely quiet. 'We were all very happy to receive your dear husband's letter,' wrote Hermine eventually on 20 April 1942 from 109 Worple Road, 'his letters are so lovely.' She was experiencing pain in her feet and could hardly walk, meaning that she could not enjoy celebrating her own 50th birthday. And Walter? His letters were indeed lovely: 'Hello, darling love, how are you?' On 8 June he wrote from the 12th Field Ambulance in Selkirk, undertaking 'to chronicle the events of the last few days', which he was to do regularly from then on.

If we think back to the theories developed by family therapist Carlos Sluzki on the change in the family relationship as a result of the process and outcome of emigration, it becomes clear that new rules were coming into play here: Walter's rules, those of the Schwab family, those of the military Walter belonged to. Although the new norms and rituals were born out of sympathy and good will, they were still *different* rules, and Liesel had to adjust to them. She had been given nothing if not a surfeit of advice, from her mother, from her 'Vice-Mama', from Gabriel, from her friend Minni ('a woman must – "if she is in love" – be able to give up a lot of her "self"'), and now the situation was this: she had a husband, and, although he was far away, he kept in contact with her through his letters: 'Be good, dear, I hope you miss me and kiss you everywhere.' Initially, they were able to see each other too – Liesel was able to visit him in Scotland on one occasion.

Liesel's parents now had to loosen their grip over their daughter if their dreams of a respectable life and future for her, with a husband 'by her side', were to be realized. This, though, would again prove difficult. 'Dear Liesel & dear Walter,' wrote Hermine on 2 July 1942, 'after you left [I] still had much to say, time always goes so fast.' Mrs Schwab, as Liesel was now addressed in the letters, now had a little bit of time to pursue her own interests, one being her love of literature. Gertrude Salinger (whose books of songs and games are still available to buy) thanked Liesel for putting her in contact with Kurt Maschler and proudly announced that her book *Games to Play* had been accepted by a publisher, Evans Brothers, in London. By this stage the Blitz had come to an end and life in England was a little more bearable. However, news of the systematic murder of the Jews of Europe was beginning to come through. Alice Schwab says in the 1990 interview:

Figure 19 The Rosenthal and Schwab families, *c.* 1945. Left to right (front): Hermine Rosenthal, Julius Schwab, Liesel with her husband Walter Schwab, Anna Schwab. Behind are Harry Schwab and Ludwig Rosenthal.

At this time I was worrying about what was happening in Germany; and by that time it wasn't only Germany, but Austria, Poland, the whole of that part of the world, Roumania, Jugoslavia. The Jews were being herded into camps like animals. There were lots of other camps, apart from Bergen-Belsen. My relations in Switzerland still had contact with my father's brothers and sisters. So we did get some news. My uncle was killed in a small camp in Wurtemberg-Baden; one of my aunts jumped to her death out of a train taking her to Bergen-Belsen, or some other camp, I don't remember which. My cousin who was supposed to come to England, got homesick and couldn't bear to leave her mother. She just disappeared and was never heard of again. And her mother just disappeared.

I had one cousin who came over to England in 1939 just before the outbreak of war. His wife was still in Germany and, on the way to the train, with her father, which would take her to the boat sailing to America, they let her father go, but took her away; she was never heard of again.

People were constantly disappearing. On my mother's side, her sister and brother-in-law went from Stuttgart to Holland. There they were arrested and taken to a big camp at Westerbork where all the Jews in Holland were first taken. From Westerbork they were sent to Bergen-Belsen. As it happened, there was an arrangement for German nationals living in Palestine to be exchanged for Jews. It cost a lot of money – the Nazi's didn't do it for nothing! My family in Switzerland and other relations produced the sum needed and the exchange was arranged. My aunt and uncle were on their way to Palestine, in exchange for two people in Palestine who would go back to the

Fatherland. [...] Unfortunately, my uncle became very ill on the way, he was dying and his wife wouldn't leave him. Eventually he died and she was sent to another concentration camp. By that time, the Russians were already on the doorstep; they rescued her, but she also died.

Here, she was summarizing all the news she had heard about the fate of the members of her family who had 'disappeared'. At the time, news came piecemeal; only Hede and Jakob Wertheimer in Switzerland could stay in contact with relatives for a time, partly through the Red Cross, and they also tried, unsuccessfully, to rescue Luise and Richard Loeb. Other information, such as the death of Minni Stern and her mother Helene, could only have reached Liesel after the war. We will therefore return to the letters and to 20 November 1942. Joan, waiting at home for the birth of her twins, discussed with Liesel the terrible news reaching them from the continent:

Yes, Liesel, I am sorry to hear of the frightful things that are happening to the Jews. The worst part of it is that there is nothing one can do. It is dreadful. In a way the best way to think of the problem is to think of the killing of the Jews as part of the war and no more dreadful than the killing of so many soldiers, sailors, and airmen. This diverts attention to the war and there may be things one can do to assist the ending of the beastliness. I know that the Jews are murdered in cold blood and with torture, but I wonder if their killing is worse than the killing of some other people. One feels that when the Jews are killed this suffering is useless but the present atrocities are arousing so much feeling and understanding that the suffering may not be useless – at least not as useless as some of the sufferings of the Jews in the past. But it is dreadful for you because you know so many people who are in danger.

The first news of the Holocaust, 'scattered information about Nazi massacres of many thousands of Jews in German-occupied Poland and Russia', had reached the Allies by late 1941/early 1942.

The turning point came in late May 1942, when a courier from the Jewish Socialist Bund of Poland reached England with a shocking report. It began: "From the day the Russo-German war broke out, the Germans embarked on the physical extermination of the Jewish population on Polish soil." The Bund Report stressed that the killings were not isolated outbursts, but part of a systematic plan to "annihilate all the Jews in Europe", town by town, country by country. The report described how in villages throughout Poland and Western Russia, German troops marched the Jewish residents to a nearby forest or ravine and machine-gunned them into giant pits. The Bund also detailed the killing of Jews in the Chelmno camp in mobile death vans – trucks whose exhaust fumes were pumped back into the passenger cabin. [...] Shmuel Zygelbojm, a Jewish member of the London-based Polish Government in Exile, played a major role in publicizing the Bund Report.[37]

In November and December 1942 a number of English newspapers reported the mass murder of Eastern European Jews and asked what Germany's enemies could do to prevent it. On 5 December 1942 the *News Chronicle* became the first newspaper to describe it as 'a holocaust'.[38] These despatches must have been the cause for Liesel and Joan to exchange letters about the sense of horror they felt. Joan's reply, advising Liesel to consider even these atrocities in the context of the war and to therefore do everything possible to bring the war to an end, reflected the view of a large part of British society, as well as the British government. Although as Joan herself remarked, and could see in Liesel's letters (which have not survived), the refugees in Britain reacted differently to these reports affecting their relatives who had stayed in Germany, some of whom had already been deported.

In the meantime Liesel (with Walter, and yet without him) had moved house to a new address at 22 Lissenden Mansions, NW5. At the beginning of March 1943 Joan proudly announced the birth of her twins, Richard Daniel and Richard Robert, 'perfect babies [who] understood the feeding arrangement after one lesson'. Their father Richard was away fighting, however: 'news come through at long intervals, I am very worried'. She recommended that Liesel read Arthur Koestler's books *Darkness at Noon* and *Scum of the Earth*. Koestler, born in Budapest in 1905, had gone to Palestine in 1926 as an enthusiastic Zionist and from there he wrote reports for the *Vossische Zeitung* newspaper. In 1930 he became deputy chief editor of the *B.Z. am Mittag* newspaper and joined the Communist Party at around the same time. In 1937 he travelled to Spain as a war correspondent, was captured by Francoist troops and summarily sentenced to death as a spy before the British government intervened to save him. Back in Paris, when Stalin's show trials began he turned away from communism, joining Hans Sahl, Manès Sperber, Ignazio Silone and others in the group of 'Renegades'.[39] This group stood almost alone – persecuted by fascism and with their Communist hopes dashed – and in a position of great danger developed important ideas on democratic society and culture in Europe. In 1940 Koestler came to England, and *Darkness at Noon* was published the same year. He worked for the *News Chronicle* and was one of the leading intellectual figures in the community of German-Jewish exiles in Great Britain.

Max Victor wrote a long letter from New York on 8 April 1943. They had successfully managed the initial, superficial adaptation to their new country, 'but the real and longrun assimilation takes years and is perhaps even impossible for our generation'. Their elder daughter Ursula was even having more difficulties than her younger sister Hannah, but both of them liked it there and were enthused by the idea of the land of the free. They attended a good school together with Walter Flegenheimer from Heilbronn. The Victors heard from Heinz Gumbel in Jerusalem around every six weeks, and Trude added: 'Paul Scheuer is our most faithful Heilbronner friend, he is an excellent student but still single.'

As in many émigré communities, it was the former home city of Heilbronn – now so far away, taken away from them by the Nazis who still ruled it – which formed the common reference point for individuals and families in the United States, Palestine, Britain and everywhere else. We will explore this again in the last chapters of this book, as Max and Trude Victor were to be among those who re-established contact with their former home town once the war was over.

Erwin Rosenthal was a key figure in maintaining the links between émigré Heilbronners. Somewhat surprisingly, so far he had only appeared briefly in the letters. Alice Schwab mentioned him:

> *My cousin and friend, Dr Erwin Rosenthal, came to England in 1933 and eventually settled in Cambridge where he became a don at Pembroke College. Through his help, one of his sisters settled in Manchester, but his other sister disappeared in a concentration camp.*

His obituary in *The Times* gives more information on Erwin Isak Jakob Rosenthal, who was born on 18 September 1904 in Heilbronn and died on 5 June 1991 in Cambridge:

> *Erwin Isak Jacob Rosenthal was born at Heilbronn, Württemberg, and studied Semitics – particularly Arabic and Hebrew – at the universities of Heidelberg, Munich, and Berlin, numbering Bergstraesser among his teachers. His first publication, on the political philosophy of the 14th century Tunisian historian Ibn Khaldun, appeared in 1932. […] During his student days he met Martin Buber who made a Zionist of him. […]*
>
> *When Hitler came to power Rosenthal was baulked, as a Jew, of any prospects of making an academic career in Germany and he came to England. He was sympathetically received at Cambridge and shortly afterwards the Goldsmid lectureship in Hebrew at University College London was made available to him. In 1936 he moved to a lectureship in Semitic languages […] in Manchester. […] The outbreak of the war brought personal problems, and he was not entirely happy at Manchester. He was in due course attached to the Foreign Office and also became involved during the aftermath of the war in adult education both among civilians and the forces. […]*
>
> *The fruits of an extended tour of Islamic countries were embodied in his Islam in the Modern National State (1965), a counterpart to his Political Thought in Medieval Islam, which had been published in 1958. In between there had come a book on Judaism and Islam and a study, in German, of the Greek heritage in Jewish religious philosophy, entitled Griechisches Erbe in der jüdischen Religionsphilosophie des Mittelalters. Rosenthal liked the life of Pembroke College, of which he was a fellow and, although perfectly at home in England, recognised, good-humouredly, that he would always be marked out as a foreigner.*[40]

I attempted to find out more about Erwin Rosenthal, and with the help of his daughter-in-law Ann Rosenthal, and after a few detours, I ended up in Buenos Aires. Erwin was the 'favourite uncle'[41] of Margarita 'Hex' Munk, who was ninety-six years old when we began corresponding. Her sons Thomas and Peter were able to stop her 'clearing out' her papers, but they could find no letters concerning him, only obituaries.

On 20 May 1943 Erwin wrote from 31 Oak Road, Withington, Manchester.[42] The letter – asking after Liesel's parents, whom he had been unable to reach on the telephone, and asking her to find a flat in London for a friend's son – suggests that he and Liesel had been in contact with each other for a long time. He himself planned to come to London at the end of May and hoped to see her. He could also conceivably still be called up, as he was 'of military age'. On 28 September he wrote again and invited her to come to Manchester to escape her 'boredom'.

> *I can only hope to watch our "Familienglück"* [family happiness] *will not depress you in your present state of childlessness. It is never too late and this war will come to an end sometime. Let us hope in 5704* [the new Jewish calendar year had just begun] *and that you may settle down with your Walter happily for ever after!*

He was still working at the university (and 'barely on speaking terms' with his colleague Robertson – 'he hardly speaks'), but now his wife was looking for a part-time job. As he had done in other, shorter, letters he proudly described what his children Thomas and Miriam were doing.[43] He was teaching a course called 'Central Europe before the War and after', which was far away from his own field of research: 'I know precious little about it, but trust in the Lord and his inspirations.' Religious rituals – like observing the feast days at the Schwabs with a 'Yomtov dinner' to celebrate the new year – and family life are two fundamental components of the Jewish community, and both could easily fall by the wayside in wartime. Here, in a matter-of-fact, everyday way, they appeared again. Erwin had done his duty and started a family, of which he was clearly proud, and Liesel was now tasked with the same; at least, that was how Hermine saw it. She and Ludwig had left London for a while, recuperating with their friends the Schwarz family in Hindhead.

> *I wish you dear children all the best, keep making your way on the right path for our happiness & stay healthy for us. For you dear Liesel I particularly wish that your & our dear Walter will come home safe and well soon & you can lead a happy family life!*

Margaret had also got married and signed her letters 'Margaret Freudenthal'. Children were being born, wedding ceremonies held, a (positive) end to the war seemed to be in sight, and all those involved – or rather, all those who were rescued – could imagine a future again. Appointments were being made again, such as with Georg Schwarzenberger, editor of the *London Quarterly of World Affairs* and professor at University College London, who wrote to Liesel on 23 December 1943 hoping to meet her: 'I want to hear from you a lot about common friends.'[44]

The Wehrmacht had withdrawn from the Caucasus after the defeat at Stalingrad, while the Red Army had retaken the Ukraine and was marching westwards. Grand Admiral Karl Dönitz of the Germany Navy had called off the Battle of the Atlantic in May 1943. The Afrikakorps had surrendered, meaning that family friends in Palestine were no longer threatened by a German invasion. The Allies had landed in Italy, Mussolini had been overthrown and Italy had declared war on Germany. The Tehran conference between the leading allied powers, where a new post-war European order was discussed, had just taken place. Allied bombing raids on German cities were becoming more and more intensive.[45] Hans Schloss sent greetings to Liesel, and with this the correspondence of 1943 came to an end.

6

'Thinking of Germany.'
From a broken picture book

The new year began with sad news. Carl Ellern, Anna Schwab's twin brother, wrote from Tel Aviv on 27 April 1944 that Ludwig Kahn, husband of Liesel's cousin Leonore, had died in Palestine. This was just one of a number of reasons why Liesel was again somewhat despondent during the early months of 1944. Her brother-in-law tried to cheer her up: 'Of course you are bored stiff! Of course you wish Walter were home […]. Please try to be a little bit more cheerful, for your sake and for the old people, & remember it could be far, far worse.' He had been able to see his brother briefly when they were stationed together in Italy in June 1944. Walter had contracted amoebic dysentery and was in the hospital for tropical diseases for months, but had been well looked after and had now recovered. He writes on 16 July:

> I don't know where they'll send me – not home I'm afraid but I've asked for a division or corps job. We'll see what happens. Still things are going so well, especially the Red Army, that it can't last very long. […] Lots of love, darling, you know how much I miss you and dream of you. Be good, careful and faithful.

Erwin Rosenthal had indeed been called up and wrote on 30 August from a 'training battalion' of the Royal Army Service Corps in Woking. Max Victor wrote from New York on 27 September, consoling Liesel that, even though she was not currently able to enjoy married life, she would as a result enjoy it even more later. Trude, ever practical, asked what life in London was like: 'How is it with the lights on?' There were domestic problems at 22 Lissenden Mansions, where more friends were living, although their letters are almost indecipherable and their names illegible. The problem centred on a woman, Philippa, who was besotted with her boyfriend Arthur (one of the housemates) and wanted to move in with him. 'The flat question' was bothering Harold Ellern, Walter Schwab's first cousin, who wrote from France on 20 November, and he hoped for his 'dearest cousin' that this would be the last new year without Walter and her friends.

So far my attempts to construct a story from the letters have worked reasonably well. Only occasionally have I needed to deviate from the chronology or add explanations as to who or what is being referred to, as the news reported in the letters – our sources – has always fitted together and made sense. Now that we have reached 1944, however, the relative dearth of letters makes this almost impossible. Everything is fragmented and hardly any of the surviving documents make reference to another. 'From a Broken Picture Book' ('Aus einem zerrissenen Bilderbuch') is the title of a collection of short texts about Heilbronn written by Fritz Wolf, and this description could well apply to these letters too. While Heilbronn's Jewish emigrants and political refugees, including Erwin Rosenthal, Max and Trude Victor and Georg Schwarzenberger, were sending letters to each other, they still did not know what had happened to their friends and family members who had stayed in Germany. And their home city was about to be destroyed. Philippa's letter, in which she expressed the hope that the tedious flat situation could be settled once and for all when Walter returned, was written on 20 September. Then, remarkably, on 30 November historian Cecil Roth wrote a letter offering 'our old flat, at the top of the building' as an alternative place to live. The next letter in the collection, a request from Erwin Rosenthal for Liesel to send some Hanukkah candles to his wife Elisabeth, is dated 5 December 1944. The night before, the city of Heilbronn was almost completely destroyed.

4 December 1944 is a day in history so deeply engraved on the consciousness and cityscape of Heilbronn that generations will pass without it being forgotten. That night an air raid completely destroyed the historic city centre and caused widespread damage in other parts of the city. Almost 7000 people lost their lives.[1]

4 December: at 19:18 the Royal Air Force began its attack on Heilbronn by dropping flares. In total 238 aircraft were deployed by the British, dropping a total of 830,500 kg of high-explosive bombs and 430,300 kg of incendiary bombs and flares. Heilbronn's air raid defences consisted only of small-calibre guns which were ineffective against high-flying aircraft.

The buildings in the city centre were mostly of half-timber construction. As a result, the firestorm unleashed by the British made rescue efforts and attempts to extinguish the blaze all but impossible. As if that were not enough, water supplies were cut off and the fire station in the city centre was hit along with all its equipment. During the raid the main switch room at the power station was also bombed, leaving the city without electricity.

An area of 2.5 by 2 kilometres in the city centre was completely destroyed by high-explosive bombs and the ensuing firestorm, and in total 62 per cent of the city was destroyed. More than 6500 people died in the attack, entire families perishing in the flames. Most were asphyxiated in the air raid shelters where they had taken refuge, as official instructions considered these the safest place to go. Those who tried to escape the firestorm ran the risk of being burned alive. However, many who left the air raid shelters did manage to reach the outer parts of the city and survive the attack.

During the night many of the surviving Heilbronners fled to the surrounding areas, many taking no more than the clothes on their backs. Fire brigades from neighbouring towns rushed to Heilbronn to try and extinguish the blaze, a task made extremely difficult by the heat, which made the city centre inaccessible. Initially, water supply lines had to be laid from the River Neckar.

5 December: During the morning the fire in the city subsided considerably. National Socialist welfare organisations, the Wehrmacht and volunteers from both the immediate surrounding areas and places further afield like Stuttgart, Ludwigsburg, Crailsheim and Pforzheim provided coffee, stew and sandwiches for the bombed-out residents. Security services and Organisation Todt workers constructed makeshift paths through the rubble-covered streets and brought the first bodies out from the cellars, which were laid in rows wherever there was space.

Distraught parents and children wandered through the streets looking for their relatives. In the evening the Nazi district leadership announced over loudspeakers that the number of dead had reached 4000, and the number of missing 3000. No-one believed these figures; the talk was of 18–25,000 dead.

6 December: work began on digging a mass grave for the victims of 4 December in the "Köpfer" area to the east of the city, which later became the Memorial Cemetery (Ehrenfriedhof). In addition to local authorities and police, who registered the deaths and looked after clothes and valuables, 40–50 prisoners from the concentration camp at Neckargartach, most of whom where foreign labourers, were made to carry away bodies.[2]

The raid would shape Heilbronn's collective memory, both physically and mentally, for the coming decades. There are numerous examples of how city representatives, and former residents such as Theodor Heuss, the first president of West Germany, struggled to find the appropriate words to describe the suffering, not least through contact and discussions with those unhelpfully lumped together in the City Archives as 'Foreign Heilbronners' *('Auslandsheilbronner')*. 'Broken', 'fragmented', 'destroyed' – these words have often been used to describe the relationship between Heilbronn and those driven out of their home city, those who fled and those who chose to emigrate. Now they applied to the city itself and the *other* experience of those who stayed.

From Britain, of course, things seemed very different. 'Dear Madam, Greetings for a Happy Christmas and a victorious New Year. Also many thanks for the very useful parcel. Your kindness is greatly appreciated,' wrote L Coole from 16, Park Parade on 20 December. That marked the end of the correspondence from 1944. On 12 January 1945 Liesel's brother-in-law Harry wrote, addressed from 125 Con. RASC, BAOR. This was the British Army of the Rhine, officially 'formed on 25 August 1945 from 21st Army Group. Its original function was to control the corps districts which were running the military government of the British zone of occupied Germany', although the term was in use before then.

The war was unquestionably in its final phase, and Harry hoped 'that we'll be home this year'. Walter had contracted amoebic dysentery, and Harry wrote of his hope that it would not be too long before he could travel again. After the Allied landing in Normandy in June 1944 and the subsequent liberation of France, Aachen had become

Figure 20 A view from Götzenturmstraße in the northern direction © Stadtarchiv Heilbronn, Landesmedienzentrum Baden-Württemberg

the first German city to be occupied, captured by the US Army on 21 October 1944. The letter also gives us important information about someone who had barely featured in the letters of recent years: Liesel's brother Helmut (Jack). Born in 1924, in this final year of the war he had been called up: 'Is your brother in Germany yet? I presume he's in the American sector & therefore rather out of range of my brother-in-law-ish eye.'

By now Liesel had moved to 40 Lissenden Mansions. Lotte Fink wrote from Sydney to this new address on 28 March 1945:

The Allies have entered Frankfurt on my birthday, last Monday. I do think the war will be over soon. How wonderful that will be. Only my poor mother is probably no longer alive to enjoy peace and the happiness we could give her here. […] I have been elected Vice-President to the Association of Refugees here and we are doing a lot of work. […] How are you keeping? Have you any children? Do not wait till it is too late. How is your husband? […] How is your English? F. is perfect, he has the biggest vocabulary of all refugees, but of course still some sort of accent.[3]

With the end of the war imminent and Germany's liberation in sight, clearly many thought it was time to take stock. How had all those involved been affected by the events of the past twelve years? In which parts of the world were friends and acquaintances scattered? ('A friend of ours who married and went to South Africa visited Liesel Victor and found her a bit crazy, but nice and a successful beauty specialist, her husband being in the forces,' wrote Lotte.) What had happened to their relatives in Europe? And how did those once so familiar places, in this case Frankfurt, where Liesel had got to know the Finks (and Leopold Lichtenstern), look after twelve years of Nazi dictatorship and six years of war?

It is still too early to answer these questions, but many of the letters of the coming weeks and months are shaped by them. By now all Liesel's correspondents, from Erwin Rosenthal and Lotte Fink to Martha Sussmann, with whom Liesel had spent her first few weeks in London (she was born in England, daughter of Saemy Japhet), wrote exclusively in English and had – like Lotte and her husband, who had been naturalized in Australia[4] – truly arrived in their new homelands. But the Allied advance brought Germany back into view. Any homesickness this might have stirred in the correspondents was overshadowed by news from the liberated concentration and extermination camps:

> *Following several days of cease-fire negotiations between the Wehrmacht and the British Army, British troops took over the Bergen-Belsen concentration camp without a fight on 15 April 1945. Shortly beforehand, the SS had destroyed the camp's administrative files to erase all written evidence of their crimes. The British soldiers were utterly unprepared for the inferno they encountered when they entered the camp. For thousands of the at least 53,000 prisoners, liberation came too late. Although the British Army and various relief organisations quickly arranged for medical aid, another 14,000 liberated prisoners had died of the effects of their imprisonment by June 1945 alone.*
>
> *When the British soldiers took over the camp, they disarmed the remaining SS personnel and placed them under arrest. In the following days, both male and female SS members had to dig mass graves in the grounds of the former camp and bury tens of thousands of bodies.*
>
> *The British troops were accompanied by military photographers and cameramen whose job it was to document the conditions in Bergen-Belsen and the emergency aid measures initiated there. The hundreds of photos, film reels and notes they took from the day of liberation through June 1945 give some indication of the extent of the crimes committed in Bergen-Belsen. Many of these photographs were published around the world, and they have had a lasting impact on the memory of the Nazi concentration camps worldwide.[5]*

As a result of this, in Britain the word 'Belsen' has become as symbolic of the Holocaust as 'Auschwitz' is in Eastern and Central Europe. Liesel asked the soldiers she knew for further information, and Harold Ellern replied on 30 April 1945:

> *I quite agree with what you say on the subject of Belsen, but I am afraid that I can't help you in your search for your relatives. Roughly the position is this: There were 39 000 people in the camp and NO RECORDS whatsoever. They had been destroyed by the SS previously and in any case several thousand had been admitted since then.*

> When the British troops entered all the gates shutting the various compounds off from each other were opened and all 39 000 or at least all those who were physically able to, started walking around. Next: The only solution was feeding and evacuating, for there was no hope of ever cleansing the camp from disease, so by now only God knows where everybody has got to. Lastly, as I told the family, all persons on the exchange list and all complete families had been removed in direction Theresienstadt 2 or 3 days previous to our arrival, 7000 people in all, and by what you tell me your relatives are almost certain to be amongst them [...], all you can do is hope that they are among those we'll be able to save.

Harold wrote again on VE Day (8 May 1945): 'We remember too many sacrifices that have been asked of us and our people. The final balance of Hitlerism will reveal the shocking number of his victims, but yet we have survived our enemies once more.' This was a sober, accurate appraisal, and this is perhaps the ideal opportunity for us to ask what had happened to Helmut Rosenthal, now known as Jack Rosen, and to reconstruct with him the transition from wartime to the post-war period; he was to become the first member of the Rosenthal family to travel to Germany and, from there, send his impressions to his family and friends.

We first met Helmut as a child, seeing him through the eyes of his mother. We saw him as a schoolboy who sometimes had difficulties with his studies, particularly when more and more of his friends from Heilbronn emigrated away with their families. We saw him as a 'dear boy', whose parents worried greatly about his future, and at his *Bar Mitzvah*, where he spoke so beautifully in the synagogue, 'like no other boy before him'. We saw how Hermine and Ludwig tried to keep him with them as long as possible before Liesel was finally able to bring him to Britain. In her collection of letters there were at first only undated slips of paper (or some with just the day and month), and it is impossible to know where they fit into our chronology. The first letter from him that she kept came in June 1937: he wrote from a children's home in Bad Kissingen, still in German, and Ludwig wrote the address ('by Mr. Patrick Dobbs, Birmingham') for him. Helmut asked Liesel: 'I can't write in English, so write in German.'

There are hardly any personal details about him to be found in the documents from the time when preparations for his emigration were being made. Instead they reveal the discussions that took place between Liesel, Ludwig, Hermine and their relatives in Zürich. The first document from his time in England is a timetable from Beaconsfield College: 'Monday: Arithmetic, Algebra, French – Hebrew, English, Geometry, Algebra – Walk/Lunch – Latin, Drawing, Hebrew', followed by 'Nat. Study, History, Literature, Scripture, English letters, Gen. Knowledge' for the rest of the week. This was a demanding curriculum, introducing him to the English education system and everyday life in Great Britain. From then on he wrote regularly to Liesel, asking for stamps and on one occasion for money to buy batteries for his bicycle. He soon began to sign his letters 'Jack', and English words appeared ever more frequently in his German letters, while at the same time he began to make mistakes in his written German. He became unhappy in Brighton, and asked his sister to find a family for him in London to stay with and a job which would not require a school leaving certificate. He looked forward to his parents' arrival ('How are our parents? Are they getting on with each other? I am so happy that they are across the Channel') but was not particularly keen on living with them. He followed the goings on in the family and wrote to his Aunt Emma when the house Ludwig had been born in had to be sold ('It wouldn't hurt you to include greetings at the end of your letter,' he told Liesel).

At some point during 1939 his German disappeared, and from then on he wrote solely in English.

> *On Wednesday morning I met the parents at 9.35. Then we had a quarrel about the tram. Mother wanted me to go with the old thing, at last I went by underground to Tottenham Court Road. From there I went to the Bloomsbury House. Then I waited for about 1 ½ hours. Then they arrived. Mother shouting German on the street as usual. We went inside the Bloomsbury House and inside she suddenly started talking English. We waited for about 1 hour then we were called in and of course achieved nothing. Then we went to the British Museum and had our dinner there. I wanted to go to Halevy's, and now we had a quarrel about the bus fare.*

Just as we can describe Liesel's experience of emigration as a process of emancipation (and not just from her parents), Helmut's life in England can be read as a sign of his growing up. He had adjusted to the rules of his new homeland and had now mastered the Underground, while Hermine still clung to the 'good old' trams she was so familiar with. Now it was she who was breaking the rules: aid organizations repeatedly had to remind emigrants not to speak German in public. A postcard distributed to the emigrants, preserved alongside the letters, appealed to these 'Guests of Great Britain' to behave with the appropriate politeness.

Unfortunately, there is now a considerable gap in the correspondence. I am therefore not in any position to say what Jack's experiences were during the war and how he came to join the military. In November 1945 H G Rosenthal, APO [Army Post Office] 757, US Army, wrote a letter from Paris: 'Dear sis & brother-in-law. Arrived here safely after the roughest crossing ever made. I was seasick all the way. Leaving Paris tonight.' His handwriting had grown up too. On 23 April 1946 he wrote to 'Dear Sis & Wally' (Walter must have recently returned):

> *I have just received a Reg. Letter from your exboyfriend Lister which made me so wild that I cannot but write to you and tell you about it. Inside the REG. envelope was a letter to me and another letter for a German. Now I have been told when joining this organization not to deliver letters to Germans and if I do that I will lose my job. I don't mind doing a favour for a friend but this is something I will not do.*

Lister (Leopold or Poldi Lichtenstern) was clearly trying to use Jack to make contacts in Germany, but Jack thought it too much of a risk. On 16 September he wrote:

> *Dear Sis and Walter, I just send you some pictures which I took on my last Rhine boat trip to show you my photographic genius. The building on one of them is the Casino behind the IG Farben building, where I sometimes go and taste some of the good food they serve there.*

SIE SIND GAESTE GROSSBRITANNIENS.

Hoeflichkeit und gutes Betragen werden Ihnen ueberall herzliche Aufnahme und Sympathie zusichern.

Sprechen Sie nicht laut auf der Strasse, besonders nicht am Abend.

Nehmem Sie Ruecksicht auf die Bequemlichkeit anderer Leute und vermeiden Sie, deren Eigentum und Moebel zu beschaedigen.

Vergessen Sie nie, dass England's Urteil ueber die deutschen Fluechtlinge von IHREM Verhalten abhaengt.

ACHTUNG.

Deutschen Fluechtlingen wird dringendst geraten, aeussert vorsichtig in ihren Gespraechen zu sein.

In Ihren eigenen Interesse empfehlen wir Ihnen dringend, keine Arbeitsangebote irgendwelcher Art anzunehmen, ohne vorher die Erlaubnis der englischen Regierung eingeholt zu haben.

Figure 21 Code of conduct for German refugees. Above: 'You are guests of Great Britain. Politeness and good behaviour will guarantee you a warm welcome and sympathy everywhere you go. Do not speak loudly in the street, particularly during the evenings. Consider the comfort of others and avoid damage to their property and possessions. Never forget that England's judgement on German refugees depends on YOUR behaviour.' Below: 'Warning: German refugees are strongly advised to take extreme care in their conversations. In your own interests we strongly recommend that you accept no offer of work of any kind without previously having obtained permission from the British government.' © Baroness Julia Neuberger, Private Collection

He visited Darmstadt, Offenbach and Limburg, read voraciously, took photographs and bought scarves and other things which he sent to Liesel. And he had a girlfriend, Lilli – 'my girl and I went to the theatre last night and saw "Ariadne". It was very nice but damnably cold.' The rest of his letters say little of any importance, although he was not particularly happy that so many people were writing to him, asking him

> to visit their friends or send parcels there [...]. Uncle Siegfried Rothschild is asking me to visit a friend of one of his friends in Frankfurt or Mannheim. So is mother, so is Mr. Lister [...], please Liesel put a stop to it.

For him, Germany was a temporary workplace (which he viewed from an English perspective: 'One of our lieutenants took us to a kraut-house where he searched for stolen goods'), but it was simultaneously a cemetery:

Figure 22 Jack Rosen (Helmut Rosenthal) as a soldier © Baroness Julia Neuberger, Private Collection

Tomorrow I am going to Esslingen and will look for grandfather's grave in Cannstatt cemetery, a thing which I don't mind doing. But to look if this or that one still lives there I have no time for.

On 24 May he announced that he was returning from Germany and asked Liesel to help him look for a 'decent job': 'I wish to work hard to become a man of the world and not live on my savings.' He gave short shrift to Lister's suggestion that he find a nice German girl, as he already had a girlfriend and did not need another, 'and certainly not a German one'. Lilli wrote on 20 February 1947 that 'Schecki' [Jacky] had 'saved [her] from two drunken Americans'. However, Jack would not be the one to build bridges with Germany.

On 20 May 1945 Jack and Liesel's cousin Erwin Rosenthal wrote from an unexpected location:

Cairo is a very interesting place, an extraordinary mixture of East and West, and not of the best features of either. But it has its attractions, no doubt. And yet, one can't get over the crass contrast between enormous wealth and abject poverty next door. […]

I'm trying to get my family out but so far can't even make application yet. We would send Thomas to a kibbutz in Palestine. Won't you go and see Elisabeth? She would be so glad to see you, so would the children. Do you know that Hex has a boy, Peter Victor? Another bit of news is, I am afraid, very terrible. Else died a day before her release from Theresienstadt to Switzerland, so people who escaped wrote to Liese Schwarzenberger. Isn't it terrible! And not a word of her husband and Hannelore who would have been 21 last week. Werner whom I met here was terribly upset, he was so absolutely certain he would see his people again that the news gave him a terrible shock. He is now stationed a good distance from Cairo but comes in occasionally. He came back from Palestine very enthusiastically. I am much looking forward to going there on a holiday, perhaps in autumn. […]

Do you feel any relief since the European war is finished? Is there a chance of Walter coming back soon? How are your in-laws, my generous hosts? And how are your parents & brother? Please give all of them my kindest regards. How is Anna Schwab in her health? I feel I ought to write to them. But I just can't bring myself to do it (what a Germanism!). […] Heinz has an atelier of his own opposite the Bezalel School. […] Now Liesel, be nice and write me sometime soon.

To a certain extent this letter addresses many of the themes we have encountered before in this story. Like Liesel, Erwin Rosenthal had become an English citizen (gaining citizenship at the start of 1940), and he was struck by his use of a German expression in his English writing. In Cairo his perspective was that of a British officer with a privileged position (he was unable to say so in his letters at the time, but, as he later put it in a short biography he sent to the City of Heilbronn, he 'was responsible for looking after German POWs'). His view of Palestine was naturally that of a German Jew who had friends there (like Heinz – by then David – Gumbel) who in light of the Nazi dictatorship decided to embrace this Zionist alternative.

Germany itself was now no more than the country where all the terrible news was coming from; it was around this time that the Rosenthals learned of the death of Aunt Luise Loeb. Hermine wrote to Liesel and the Schwabs on an undated postcard: 'I am so unspeakably sad that my lovely sister had to die. How happy I was, we all were, when we had the news that she was alive. Words cannot express how difficult it is for me now.'

In this situation it was important to ensure that she had friends and family around her, even if only through letters. Liesel again was a key contact: 'I wish [...] you and I could spend many an evening at our house as I spent them in your flat, enjoying your hospitality no less than your company.'

Trude Victor wrote from New York in a similar spirit:

Since we haven't heard from you for such a long time, we should like to know a lot of things, how you are, whether Walter has returned in the meantime or when you expect him back and how the end of the war affects your life. [...] Imagine we got the other day a letter from Tannenbaums, who could stay in Amsterdam in their old apartment (Leonardostraat 6), it sounds like a miracle but it is hélas [alas] a singular case and we have not got any news from all our other friends.

And how indeed was Liesel? Her friends wrote of illnesses, headaches and 'depressions'. In light of all the news from far-off places, had she thought of leaving England? Walter wrote on 23 June 1945:

I had thought myself one time of emigration to New Zeeland especially, but I don't think it is a very good idea, because it is a rather different sort of people who are wanted there. No, we'll stay in good old England and probably not make a lot of money but a decent living and live the way we want to live. I have told you before that I have no worries for the future [...] because I know what advantages I have in brains and education.

He had, he hoped at least, 'about 6 more months to do'. Then he asked how she expected the elections to pan out – he reckoned that the Labour Party would win. Walter himself was active in the Labour Party, 'and then we must hope they act promptly and efficiently'. Liesel, too, was known for her Labour sympathies; a Mr Schwarz wrote of his disappointment when the election results were announced that her name was not listed among the new members of the Cabinet.

The hackneyed cliché 'life goes on' is, sometimes, justified. On 5 July 1945, in the first general election for ten years, war hero Winston Churchill was voted out of office and Clement Attlee's Labour Party won with a considerable majority. This victory had consequences both for life in Britain and the ongoing British Mandate in Palestine. Churchill had rejected the White Paper of 1939 and its restrictions on Jewish emigration; by contrast, in the three years until the state of Israel was founded in 1948 the new socialist government tried to prevent by violent means what it saw as 'illegal' immigration by Holocaust survivors waiting in so-called displaced persons camps to leave for Israel. (This was to provoke heated discussion – Trude Victor wrote from New York on 8 August 1946 that 'I am terribly worried about the situation in Palestine and deeply disappointed in your labor government.')

Walter wrote a letter from Venice on 4 July: 'I went to the ghetto here on Friday night & to the synagogue. It was a very large but very poor community and has a number of extraordinary customs. I believe many of the best were taken to Germany.' The past remained present, even after the end of the war and with all the hopes for a new beginning. 'My brother-in-law is alive in Theresienstadt,' wrote Erwin Rosenthal on 29 July,

> *very unhappy about Else's death and worried. He hopes to go to Berlin. What an aftermath! If we could only get Hannelore here at least! Sorry about all the family. I heard about Tante Caro from Schumanns already. If only Minni is alive and can get together with Alfred again. We are building a brave new world, indeed.*

It seems that Leopold Lichtenstern had travelled to Frankfurt, as Lotte Fink wrote from Sydney on 6 August:

> *In case he is still in F. please let him search for Kaethe Voegler, her last address was Diemelstr. 7, and for the Griesbachs who lived in Kettenhofweg. You know he was a socialist who had lost his job as headmaster of a school through the Nazis. I am always hoping that Nölting might still be alive and in some sort of new government and all the real Nazis found and punished. How good that people like L. are on the spot there.*[6]

Even Lotte, in far-off Australia, who found it strange to discuss these real events, listed the names of friends and acquaintances and asked Liesel if she had heard from this person or that person: 'This is not a whitty letter but to tell facts one has to abstain from jokes and then, they really would be too tuff.'

On 10 August Walter wrote again. Now that Russia had

> *joined the fight against Japan, this should finish off the pacific war pretty quickly. I reckon it will be over by Christmas, especially with this uranium bomb. The Russians have a great expert on that stuff, Prof. Kopitzer who used to be at Cambridge, working under Rutherford and then went back to Russia on holiday & they wouldn't let him come back. He was supposed to be one of the best men. I wonder if he had anything to do with this.*

His last sentence referred to the atom bombs the United States had dropped on Hiroshima and Nagasaki on 6 and 9 August 1945. A day later, on 11 August, he wrote again with the 'news about peace with Japan' and hoped: 'If this is true it is a very good thing and everything will go a lot quicker.' Above all it meant that his hope of returning home could be fulfilled. 'I kiss you where you like it best and love you with all my heart.' Walter's letters were lovely indeed.

Margret Lichtenstern (Poldi's sister-in-law, wife of his brother Heinz) wrote on 10 August, thanking Liesel for 'all the lovely and beautiful things' she had sent her, including cloth, a wool jacket, soap and soap powder. 'You can certainly imagine what all these goodies mean for us, after Poldi will have told you how we have lived during the last few years' (Heinz, Margret and their children Ruth (Tutti) and Robbie were in Theresienstadt for the entire war, and survived). She continued:

Although you quickly get used to the good life again, I am consciously making sure that on a daily basis I enjoy the little things that make life unbearable if you have to do without them: a clean bed, a properly laid table, even just sitting on a clean toilet, being able to look after your health etc. etc. However, life here is still awfully complicated & extremely difficult, particularly for us, & it will take years for normality to be completely restored. But things are looking up, a scarcely believable thought.

Of course I see all that's beautiful in life with a smile and a tear in my eye, as I certainly don't need to tell you what it means to lose your parents and brother. The particularly tragic aspect of their fate is that my parents were in the last group of 300 people deported to Auschwitz, and indeed on the last transport that ever left Theresienstadt. I cannot allow myself to think of the horrible way they must have died, as by then the gassings had stopped. […] The incredible thing is that life still goes on, and you laugh now and again and feel joy.

News from Auschwitz. News of the atom bomb. And, at the same time, descriptions of nicely laid tables and goodies. Such was and is life – but historical literature seldom reflects it that way. The traditional historian, interested in structures and events, regards the goodies Margret described as insignificant, while the ethnographer or cultural historian, interested in the detail of everyday life, can sometimes lose sight of the bigger picture. These letters, however disordered and chaotic they may seem to us at times, represent a challenge for both approaches. On the one hand they show how 'world history' interferes with the lives of individuals, and how individuals and groups process such major events: see how Walter evaluates the news from Japan not merely in terms of its political significance, but also in terms of its effect on his personal life (and that of his wife and family). On the other hand, it is precisely these everyday objects – the beds, the tables, the toilets – with which people can concern themselves even in the most extreme situations, and which allow life to go on. The letters demand that we bring both fields of study into dialogue with each other. Walter was pragmatic in this respect, as this undated letter shows:

You've no business being upset because I'm not and I don't give a damn if I don't get into the Intelligence corps and if anybody thinks they don't like my German wife, I don't like them and it's not their business & I'm quite satisfied & love you very much and in any case the Intelligence corps are far more interested in my parents than in my wife.

Of all the people Liesel knew, Walter was the least inclined to treat her like a child. Instead, he often praised her: 'Have I ever told you that your English has improved a lot in the last few years?' On 17 August 1945 he wrote her a long typewritten letter: 'You don't make nearly as many spelling mistakes as you used to do, and the number of mistakes in grammar that you make is far less than when I first knew you.'

With a heavy hint of irony he complained that not just his family, but also his wife, were leaving him in the dark in terms of family news. 'The one thing that I am naturally rather interested in is the engagement of my brother.' The correspondents were still scattered around the world, or in this case at least around continental Europe, and they still had to make do with writing letters to each other.

> *Am I allowed to write to him or to her or is it still under a cloud, and what are the intentions of the young pair, when are they going to get married and are they going to wait for me to get home some time at the end of the year?*

And when he did come home, what were he and Liesel to do? Could they send their housemate Madeleine away for a while so that they could have something of a honeymoon? Would he find work in those difficult times, as industry would, he suspected, do everything it could to boycott the Labour government?

> *So I spend my time building castles in Spain and villas in Capri and inventing the most wonderful ideas of all the things I can do and would like to do after the war or rather when I get home and thinking about you my dear and the sort of life we can and will live together when we once settle down to be husband and wife in fact rather than only on paper as we are at the moment.*

Measured by the standards of Sam Barron ('I've carefully taught myself to restrain my outward expression of my emotions,' he had written a long time ago), Walter was

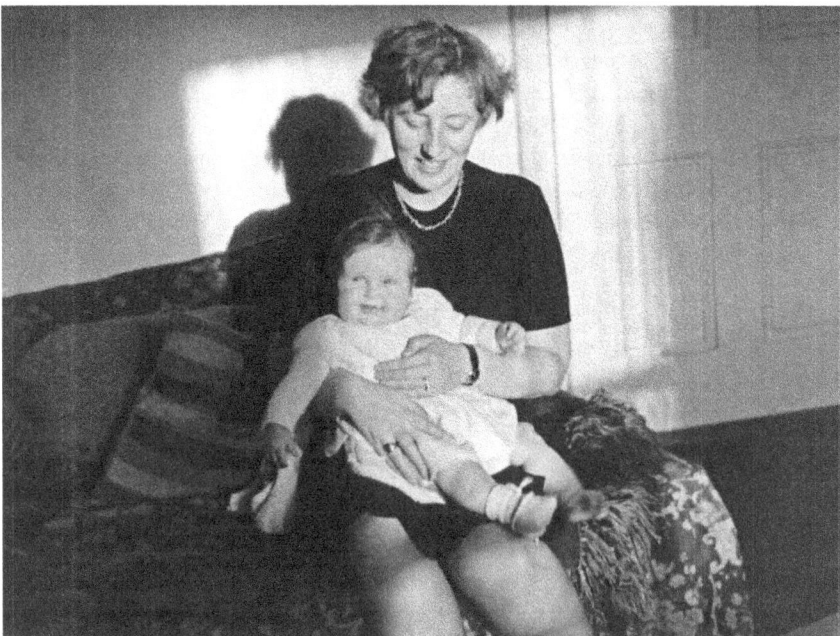

Figure 23 Liesel Schwab with her daughter Julia, 1950 © Baroness Julia Neuberger, Private Collection

becoming less and less English: 'I don't know how you feel, but it's not only the sleeping with you that I like so much, but having you by my side and knowing that you are near me', and 'I don't think you are ever out of my thoughts'.

Although there are lots more charming letters such as these from Walter, this is perhaps an appropriate point to take a step back from the story for a moment. But before we do so we should tie up some loose ends. Walter returned home unscathed in April 1946 and initially found work in 'a handbag factory', and then, on 27 February 1950 (when Liesel was thirty-five and Walter thirty-seven), their daughter Julia was born. She was to have a remarkable career as a rabbi, a politician, a chancellor of a university, a member of the House of Lords – 'in June 2004 she was created a life peer as Baroness Neuberger, of Primrose Hill in the London Borough of Camden'[7] – and it was she who passed on all these letters to me.

We must return to continental Europe. First comes Kurt Jeselson, Staff Sergeant in the Military Government of the US Army, who wrote from Wesermünde on 3 September 1945:

I was glad [...] to hear that you are well and have survived the ordeal. The latter I can say for myself, too, despite the fact that I went through the hell as so many millions had to. I arrived on the European battlefront last September and went on moving right up to the Elbe, being with a unit comparable to your Field Security Section. Then after V-E Day I switched to Military Government where I have been ever since.

I have seen quite a bit of Germany now, south as far as Heidelberg (still in its old glory). But all the rest of the cities I saw – like Frankfurt – are terribly destroyed and it is terrible to see how the punishment for all they have done has crashed down on the German people.

Margret Lichtenstern saw things rather differently. In a letter from 10 September she quoted Poldi's news from Germany: 'His reports about the situation there are devastating – i.e. for me they can't be bad enough.'

Erwin Rosenthal wrote on 7 October that he had been in Jerusalem and met Heinz Gumbel, who was a successful silversmith and teacher at the Bezalel Academy of Arts and Design: 'I would never have thought he would go in for liturgical art.' He had an assistant, Liesel Stern from Berlin, 'an old pupil of his, a very nice girl, but he doesn't want to marry her, apparently'. Erwin had also met Erich Gumbel, Heinz's cousin, 'and it was as if we had only met a day before'. And he had been to Nahariya,

where I met Fritz Wolf, too. He is a gardener (flowers) and at the Telephone Exchange (imagine Fritzle in that role, first he was the postman!), his first wife died shortly after the birth of the baby & he married again, a very nice girl, who is looked upon as the real mother by Danielle. Fritz is the local poet. I also saw Manfred Scheuer at Shavei Zion, I don't envy him with his Rexinger cattle traders. [...] Look at the world and how it manages its affairs (or rather can't) und das grosse Kotzen kann einen ankommen.[8]

It is perhaps unsurprising, after he had encountered so many Heilbronners, that a German idiom appears ('it makes me want to throw up'). Some of the names and stories mentioned in this letter deserve an explanation, and this will come when we return to Fritz Wolf – 'in Nahariya? In Heilbronn?' – and his life. On 20 January 1946 Erwin wrote again. After a difficult time in Cairo, where he had contracted hepatitis towards the end of his stay, he had finally made it back to England and was with his family: 'the children were thrilled to unpack my things.'

On 16 May 1946, for the first time (at least as far as we can tell), there came a letter from former Christian neighbours in Heilbronn. The Eckerts wrote, using the letter paper of the Rosenau Brewery:

Dear Liesel, we were so very grateful to receive your letter and we are only sad that it was not longer. We would like to know how things are going for you; what are your parents and Helmut doing? So far everything is back to normal for us. Karl and Paul are at home, only Hermann is away, as he's in America. Johanna is in Neustadt a./ Kocher, her husband in Heidelberg and he's coming home this weekend. There are now three children, two girls and a boy, to the joy of us grandparents. All of us are in good health. My husband and I are still living in the cellar, Paul has sorted out somewhere to stay underground and Karl is in the barracks they've built. Heilbronn is now nothing but a pile of rubble and debris. If only you could see it!

The Eckerts, beer brewers next to the wine merchants, were neighbours in a former life. Alice Schwab later said that 'it is quite extraordinary that, through the Red Cross, I remained in contact all the time with the girl in Heilbronn with whom I had grown up and whose father owned the local brewery'. However, no news of what happened during the war is given. Some time after this initial post-war contact, Johanna Eckert's husband, Dr Max Koppe, Professor at Tübingen and on the staff at the Max-Planck-Institut, visited Britain. Walter initially refused to meet him, saying 'I don't want to meet a German, I've just fought them', although eventually the two men met and got on very well with each other. As Alice Schwab wrote:

He said that he had had to come, because his wife had never had another friend like me, always talked about me, and that this just had to continue. Johanna Koppe, my friend, wasn't Jewish. Yet there was this re-opening of our relationship, which had broken off when she had said goodbye to me on the 16th of May 1939 [recte 1937] before I left for England. After the initial contact, they came over to see us regularly, at least once, if not twice a year, because they knew I would not go back to Germany.

We will go into this last point later. On 2 June 1946 Johanna herself wrote from Neuenstadt:

My dear Liesel! I had almost given up believing that I would hear from you again. I was delighted when Mother brought me your letter when she came to visit. Now you must write to me more often so that we can find out more about each other again. We spent so much time together when we were young that we will always have a

> special bond, don't you think? I still remember very clearly what happened when we last saw each other. It was in our garden at Fleinerhöhe, you had come from Frankfurt after being ill and we sat opposite each other on the stones by the garden path. I told you about the nightmares I often had: I was sailing down a river, banks covered with flowers left and right, but in the distance a waterfall was raging, and my little boat was headed unstoppably towards it with no escape. How often things like that come true!

Her husband, she continued, had returned safely from Russia, her brothers Karl and Paul were back at home, and even Hermann would return from a POW camp in the United States at some point.

> *I do not want to talk about the air raids and the armistice negotiations at the end of the war. I was so desperately worried about my children, my youngest daughter Petra was only weeks old when the war ended and the attack on Heilbronn, which destroyed my parents' house was two months before she was born. [...] Now you must write to me and tell me what you've been doing all these years and what you know of your parents and Helmut. Are you still working in a bookshop and still single? [...] Warmest greetings from our Ländle and write back to me as soon as possible*

Greetings from back home. Childhood, language, countryside – this was once their shared home, and old friends can write like this. Alice Schwab had nice words to say about Johanna and Max Koppe ('he was a good German, but he felt very bad about what had happened'), but I can well imagine that Liesel might have thought something was missing when she read this letter. What the emigrants had been doing 'all these years' is a question which good Germans liked to ask those who spent the war years 'outside'.[9] Johanna was attempting to resume a long-interrupted conversation. She wrote on 5 September 1945 that she 'simply couldn't imagine' that Liesel was married, that she was 'very proud of your professional career', and asked in all seriousness: 'Despite everything do you still have enough time for your husband that he doesn't get cross with you?' The two women's worlds had clearly drifted apart. She hoped 'that we can introduce our better halves to one another', though as her English was not good enough to hold a conversation she asked Liesel to 'give him [Walter] a thorough education in Schwäbisch'. Johanna repeatedly wrote 'Do you remember … ?' in her letters, and mentioned old names ('now I'll just tell you a bit about our old friends') and places:

> *Determann's bookshop has gone. During the war they moved to the Allee, but even there they were totally bombed out. In the centre of Heilbronn there is not one single house left standing, it's a pile of rubble like you can't imagine. It makes me sad every time I see it.*

The war was her main reference point, and she described what happened at its end as a 'collapse' *['Zusammenbruch']*. How did Liesel react when she read it, particularly given that just a few days later this letter from Oskar and Jenny Lichtenstern, Poldi's parents, arrived?

2 months ago we returned [to Amsterdam] *from Theresienstadt, but so far we have not been able to rest as we have had to change flat four times in this short space of time.* [...] *You cannot imagine how bad the shortage of housing is here and what difficulties the German Jews in particular have to face. But we are happy that we now have two furnished rooms and that we are in the position we had not been in for so long, of having our own bed, of using our own washstand and, if we wish, of being alone. Being forced to spend all your time with so many people, many of whom were uneducated and unfriendly towards us, was an unpleasant by-product of living in a camp. We had imagined that our return from the camp would be somewhat different, but we just have to adapt to the situation we find ourselves in.* [...]

We hadn't seen him [Poldi] *for 6 years and it was the hope of seeing him again that gave us the strength to survive and hold on through the terrible times in the camp.* [...] *As unpleasant as life in Theresienstadt was, it did give us a great deal more intellectual stimulation than the Dutch camp where we spent the first 8 months. A huge number of Jewish intellectuals from all across Europe were in the same place, such as you otherwise seldom come across, and during our time there I attended some splendid concerts and lectures which helped me escape from the misery of daily life.*

In October 1946 Liesel spent some time with the Wertheimers in Zürich, at 1 Tödistrasse (very close to Lake Zürich). This was her first visit to the continent since her holiday in Holland before the war. Back in London, on 5 January 1947 a letter arrived from Justin Hönigsberger in Regensburg. He thanked Liesel for the support she had given his sister (Emmy, likely a colleague at Marks and Spencer) throughout her illness and in the days before she died: 'I take certain comfort from knowing that in her final days there was someone with her who made the terrible isolation of being in a foreign land, away from all her family, somewhat easier and more bearable.' Whether the cause of death was pneumonia, a heart attack or contaminated medicine was not decisive in the end; 'it seems much more likely to me that her nerves failed as a result of the heavy blows the death of my 3 siblings caused her'.

Hönigsberger added that Liesel's German had 'in no way become rusty [...], you can still be proud of your mastery of your mother tongue'. Should she come to Germany in the foreseeable future, 'if only for a visit', he asked her to come and see them 'in old Ratisbon', which Emmy, deeply attached to her home city, had often talked about. Once again an image emerges of background and belonging, and each one of these homelands looked different.

Liesel was also looking for contacts, including the Determann family, in whose bookshop she had completed her apprenticeship. Hannah Determann wrote from Stuttgart on 9 January 1947:

With all my heart I wish you all the very best for the new year that has just begun! May it give the whole of humanity a little glimmer of hope! There can be very few people who have not suffered in the past few years. I would have liked so very much to bring you a little bit of joy, but for now this is not yet possible. I am so grateful to you for treasuring my father's memory, as I was extremely devoted to him. We hear regularly from my brother Franz. He's in Siberia, though the camp seems to be good. He keeps going with the hope of returning home, and we share that hope with him. Sadly we know nothing at all of my 2nd brother. And we received the terrible news that my eldest brother died in a camp in the Caucasus. It's just one blow after another! [...] And I can only give you sad news about Fritz Rothmund. He died in the attack on Heilbronn on 4 Dec. 44.

Determann's bookshop was reopened; I bought books there as a schoolboy. It has since closed, and a member of the family told me on the telephone, when I asked if they possessed any letters from Liesel Rosenthal or Alice Schwab, that after their father's death all the papers had been 'respectfully buried'.

Johanna repeatedly asked Liesel for a more detailed letter answering all her questions. Liesel said on 28 February 1947 that she had once 'written a long letter but not sent it, as it was too full of emotion towards you'. Johanna got other former schoolfriends, including Lilo, Käppi, Sylvia, Sause, Hotto and Theo, to send greetings on a postcard with a picture of Heilbronn town hall. It survived, ripped in half, and it is easy to imagine that this caused feelings to stir in Liesel which she put to paper, only to think better of it: *don't get carried away*. On 8 July Johanna again asked for letters:

I often imagine you suddenly turning up on my doorstep, as the trip to Germany you planned comes to fruition. It's lovely here in summer, so we could go on evening walks through the fields of waving corn to the forest.

Perhaps that would be too good to be true. Liesel sent parcels (Johanna thanked her for one on 15 July, at the same time both profusely and meaninglessly), but she kept her distance. That, at least, is the impression given by the letters. Their relationship became easier, Alice Schwab remembered much later, when the Koppes began to travel to England and meet up with Liesel *there*.

The various meanings of the word 'there' [*dort*] are worth considering, and David Grossman has done just that in his wonderful 1989 book *Ayien Erech: Ahavah* (translated into English as *See Under: Love*). For Momik, a young boy in Israel who eavesdrops on the conversations the adults, all Holocaust survivors, are having, the country they call 'there' becomes symbolic of the attractive and repellent aspects of life in the diaspora (from an Israeli perspective). There were, as Amos Oz also describes, 'proper towns' and verdant forests and fields of waving corn, and there was also the Nazi monster.[10] In the letters Liesel received, both from Heilbronn and from her parents, at first the word 'there' appears as a synonym for England, 'over there'. However, over the course of time the situation changes: England becomes 'here' and Germany 'there'. 'People have already come from America to visit their relatives here,' wrote Johanna, asking Liesel to do the same. Johanna's was, though, a different 'here'.

On 19 November 1947 Hannah Determann sent a 'modest Christmas greeting' in the form of an engraving of Heilbronn, 'an old friend of yours'. She added: 'As I know you have fond memories of the time you spent with my father, I fear thinking of Germany must be even more painful for you.' A short letter arrived from Erich Wesselow, who painted Liesel's portrait around this time and sent a few drawings 'as a special sign of my gratitude' on 3 December. Liesel sent parcels to Stuttgart, 'such lovely, tasty things', for which Hannah thanked her, reporting on 6 February 1948 (we are now in the last year of the letters) that she had taken some of them to Heilbronn to give to her brother Franz, who had returned from a POW camp in Russia. They sent Liesel a Heilbronn calendar, 'which I'm sure will interest you', by way of thanks. Life there was being played out 'on the edges of the city', as the reconstruction of the city centre would take years to complete.

Some time after that, a letter arrived from Ludwig. He sent best wishes to Liesel and Walter, who were on holiday in France. Writing 'in German, because it's easier for me', he thanked Walter in particular for his detailed letters, 'which you can't say about Liesel. Walter, make sure Liesel doesn't drink too much, the wine in the south of France is very strong'. Some things never change. Ludwig added that Alfred Stern had remarried 'to a Miss Göttingen from Breslau'.

Life went on. Leopold Lister had made his money selling handbags and now had his own letter paper: Leopold Lister, 49 Lancaster Grove, London NW3. He wrote on 13 June 1948 that Trude Friedlander was back from Holland, 'and my father remarked: "That only happens once, it won't happen again"' ['Das gibt's nur einmal, das kommt nicht wieder'].

How strange. While writing this book I am also investigating letters and other documents belonging to Werner Richard Heymann and Robert Gilbert, who together wrote the oft-quoted song 'Das gibt's nur einmal, das kommt nicht wieder' ('It only happens once, it won't happen again') from the 1931 film *Der Kongreß tanzt* (*The Congress Dances*), directed by Erik Charell. I am studying the time they spent in exile, Heymann in Hollywood and Gilbert in New York, and I have alluded to another song written by them, 'Irgendwo auf der Welt gibt's ein kleines bißchen Glück' ('Somewhere in the world there's a little bit of happiness'), several times in these pages. How appropriate, in terms of my writing strategy, that the correspondence ends with this. Around this time Alice Schwab bundled the letters together, tied them up with string and put them away in boxes, in the process saying farewell to Liesel Rosenthal and her youth.

7

'Your home' ['Ihre Heimat'].
Reconnecting

Max and Johanna Koppe sent their daughter Heidi at the age of seventeen to England for a few weeks to live with the Schwabs and improve her English. 'When their daughter was staying with us', Alice Schwab remembered,

> *and all the details of the concentration camps came out – I remember the accounts in the News Chronicle – she used to read it from morning to night. She had had no idea that such things could have happened. One must also remember that, while things looked wonderful at the beginning, the Germans didn't have such a pleasant war. They were heavily bombed, had terrific food shortages and life had been pretty difficult.*

These recollections were directed primarily at her child (Julia) and her grandchildren. While she attempted to come to judgement on her own life, she also looked back at Heilbronn through the prism of her relationship with the Koppes, with whom she was friends again.

> *This girl – she was seventeen years old, had no idea of what had happened. When she found out, I got really worried, she was in tears and simply couldn't understand it all. But gradually the truth dawned on her.*

Why had her parents, or her teachers, not told her about this? Johanna's brother even had a Jewish girlfriend who had emigrated with her parents to the United States shortly before war broke out, while he was called up to the Wehrmacht and saw action in Russia: 'When he returned from the army, he couldn't take it anymore and committed suicide. So my friend's family also suffered.' Alice continued:

> *As things got back to normal, my parents received quite a number of inquiries from their old friends and neighbours in Heilbronn, some feeling pretty bad about what had happened. My parents went back to visit Heilbronn in the sixties, being one of the first to be invited to come. My father had been friendly with Theodor Heuss who was born in Heilbronn [recte Brackenheim] and used to go drinking with him. Later Heuss became President of West Germany.*

> When my parents were in Heilbronn, the Oberbuergermeister came to see them and they also heard from Heuss himself. They only stayed in Heilbronn for a few days and, later, they made one or two further visits. They were pleased to see old friends and certain people made them feel welcome, but the hurt was there. The hurt was so bad that it affected my father's mental stability. He never got over the loss of his family. He lived to the ripe old age of eighty-eight, but in his last years he mostly talked about his family and what happened to them. […]
>
> My mother continued to live in the house in Wimbledon and had very good and kind friends. She still enjoyed life, but died two years later. My mother used to talk a lot about what happened and about her good friends in Heilbronn who had helped her and with whom she had been in contact.
>
> I still write to some of the old people, as far as I have been able to find them, never forgetting what they did and how they helped. Once things got very difficult in Germany and my mother decided to leave, they helped her with the packing of her possessions, saw that she was cared for, brought in food on the quiet and generally let her know that there were still people who were interested and prepared to help. And they did this despite the danger to themselves!

This chapter will focus on the questions that arise from memoirs such as these. The Rosenthals still feature, but we expand our perspective a little and consider the local and international culture of commemoration centring on the city of Heilbronn and comprising correspondents from around the world. This involves studying letters and other documents from the City Archives, as well as using information a number of families have been generous enough to provide. The general impression is that – due to the initiative of individuals – Heilbronn sought to contact emigrants, and attempted to come to terms with the local and regional Nazi past and its impact, earlier and more intensively than other places in Germany. However, once again we will leave it to Alice Schwab to give us a picture of the city, which she herself only visited much later:

> Then I started getting invitations to visit Heilbronn. The first such invitation came in 1982 when the municipality invited people from all over the world to re-visit Heilbronn for a week and be shown what happened. But I had had a cancer operation. I felt that I ought to go back to see my home town, but the surgeon thought that it was too early for me to undertake such a journey.
>
> Then, as the years rolled by, I got more and more fearful, should I or shouldn't I go? A lot of my friends and some of my relations had been back and had enjoyed their visit. The authorities in Heilbronn tried very hard to make things pleasant for them. But I was frightened. I hadn't forgiven them for what they had done and I felt that I was too upset if I went and it all came flooding back. Then in 1988 the Oberbuergermeister wrote that my husband and I should come on our own, without a group, just on our own. Walter said, "If you don't go now, you never will."

'Your Home.' Reconnecting 181

So they did go. An old schoolfriend, probably Johanna, picked them up from Stuttgart airport and took them to the hotel,

and everybody came to see me. There were class meetings in the afternoon and lunch the following day. They were absolutely marvellous. As far as they could manage it, all my old class-mates came, from all over Germany.

Together with Johanna and Heidi she visited Löwenstein, 'a lovely place which I had always liked'. She went to see 'my old home in Stauffenbergstrasse', and she and Johanna looked back on their childhood.

The night before we left Heilbronn, I met a Mr Palme [recte: Palm] who was quite an important local citizen. He now makes it his business to keep records of all the people who had been killed and he also keeps in touch with the survivors. He also ensures that the Jewish cemetery is properly maintained and he arranged, when we went to the cemetery, for my grandfather's grave to be restored. Before saying goodbye, he asked me what I felt. I told him that I couldn't have had a better welcome or a better time, and that they could see how much my husband had enjoyed the visit to Heilbronn, but I could never forget what they had done to my father and I could never forgive them for that.

The surviving documents show that from 1865 Lazarus Rosenthal lived at 5 Große Biedermanngasse before moving with his brother Jacob to 25 Götzenturmstraße in

Figure 24 The Götzenturmstraße, as seen in a postcard from the 1930s © Stadtarchiv Heilbronn, Fotosammlung, Hersteller H. Rubin & Co., Dresden-Blasewitz

1868. In 1882 he moved to number 43 on the same street. The entry for Rosenthal & Dornacher, wine wholesalers, 43 Götzenturmstraße features for the first time in the 1903 directory. This was where Jacob's son (and Liesel's father) Ludwig Rosenthal lived and worked, and his new address at 10 Mozartstraße is listed for the first and last time in the 1934 and 1938/39 directories, respectively. Not one of these buildings still stands. The Rosenau brewery founded by Carl Eckert, which Johanna Koppe's parents ran until it was destroyed, was located on the corner of Götzenturmstraße and Nägelingasse from 1860. Eckert took over the brewery in 1878, and in 1897 he relocated it to Rosenbergstraße where it was rebuilt.[1]

As Alice Schwab mentions, the most famous fellow German with whom the Rosenthals were in contact after the war was Theodor Heuss. A liberal politician, who in 1933 had reluctantly gone against his own conscience and, in accordance with DVP party wishes, voted in favour of the Enabling Act (giving Hitler the power to enact laws without the approval of the Reichstag), he became the first president of the newly created West German state, the *Bundesrepublik Deutschland*, on 12 September 1949. He replied to the Rosenthals' best wishes on 24 September in typical post-war German style, with reference to Germany's own suffering: 'Honoured compatriots, I thank you sincerely for your best wishes, remembering our shared homeland which, as you will know, suffered terribly during the war. I wish to carry out my duty so that I my conscience may be clean. With good wishes, your devoted Theodor Heuss.'[2]

This was a president writing. Could he have said more? Did he want to? His wife, social reformer Elly Heuss-Knapp, died on 19 July 1952. She had studied economics and made a name for herself as a lecturer on topics such as 'Women at home and in the workplace', as well as speaking out on collective labour agreements and the minimum wage. After the Nazis came to power she was banned from making public appearances (as was Theodor, who had been a lecturer at the German Academy for Politics in Berlin and was now blacklisted). Perhaps unsurprisingly, she had more contact than he did with the persecuted opponents of Hitler's regime, including Martin Niemöller. Many women considered her a role model as she did not merely fulfil the typical woman's role (for example by co-founding the Müttergenesungswerk, an organization for maternal health): she provided for her family by working, and even revolutionized radio advertising by inventing the jingle as an acoustic brand for companies.[3] Her autobiography 'Ausblick vom Münsterturm' ('View from the Minster Tower') was published in 1934 and a second edition was published in 1952. Theodor replied to Hermine's letter of condolence on 25 September 1952:

> *Dear Mrs Rosenthal! Many thanks for your charming letter with the eulogy from Mrs Helene Hurwitz-Strantz. I found it rather touching that the young women and girls of Heilbronn, whom my wife convinced to do social and humanitarian work almost 40 years ago, some of whom are scattered around various continents, still have such fond memories of her. With best wishes, your Theodor Heuss.*[4]

Interestingly, in recent years two new biographies of Theodor Heuss have been published. His personality seemed to combine numerous strands of German intellectual and political history, many completely at odds with each other.[5] With the help of original documents, Karl Josef Kuschel's 2013 book 'Theodor Heuss, die Schoah, das Judentum, Israel' discusses in great detail Heuss's initial ambivalence towards the 'Jewish question', his 'anti-Semitic echoes'[6] and his later attitude towards the state of Israel. Accompanied by Leopold Marx and Manfred Scheuer, on 12 May 1960 Heuss visited Shavei Zion, the place 'which you could call a piece of Swabia in Israel, or Swabian Israel'.[7] His bond with the city is made clear by this remarkable quote: 'What did Heilbronn give me? Democracy as a way of life.'[8]

On 31 October 1959 Heuss thanked the Rosenthals for their letter which 'has reached me in London'. He was, however, 'so overworked at the moment'[9] that it was not possible to meet them, as Hermine and Ludwig had hoped. Beyond politics, Ludwig viewed Heuss in the context of winegrowing. As a nineteen-year-old student in Munich Heuss had told his professor, economist Lujo Brentano, that he wished to write his PhD on 'Winegrowing in Heilbronn'. The open-minded Brentano accepted it with the lovely line, 'Someone once worked with me (or: under my supervision) on hops', as Dorothea Braun-Ribbat notes in her introduction to the new edition of his dissertation 'Viticulture and Vine Dressers in Heilbronn', published by the City Archives in 2009.[10] Heuss wrote in the preface to his dissertation that this attempt 'to portray the history and current state of winegrowing in Heilbronn has come about thanks to a vivid appreciation of the cultural characteristics of viticulture in my home city'.[11]

He opted for an extremely individual, empirical approach. In addition to national economic considerations he placed the particular 'character of the situation of the Wengerter' (as wine growers in the region are called) to the forefront of his investigation. The Wengerter were a group of people, in a city of trade and commerce, who stayed true to their agriculture and winegrowing even in a time of great industrialization, 'and [they] possessed a distinctive cultural identity'. In addition to an A-Z list of winegrowers, the excerpt from the 1929 directory included in the new edition contains the names of wine merchants familiar to us: Rosenthal & Dornacher, wine wholesalers, 43 Götzenturmstraße, and Rosenthal Lazarus, wine wholesaler, 60 Cäcilienstraße. This makes it even more astonishing that the Jewish wine merchants, who had contributed so much to the increased spread and sales of Swabian wine, are not mentioned anywhere in Heuss's dissertation.

This memory loss – my relatives, who have owned vineyards in the neighbouring village of Gellmersbach for generations, have not heard of the Rosenthals either – is profound. More than anything else, memories of the destruction of this way of life by the Nazis have been superimposed by memories of the city's destruction during the war. As Heuss wrote in the preface to the 1950 edition:

> *The city of Heilbronn, and the evidence of its history, was destroyed on 4 December by a hail of bombs. Only the façade remains of the wonderful old City Archive, whose delightful rococo inspired this young student to make such eager and enthusiastic efforts to decipher the old documents it contained. The narrow, angular streets, where a good number of the winegrowers lived, where the young man gained a free education and the old man made such good friends, were burnt to the ground; unable to defend themselves in the deep cellars, which had become prisons, one hundred and fifty of the roughly three hundred winegrower families, who had lived in this prosperous city for centuries, were extinguished in half an hour of death and destruction.*[12]

While in the 1950s Heilbronn's own suffering was afforded greater prominence, as the 1960s began memories of Jewish Heilbronn increasingly came to the fore. This was without question the initiative of certain individuals, but the city authorities also provided support for it. I have frequently quoted from Hans Franke's 'Geschichte und Schicksal der Juden in Heilbronn', and this pioneering work – the first in Germany to comprehensively document the history of the Jewish citizens of any city, from its beginnings to the present day – shows that the city sought to come to terms with its Nazi past, and the memories of the Jews who were driven out or murdered, earlier and more intensively than anywhere else in Germany.

Franke was born in Munich in 1893. He first worked as a journalist in Berlin, Leipzig and Zwickau, where he was theatre critic at the *Zwickauer Neueste Nachrichten* newspaper, and on 1918 his first volume of poetry, 'Meine Welt' ('My World') was published. He moved to Heilbronn in 1919, where he began working at the *Heilbronner Zeitung* newspaper before becoming features editor at the prestigious *Neckar-Zeitung*. Two of his plays were performed at the local city theatre. On 19 November 1933 Franke was assaulted by Nazis in his home, and he lost his job at the Neckar-Zeitung on 2 February 1934. He made a living in the Third Reich as a writer before he was called up to the Wehrmacht in 1944, becoming an American POW in spring 1945. He returned to Heilbronn in 1949 and became editor of the *Neckar-Echo* newspaper.

In 1960 Franke began work on 'History and Fate of the Jews in Heilbronn – From the Middle Ages to the era of Nazi Persecution 1050–1945', which was published in 1963. Some of his expressions are indicative of the uncertainty with which people in the early 1960s approached the subject of the persecution of the Jews, but that does not detract from his achievement. He planned to visit Israel, but before he was able to do so he died at Hasenhof in 1964.

As part of the research for his book, Franke sent out questionnaires to Jewish people who had emigrated from Heilbronn. The questionnaire filled out by Ludwig Rosenthal survives, both in Alice Rosenthal's documents and in an exhibition at the Heilbronn City Museum:

Name: Rosenthal, Ludwig. Date and place of birth: 6.2.1880, Heilbronn. Marital status on 1.1.1933: married, 1 daughter and 1 son. Residence in Heilbronn on 1.1.1933: 10 Mozartstr. Which profession did you practise in Heilbronn? Wine merchant. Self-employed? Yes. Current profession? Man of independent means.

Father's name and surname: Jacob Rosenthal, 2.7.1830. Mother's name and surname: Betty Rosenthal, 25.1.1843. Which profession did your parents practise in Heilbronn? Wine merchants. When did your ancestors move to Heilbronn? 1860. Where from? Laudenbach, Mergentheim.

When did you leave Heilbronn? 9 April 1939. Where did you go? London. In which country are you now permanently resident? England.

Which societies did you and your parents belong to in Heilbronn? 'Verein Einklang'. Did you hold any honorary posts and if so, which? Chairman of the Heilbronn POW association for many years. Did you take part in the 1914–18 war? Yes. Decorations? Iron Cross, 3rd Class.

Were you, your parents or other relatives living in Heilbronn at the time deported [to the camps]? My brother Max Rosenthal, formerly resident at 6 Clarastr., his daughter Eugenie Rosenthal. My sister, Mrs Helene Eisig, her daughter Hansi Metzger née Eisig, Hermann Eisig, his wife Melita and their son Hans Eisig, resident at 10 Bergstraße, my sister, Mrs Emma Dornacher, formerly resident at 6 Clarastr., my sister Mrs Berta Stern, 20 Schillerstr., Heilbronn.

Which of the above persons would you describe with certainty as a victim of the Nazi regime? All of the above.

After this initial questionnaire, may we contact you again with questions concerning the history of former Jewish residents of Heilbronn? Yes.

Address: Ludwig Rosenthal, 116 Kenilworth Avenue, Wimbledon Park, London SW19.

The Rosenthals had in fact made contact with their home town much earlier than this. The first letter I have found in the City Archives was sent on 20 April 1950, when Ludwig and Hermine were still living at 109 Worple Road, Wimbledon. In what was remarkably neat handwriting by his standards, Ludwig wrote:

Dear Mr Mayor, I thank you most sincerely for the many letters concerning the city of Heilbronn & my family & I have read them with great interest. I have no doubt that your drive and energy will succeed in having Heilbronn completely rebuilt over the course of time & I wish you complete success. Once again many thanks for the brochures, I remain, with best wishes, your Ludwig Rosenthal.[13]

Emil Beutinger (1945/46) was the first post-war mayor, appointed by the military government. Paul Metz (1946–1948) followed, elected by the city council. The man Ludwig was writing to here was Paul Meyle, elected mayor in 1948. He had spent the war working as a businessman for the Knorr food company, and it seemed that there was no stain on his character. On 20 August 1950 Ludwig thanked him again:

It really was extremely considerate of you to send us a Heilbronn travel guide & it was of great interest for all of us to read about all the places to visit & buildings we once loved. […] It is not out of the question that we will visit Heilbronn & Stuttgart again, as we wish to visit the graves of our relatives. We hope that under your proven leadership Heilbronn will regain the prestige it once had. We are glad to hear that the Zügel, Brenner-Schilling, Determann & Kachel firms are flourishing businesses again, we still have fond memories of them.

The Rosenthals named more addresses in the city, making their personal contribution to the creation and development of a new network of 'foreign Heilbronners'. As we have seen throughout this book, this group had kept in touch with each other as much as they could, but now the city itself became a point of contact again. The mayor's office announced on 14 November 1950 that they had 'taken the liberty of publishing one of your recent letters in our city and district gazette, so that the residents of Heilbronn can take part in the correspondence with those Heilbronners living abroad'.

Hermine wrote on 20 August 1952 that she had organized an 'Evening for the Friends of Heilbronn' the previous Sunday, when she had shown her friends the brochure they had been sent. 'We are glad that Heilbronn is being rebuilt so beautifully and so quickly.' However, she added, 'I would be interested to know what now stands on the site of the Heilbronn synagogue, as my grandfather Dr Engelbert was its first rabbi.' Paul Meyle himself replied on 17 September 1952:

As always, I was delighted to receive your letter from 20 August and it is gratifying to know that you have meet-ups with all those who feel a connection to their home city of Heilbronn at a "Day for the Friends of Heilbronn". Now you ask what stands on the site of the Heilbronn synagogue, whose first rabbi was your grandfather Dr Engelbert. The land between the Allee and Gymnasiumstraße, the former Friedenstraße, was acquired some years ago by a Mr Ludwig Stern from Heilbronn-Neckargartach, who built a cinema there. The entrance to the cinema is on Gymnasiumstraße, and the area adjoining the Allee, i.e. the specific area where the synagogue stood, initially lay unused for some considerable time. Herr Stern was forced to sell his company about a year ago. The new owner of the cinema and the whole land has cleared the area between the cinema and the Allee and rented it out to the owner of the café based on the first floor of the cinema. I must also inform you that the land did not belong to the city; in the course of its recovery it was instead managed by the Israelite Community, which in turn sold it to Mr Stern. If you ask me what I feel about it personally, I would openly admit my wish that another purpose had been found for the land. However, it was not possible for us to influence the sale to Mr Stern or what he intended to do with the land.

Like in many other cities, the few Jews living in Heilbronn in the immediate post-war period had other things to worry about. In many cases the land on which the synagogues destroyed in 1938 stood was sold after 1949, not just because the Jewish congregations needed the money (which they certainly did), but because they could not imagine that a Jewish community would ever re-emerge in these places. They viewed themselves as communities to be wound up, and focused on enabling the survivors – including those in 'mixed marriages', those in hiding and the displaced persons from Poland and Hungary who had survived the camps – to leave Germany in an orderly fashion and resettle elsewhere, preferably in Palestine or, as it became on 14 May 1948, the State of Israel.

And there is another factor to consider: the idea of memorials, through which historical memory is tied *to* places and conveyed *through* places. This is by no means new. Memorials had been maintained and visited by interested travellers for some time before this, including in a Jewish context; just consider the imposing monuments to the mediaeval Jewish presence that Worms and Speyer represent, for instance, or the tombs in Jewish cemeteries. To some extent this was spurred by the reawakened Jewish historical consciousness of the late nineteenth century, when European Jews were faced with the threat of increased anti-Semitism across many parts of the continent and chose to leave. But the fixation on the significance of particular *places* is a result of the belated attempts to address this issue from a historical standpoint during the 1980s, an era of historical workshops and of numerous local initiatives in Germany to come to terms with the past. In the context of a specifically Jewish culture of memory, in which words, religious texts and the ritual of time-bound commemoration (often on a yearly basis) are given prominence, the desire of well-meaning non-Jewish neighbours and their descendants to identify certain places and hold commemorations *there* is sometimes treated with scepticism. I still remember when, as students of empirical cultural studies at the University of Tübingen in the mid-1980s committed to preserving the former synagogue at nearby Baisingen, Rabbi Joel Berger told us in no uncertain terms that as far as he was concerned the building, which had for many years been used as a barn, was just that: a barn. Without the presence of the Torah scroll around which practising Jews can gather, a 'former synagogue' is not a synagogue anymore.

This makes Hermine's question regarding what had happened to the Heilbronn synagogue, and Mayor Meyle's somewhat defensive attempt to justify it, all the more remarkable. He was factually correct: the Jewish Restitution Successor Organization (JRSO) sold the land on which the synagogue destroyed in 1938 had stood, and whether this Mr Stern ('a Heilbronner of Jewish faith'[14]) or someone else had built a cinema there, or indeed a barn, is of no legal consequence. But from a moral and historical/political standpoint it did matter, and Meyle knew this, as his stated 'wish' that it had been different makes clear.

The culture of commemoration has developed so much in the past few decades in Germany that almost every location of a destroyed synagogue has been identified, provided with information boards or even turned into a memorial or museum, all in the name of redefining the space to make clear its significance. Indeed, in some cases the synagogue has been rebuilt, a process which rabbis such as Joel Berger found moving and to which they gave wholehearted support. Today there are numerous memorials in Heilbronn to the history of the Jewish community. A plaque commemorating the Jewish victims of Nazism was unveiled on the Allee on 9 November 1966, and in 1996 the nearby dome memorial followed, intended to commemorate the dome of the former synagogue.

In 1952 all this was still a long way off. Yet the correspondence between the Rosenthals (who were Heilbronners now in London, or perhaps *former* Heilbronners now in London) and Mayor Meyle suggests that something variously described (most notably by Edward Soja[15]) as a *thirdspace* was developing. The historical record shows that there is a city called Heilbronn. Local memory is that it was almost completely destroyed by British bombs on 4 December 1944, and under Meyle's leadership its reconstruction, which so impressed the Rosenthals, had begun. But for Hermine, Ludwig, Liesel and Helmut, and for those who suffered a similar fate as them, the Heilbronn to which they (and Theodor Heuss) were so tightly bound had lost its soul and its identity already in 1933. Not only had they been forced to leave their 'things' behind, they had been unable to take their relatives with them – relatives who, with the help of many Heilbronners and despite the resistance of a brave few, were taken from their homes and sent to their deaths. Their Heilbronn (which Fritz Wolf reflected in his poetry and stories) had disappeared long before December 1944; instead they had taken it, or the memory of it, with them when they emigrated. When these two perceptions of the city collided, as they did in the Rosenthals' correspondence with Meyle and Heuss, a third emerged. This was a Heilbronn in thought, in memory, in hope: a literary Heilbronn.

Hermine and Ludwig wrote to Meyle on 15 January 1954, thanking him for sending information about the city (which included a brochure called *Rebuilding Heilbronn*) and saying that they would like 'to see the rebuilding of the city for ourselves' at some point. Hermine was more specific on 28 December 1954: 'My husband and I intend to travel to Heilbronn in the spring to visit the cemetery. Of course we will have a look around the city & visit our friends who have stayed loyal to us.' With greetings to master butcher Fröschle and his wife.

Their first visit took place the following May, although sadly no information about it can be found. Paul Meyle planned a visit to London in early July 1955 with a delegation from the Foreign Office and hoped to meet the Rosenthals, but unfortunately, as he wrote in an official-sounding letter on 19 July, 'my intention to visit the Heilbronners

Figure 25 Mayor Paul Meyle © Stadtarchiv Heilbronn, Fotosammlung, photographer: Fotograf Ottmar Schäffler

living in London or to organise a meeting with them was unable to be realised'. With all his engagements at various 'government offices and authorities' there was no time 'to arrange private matters'. 'Private matters'? What a strange way of putting it. It was a real shame that the chance for the two perceptions of Heilbronn to meet was missed. 'It was much to our regret,' wrote Hermine on 3 August 1955,

> that you were unable to spend a pleasant afternoon or evening with us during your stay in London, we would have been delighted to meet you. In any case we were very glad to read in your letter that you took many lovely & good impressions of England back to your home with you.

To *your* home ['in Ihre Heimat']. Whoever would have thought that Hermine Rosenthal, whose letters and postcards to her daughter were often so jarring for us to read, would become an expert at diplomatic correspondence? 'There's always another time,' added Ludwig. They wrote on 28 September 1955: 'We are interested to see that the city is thriving, particularly as we were able to see it for ourselves during our last visit in May.'

So letters were regularly sent, along with brochures, calendars and boxes of English tea. Meyle wrote on 13 December 1956 that he was soon to travel to the United States, 'and I am already looking forward to meeting and speaking to the Heilbronners – or at least some of them – living in the USA'. For him this was a real opportunity to help 'the Heilbronners living abroad and the friends of our good old city of Heilbronn' form a connection to the city, and he also sent lists of addresses. He had great success with the Rosenthals; they wrote to him on 2 April 1957, mentioning 'our stay there last autumn'. Heilbronn was now *there*. 'We haven't forgotten our home city either,' they wrote on 9 December 1957, 'even if it is sometimes melancholy to think about.' They were 'pleased to see the rebuilding & the improvements', and on 17 December 1959 they promised to pay a visit to 'our little Swabia'. This time it was *our* Swabia.

Meyle's secretary, Clara Wahl, played a key role in putting the city in contact 'with Jewish families from Heilbronn', and for this she was awarded the Gold Medallion of the City during a 'Week of Encounters' in June 1985. Mayor Weinmann said in his speech:

> Miss Wahl was secretary to the owner of the Victor leather shop before and during the early years of the Third Reich. Her antifascist, humanitarian beliefs led her to remain loyal to the family during the boycott, help many other Jewish families in Heilbronn and support them while they made plans to emigrate. She re-established the threads of contact with these former Heilbronners soon after the war and extended these to others who had been affected.[16]

On 3 February 1960, to mark Ludwig Rosenthal's imminent 80th birthday, Meyle sent

> very best wishes in the name of your home city. Of course at this time your thoughts will drift back to the many different stages of your life, including to your home city of Heilbronn. As well as many painful memories you will also associate many

> happy times with our city. Even though unfortunately very little of the old Heilbronn remains, it is still a piece of home.

He was skating on thin ice here, and it is easy to imagine that the mayor's office thought long and hard about how best to phrase this letter. But his efforts were rewarded. Hermine wrote to him on 23 December, praising the successful rebuilding work,

> which I was able to see with my own eyes during my short stay in Heilbronn during the month of August. I also visited the graves of our relatives & was moved by how beautifully presented everything was in the cemetery.

Both were assiduously 'studying' the books they had been sent and on 8 May 1961 they wished Meyle 'many more years at the helm of the city of Heilbronn & the surrounding area to complete your work'. For the next two years Ludwig was very ill, and so the Rosenthals' next letter did not come until 18 August 1963, along with another invitation to visit them in London. A visit to Swabia to celebrate their golden wedding anniversary had to be cancelled as a result of his illness. On Meyle's behalf, Deputy Mayor Dr Nägele sent Hermine and Ludwig congratulations on their golden wedding anniversary on 23 July 1964:

> Through the grace of God's will you have walked together through these 5 decades, surviving many of life's adversities and dangers in addition to the difficult times of two wars. You can look back on your life's work with satisfaction and a just sense of pride.

The Spectator reported on the rebuilding of Germany in October 1964 in an article called 'Housing: German Style', picking Heilbronn as a case study, and the Rosenthals sent the cutting to Meyle and Dr Nägele on 18 October. On 8 January 1965 they wrote again: 'We were so sad to hear of the sudden death of dear Hans Franke & we wish to send our condolences to his family. He sent us such a lovely letter last summer.' They also thanked them for the 'Heuss anecdotes' they had been sent,

> as we knew Pres. Heuss personally & we received various lovely letters from him here, of which I am proud. The list of names of emigrated Heilbronners is of great interest to me.

In March 1965 they sent another thank you note, this time for a book on 'famous Heilbronner Robert Mayer'.

> We remember the Robert Mayer statue by the town hall especially well, as when I was a child my mother, who was from Heilbronn (née Engelbert), told me so much about the great man. Now I am busily reading his works.

This was discourse concerning background and belonging. It was cautious, but there were many common reference points, more than in London: 'It is wonderful to see how our home city has developed in such a short time,' they wrote (by then Hermine was probably writing on behalf of Ludwig). 'You can see that "Heilbronners" still have wine in their blood, which gives them strength to work.' There were also family connections in a text commemorating 'distinguished privy councillor Dr Bruckmann', as he was 'a personal friend of my grandfather, Dr Engelbert' and had given the rabbi 'a wonderful silver bowl'. In London they ate with Bruckmann silver every day.[17]

On 13 July 1966 Hermine sent a letter to the city administration expressing her sadness that Meyle was to leave office. The city's 'friends abroad' would be forever grateful for his work.[18]

Exactly a year later, on 13 July 1967, Ludwig Rosenthal died in London. 'He was a Heilbronner in body and in soul,' wrote Hermine to Meyle, who immediately replied:

My dear Mrs Rosenthal, many thanks for your letter from 13 July 1967. Sadly I learn from it that your dear husband, Mr Ludwig Rosenthal, has been called away to the eternal home. On behalf of myself and the city of Heilbronn I send you my deepest sympathies at this great loss.

She replied on 8 August:

Please accept my sincerest gratitude for your loving sympathies at the terrible loss of my beloved husband Ludwig Rosenthal. After 52 years' happiness together it is very hard for me to be alone.

A postmark from 18 December 1967 confirms that Hermine's Christmas card had arrived: 'Hope you have the merriest Christmas ever'.

Dear Mr Mayor, please accept my sincerest gratitude for the wonderful calendar, your lovely letter & the list of names. I have never been able to forget "Heilbronn" & will visit my former home city again this coming year. Once again many thanks and yours sincerely, Hermine Rosenthal.

Although it was normal to highlight words with quotation marks, the 'Heilbronn' here can be read as a perception of the city which no longer existed: *her* Heilbronn which she *could not* forget, even if she might sometimes have wanted to. Even in a text as short as this, such ambivalence can still be found.

8

Digression: 'Now in ruins.'
The house in the Götzenturmstraße

In all these letters, marked by mutual respect and just as strongly by a complex relationship with 'home', it is interesting to note that one matter was not discussed, even though it was of great significance. A file contained in the City Archives labelled 'Compensation files' contains documents concerning the building at 43 Götzenturmstraße: '2.32 ares, residential property and yard, former owner Rosenthal Babette, widow, née Wolff, beneficiaries: Ludwig Rosenthal, Alfred Stern'.

So what did happen to the house? Julia Neuberger had no information, and Alice Schwab said nothing about it in her interview. It was no little 'Häusle', as Swabians are often wont to call their home, but a large townhouse owned by the family since 1868/69, located on the edge of the city's old town not far from the River Neckar.

The file[1] begins with the last letter in the chronology, an invitation (at least for the cultural historian who does not believe he can reconstruct things as they once were) to step down in the archive and look at the past from the perspective of the present. On 8 August 1968, more than half a year after Hermine Rosenthal's last letter ('merriest Christmas ever') to Paul Meyle, Heinz Krüger, a member of the city's administrative council, replied to a letter from Philipp Cromwell, a lawyer who ran a law firm in London and Nuremberg focusing on compensation cases. The letter referred to the 'Compensation case Ludwig Rosenthal v the City of Heilbronn; specifically: claim for war damages'.

> *Regarding this case, we very much regret to inform you that we cannot acquiesce to your position. We remain of the opinion that the payment of DM 7000 compensates all respective claims and also satisfies the claim for war damages based on the merits of the case. This arises from examining the file and establishing how the sum of DM 7000 was calculated. […]*
>
> *Although we will ensure that Mrs Rosenthal receives everything she is entitled to, in this instance we are unfortunately unable to fulfil your wishes.*

A 'Building Report' from 20 May 1893 states:

> *Jakob Rosenthal, wine wholesaler, 43 Götzenturmstraße, has declared his intention to erect a steam apparatus in the south-facing laundry room on the ground floor of his residence.*

This establishes who owned the property in 1893 at least. But by 1949 it was not so clear. The Land and Property Department reported to the mayor's office on 20 June 'regarding the compensation claim for the property – now in ruins – formerly belonging to wine wholesaler Jakob Rosenthal at 43 Götzenturmstraße in Heilbronn'. The first layer of the story was then uncovered, as the Land and Property Department described 'the acquisition of the property by the City and the use of the same until its destruction':

> *Max Rosenthal, merchant and wine wholesaler in Heilbronn, had deregistered his wine-wholesaling business on 1 April 1938 and subsequently offered to sell the basement belonging to him underneath the property at 11 Bahngasse, accessed from the Keltergasse, to the City Council for 1600 RM. The City Council chose not to acquire the basement at the time as it had no use for it. […] Wine wholesaler Ehrmann subsequently purchased Rosenthal's basement.*
>
> *In 1939 Rosenthal also offered to sell his residential property at 43 Götzenturmstr. to the City Council. In the local land register, Book No. 3450, Section 1 No. 1 the owner was listed as:*
>
> *Babette Rosenthal née Wolff, widow of Jakob Rosenthal, wine wholesaler in Heilbronn. Widow Rosenthal died on 27 December 1938 and according to her will from 7 March 1938 left behind: 1/2 to her daughter Berta Stern née Rosenthal, widow of Hermann Stern, merchant in Heilbronn; 1/8 to her son Max Rosenthal, local merchant; 3/8 to her son Ludwig Rosenthal, local merchant.*
>
> *These three beneficiaries sold the property they were living in at 43 Götzenturmstraße, 2 ares 32 m², residential property, yard, walls and recesses, at a price of 16 000 RM to the City Council on 1.6.1939. The value of the property was assessed to be 28 000 RM at the time. The price was so low as it was a very old building in the city centre, it was in very poor condition, the flats were in a very worn state and the living spaces had been unfurnished for some time. […] Everything was in a neglected and run-down condition. […]*
>
> *Ownership of the property was transferred to the city on 1 July 1939. The City Council subsequently had the property restored at considerable cost – around 15 000 RM – and rented it out to the Fleinertor district group of the Nazi party at a yearly rate of 1560 RM.*
>
> *The property was completely destroyed on 4 December 1944.*

The report concludes that the 'beneficiaries' had a claim against the City Council amounting to 35,800 RM (value of the property in 1939 and rent income) while the City Council's claim amounted to 30,860 RM (purchase price in 1939, restoration, taxes and administrative costs). If the City Council retained the ruined property, the claimant would therefore be entitled to the sum of 4,940 RM, 'converted 10:1' to make

494 DM. If the property were returned to the beneficiaries, the Land and Property Department calculated a sum of 8,110 DM. This is, as I stated above, only the first layer of the story to be uncovered; the low purchase price of 16,000 RM cannot be justified solely on the basis of the poor condition of the property and its alleged 'neglect'.

This becomes clear in a letter written by lawyer Paul Kleine, 65 Moltkestraße, from Heilbronn to the Central Registry Office in Bad Nauheim (the last residence of Alfred and Minni Stern before he emigrated and she was deported) on 27 December 1949. Ludwig Rosenthal, merchant in Wimbledon, and Alfred Stern, believed to be in New York, were listed as the 'beneficiaries' of the compensation claim both for the house and for other assets. Both were acting in the name of their murdered relatives, and the letter also gave the 'particulars of those persecuted: Rosenthal Max, merchant, last residing in Heilbronn, deported from here to Theresienstadt; Mrs Emma Dornacher, widow, last residing in Heilbronn, 7 Klarastr., later in Frankfurt, died on the transport to Theresienstadt (at the time of her dispossession she mainly lived in Heilbronn and only after all her assets were seized did she live in Frankfurt)'. Kleine then described the dispute:

Those persecuted, Max Rosenthal and Emma Dornacher, had each inherited 1/4 of the property at 43 Götzenturmstr. on the death of their mother, Mrs Babette Rosenthal née Wolff. The property was a residential and business property plus a basement. The deceased Babette Rosenthal had been offered 55 000 RM by the City Council for the property before the persecution of the Jews began. After the death of the deceased, under pressure from the City Council the property was sold at a knockdown price said to be 16 000 RM. […]

At the instigation of Mayor Kölle, Heilbronn City Council forced the heirs of the deceased Babette Rosenthal to sell the property at 43 Götzenturmstr. to the City Council at a price far below its assessed value and even further below its market value. The exact details of the sale are unknown to the beneficiaries.

Both Max and Emma also had their shares and bank balances seized. Ludwig and Alfred, as their beneficiaries, demanded compensation for these damages as well as for the insufficient purchase price Max and Emma had been pressured into accepting by the Nazi administration. Another letter in the file reveals how much the Heilbronn Land and Property Department initially relied on the Nazi version of events. Deputy mayor Hugo Kölle, as the 'Commissioner for official valuation of buildings in the Heilbronn district' and 'authority on price regulation', signed a letter to the 'Württemberg Minister for Economic Affairs' on 2 June 1939:

According to the purchase contract from 1 June 1939, the beneficiaries of the Jew Babette Rosenthal, née Wolff, widow of Jakob Rosenthal, former wine wholesaler in Heilbronn, sold the Heilbronn property: Building 43 Götzenturm-straße, 2 ares 32m², residence, yard, walls and recesses, to the City Council of Heilbronn for 16 000 RM. […]

The building in question is very old and is located in the old town. The inspection revealed that the house is in very poor condition. The necessary repairs will require considerable financial outlay. The house has been inhabited exclusively by Jews. The flats are in an extremely worn state. The existing ovens and stoves are mostly defective and the living spaces have been unfurnished for some time.

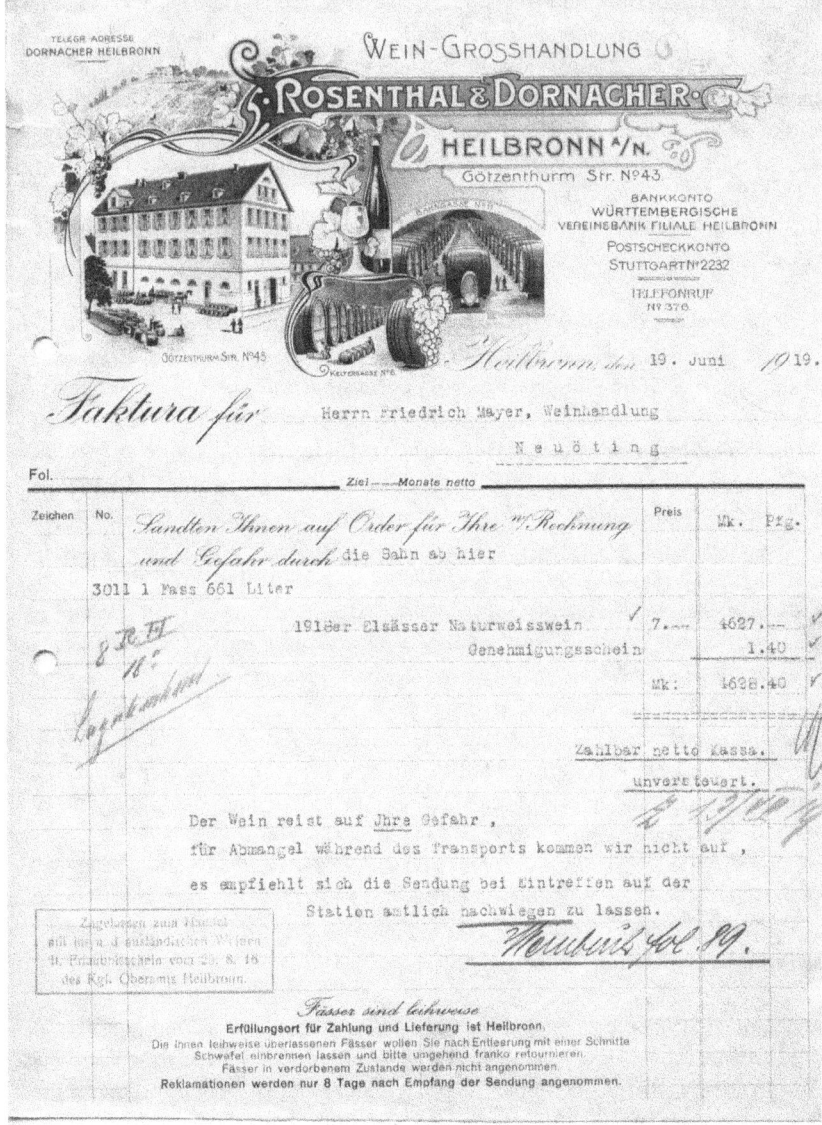

Figure 26 Letterhead of Rosenthal and Dornacher Wine Wholesalers, 43 Götzenturmstraße, 1919 © Stadtarchiv Heilbronn E002-914, Einblattdrucke

In 1948, when the first compensation claims were lodged against the City Council, this letter was copied almost word for word, although whoever did so was careful enough to remove the negative references to the Jewish residents. A copy of the contract from June 1939 also survives, in which Berta Sara Stern and Max Israel Rosenthal 'appear in person'; it shows that they were forced to sell their mother's house for a price

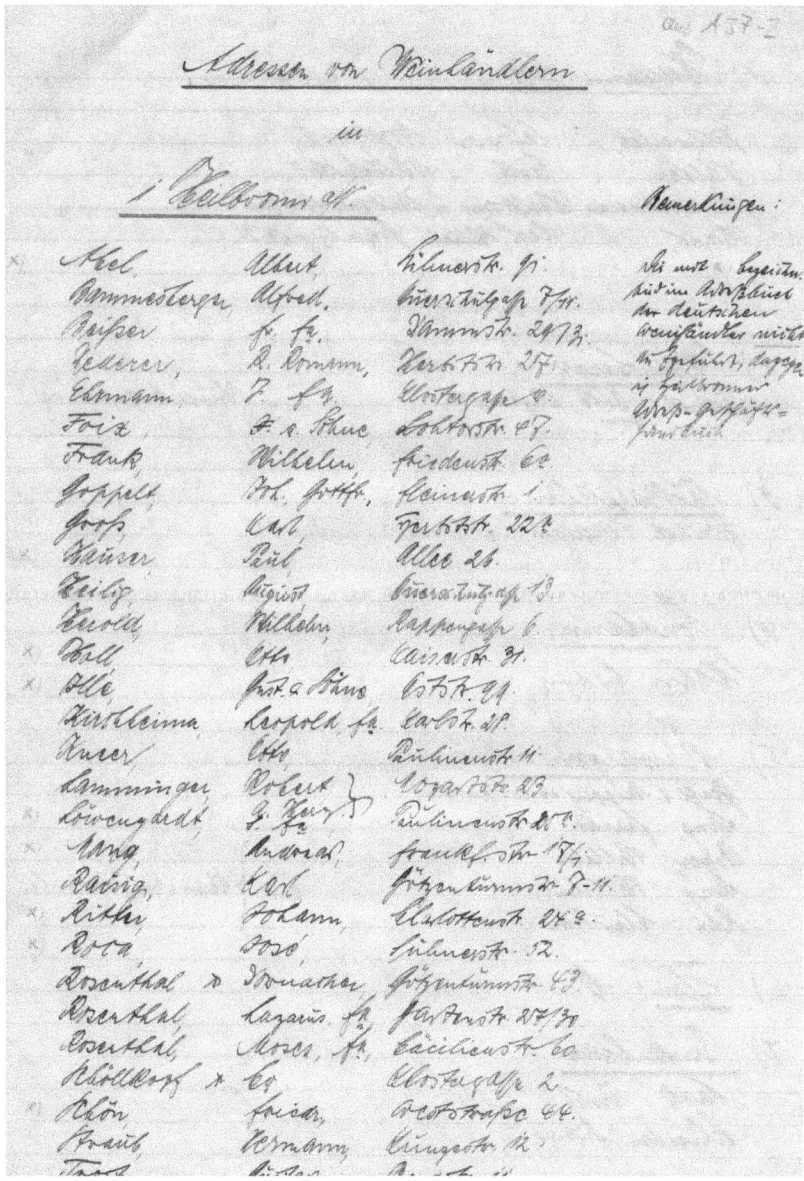

Figure 27 List of the Heilbronn wine merchants

far below its real value. As both were victims of the Holocaust, Ludwig and Alfred were the claimants – with Kleine as their lawyer – against bailiff Krüger, representing the Heilbronn City Council, when the case came before an arbitrator for compensation in Stuttgart magistrate's court on 17 October 1950. The initial settlement obliged the defendant (Heilbronn City Council) to pay the claimants 5,000 DM 'as compensation for all claims' regarding the house. A second hearing on 7 November 1951 adjusted the compensation to a total of 7,000 DM.

By January 1952 the City Council had still not paid the compensation for 'reasons of foreign currency', but Kleine made clear to them how 'legally incorrect' this position was: 'Foreign currency regulations are intended to prevent money being transferred improperly. This is not the case here.' The money could be transferred either to him or to the appropriate bank in order to then be transferred to the claimants. The case was still not settled, however. On 3 November 1958 the public compensation attorney at Stuttgart magistrate's court asked Heilbronn City Council for information concerning whether in 1939 the 16,000 RM was paid at all, and if so to whom:

> *As we believe that the money was taken by the German Reich, we kindly ask that you inform us where the purchaser paid the money into and whether the money was seized by the Heilbronn Finance Office or by another body.*

Krüger replied on 20 November that it was

> *unfortunately no longer possible to establish – for reasons of which you will be aware – where the money was transferred to at the time. There is no doubt about the payment itself. […] It is safe to assume that payment was made into a frozen account and that the sellers were unable to access the money. If the money was seized then it would not have been our direct responsibility but the bank's.*

Cromwell's attempt to get compensation under the Equalisation of Burdens Law for Hermine, as a widow, also failed. In 1968 the file was closed.

9

'How was the wine harvest?'
Heilbronn from afar

It would be a worthwhile exercise to search for traces of 'Heilbronn' in memories, in letters, diaries and manuscripts, wherever in the world they may be. That, however, is beyond the scope of this book. But the thought of searching for Heilbronn from afar arises when reading Arthur Reis's *Der Eiserne Steg* (*The Iron Footbridge*), initially written under a pseudonym before being published under his name in 1986 by a committee of local citizens. Half autobiography and half novel, Reis describes life in Tel Aviv. He rented a flat on the corner of Bialik and Idelsohn Street, not far from Tel Aviv City Hall and with Hayim Nahman Bialik's house one block further away. This is his description of the neighbourhood:

> As well as the nearby Bialik House, Arthur's new neighbourhood exuded a special cultural atmosphere. It was not uncommon to bump into such leading lights of the new Hebraic literature as Shaul Tchernichovsky and Avraham Shlonsky. The house belonging to Theodor Zlocisti, a famous figure in Zionist history, was directly opposite Arthur's flat. At the time it was inhabited by two well-known Tel Aviv doctors, Dr Steckelmacher and Dr Stahl. On the upper floor of the house next door lived Dr Hildesheimer, whose home concerts were always a special joy for most of his neighbours. Famous surgeon Dr Aschermann's house was built not far from Arthur's flat, above which Dr Alex Bein's parents lived. Bein was the author of a definitive work on Theodor Herzl, and he and Arthur were both former members of the "Blau-Weiss" Zionist youth movement. Dr Pinchas Rosen, formerly Felix Rosenblüth, who had cofounded this movement which was so important in the history of Zionism, was now on the Tel Aviv City Council, whose members regularly passed by Arthur's flat on their way to meetings at the Iriya. Dr Karl Schwarz, a former museum director in Berlin, did not shy away from personally recruiting him as a member of the Museum Society at 23 Bialik Street.[1]

The 'Chevre' circle met at the 'Aunt Rosa' café on Sheinkin Street, where friendships were formed and new arrivals found all kinds of different professions: at 'Maspero', a cigarette factory, at the new advertising agencies, on building sites. And the circle included more than just German emigrants: Arthur married Fela Majerovicz from

Poland, who had got into Israel through a sham marriage and who had fallen out with her first housemates in Tel Aviv over how chic and elegant an emigrant should dress. She worked at the 'Holender' hat store on Ben Yehuda Street. At their wedding Arthur's top hat was missing, 'which his mother Sophie had given to one of his many visitors from his old home of Heilbronn to forward to him. On this momentous occasion in his life he thought a lot about his mother and siblings, about the question of their emigration to this country and whether they would be able to adapt to the difficult living conditions here.' The worry was ever-present: 'Although the stories from back home showed that his relatives were in good health, their silence concerning the ever-increasing pressure the new Nazi regime was exerting on them and other Jews was even more telling.'[2]

This was how the Heilbronners forced out of Germany kept in touch with each other in Tel Aviv in the 1930s. None of them could have imagined that they would receive an official invitation to visit Heilbronn decades later. These visit programmes, which took place in many German cities primarily in the 1980s, offer researchers of German-Jewish history new perspectives, in particular in the fields of memory culture and commemoration policy. Gal Engelhard wrote his dissertation at the University of Haifa on institutionalized visits of German-born Jews and their offspring to their native hometowns in the 2000s,[3] focusing on visits to Nuremberg, Leipzig, Halberstadt and Rexingen. Working as an ethnographer, he accompanied those who travelled, most of whom came from Israel. He attended the official events they were invited to, listening to many mayoral speeches in the process, and conducted interviews with those involved. He noted the dynamic which arose from the tension between the emigrants' former hometowns and the places they were now living in, a tension which intensified through the experience of the trip.

Lina Nikou investigated 'Invitations to the old Homeland: Visit Programmes organized by German Cities for the Victims of National Socialist Persecution since the 1960s' in her dissertation for the Research Centre for Contemporary History at the University of Hamburg. She interprets the visit programmes as part of a German (given the historical context, primarily West German) policy of historical memory. An analysis of these visits, of the programmes, the intentions of the organizers and the reactions of their guests, can offer us valuable insights into the development and progression of this policy in terms of both local histories and the German-Jewish relationship as a whole.[4]

Anja Kräutler has also studied this subject, and she has shown the important function that these visits often had for the guests:

> *Frequently, group visits provided an opportunity for relatives scattered all over the world or former classmates, friends and acquaintances to see each other again for the first time in decades. It was not uncommon for them to learn of the fate of others only after the invitation to visit Germany, and so of all things it was their stay in the country from which they were once expelled that became a "family gathering".*[5]

Alice Schwab and her husband did not take part in any of these institutionalized events, although she did pay a private visit to Heilbronn at the invitation of the city. It is, however, interesting to place her experiences (and those of her parents) in a wider context. What was the relationship like between the city and those it called 'Foreign Heilbronners'? Searching for them, one will quickly come across famous names, such as novelist Victoria Wolff (1903–1992) born Trude Victor, not the same Trude Victor we know as Liesel's friend:

"My childhood was wonderful ... " This was how Trude Victor, born in Heilbronn, summed up her early life after many years' living as an author in the USA, her name changed to Victoria Wolff. The daughter of a Jewish leather factory owner, in 1917 she began attending the Realgymnasium grammar school in Heilbronn and took her final exams there in 1922. She abandoned the chemistry studies her father wanted her to complete and dedicated all her efforts to making the most of her journalistic and writing talent.

She continued to write after her marriage to textile manufacturer Dr Alfred Max Wolf and the birth of their two children in 1926 and 1928. Her first novel was published in 1932. After Hitler came to power she was no longer allowed to publish works on account of her Jewishness.

She therefore left Germany with her two children as early as 1 April 1933, while her husband initially stayed in Heilbronn. In 1947 the marriage was dissolved. Via Ascona and Nice she managed to emigrate to the USA in 1941. There she married Dr Erich Wolff in 1949 and adopted the "ff" in his name; he is supposed to have said to her "After me you can't marry anyone else, as there is no Wolf with three 'f's!" Despite trying circumstances she was able to publish a series of books; in addition to novels, short stories and essays she also wrote Hollywood scripts. She was friends with Erich Maria Remarque and Leonhard Frank, amongst others. Her literary output is notable for addressing the conflict between the emancipated woman and the conservative man.

After the end of the Second World War she resumed contact with her old home and was a frequent visitor to Heilbronn between 1949 and 1985. She died on 16 September 1992 in Los Angeles.[6]

The extensive memoirs that her first husband, Alfred Wolf, left for his grandchildren have been preserved in the City Archive.[7] He and Victoria emigrated to the United States where they eventually divorced, although they remained close. She also kept in touch with his brother in Israel, Dr Fritz Wolf.

Another prominent (non-Jewish) figure who features repeatedly in the archives is 'Citizen of the world from Heilbronn' Will Schaber.[8] Michael Groth, who has studied the emigration of journalists from Germany (primarily from Berlin) to the United States, gave a description of Will Schaber in 1985:

Even after 46 years in New York, Will Schaber's language betrays his Swabian roots. [...] He is, so to speak, the "archivist" of emigration to New York. His aim is to document a piece of German cultural history: the story of those people who were forcibly driven out of their homeland in 1933, most of whom have not returned.

Schaber was born on 1 May 1905 in Heilbronn. His father was a master engraver and social democrat, and his mother came from a long line of winegrowers – Heilbronners can scarce be understood without reference to wine. Schaber, who felt aligned to the peace movement during the Weimar Republic, was briefly a trainee at Erich Schairer's independent Sonntags-Zeitung newspaper before moving to the social democratic Neckar-Echo. In 1928 he headed to Berlin, and he later worked in Saalfeld, Thuringia. In 1927 he married actress and cabaret artist Else Rüthel. In 1933 they left Germany together for Estonia, and he subsequently worked at the Tagesboten newspaper in Brno, Slovakia.

After Else's death in 1938 Schaber travelled to New York, initially with a visitor visa, and made a living there by writing articles for Swiss newspapers and for the German-language *Aufbau* magazine, described by Atina Grossmann as a 'family bible' for German, and above all for German-Jewish, immigrants. He worked for the 'British Information Services' for many years, and in 1965 he became editor of *Aufbau*. He was a regular guest of author Oskar Maria Graf's 'Stammtisch' in Yorkville and attempted, as Groth wrote, 'to summarise the experiences of his generation'.[9]

Groth believed that Schaber would have returned from emigration if Fritz Ulrich had offered him a job at the *Neckar-Echo*. Ulrich's appointment as Württemberg Interior Minister ensured that this remains conjecture, although Schaber did visit Heilbronn and gave a number of speeches, not least of which was a public reading of his memoirs focusing on the city's happier times: 'The city of Heilbronn has always possessed a marked democratic character. As a true bastion of journalism, Heilbronn was of great importance for my later career.'[10] Schaber consequently became a key figure at the interface of pre-war life, emigration and reconstruction, all of which will concern us in this chapter. This was another description of him:

When the tall, aged man begins to speak his roots are unmistakeable. Schaber is still a Swabian. "Yes, of course!" he reacts with mild amusement, "I'm a Heilbronner!" And after a short pause he adds: "But I am just as much an American, and a New Yorker too." He calls himself a citizen of the world, and he's rather proud of it too. This is a man who comes from a modest family home, born in 1905 in Heilbronn, on International Workers Day of all days. His father was a social democrat and master engraver, while his mother came from a long line of winegrowers. Memories? Most have been wiped. His family died in one of the last Allied air raids in December 1944. "Seven thousand people died in the inferno in Heilbronn", he says quietly, shaking his head.[11]

Schaber was a close friend of Hans Franke and shared his opinion that Christians and Jews lived alongside each other better there than in other places:

There were some tensions between the two sides. I must say, however, that in general the Jews of Heilbronn were respected by the non-Jewish Heilbronners, above all as a result of the prominent Jewish businessmen, whose fairness and passion for their craft was known and treasured. In contrast to other regions and cities in Germany, there is no doubt that we had less anti-Semitism.[12]

The local authorities and the people of Heilbronn would of course have been pleased to read this. But Schaber could indeed give specific examples. Rabbi Dr Max Beermann, who taught at the adult education centre; journalist Thekla Sänger-Mai, daughter of a respected businessman (later, in New York, she was to 'keep the Heilbronners together in a small organisation'); Jewish supporters of the theatre, including furniture salesman Hermann Kern; lawyer Hugo Kern; banker Abraham Gumbel, who wrote under a pseudonym for the *Sonntags-Zeitung* newspaper; Alex Amberg, leather shop proprietor and council delegate at the Württemberg Jewish Congregation; Philipp Rypinski, director of the City Theatre. Taken together and without quotation marks, these people were what Hermine Rosenthal meant when she used the word *Heilbronn*. Schaber's efforts (along with those of others who were less prominent) to highlight these people and the work they did for the city's cultural, economic and social life succeeded in restoring the city's memory of those once driven out and murdered. Editor Gerhard Schwinghammer believed that the story of the prodigal son 'will one day have to be rewritten as the story of the prodigal sons of Heilbronn'.[13]

Individual emigrants (like the Rosenthals) had been visiting from as early as Paul Meyle's period of office. The yearly greetings sent by the city and the incipient attempts to confront its history made them more receptive towards their former home. David Heinz Gumbel, whose letters to Liesel from Jerusalem featured frequently in the correspondence we have read, sent a message of thanks for a plate decorated with the Heilbronn coat of arms in December 1958:

As I took my first steps in my profession as an apprentice steel engraver at Peter Bruckmann and Sons, this was a particularly lovely reminder of the city where I spent my youth.[14]

His cousin Erich Gumbel expressed his gratitude that the city was to rename a road at the foot of the Wartberg hill after his father, lawyer Dr Siegfried Gumbel, in a letter from 6 April 1963:

Such a token of recognition on the part of his fellow citizens would have been a source of great happiness for my father, were he still alive. He always regarded himself as a true son of his home city and gave his heart and soul to work for its wellbeing. If I should ever find myself in Heilbronn, I would gladly take the opportunity to come round and speak with you.[15]

Dr Manfred Scheuer, mayor of the Shavei Tzion settlement on the Mediterranean Sea, was himself an important transnational contact for emigrants from the whole of Württemberg, and he sent a list of more than twenty names and addresses to the City Council following a request from Paul Meyle on 17 February 1958. Meyle also sent a cheque for over 500 Deutschmarks to help construct a memorial to Otto Hirsch, the former president of the Higher Council of Jews in Württemberg, in Shavei Tzion.

On 2 June 1964 Julius R Scheuer wrote a thank you letter from New York for post he had received from Heilbronn:

> *It restores one's faith in the good of humankind and shows that the nation of poets and thinkers, of whom we were once so proud, has not quite been extinguished. Although the graves of my loved ones are there, it was my firm intention never to set foot on German soil again. This book* [Hans Franke's 'History and Fate'], *which is now indispensable for the history of Heilbronn, has shaken this conviction somewhat.*[16]

Hans Franke's book had made an impression in Shavei Tzion too, and Manfred Scheuer asked Meyle to send his thanks and praise on to Franke in a letter on 18 February 1964. Manfred and Sofie Scheuer, good friends of the Rosenthals, sent thanks for news they had received from the 'old home' on 15 December 1969 and announced that they planned to take a detour to Heilbronn during a visit to Stuttgart. Over the course of the following years many private visits took place, which are well documented in the letters. In the 1980s the visits became more institutionalized.

In February 1983 Dr Manfred Weinmann became mayor. In a letter to 'Dear Heilbronn friends all around the world' he introduced himself as a Heilbronner by birth whose father had been killed shortly before the end of the war. After giving an update on some of the latest developments in local politics, he came to the main reason for his letter:

> *We would like to invite our former fellow Jewish citizens, and indeed everyone who in the years of the Third Reich, 1933 to 1945, was forced to leave the city for religious or political reasons, to a one-week visit at the city's expense. I see this as a step on the path to reconciliation, as a gesture of goodwill, hope and community, and as a token of our belonging together. We all know the terrible things that took place during that time. Unfortunately we cannot make it un-happen. But we should always be willing to stretch out the hand of friendship when the other side is ready to do so. This is how we view the invitation to visit the city of Heilbronn.* [...]
>
> *For now I simply ask for a short message to indicate if you wish to accept the city of Heilbronn's invitation. We have already started to plan a few of the details, and a "Citizens' Committee for the Encounter with Former Jewish Citizens of Heilbronn" has been established.*[17]

He suggested two dates: one in autumn of the same year, 'when it is particularly beautiful here in Heilbronn', and the other in summer 1985 to coincide with the Neckar Festival. He enclosed a list of the addresses the City Council was aware of, and asked for those who could to add more.

'The City of Heilbronn Receives Jews and Emigrants' ran the headline in the *Heilbronner Stimme* on 18 September 1984. In addition to the local authorities, the citizens' committee under the leadership of Rolf Palm and journalist Uwe Jacobi – who had contributed a great deal to the process of confronting the city's Nazi and post-war past[18] – was responsible for organizing the visit. Before the guests arrived the exhibition 'Heilbronn Through Maps' was officially opened, and on 14 September the citizens' committee arranged a wreath-laying ceremony at the memorial stone for the synagogue on the Allee before another exhibition, 'Four Artists From Israel', was opened in the evening. After Mayor Weinmann's official reception and a tour of the city the visitors attended another exhibition, '50 Years of Aufbau', officially opened with a speech from Will Schaber on 'A Newspaper as Home'. Every one of the guests will have been aware of *Aufbau*, and this 'Home' was a reference point they all shared. After a visit to the theatre and an organ concert the party headed to the Jewish cemetery at Breitenloch, and in the evening a discussion on the topic of 'Jews and Christians' was organized. A plaque dedicated to resistance fighter Gottlob Feidengruber was unveiled before a trip down the River Neckar on board the 'Trollinger' and a farewell evening celebration with the mayor rounded off the programme.

This was a varied range of activities, as was typical for these institutionalized visits. Representatives of the city and its inhabitants officially welcomed the guests and accompanied them throughout the programme, in which the latest developments in the city – local pride at what had been achieved – and commemoration of the past were combined and reflected in each other.

As far as I can tell, the first text to critically engage with such visits was published by Wolfgang Benz.[19] He focused on the various motives of the hosts and the visitors, whose encounter yielded a productive dialogue in the best case scenario but misunderstandings on other occasions. This is clear in some of the reporting: for instance, an article in the *Heilbronner Stimme* on 19 September 1984 describing the group's tour of the city was given the headline '77-Year-Old Woman: "That's Called *Neckargaartlch*!"' The woman in question pronounced the name of the village of Neckargartach in the vicinity of Heilbronn like a true Swabian, and the fact that she could still speak some of the dialect was interpreted by the reporter as a sign of her bond with the city. Another visitor, the article continued, had 'not only come back to her home city without a single grudge, but with an almost passionate readiness to find everything lovely'. She knew that the inhabitants of the Böckingen area of the city were known as 'Pirates' ('Seeräuber') and, as the reporter saw it, took an almost childlike joy in saying so – reading between the lines, the impression is one of how nice it would have been if she were still a child of her home town and everything had turned out differently. She had laughed a lot during her stay, leading the reporter to state: 'Could there be a better compliment for the city?' Admittedly she could 'of course' not forget that when she was a young girl she had followed the advice of her family doctor to 'get out of here!', and the pain of emigration, the 'suffering and tears which shaped her life for many years', would never leave her. But she was not one for looking back and was prepared to 'forgive'.

Such forgiveness was not the direct aim of the visits, but the organizers were hoping for recognition of their efforts at least. The mayor's invitation anticipated a positive reaction of goodwill, reconciliation and even friendship that they hoped the visit would generate. The City Council has archived all kinds of sources concerning the 'Weeks of Encounter', which began in 1984, as part of its efforts to document 'the visit paid to their home city by former Jewish citizens and political emigrants from Heilbronn', including speeches, pictures and newspaper reports. These sources are of great interest to those investigating the question of how local German communities, press and authorities perceived their own history. Whenever someone felt 'homesick' the city could, through its invitation to visit, assume the role of the helping hand and healer. Accepting the invitation was 'proof of loyalty', as a letter from the mayor's office from November 1987 states.[20] Did that mean those who declined the invitation were disloyal? The city of perpetrators, of bystanders, with only a few who resisted, stretched out its hand – were those who did not accept it guilty of betraying their homeland?

Many visitors were delighted to return to the city; they gratefully accepted the invitation and ensured that relations were cordial during their stay. Marine chemist Paul Scheuer, living in Hawaii, had many friends in Heilbronn. Heinrich Horrowitz, living in Israel and still proud to have been awarded a prize for his reading of Schiller's poem 'Der Taucher' in 1933, said that making the trip was 'a dream come true'.[21] But other guests were critical. Victoria Wolff, though glad to receive regular greetings from the city and particularly pleased to be sent address lists of those who had 'left', told the mayor in an undated letter after her visit in 1985 of how a former schoolfriend had told a 'massive lie' to try and show that 'his character was not stained by Nazism': he asserted that she had been his best friend and that he had 'helped her whenever she was in danger', even though she had emigrated long before then. In another letter from her on 16 July 1985, however, she wrote that she found the visit itself 'so shocking and beautiful that it has left a deep mark'.[22]

Right from the start, the correspondence between 'Foreign Heilbronners' and representatives of their home city made clear the importance the former group attached to the cemeteries and graves of their relatives. For many, visiting the family grave was the main reason for making the trip, and they tended to measure the respect they were accorded by the condition of the cemeteries. This is exemplified by an extremely sceptical report written by Richard F Gummers, which he himself titled 'My Return to the Birthplace Which Drove Me Out':

> *I had mixed feelings and took some time to decide whether or not I should accept the invitation. Eventually I decided to go and accepted the invitation, primarily to visit my mother, brother and grandparents' resting places and to say prayers by their graves. […] The mayor of Heilbronn welcomed us and asked us to place our trust in the new generation which is now responsible for the towns and cities, for the German states and for the country as a whole. He also regarded the encounter as moral restitution for the injustice and persecution, for the humiliation and all the adversities we had suffered during the Hitler regime. […]*
>
> *Everyone kept their thoughts to themselves while we walked through the cemetery. I found my grandparents' and my brother's graves to be in a good state, though my mother's grave was in poor condition. […] The mayor promised that the grave would be restored. I also felt that the cemetery was missing a plaque with the names of the Heilbronn Jews who died in the concentration camps. They are the forgotten.*

> *After visiting the cemetery there took place an encounter with 40 members of the church community who, all middle-aged, wanted to know more about our experiences of emigration. Many of us spoke of our flight and our experiences in our new homes, and we spoke of how difficult it had been to build a new life. In my opinion, however, the despair and bitterness we had all known after having had to leave our country could not be felt. […]*
>
> *The citizens of Heilbronn treated us marvellously during our stay. They gave us the feeling that we were truly welcome, and for our part we were prepared to forgive and build bridges. Yet despite the wonderful reception we were given in Heilbronn we can never forget the persecution, the concentration camps and the injustice we suffered in the name of Hitler and his Nazi regime.*[23]

He did not mince his words. However, this did not stop the local newspaper from printing part of his account with the headline 'We Have Forgiven and Built Bridges' on 20 September 1984. Reading the speeches given during the Weeks of Encounter gives the impression that the hosts, politicians and church representatives were completely at peace with themselves; it is the visitors who have provided us with more nuanced perspectives on these events. Arthur Reis, from Tel Aviv, gave an acceptance speech on behalf of the invited guests on 24 June 1985:

> *It is less than a generation ago that we, in the flower of our youth, together with the members of our family and our people, were branded as Jews, stripped of our rights, humiliated, driven out and displaced. A large part of European Jewry was killed. Many of those who suffered the unimaginable torture and suffering still live among us.*
>
> *Before the brown darkness descended over this city we grew up happily in Heilbronn, and our roots with it and its people ran deep. We loved our Jewish and non-Jewish friends. The Wool Hall and the Hammelwasen fairground, the swimming baths on the Neckarhalde, the old cemetery and the Wartberg, the Köpfer and the Jägerhaus were a part of our being. The City Theatre and the Harmonie concert hall, art, literature and culture as was then understood, were as much a part of us as the air we breathe. Social responsibility and professional ethics, love for the work we did and the democratic ethos of this city were passed down to us from our forebears.*
>
> *In social, religious and political matters there were of course divisions, differences of opinion and groupings among the Jewish citizens of Heilbronn at this time. Although the liberal idea of the "Enlightenment" and emancipation in the spirit of Lessing and Mendelssohn, Gabriel Riesser and Abraham Geiger brought the Jews of this city greater freedom and prosperity, it also meant assimilation to their surroundings and estrangement from their roots. This estrangement frequently took from them the basis of their inner strength to assert their identity when faced with the unremitting, dishonest and shameful anti-Semitic hatred of their foes.*[24]

This was written, and spoken, from the perspective of a man who was brought up in a family adhering to Samson Raphael Hirsch's modern orthodoxy and who became a Zionist in his youth. He stated that 'Instead of Jewish youths we wanted to be young Jews', and he also spoke of his interest in the difficult growth of Israel as a state, of the problems the 'young Swabian Yekkes' had learning Hebrew, which they had already attempted to learn in Heilbronn, and of the clashes with the city's more assimilated Jews, who 'wanted nothing to do with this' and who were split on how to react 'when the brown flood tore our former home city asunder'. Reis cited the early initiative of Paul Meyle and his secretary Clara Wahl, as well as their request that former Jewish citizens should not merely make contact with the city but also 'help with the research into the fate of its former Jewish citizens'. He mentioned Hans Franke's seminal study[25] and looked back on the first visits that Heilbronners, including Willi Söhner and Kurt and Susanne Scheffler, had paid to Israel. He praised the research carried out by Uwe Jacobi and Albert Großhans into the local history of National Socialism and highlighted the efforts of Hartmut Gräf, a local teacher who, together with his students, had begun the process of documenting the graves in the Jewish cemetery and of restoring them.[26]

This emphasis placed on the small steps and the significance of personal initiative is a much more pragmatic, and therefore better founded, approach than talking of 'reconciliation' and 'forgiveness'. Rabbi Dr Lehmann gave a speech on 27 June 1985 at St. Kilian's Church – whoever would have thought that he, who was forced to leave Heilbronn as a child as he could no longer attend school there, 'would ever speak at St. Kilian's' – which he ended with this warm thank you to the hosts: 'You have done so much to give us the feeling that we are back home, even if it is of course only temporary'.[27]

Responsibility for organizing the city tours fell to Rolf Palm.[28] In the course of my research for this book I wrote to his daughter, and after a friendly reply I spoke to her on the telephone. She soon noticed from my accent that I was not a Berliner. 'No, a Heilbronner,' I said. 'Even!' she replied. She now understood my interest in her father's home city and his work, and she was very willing to talk. One of the first things she mentioned was how during the Nazi period her father, who owned the Palm fashion store on Fleiner Straße, asked a member of staff to work in the evening so that the 'the Jewish ladies and gentlemen', who were not allowed to enter the shop during the day, could buy their clothes. This was an extremely courageous act. His mother, by contrast, worked 'in the Lodz ghetto' during the war and did not approve of her son's actions: 'both these things can be found in one family'. Rolf Palm was born in Heilbronn in 1914 and saw the synagogue burning in 1938: 'Everywhere the mood was gloomy. Many said: God will not be pleased that a temple was set alight.' It was this conviction that led him to his future work.

After the war, Palm began to research and re-establish contact with his former school friends (although it seems an obvious thing to do, no-one else had yet done so). While the first invitations in the 1950s and 1960s were initiated and organized privately (a consequence of which, unfortunately, is that they were not documented in correspondence or other sources), they did form the basis for the institutionalized visits of 1984–1987, arranged with the help of the citizen's committee to which Palm belonged. His preparation for the city tours was meticulous: a list of all the places visited survives, including 43 Götzenturmstraße and a reference to the Rosenthal & Dornacher wine business. This list represents a topography of the city's Jewish past, but it also makes clear its destruction. Palm did not spare the details of its aryanization either: '28 Bruckmannstr.: Josef Kahn, later Kreisleiter Drauz'.

The encounters helped foster more academic research. The 'Palm file', residing in the City Archive, contains a comprehensive family file and a list of the graves in the Jewish cemetery. It also documents 'the history of the families, of all businesses, tradesmen and members of the liberal professions in Heilbronn, making clear the scope and significance of our city's former Jewish population', as the Friends of the City Museums wrote in a letter from 6 March 1989.[29] In the course of putting the file together Palm exchanged many letters with emigrants; they provided him with more contacts, which in turn spurred the 'Foreign Heilbronners' to get in contact with each other. A letter written by Arthur Reis from Hod Hasharon to Gerda Avnon in Jerusalem on 1 September 1986 is typical of this:

Dear Gerda, if I am mistaken then please forgive me for addressing you in this way. However I am sure that you are the former Blau-Weiss girl Gerda Gans from Hall, with whom we often spent time together in the Heilbronn Bund in our youth. If so, I certainly need not introduce myself to you any further.[30]

He then asked her, 'with regard to Mr Rolf Palm's question', for information on possible common ancestors. In her reply on 16 September she wrote of her visit to the cemetery and invited Reis to visit her in Jerusalem.

Lotte Reches, another Heilbronner by birth, wrote to Palm from Haifa on 12 December 1986:

We all value your tremendous work so very much, and we thank you for carrying out such thorough research. – What news is there of Heilbronn? How was the wine harvest? [...] You are all very aware that a good wine makes for the best stories.[31]

Wine really did represent a common theme among Heilbronners, and Palm went to great efforts to fulfil some of their other wishes. 'It was so terribly, terribly nice of you to send me the beautiful down pillow', wrote Lillian Rosenberger on 5 April 1988 from Cresshill, New Jersey.

But these courtesies and stories were just the beginning of Palm's work. He knew how important the Jewish cemetery was to the emigrants, how concerned they were that their relatives' graves were looked after – in March 1987 Arthur Reis sent him a long poem called 'Jewish Cemetery in Heilbronn' – and how deeply they wished for some form of memorial to those deported and murdered. Palm was therefore commissioned to create a 'Deportation and emigration list'[32] on behalf of the city, which also sought to correct the errors in Hans Franke's work and, more importantly, to serve as the basis of a planned memorial plaque. Erwin Rosenthal wrote from Cambridge on 12 March 1987: 'It is so wonderful and commendable that my home city is to construct a memorial at the Jewish cemetery. All the former Jews of Heilbronn will welcome it with gratitude.' Liese Rothman from Skokie, Illinois, was also impressed: 'Your lovely letter helped us,' she wrote on 1 March 1987,

> *make the decision to come to Heilbronn, and the list of those involved has names of old friends I have not heard for years. The dedication of the memorial, however, is a major reason for our trip.*

Palm received this heart-warming letter of praise from Mordechai Schkodi, writing from Givat Haim, on 17 November 1991:

> *In the last 25 years I visited West Germany a few times and each time I had the opportunity to visit cemeteries in various towns and cities. It is hugely gratifying to be able to say that the best-kept of all of them is in Heilbronn, my home city, where there is also a special memorial stone. [...] Dear Mr Palm, a non-Jew of our generation needs courage and, moreover, a warm, inner humanistic conviction to actively tackle the heavy burden of memory, which we cannot shake off, even more so when it is close to home and on a personal family level. Your diligent collecting of documents to ensure that the memorial contains every single name, making it whole and incontestable, reflects this. Dear Mr Palm, you have succeeded. No man, only God, can reward you for it.*

This section has traced the encounters primarily from the Heilbronn perspective. To examine the other side, with which we can study Heilbronn from afar – from Israel, from the United States, from Great Britain – it is useful to consider a speech given by Rabbi Joel Berger on 22 June 1987 in the main council chamber in the City Hall. 'At a time', he said, 'when your home and birthplace welcomes and celebrates you as children who have returned home', he focused on the biblical tale in which Moses was instructed by God to send spies to scout the land of Canaan, telling them: 'And see the land, what it is, and the people that dwelleth therein':

> *In a certain sense, I believe, dear brothers and sisters, that you are like those former scouts sent out into the Promised Land. The decision to undertake this journey to the place where you spent your childhood and youth cannot have been an easy one for any of you. It can never be forgotten or forgiven how this old free city once forced you out. This visit asked more of you than just to confront these bad memories. [...]*

> *You have clasped these stretched-out hands and, like those scouts, want to know: What became of this country, Germany? How do its people ... how do they view their past and present? What became of its cities, in which so many Jewish people once built manifold monuments and works of German and Jewish culture and creativity?*

> *I do not feel able to describe the image of this country objectively or with the appropriate perspective. I can, however, say that the decision to invite those once so monstrously persecuted and driven out to visit this city, to show them that their old home needs them, that their old home is a place enjoying a blossom of moral,*

decent democracy ... this decision is an expression of the free will of the free citizens of this city. [...] When you go home to those you love, tell them that a small Jewish community is stirring in the Heilbronn region: that 15 Jewish children here are learning Torah every week under the guidance of expert teachers [...].[33]

In the City Archives there is a list 'of the Heilbronners living abroad', which includes not just Jewish emigrants but those who moved abroad for various, mostly economic, reasons.[34] However, the list – containing thirty-three entries for Israel alone – does give an insight into the transnational dimension of the history of German-Jewish emigration. The biographies which make up part of the file are mostly short, though some go into great detail, and they do more than just illustrate; as Erwin Rosenthal put it, they stand for the ambivalence of a term like 'loss', in contrast to the old cliché of the 'contribution' made by Jews to German culture:

I feel that we must acknowledge the enormous efforts modern-day Germany has made to rehabilitate its former Jews and to accept what the country lost through Hitler's "Final Solution".[35]

Erwin Rosenthal – Liesel's cousin, whose letters we have cited at length in this story – wrote this after his impressions of a visit to the city where he was born. He continued: 'I was moved when I visited my parents' graves at the well-preserved Jewish cemetery and when I stood in front of our house on Cäcilienstraße, familiar and strange at the same time.'

Well-intentioned though it was, if the idea – as the rather too euphoric newspaper reports made much of – behind the visits was to reduce alienation and develop a new sense of trust, then these documents show us how difficult those involved found it. Alice Lion, née Adler, wrote from Nahariya:

My mother wanted to go to America. Unfortunately she missed her chance, was taken to Theresienstadt and gassed at Auschwitz. My sister lives in Chicago – Nellie Richeimer from Stuttgart. My brother Robert was severely injured at Dachau, had to leave immediately and died a few years later in El Paso. My mother has an entry at Yad Vashem in Jerusalem. Shalom.

This, not 'Neckargaartich!', was the reality of life and memory for the Heilbronners living abroad. However, they had taken a piece of 'Heilbronn' – to use Hermine Rosenthal's quotation marks again – with them to their new homes. Frank L Herz, born in 1908, wrote from Southbury, Connecticut:

My family has deep roots in Württemberg. My great-grandfather Lazarus Herz (1809–1888) moved to Heilbronn from Kochendorf. [...] In 1933 I was in my third year as a trainee lawyer at the Gumbel, Koch and Scheuer practice. [...] The political upheaval of 1933 hit my family like a thunderbolt, though it was not a surprise. We had not completely ignored the dark clouds on the political horizon. My career in Germany was over. My father found it hard to grasp that his position in society and his well-established relationships with neighbours and customers, his brother's "hero's death" – that none of all these bonds would prove lasting or of significance any longer. The family decided that if we had to leave we had better do it immediately. [...] My parents' German origins played a very large role in their life; they were nothing but Swabians, and the United States always remained a foreign country to them. My brother never neglects to visit our grandparents' graves in Heilbronn and Hechingen during his yearly visits to Germany, and he meets up with his old schoolfriends in Heilbronn. My own son spoke only German until he was 5 years old and shows an interest in his background. But that's where it will end. When I visited Germany for the first time in 1960 Heilbronn seemed to me no longer the same city that I had known. I preferred to leave my memories untarnished and have never returned.[36]

Heilbronn, too, emigrated and never came back. It is easy to imagine how a well-meaning local newspaper editor gave this report the headline 'We Always Remained Swabians', and that would not even be entirely wrong. But neither would it be quite right. James May (born Julius Mai in 1921, the son of Heinrich Mai and the aforementioned Thekla Sänger) is a name known to many in Heilbronn. No other emigrant has engaged as intensively with national and local politics as him, and certainly no-one has written so many impassioned letters to the *Heilbronner Stimme* newspaper. In particular, one from 1982 stands out: 'No-one in Heilbronn cares about Jews!' was written after a talk with teachers and school pupils, whose ignorance and unwillingness to learn shocked him. This was part of his story:

In 1931, Hitler was gaining power and anti-Semitism started to grow. I was one of three Jewish children at a private school of 200 students. The professors started to treat us badly – they wouldn't grade our homework, so we weren't promoted to the next grade. During recess, the others kids began to mistreat us. I was beat up and urinated on by some of the students and the teachers did nothing to stop them. Then my parents received a registered letter from the school, stating that I could no longer attend their school since I had failed my classes. But the worst thing that happened to me was the day I went to my friend's house and his mother opened the door and said, "Richard doesn't go to the opera with Jews", and she slammed the door on me.[37]

As a teenager he was sent, alone, to New York. His ship was greeted with huge, cheering crowds when it docked, though, he remembers, this was for General John J Pershing rather than him. He began an American life:

Within 48 hours of arriving in the United States, May had seen the governor of New York, the mayor of New York City, had a new identity and was introduced to some very different types of food. "They fed us some meat in a bread roll and a thick cold milk drink, that was my first hamburger and milkshake," he said.[38]

During the war May worked as a code breaker for the Pentagon, and later at a studio designing flooring. In retirement he moved to Santa Fé, New Mexico. And wrote his letters to the editor. Is he a Heilbronner?

Are the 'Heilbronn afternoons', which his mother organized as a get-together for Jewish refugees from the Swabian lowlands in New York, a Heilbronn event?[39] Does the middle-class settlement of Shavei Tzion in Israel, whose 'mayor' was lawyer Manfred Scheuer, really have a 'Swabian character'?[40] All these memories, or perhaps we should say fragments of memories, concerning the city and its efforts to commemorate its past do, when considered as a whole, help paint a picture: not 'of', but nevertheless 'from' Heilbronn, and in particular from a town which no longer exists.

Fritz Wolf has tackled these questions more intensively than anyone else. His name features in the Rosenthal/Schwab family stories (Julia Neuberger wrote, 'my mother thought about marrying him, he was known as Fritzle Wolf', but Liesel's marriage plans are a chapter for themselves), and he appears again and again in local memory too. If the documents are completely correct, which given the time elapsed cannot be established with any certainty, he first made contact with Heilbronn on 9 June 1957 in a letter to mayor 'Maile'. Headed 'Dr Fritz Wolf, Naharia, Herzl Str. (Israel)', he wrote:

One hundred years after my grandfather W M Wolf founded his eponymous firm in Heilbronn (in 1961 it would have celebrated its centenary) – twenty five years after I was forced to leave Heilbronn – and twelve years after Hitler was defeated, I thought to myself that one should attempt to forget the horrors of the past and only think of the best parts of it. This letter contains the question: WHAT IS HEILBRONN DOING?

I have Doctor Hugo Kern in Tel Aviv and Dr Manfred Scheuer in Shavei Tzion to thank for the few scraps of news I have received, including the fact that you are in office. Both men were once well-known Heilbronn lawyers. What is Heilbronn doing? By this I mean more than just the people, the Wartberg and St. Kilian's and the smell of the early-morning mist over the Neckar Valley. What became of all that between 1925 and 1939 was the old, decent, "democratic" Heilbronn society? Could you possibly send me something, such as a chronicle or a contemporary report from the time immediately after the world war? I would be delighted to read one. Send my greetings to Heilbronn! Perhaps not the actual Heilbronn, which I do not know at all – and perhaps not a Heilbronn which no longer exists and which lies in rubble or in graves – rather the "idea" of Heilbronn. I did, after all, study philosophy at the Realgymnasium grammar school next to the Friedenskirche with Professor Dr Schopf.[41]

This is perhaps the most perceptive letter I have ever read in this context. For him, his memory with which he now confronted the city (a friendly confrontation, as he was a very friendly man) produced a sort of 'Heilbronn as a spiritual way of life', in the same way that Thomas Mann viewed his Lübeck. This was an 'idea' of the city of which he was once part, which he could not let go even a quarter of a century since his emigration, in the midst of a life in Israel about which we are soon to hear more. There were the 'horrors of the past', and the attempt to forget them. There was an image of the city, and its river, which lived on in Israel (and in other places).[42] Paul Meyle, too, was a perceptive man, and he answered in person, writing from his perspective and with his agenda:

I was delighted to read the kind words you found in your letter. I found it most pleasantly moving to find out that you have now found your way back to your home city in a spiritual sense. Much has indeed changed in the intervening years and decades in Heilbronn, and those who come here to refresh their memories of this or that building or this or that street do so in vain. But I believe that in their hearts Heilbronners have remained true to themselves, true to what they were prior to 1933 – namely hard-working, decent, liberally minded citizens. If you have not done so already, now would be a good time to visit your home city once again. We could chat about former times and about the exemplary reconstruction of this city, which has progressed so much thanks to the willingness of its citizens to help. To give you a picture of the city I have taken the liberty of sending you various texts on Heilbronn, published over the course of the last few years, with this letter.

With this letter the City Archive, which for a number of years had been 'in regular contact with numerous Heilbronners living abroad', added Fritz Wolf to the file. It is not easy to tell if the two men were speaking on the same level and of the same subject, but on 16 July 1957 Wolf, with his keen, critical mind, sent his heartfelt thanks for Meyle's time and efforts. He congratulated the city on having a mayor

who appreciates that the writings of his city are so perfectly appetising and aesthetic, and who pays them the respect of elevating them to the level of works of art or a scientific paper.

He also described the experience of reading about the city's past and present. This is another insightful, sensitive letter, yet one which was at no point conciliatory in its tone. It deserves to be quoted at length:

It was with the most mixed of feelings that I spent many hours reading and studying the pictures. I dedicated a good few hours to comparing the pictures at the beginning and at end of the "Blüte, Untergang, Wiedererstehen" ["Blossom, Downfall, Resurrection"] book alone: I looked for the old Heilbronn and only found it in certain wistful hints. New streets, canals, buildings – a new Swabian courage and determination to rebuild! I read the names of those living and mourn the deceased! And as you, dear Mr Mayor, are without doubt a fine example of humanity, please allow me to make some remarks on the ever-recurring memory of 4.12.44, which can perhaps have an even more lasting positive impact as they are addressed to a person who is in a position to make a real difference.

There is no doubt that Hitler was intentionally not discussed in any of the texts. It is as clear as it can be that today the situation is still somewhat "delicate", and that everyone feels a quite natural need to forget. For the same reason it is understandable and justifiable that there is not one word on the former Jews of Heilbronn: only when Hitler is mentioned must the Jews also be mentioned – and if the Jews are not mentioned, Hitler's name need not be invoked either. The following remarks therefore have nothing to do with personal resentment at the fact that we Heilbronn Jews, too, are to be counted as living or dead victims and essentially forgotten. It is sometimes hard not to get the impression, however, that many wish to suppress, ignore or even feel a little self-pity for what happened.

I see a danger in this, as every recovery process (and is our correspondence not an example?) relies on acknowledgment and not on staying silent. Specifically: all too often one gets the impression that 4.12.44 is seen as a mere misfortune, as if it were an earthquake or a flood. Under no circumstance should we go too far in the opposite direction and speak of self-inflicted guilt: what decent person could acknowledge the concept of collective guilt, who in this world is without sin and who could call an innocent child guilty? So let us not speak of guilt! But as a member of the nation which effectively invented the pragmatic writing of history [...] I can assert that there should be no talk of mere "misfortune" and that talk should instead be of historical cause and effect. There is a deep and terrible connection between Hitler, the Jews and 4.12.44. [...] Such things can only heal with time, and so it will be a little time yet before we meet in Heilbronn.

This letter might be considered the beginning of the politics of commemoration in Heilbronn, which served as the basis for Hans Franke's book. However, Meyle's reply on 13 November, in which he recognized that Wolf's 'desire for understanding' was 'objective' (while 'many of your fellow believers consider things subjectively'), was rather unconvincing, and his reference to the 'sacrificial death of the people of Heilbronn, to whom Jews and Christians belonged in equal measure',[43] was even less so.

But no matter what our reaction is today to Wolf's letter 4.12.44 was no accident; you must mention Hitler by name, and you must remember the Jews, otherwise the recovery you prematurely celebrate cannot take place – it will certainly have had an impact at the time. He closed on a reconciliatory note: although he could not accept the rather casually phrased invitation to come and 'chat', he did hope for greater contact between Germany and Israel (in 1957 no diplomatic relations had yet been established) and that the mayor would visit Israel, where they would drink not Trollinger but Carmel wine, 'also a good drop'.[44]

Shavei Tzion and Nahariya welcomed another visitor in May 1960: Dr Theodor Heuss, president of West Germany. On 21 May Fritz Wolf, the poet, gave a speech in rhyming form, and he was wise enough not to talk about guilt or the writing of history. Instead he discussed the Hebrew language and, using a few Hebrew words, Israel. Although Heuss was amongst Swabians – 'with Maedle and Flaedle, with Taenzle and Haensle, with Draechtle and Naedle, with Schwaenzle and Pflaenzle' – pure Swabian folklore was never to be expected from Wolf. As a cultured man educated at the Karlsgymnasium grammar school, he said, the president would take an interest in languages and seek to 'understand the Jews', rather than be like the 'Pfleiderer' know-nothing who saw Hebrew text reading from right to left and said, 'No wonder no-one talks to the Jews.'

The self-irony was unmistakeable: 'We have the Israel Philharmonic Orchestra/ We have Ben Gurion, there is no-one better/We have the lowest point on earth/Of money we have the greatest dearth.' Even the complex issue of reparation could at least be mentioned in dialectal form, in the same breath, no less, as the difficult integration of German Jews, the 'Yekkes', into the nascent State of Israel: 'We make the Germans pay more than their due/Though speak their language they dare not do.' Wolf used the term 'Sabra' to introduce Heuss to the 'new' Israelis (and a new Jewry) in the spirit of Zionism: 'They lounge around on the sofa there/Shout like only a schoolchild dare/With hand and fist they're ever stronger/The Jewish fear, it is no longer'. The poem closed with a 'Shalom', and his wish was as follows:

> *Shalom to all the Arabs out there/And "anachnu" [we] in Israel's care,*
> *Shalom to the end, I hope not in vain/To those who caused us suffering and pain,*
> *Between Jews and Christians – of this I am sure –/Professor Heuss, be our guarantor!*

Hanna Frielinghaus-Heuss, Theodor Heuss's niece, was also in the party which visited Israel, and she gave a detailed account of her encounter with Wolf in Nahariya.

> *There strolled a slim, good-looking man over the lawn, whose gait immediately reminded me of a figure from my childhood days in Heilbronn: it could only be Fritz Wolf! I saw him in front of me, how he used to walk along the Friedensstraße, head tilted back, eyes fixed on somewhere far in the distance, satchel askew over his shoulder – for me the embodiment of a head in the clouds. He sat next to me and in a conversation where "Do you remember?" was asked over and over we effortlessly glided back through time and space to a 1920s and 1930s Heilbronn. […]*

> *Fritz Wolf spoke of the two lives he had lived: a sheltered life in Heilbronn which produced a German schoolboy and student, and a stormy life in Nahariya which made him an Israeli. […] He wrote me many letters concerning his second life in particular, with which memories of his first life kept interfering.*

Meyle thanked Wolf for sending him the poem on 15 June 1960 and expressed his delight at the 'warm words'. In the same 'spirit', he added, the Heilbronn Homeland Days (Heimattage) at Whitsuntide had taken place,

> *when I sat together with Heilbronners from around the world and we called up each individual guest by their country of origin. A small world was gathered in the Wartberg Hall, a world which had one thing in common: love of their home city and the wish that peace may prevail for all of us.*

It was at this time that Hans Franke was writing his book. Just as Rolf Palm did for his file, Franke collected information on the fate of the Jews driven out of Heilbronn. Wolf provided this account:

Figure 28 Fritz Wolf during his visit to Heilbronn in 1985 © Stadtarchiv Heilbronn, Fotosammlung, Fotosammlung, photographer: Mathäus Jehle

I was born in 1908 and was the typical spoilt child, even more so as my emotionally driven mother was by the standards of the time rather old, namely 31. I was the result of a loving marriage to a handsome gentleman and businessman called Julius Wolf, already part-owner of what later became known as the knitwear offcut sorting plant, WM Wolf AG […]

Until 1933 my life followed the model of many well-off Jewish boys in Württemberg: three years of preschool, nine years of Latin, school leaving exam at the Realgymnasium grammar school in Heilbronn, four years studying law at the Universities of Heidelberg, Munich, Berlin and Tübingen, trainee exams, doctoral exams, two years of training in the judiciary. And then, right at the beginning of my third year of training at a legal practice, the Third Reich suddenly came into existence. Immediately, as early as May 1933, I left Germany.

First he went to Italy, where he wanted to become a ladies' hairdresser – a typical plan, he wrote, for those 'whose intellectual aspirations had been destroyed by barbarism' – before eventually becoming a musical instrument and machine oil salesman. He later emigrated to Palestine. His brother-in-law, former lawyer Dr Oskar Mayer, acquired a plot of land (a *meshek*) for him in Nahariya, where he struggled 'as a gardener and chicken farmer'. He married and became father to a daughter, Daniela. After his wife Paula's death he found a new companion in Ruth Mamlok from Breslau, who became mother to his son Uri. 'Together with her I was able to build a home – both symbolically and eventually in reality.' He took a job as a post office clerk and also gave piano lessons in the evenings.

> *And eventually I wrote large, evening-filling musicals for Nahariya, the "Nahariyade", the "Grosse Parnosse" and "Abrakadabra" or "The Miracle of the East" – all the lyrics and a good part of the music I wrote myself* [...].

In an appendix Wolf told of how his parents visited him and his sister in Palestine in 1937. Cäcilie Wolf died of a heart attack on the return journey on 10 June, as a few of the letters sent to Liesel mentioned, 'though people say, much more accurately: she died of a broken heart'. Shortly before the outbreak of war his father managed to escape to England, where he died after an operation in September 1939.

The story of Fritz Wolf's life in Israel is for another book; there are a great number of unpublished manuscripts in the archive at the German-Speaking Jewry Heritage Museum in Tefen, Galilee. Lena Kreppel analysed sections of his work in her dissertation *German, Jewish, Israeli: Construction of Identity in Autobiographical and Essayistic Texts by Eric Bloch, Jenny Cramer and Fritz Wolf*. Her father Klaus Kreppel has also studied the history of German Jews' settlement in Nahariya in depth, and together with schoolchildren from its twin city of Bielefeld in Germany he successfully restaged the *Nahariyade*, for which David Vitzthum made a lovely film.[45] In 2001 Armin Wallas, with whom I had visited Fritz Wolf together the year before, published 'Das Sülmer Tor' (referring to the Sülmer Gate in Heilbronn) in the *Mnemosyne Magazine for Jewish Culture* which he edited. In this text Wolf used his childhood memories, written while sitting at a desk 'in a very different country',[46] to tell the story of his family, his grandfather and founder of the business, and in particular his great-great-grandfather Anschel Wolf.

> *I must keep moving forward and shake off this compulsion, which holds me in an iron grip, to think back to the time when the old, proud, free city of Heilbronn tolerated no Jews within its walls, and barely allowed them to enter the city for even a day.* [...] *Why is it that I cannot help but see the city before me, this proud, beautiful and cursed city, which I so loved and which caused me so much suffering, and in the same instant this ragged, wretched ancestor whose name I barely know, without whom I would not be here. Why are my thoughts stuck there: at the Sülmer Tor?* [...]
>
> *I often walked through the city. Its name is engraved with silver pen in my mind, but the pen is now a rusty nail which has poisoned me. I walked every route a hundred, a thousand times: to school; to the railway station; to the sorting firm on the Salzstraße so I could walk home with Papa; along the Allee to the theatre; to piano lessons on Gartenstraße; to the Olgaplatz, where my sweetheart lived;*

through the rubble of the "Hohle" up to the Wartberg; through the Karlstor to the ruins of the Weibertreu castle in Weinsberg. The fire brigade band played in the Harmoniegarten and the young women wandered around; the bells in the Friedenskirche tower rang; the Schießhaus came into view, the Bläß'sche Palais, the little house on the Trappensee; sturdy steeds, young girls singing, carts clattering by, taking the grapes into the cellars. Flags fluttered throughout the city, celebrating the early victories of 1914. From the Neckar Bridge I looked down into the river – that was my Neckar.[47]

As an author Fritz Wolf is still to be discovered, but here our interest is in him as a letter writer. There is a long gap in the correspondence with the city, in all probability a problem of missing documents rather than of actual silence. This book is not about Fritz Wolf, so I will not attempt to look for these missing sources.

Our primary concern is to understand the story of Liesel Rosenthal and the city she was forced to leave in May 1937, and to find as many sources as possible to help us. On 25 February 1984 Wolf congratulated the new mayor Dr Manfred Weinmann on his appointment, and thanked him and his predecessor Dr Hans Hoffmann for the Christmas parcel containing a calendar, special coins commemorating the inauguration of the new City Theatre and the annual round robin. He reported that his brother Alfred – Victoria Wolff's first husband – had died in Atlanta, and, prompted by the city's invitation to visit, provided more information on the family. They had lived at 16 Moltkestraße, in 'a house adjoining the Friedensstrasse which belonged to Mr Henry Oppermann', that is, in the same house as Melitta and Hermann Eisig and their son Hans, who despite the efforts of Liesel and Hans Schloss had not managed to emigrate. He also detailed his thoughts on the invitation, which he could not accept, only partly for practical reasons:

This is for me and my Swabian-Talmudic manner, as a "ponderer" and "deep thinker", a much more thought-provoking offer than it is for those creatures who do not burden themselves with such things. [...] It differs greatly whether one is visiting long-time friends – and a great deal of Heilbronners, and Hanna Frielinghaus from the Heuss family, belong to that group! – or whether one accepts an official invitation from the city of Heilbronn.

There are oh so many who would make things easy for themselves and quickly and firmly give their yes or no – a yes to this "timely opportunity" for shaking hands and forgetting, for building bridges and perhaps even for reconciliation at however deep a level, or the reverse: a harsh, bitter no to the nightmare of memory.

I belong to neither group. Here the question is not one of guilt and forgiveness, nor one of protracted healing processes – something happened here which I can only describe as a spiritual rupture, and it cannot be made clear enough to the well-meaning, decent people involved in this that they should take great care with what they are doing. The feeling of disintegration is stronger and more terrible the more one was connected to this city through the generations and through one's own experiences.

It is much easier to forget the Wartberg Tower and the "Knoepfle", the Town Hall Clock and the octagon of St Kilian's than the jagged autumn colours of the maple leaves on the Friedensstrasse by the Karlsgymnasium and the September mists, rising so white and gentle to reveal a sweet and cloudless blue sky ... Please, distinguished Dr Weinmann whom I do not know, excuse this sentimental detour.[48]

A year later, in July 1985 during the Federal Garden Show, the Wolfs did travel to Europe, first to Belgrade (where his third wife Fritzika Horwitz came from) and then to Heilbronn. His subsequent thank you letter to mayor Weinmann on 1 August 1985 was rather more pragmatic than his previous letters.[49] Although the 'unprecedented horror of the German-Jewish tragedy' featured heavily, he felt the encounter was better served by dialogue with real people than by clever speeches and long books. The city's 'Jewish Week' had made such dialogue possible, and if he had any further advice it was to provide much more opportunity for it. It was almost taken for granted that the visit was 'a model of smooth organization' and that the city had impressed the guests with its cultural offerings, cleanliness and courteousness. He suggested that a 'Day of Personal Encounters' would be a desirable addition to the programme, as he had been most affected by conversations with a former Luftwaffe pilot and the daughter of an SS general. They had been difficult conversations for sure, but they were of more use to him than yet another excursion or formal speech.

In particular Wolf singled out the work of Weinmann's assistant and 'Public Relations lady' Eva Niklasch for praise, citing her discretion, her tirelessness and the sense of calm she exuded. He exchanged further, 'unofficial' letters with her: 'For me you are a sort of "symbolic figure" uniting the old and new Heilbronn,' he wrote to her on 8 January 1986, 'a modern, unromantic "Katie of Heilbronn" so to speak, and moreover the "key figure" who connects the Heilbronn administration with its former Jewish citizens.'

He discussed the new anti-Semitism in Germany: the controversy surrounding *Der Müll, die Stadt und der Tod*, a play by Rainer Werner Faßbinder whose premiere in 1986 was stopped by the Jewish Congregation of Frankfurt occupying the stage, the oft-repeated accusation that the property market in Frankfurt was 'in Jewish hands' and the comparison 'between the Arabs in the occupied territories and the Jews persecuted by Hitler'. All this had to be discussed during the visits, even if a few of the Jewish guests would have preferred to simply 'enjoy a pleasant visit', to serve 'a truth which does not simply avoid and turn a blind eye, and a younger generation which has no idea what Jews are'. The problem of 'Jewish-Heilbronner relations' concerned him greatly, and his unyielding desire for total honesty is truly admirable, even if, as he wrote in another letter to Mrs Niklasch, the issue had been put to the back of his mind again after his return: he had too much on his plate with 'our Israeli problems'.

We have Mrs Niklasch to thank for ensuring that Wolf's work was finally published. In 1986 the City Archive publications department published his book *This Was My Heilbronn: From a Broken Picture Book*, with a foreword by Hanna Frielinghaus-Heuss (quoted above). The cover featured a picture of the town hall with its oft-described clock, underneath which stood the phrase 'Time hurries, divides, heals' ('Die Zeit eilt, teilt, heilt'). His sketches of the old Heilbronn, 'The Tambourine Major', 'Art Lessons', excerpts from 'The Sülmer Gate', 'Heilbronn VfR Football Club' and 'Christmastime', were lovely to read, but harmless. Missing were Wolf's feelings of disintegration and the direct mention of difficult issues which characterized his letters. However, at long last he had a published work, and this gave him great joy.

He wrote to Wilfried Hartmann, head of the publications department, on 20 January 1987 that he had received plenty of positive reaction 'to the little Heilbronn book', including from his 'ex sister-in-law Victoria Wolff in Los Angeles'. He also invited Hartmann to 'come and visit us here! We don't bite! It is in any case an interesting country, and a welcoming one too.' Hartmann and Frielinghaus-Heuss were also attempting to find a publisher for his poems: 'to "see me in print"? What childishness! What I want is to reach out and touch other people's hearts.'

> *See, the wife studies the sunken buildings and squares,*
> *I myself read what is written about the monument,*
> *I see the gates in front of me, oh so many old friends:*
> *One a tobacconist and another a quality tailor,*
> *She played tennis with us, and she knew nothing of the horror.*
> *Misery and bestiality, tragedy of Jewish history.*
> *What remains in memory is but a shadow of what once was.*

Wolf sent the complete poem to mayor Weinmann on 31 December 1988. Three years later he tried to obtain German citizenship for his grandson Itai, whose mother Daniela had taken her own life. His attempt was in vain, as he told Mrs Niklasch in a letter on 3 June. Lonely and somewhat bitter, Fritz Wolf wrote his last surviving letters in the late 1990s. On 23 October 2006 Wilfried Hartmann wrote to the new mayor, Helmut Himmelsbach, that Itai had called to let him know 'that his grandfather died early on Sunday 22 October in Nahariya at the age of 98 after a long illness'. With his death a unique, Heilbronn form of memory culture from afar came to an end.

'On the 27th of February, 1950, my daughter Julia was born,' says Alice Schwab in the 1990 interview. After a long, complex story Hermine and Ludwig Rosenthal's wishes had finally come true, and Liesel had done what they expected of her. Moreover, it was of her own accord and in the context of a happy, lifelong marriage to a man, Walter Schwab, whom her parents more than accepted. The Liesel who arrived in Britain in 1937 as a domestic servant would never have dared believe that this little Julia would go on to become the UK's second female reform rabbi and a politician active in numerous charitable organizations, ennobled for her services and made a life peer in the House of Lords.

At long last, Alice focused on herself in the final passages of the 1990 interview. After Julia's birth, by which time she was already thirty-five, she worked for the Association of Jewish Refugees and their United Restitution Office: 'They had started an employment agency and I looked after the men's section.' She then worked for Youth Aliyah, running their greeting cards (Rosh Hashana cards) department, and as part of her work she commissioned designs by Jewish artists from all over the world, among whom were many Israelis, including Mané Katz. It was a job she found extremely fulfilling.

Figure 29 Alice Schwab with her daughter Julia, 1955 © Baroness Julia Neuberger, Private Collection

She subsequently began her own project, 'an Over Sixty Employment Bureau for the Citizens Advice Bureau in Old Street'. At the same time she was active at the Ben Uri Art Society in Soho, which had been founded in the East End, and this activity increased after she ended her work at the employment bureau. She organized art exhibitions and played a leading role in the creation of the 'Permanent Collection of Works from Jewish Artists', with which Walter also helped once he had retired. References to her work can be found above all in the 'Art Notes' she wrote as art correspondent for the *AJR Information* journal: exhibition reports, contacts with artists and books, which Hermine had once so strongly warned her against.

'My pre-War and wartime experiences had a great influence on my life. You can never forget what has happened and I sometimes wake up in the night thinking of this cousin or that relation.'

She oversaw the acquisition of a Düsseldorf exhibition 'Verjagt, ermordet' ('Chased out, murdered'), focusing on the fate of Jewish children in Germany after 1933, for the Ben Uri Gallery and watched Holocaust documentaries on TV. She twice travelled to Israel and met David Heinz Gumbel, by then a renowned silversmith, and collected prints and lithographs. She reminisced about old friends like Max Victor, who we have encountered in her letters, and about names like Betty Duchin, 'my oracle, a good, clever and kind woman with whom I have maintained a close friendship for more than fifty years', Annemarie Meyer, former 'secretary of the Warburg Institute' [Annemarie Meyer was also a cousin of Walter Schwab's and part of the Tietze family, department store owners in Berlin], and her cousin Anne Baer, 'who is always present with help when there is need'. These three people did not feature at all in the letters, a further and necessary reminder of the problematic nature of such sources. She expressed her gratitude to Britain – 'I am most grateful to this country for all the friendship and help that has been given to me over the years' – and the last few sentences of her interview were addressed to her daughter Julia and her children Matthew and Harriet: For I came from a community with close family attachments and this still remains with me.'

Her obituary was published in *AJR Information* in July 2001:

Alice Schwab, former AJR Information arts correspondent, has died aged 86. She was born Lisl Rosenthal in 1915 in Heilbronn where her parents were wine merchants. Although her first love was art, Alice took practical training as a bookseller. After arriving in England in 1938, her first position was with a much-admired Quaker family, following which she went to live with relatives in London and to work for the Jewish Refugees Committee at Bloomsbury House to assist Anna Schwab who became her mother-in-law when she married Walter in 1942. In 1939 Alice joined Marks and Spencer, determinedly coping with the bombing of an East London store.

After the birth of her daughter Julia in 1950, Alice concentrated her efforts in support of AJR's Employment Bureau, and later Children and Youth Aliya. From 1975 the Citizens Advice Bureau benefited from her help in finding employment for the over 60s. A lifetime's devotion to collecting and appreciating art led her to accepting the important position of AJR Information's art correspondent, from where she informed and guided her regular readers for a quarter century.

Alice was a delightful person blessed with a warm gregarious personality who will be remembered with affection by her many friends at the AJR.[50]

The last sentence in the German edition was: Perhaps, with the help of this book, the memory of Liesel Rosenthal and her family, the Rosenthal wine merchants, can be brought back to Heilbronn. This has indeed happened, in January 2016 the city of Heilbronn hosted a wonderful reception for Julia Neuberger and for the book, and since then the city archives have used it to introduce pupils in local schools to the history of the Nazi regime and its victims in their city and beyond. I can only wish for a similar development in the country Liesel has made her home – and in the language that most people in this book, including its author, speak with an accent.

Notes

Introduction

1. These letters and postcards left to us are not individually referenced. In this first example I have filled in the abbreviations to make it more readable but will not do so from this point on.
2. Most of the parents' letters and postcards have been written in German and appear here in an English translation made in 2016. The mother sometimes tried to write parts of her communication in English (see, for example, the use of the word 'ready' in the following example). While it is difficult to maintain the local nuances in translation, the translator has tried his best to make these linguistic switches visible.
3. http://sounds.bl.uk/Oral-history/Jewish-Holocaust-survivors/021M-C0410X0089XX-0001V0 [27.11.2016].
4. For this type of documents – in contrast to letters detailing recent experiences – Pierre Bourdieu's 'biographical illusion' is more appropriate: imagining (and believing in) a 'life story with an inherent purpose and logical development towards fulfilment'. (Lamprecht, *Feldpost und Kriegserlebnis* (2001), 21. See Bourdieu, *Die Biographische Illusion* (1998), 76).
5. See WerkstattGeschichte 60 (2013): *Korrespondenzen*. In the editorial Ulrike Gleixner and Dorothee Wierling write that we should 'analyse the respective rules according to which correspondents express their desires and concerns in written form, in letters or other written communications'.
6. Matthews-Schlinzig/Socha, CfP, What is a letter? (2014).
7. Matthews-Schlinzig/Socha, CfP, What is a letter? (2014).
8. Häntzschel, *Der Brief – Lebenszeichen* (2013), 20.
9. Ibid.
10. Häntzschel, *Der Brief – Lebenszeichen* (2013), 27; Brinson/Kaczynski, *Fleeing from the Führer* (2011).
11. Helbich, *Tagungsbericht* (2003): 'The gaps appeared like yawning chasms. There was not one specific example of multidisciplinary, thought-provoking interpretation, or even "de-coding", both of which have been so highly praised. No attempt at a transnational comparison of letters or letter-writing culture was made. The problem of transnationality in letter writers, often mentioned in the context of emigrant letters, was only referred to in passing. There was a report on representativity, but none on its relevance. No-one discussed illness, death or religion, which play such a large role in the letters. No-one took the opportunity to carry out an emotional-historical investigation of material more suited to one than almost anything else. And no-one attempted to specifically examine the development of identity.'
12. Post/Struck, Workshop *Schreiben in die alte Heimat* (2014).
13. Schlör, *Menschen wie wir mit Koffern* (2012); see Bischoff/Komfort-Hein, *Vom Anderen Deutschland* (2012).

14 Lamprecht, *Feldpost und Kriegserlebnis*, 22; see Gestrich, *Einleitung: Sozialhistorische Biographieforschung* (1988), 5; Rosenthal, *Zur Konstitution von Generationen* (1994).
15 Bourdieu, *Sozialer Raum* (1985).
16 Saraga, *Berlin to London* (2019); Gilbert, *From Things Lost* (2017).
17 Lamprecht, *Feldpost und Kriegserlebnis*, 25.
18 Albeit in relation to German families and their relationship with Nazism; see Fetscher, *Die eigene Familie as Nazi archive* (2013); for more on the 'distinct family ethos' of Jewish families, see Gebhardt, *Das Familiengedächtnis* (1999).
19 Neuberger, speech by Baroness Julia Neuberger DBE (2006).
20 Zeichner, *Kolomea Research Group Names of Interest*: '[Halpern] is one of the most widespread Jewish names. It is derived from the city of Heilbronn in Wurttemberg, Germany, where it was first assumed about four hundred years ago. There are many variations and some are: Heilpern, Halper, Helpern, Heilbrun, Heilbronner, Heilprun, Alpron, Alpern, Galpern and Halprin.'
21 Heilbronn (Municipality): *Jüdische Geschichte/Synagogen bis 1938*. In *Alemannia Judaica*. The volume used as the basis of the website, partially revised, is happily freely available online. See Franke, *Geschichte und Schicksal der Juden in Heilbronn* (1963), online edition 2011.
22 See Schrenk, *Heilbronn um 1933* (2013).
23 Krusemarck, *Die Juden in Heilbronn* (1938), 31.

Chapter 1

1 The novel tells the story of a German who emigrates to New York and has a career as an opera singer whilst getting mixed up in numerous intrigues: 'The novel *The Career of Doris Hart* can be read as a critique of media society and mass consumption: artificiality and media prostitution.' (OCHS, *Vicki Baum* (2009)).
2 Amongst his best-known works are the silver case for the scroll containing the Declaration of Independence of the State of Israel (1948), a mezuzah for the Israeli Supreme Court and numerous ritual objects. See *Forging Ahead*, Wolpert and Gumbel (2012). The Heilbronn City Archives sent further information (email, 19.11.2013): 'The merchant Sigmund (Siegmund) Gumbel had two sons, Bruno (1905–1939?) and Heinz (1906–1992). Heinz was a steel engraving apprentice at the Bruckmann factory (D003-125) from 4.6.1923 to 24.12.1924. He later gave his profession as silversmith. [...] Heinz Gumbel emigrated to Palestine in 1936 and his parents followed in 1939. The Gumbel & Co factory closed 30.11.1938, and was succeeded by the firm Schober & Bruckmann' (probably as part of 'aryanisation', B11-374).
3 Their friendship was a lasting one; in 1964 she and her daughter Julia came to visit Jerusalem and they met up with him.
4 According to the address books, between 1917 and 1931 the family lived in the Stauffenbergstraße, number 12 on the ground floor, in a block of flats built in 1909 by Alfred Weisert. A few houses further down, at number 6, was the residence of the Eckert family, who were brewers (the brewery itself was numbers 2 and 4 on the same street) – we will discuss them in more detail towards the end of this book. The Stauffenbergstraße was renamed Innsbruckerstraße in 1938 and is one of the few streets not to have reverted back to its former name after 1945.

5   Register of rabbis in Jewish communities in the Baden-Württemberg region. In: *Alemannia Judaica*.
6   Lotte Fink worked in the sexual advice centre at the League for the Protection of Mothers in Frankfurt. See Usborne, *Ärztinnen und Geschlechteridentiät* (2002), 82.
7   For the history of Nazism in Heilbronn see Grosshans, *Das nationalsozialistische Regime* (1981); Schlösser, *Die Heilbronner NSDAP und ihre 'Führer'* (2003); Dies, *Richard Drauz, NSDAP-Kreisleiter von Heilbronn* (1997).
8   https://www.thebritishacademy.ac.uk/blog/untold-stories-jewish-women-domestic-servants-britain-escape-nazis, blogpost from 19 July 2019. She adds in her project description: 'It is hardly surprising that the refugee domestics failed to garner the same kinds of laudatory accounts that have attached themselves to the Kindertransport and to the refugee academics and scientists who were brought to the UK in the same period. It would have been difficult to claim similar uncomplicated humanitarian motives for a quid pro quo arrangement in which thousands of women were offered rescue, but only on the condition that they labour away in private homes. Nevertheless, 20,000 Jewish women were saved, and their stories provide a fascinating study of the refugee experience as well as of contemporary British society.' See also Kushner, An Alien Occupation: Jewish Refugees and Domestic Service in Britain, 1933–1948 (1991), 553–87.
9   Tony Grenville calls them 'a respected Quaker family' (Email from Anthony Grenville (25.11.2013). Julia Neuberger is doubtful, since 'one daughter, Beatrice Painter, whom I met after my mother died, assured me that they were not'.
10 There are several archives and publications on the specific role of the Quaker community in rescuing German Jews, as can be seen in the following excerpt from an email (06.02.2014) from the Birmingham Archives, though no reference to Alice Rosenthal or the Dobbs family could be found: 'Thank you for your email regarding Quaker families in Birmingham. I have spoken to our Collection Curator, Dr. Sian Roberts, who has been involved in bringing in a substantial collection of records from the Society of Friends, and has done some research in this area. Dr. Roberts has not come across any information relating to Alice Rosenthal or the family name of Dobbs […] Amongst the collection of Quaker records we received is a volume of Refugee and Alien Committee minutes dated 1938–1944 (FA Box 114).' See Oldfield, *The Role of British Women* (2004).
11 'It has been impossible to identify any historical figures who could have been the inspiration for the title figure, supposedly the daughter of a Heilbronn weapon maker. Moreover, the stories from the late Middle Ages about her are most likely an invention of the poet [Heinrich von Kleist]. […] *Katie from Heilbronn*, a theatrical box office hit in the 18th century, is therefore entirely fictional. Only after the success of the play did the imposing mediaeval building with renaissance bay windows in the market square begin calling itself Katie's House, the supposed residence of Kleist's heroine. Every year in Heilbronn two young girls are given the title of Katie of Heilbronn, and they serve as symbolic ambassadors of the city on official occasions.' https://www.heilbronn.de/info/wein_und_neckar/kaetchen/ [14.11.2014].
12 Walter Baer, also from Heilbronn, who eventually married Liesel's cousin Anne Baer.
13 For the situation of German-Jewish refugees in Birmingham, see also Zoe Josephs, *Survivors. Jewish Refugees in Birmingham, 1933–45*. Oldbury: Meridian Books 1988.
14 Benz (Ed.), *Das Exil der kleinen Leute* (1991).
15 Prinz, *Voraussetzungen jüdischer Auswanderungspolitik* (1936), 10.

16 Sahl, *Memoiren eines Moralisten* (1991), 215. The last sentence refers to a German proverb, 'Bleibe im Lande und nähre dich redlich'. See also Reiter, *Hans Sahl im Exil* (2007).
17 See Schlör, *Reisen als kulturelle Praxis* (2014).
18 There is, however, a remarkable collection of letters kept by the Berlin Senate Chancellery since 1969, stored on the top floor of the Rotes Rathaus (town hall) alongside copies of *Aktuell* magazine, regularly sent to emigrants from Berlin. It is an extraordinary treasure trove, which Gal Engelhard and I were able to scour thanks to the friendly help of Heike Kröger. Renate Steinitz has documented the expulsion of family members over the whole world in *A German-Jewish Family Scattered: The Story of One Branch of the Steinitz Family* (2008). There is also the Leo Baeck Institute in New York, London and Jerusalem (with an office in the archive of the Jewish Museum in Berlin, headed by Aubrey Pomerance), as well as the extremely impressive German-Speaking Jewry Heritage Museum in Tefen, Israel. Furthermore, there are a number of important initiatives aimed at preserving these historical documents, such as the Moses Mendelssohn Center in Potsdam in its project 'German Jewish Cultural Heritage' (see http://germanjewishculturalheritage.com/home [17.09.2014]). But many private documents such as these continue to be lost.
19 Current trends in German-Jewish historiography can be seen in the response to a conference at the Hamburg Institute for the History of German Jews, 'German-Jewish history as an object of historiography – a summary. Significance and shifting of German-Jewish history to German history', which was published by Moshe Zimmermann and Andreas Brämer in *Transversal: Journal for Jewish Studies* 14.1 (2013) with the title 'On German-Jewish Historiography'. The title makes clear that emigration was (as is so often the case) not part of the debate. Ours is a 'German history' only in a very limited sense.
20 See Paucker, Speaking English with an accent (2017).
21 Kreppel, *Wege nach Israel* (1999); Ibid., *Israels fließige Jeckes* (2002); Ibid., *Nahariyya – das Dorf der 'Jeckes'* (2005).
22 Wolf, *Das war mein Heilbronn* (1986); Ibid., *Heilbronn bittersüß* (1993).
23 Schmidinger/Schoeller, *Transit Amsterdam* (2007); Kröhnke/Würzner (Eds.), *Deutsche Literatur im Exil* (1993); Franke, *Paris – eine neue Heimat?* (2000).
24 Gregory, *Geographical Imaginations* (1994).
25 Boas, *The Shrinking World of German Jewry, 1933–1938* (1986); see also Guy Miron, The Lived Space of German Jews under the Nazi Regime (2013), Ibid., Waiting Time in the World of German Jews Under Nazi Rule (2015).
26 Franke, *Geschichte und Schicksal* (online edition), 207.
27 Ibid., 208.
28 Franke, *Geschichte und Schicksal* (online edition), 210.
29 See *Festreden* (1927), 17f.
30 Christine Hartig is working on a project called 'Changing Relationships between the Generations in Jewish Families under the Pressure from Nazi Persecution'. She wrote to me in an email (29.05.2007): 'The effects of the persecution on family relationships and the reactions of Jewish organisations to the changing nature of childhood and parenthood are key questions in my investigation. In addition to publications from Jewish organisations, testimony from Jewish families will form the majority of my sources.' The project is not yet finished, but Hartig was able to tell me in an email (9.10.2014) that 'In my investigation, once their children had emigrated, parents urged them even more strongly to behave, adapt etc. as a way in to society in exile.

In light of the persecution, however, these expectations were expressed in new, increasingly demanding ways.'

31 Anthony Grenville summarized the situation of domestic servants thus: 'Responsibility for refugee domestic servants rested with the Ministry of Labour until late 1938, when it was taken over by the Home Office; as the latter was less influenced by trade unions wishing to keep immigrant labour out of Britain, the change benefited the refugees. But the wage rates for domestics remained paltry: many refugees were paid the fixed minimum of 15 shillings per week. The task of administering the admission and allocation of refugee domestic servants passed to Bloomsbury House, where the Domestic Bureau coped as best it could; it is not fondly remembered by its former clients.' Grenville, *Refugees in Domestic Service* (2008).

32 For now this is the information I have received from Anjali Pujari, city archivist in Offenbach: Gustav Gabriel was born on 12 February 1877 in Hildesheim, in the district of Oppenheim, and his wife Johanna née Cohen was born on 5 November 1882 in Bochum. According to the 'Jewish registration file of the archive' they emigrated to Bombay on 10 October 1938, and on 18 December 1939 their Hessian (German) citizenship was revoked. 'At the moment this document was supplied' as was stated on the rear of the index card, they regained German citizenship on 30 July 1957. Their children Elisabeth and Gerhard were born on 29 August 1905 and 3 October 1907 respectively in Offenbach. Gerhard Gabriel has his own index card which states that he lived variously in Bochum and Dortmund (1926/27) as well as in Danzig and Soppot (1928), but kept returning to his family home in the Hermann-Göring-Straße – as it was known after 1933 – before leaving for Bombay on 18 October 1932.

33 Email from Roman Rosenstein (27.12.2013).
34 Email from Joachim Hahn (03.10.2012).
35 Wertheimer, Simon. In: Wertheimer family database.
36 Artist Gunther Demnig started the 'Stolpersteine' project in Berlin-Kreuzberg in 1996, the idea is to remember the victims of National Socialism by installing commemorative brass plaques in the pavement in front of their last address of choice; see http://www.stolpersteine.eu/en/home/ [03.03.2020].
37 For a detailed and critical perspective on the British Jewish refugee aid organizations, see London, Jewish Refugees, Anglo-Jewry and British Government Policy, 1930–1940 (1990), 163–90.
38 Shatzkes/Sherman, *Otto M Schiff* (2009).
39 *Otto Schiff Dies in London* (1952).
40 Springer, *How We Did It*.
41 Lowenthal, *Bloomsbury House* (1986), 267.
42 Lowenthal, *Bloomsbury House* (1986), 267.
43 Lowenthal, *Bloomsbury House* (1986), 270.
44 See Reitmann, *Die Allee in Heilbronn* (1971).
45 Goldberg, *Wie der Wein in Mitteleuropa jüdisch wurde* (2014), 229. See Keil/Zillien, *Der deutsche Wein 1930 bis 1945* (2010).
46 Goldberg, *Wie der Wein in Mitteleuropa Jüdisch wurde*, 230.
47 Heuss, *Weinbau und Weingärtnerstand in Heilbronn a. N.* (2009).
48 Goldberg, *Wie der Wein in Mitteleuropa jüdisch wurde*, 234.
49 Goldberg, *Wie der Wein in Mitteleuropa jüdisch wurde*, 238.
50 Goldberg, *Wie der Wein in Mitteleuropa jüdisch wurde*, 238.

51 Fischer, *Vertraute Handelspartner – geächtete Handelspartner* (2012).
52 Email from Klaus Fischer (17.08.2013).
53 Ibid.
54 E.G.L., *Jews in the German Wine Trade* (1965), 11. Thanks to Tony Kushner for discovering this source and to Tony Grenville for identifying the author: 'He was one of the three founding editors of the journal AJR Information, but only very briefly, as he went back to Germany with one of the Jewish Relief Units in 1946.' (Email from 27.12.2014).
55 *Schatzki, Walter*, in: *Frankfurter Biographie: Personengeschichtliches Lexikon*, vol. 2: M-Z. (1996), 263. For Schatzki's work in Frankfurt, see Fischer, *Der Sortimentsbuchhandel* (2012), 360; see also Rosenthal, *Continental Emigré Booksellers* (1986).
56 Jewish Migration: Aliens Act. In: Jewish Virtual Library.
57 See the text of the Aliens Restriction (Amendment) Act 1919 in the National Archives.
58 Smith, Foley. *The Spy Who Saved 10,000 Jews* (1999).
59 Francis Foley, *Great Britain. The Righteous among the Nations*. Yad Vashem. The documentation on Foley's work at the British embassy in Berlin can be found in: Frank Foley, *Documents from the British Archives*.
60 See *London: Whitehall and the Jews, 1933-1948* (2001), Kusher, *An Alien Occupation* (1991), Cacciottolo, *Nazi Persecution Saw Jews Flee abroad as Servants* (2012).
61 Writer Thaddäus Troll [Hans Bayer, 1914-1980], whose role as a war correspondent has recently been disputed, is quoted as saying: 'The most important chapter for Swabians, their things. If I give something away I don't have it any more. Their things, that is their earthly possessions, Swabians' belongings they hang on to for dear life. Swabians work to own things, but in general are incapable of enjoying them when they get hold of them. They soak up money like a sponge without spending it, without exchanging it for things which make life worth living. The poet Otto Rombach once asked a woman when she sighed "We won the lottery!" what she planned to do with the money. "Ha, keep it!" she answered. Keep it, enjoying the sense of owning it, counting their money – that's more pleasure than money can buy when they actually spend it.' (Deutschlandradio Kultur). See Bausinger, *Die bessere Hälfte* (2002).
62 Systematic research has not yet been carried out on the role of Switzerland as an intermediate stopping point and as shelter for emigrants, from where they could send letters and money wherever they liked. A conference at the University of Berne in February 2015 focused on the topic of 'Exile. Asylum. Diaspora. The role of Switzerland in the 20th century.' See also Pritzker-Ehrlich, *Jüdisches Emigrantenlos 1938/39 und die Schweiz* (1998).
63 The topic of 'Marriage and family in the Jewish community' is far too complex to be discussed here. A readable overview can be found in *The Marriage Issue* (Spring 2013).
64 José C Moya and Adam McKeown point to the key role family networks have in spreading information, rules of behaviour and habits in migration processes. Moya/McKeown, *World Migration in the Long Twentieth Century* (2010), 30.
65 Sluzki, *Migration and Family Conflict* (1979), 380.
66 Sluzki, *Migration and Family Conflict* (1979), 382.
67 Sluzki, *Migration and Family Conflict* (1979), 386.
68 Sluzki, *Migration and Family Conflict* (1979), 388.

69　The organization founded by Dorothy Buxton was principally concerned with rescuing Jewish children from Nazi Germany and took part in preparing the 'Kindertransports', on which around 10,000 children from Germany, Austria, Czechoslovakia and Poland came to Britain after 10 November 1938. The Kindertransports have become another focus of current academic research. See for instance the articles by Jennifer Craig-Norton and Tony Kushner on the 'Kindertransport Conference' at the Leo Baeck Institute in London (2013).

70　Lamprecht, *Feldpost und Kriegserlebnis*, 37.

Chapter 2

1　Translloy India PVT LTD. Business profile.

2　Institutions, Monuments & Structures in India Contributed to by the Jews. Jews of India.

3　World ORT News. *ORT India a Year on from the Mumbai Massacre*, 09.12.2009. Hugo Gabriel Gryn (25 June 1930–18 August 1996) was a British Reform rabbi, 'probably the most beloved rabbi in Great Britain' (Albert Friedlander). Born Berehovo in Carpathian Ruthenia, he survived the Holocaust, as did his mother, whereas his brother was murdered in Auschwitz and his father died a few days after he and Hugo had been liberated from Gunskirchen, a sub-camp of Mauthausen, in May 1945. Gryn moved to the UK in 1946 and later trained as a rabbi in America after which he spent several years in Bombay and New York before finally moving to London in 1964, where he served in one of the largest congregations in Europe, the West London Synagogue, initially as assistant rabbi and later as senior rabbi, for thirty-two years. After his death, his daughter Naomi Gryn edited his autobiography, *Chasing Shadows*.

4　David Gabriel adds: My sister Miriam and I knew nothing at all about Liesel. That is not until we heard from Prof Joachim Schlör and the letters my Father, Gerhard Gabriel apparently wrote from 1935 onwards to her. From the translations provided by Prof Schlör of letters my Father and his own Parents had written to Liesel, it is clear they thought highly of her. In late 1937 (or maybe it was early 1938) when life for Jews in Germany got ever more intolerable, my Father brought his parents out to India. Reading the letters that Liesel's Parents had sent to her it appears as though Liesel had been put under tremendous pressure, by her own parents, to go out to Bombay and marry Gerhard. In early 1938 she did go to Bombay, but only for a very short time. What then made her finally decide against making a life with Gerhard in Bombay is something we are unlikely ever to find out more about. But whatever her reasons, she clearly upped and left quite abruptly. From the translations of various letters that our father had written to Liesel (letters that she never threw away) I am satisfied that throughout, our father Gerhard Gabriel had acted as a perfect and honourable gentleman towards her. Later in 1938 (I am not sure when) our Father married a German Jewess by the name of Helga. They had no children. And when that marriage ended, he married our Mother, Vera Levin, in 1945 and together they first had a baby girl, Miriam in 1946 (who lives in Israel) and then a baby boy, David in 1948 (who lives in London).

5　According to the Jewish registration index in the Offenbach City Archives, Gerhard Ludwig Gabriel was born on 3 October 1907 in Offenbach as the son of Gustav Gabriel, teacher, and his wife Johanna (née Cohen). In 1926 he was registered as living in Bochum, in 1927 in Dortmund, and in 1928 in Danzig and Soppot. By the end of the same year he was living in London, and on 18 October 1932 he finally left for Bombay. My thanks go to city archivist Anjali Poujari for sending me the index files (email from 9 June 2015).

6 Hermine was to write on 29 May 1938: 'Dear Liesel, you write that you don't love Gerhard, tell me, isn't it nicer to know the man loves you?'
7 On the importance of books and libraries in German-Jewish emigration, see Jessen, *Vergangenheiten haben ihr eigenes Beharrungsvermögen* (2012).
8 This was how the Indian telegram service wrote it. The last section should of course have read 'Bangemachen gilt nicht, Kuss Gerhard' ('No need to be afraid, kisses, Gerhard').
9 More detailed information on individual developments can be found at *Chronologie des Holocaust, 1938*.

Chapter 3

1 On the appeasement policy see Faber, *Munich* (2009). Information on the children from the Basque Country who were taken in, particularly in Southampton, can be found on the website BasqueChildren.org.
2 Julia Neuberger recalls: 'When my father wanted to make me feel badly, he would always say "You remind me of my mother." My grandmother, Anna Schwab, was a formidable character. We have a portrait of her in our drawing room, sitting behind a desk at Bloomsbury House, surrounded by people, painted by Rose Henriques. She chaired the welfare committee of the Refugee Committee in the 1930s, and worked tirelessly to get more refugees into the UK, fighting constantly with the Home Office, as she found lodgings, work, and helped desperate people get their families out where possible. But she could be impossible, and was uncompromising in her belief that social justice, making the world a fairer place, was more important than anything else. She was also a very orthodox Jew, unlike me. I believe my grandmother's ruling passion for social justice, helping the disadvantaged, fighting the authorities to get what is right, is absolutely what Judaism – all of Judaism – is about.' Neuberger, *Message of Reform Judaism* (2012).
3 LSE [London School of Economics] History.
4 On Aby Warburg's life and work see Treml/Flach/Schneider (Eds.), *Warburgs Denkraum* (2014). Further information on the Institute can be found on the website of the Warburg Institute in London.
5 See Gombrich, *Gertrud Bing, 1892–1964* (1965), 1–3.
6 See Neter, *Die jüdische Wohlfahrtspflege in Mannheim im Jahre 1929/30* (1930). Letters to Mrs Neter can be found in the Memoir Collection at the Leo Baeck Institute in New York – still a largely neglected resource.
7 This could refer to Dorothy Evelyn Stanley, who visited Heilbronn in September 1984. She was born Dorothea Peiser in Nuremberg in 1909 and did an apprenticeship at the Stritter bookshop in Heilbronn.
8 See Erel (Ed.), *Jeckes Erzählen* (2004).
9 In a review of Per Leo's *Flut und Boden* (Stuttgart: Klett-Cotta, 2014) Christoph Schröder speaks of 'that hackneyed idea everyone fears in family stories: it is the box full of your grandfather's books and personal documents which the grandchildren

living in the family home dig out from behind the curtain'. I am not sure what exactly 'everyone' fears here. Schröder, *Gutes Haus, schiefe Bahn, SS-Karriere* (24.02.2014).

10 My search for information on Liesel's time at Marks & Spencer was unsuccessful. Hannah Jenkinson, who works at the company archives, wrote to me in an email on 19 September 2012: 'Thank you for your enquiry to the M&S Company Archive. Unfortunately the Archive does not hold employee personnel records. However, I have carried out a search of our collection in the chance that we may have letters or photographs relating to Alice (Liesel) Rosenthal, but I'm afraid I haven't found any records.'

11 Email from Julia Neuberger (25.05.2013).

12 Franke, *Geschichte und Schicksal*, Online edition, 121–3.

13 Flora Solomon improved staff conditions at Marks and Spencer. Liesel knew her as she helped refugee children in the 1930s. She was the mother of Peter Benenson, founder of Amnesty International.

14 Hannah Arendt, according to the publicity material for a new volume of letters, 'was a "genius for friendship" (Hans Jonas) and possessed a gift for love. In her captivating letters we get to know not just the private side of this great thinker, but also the inspiring power of friendship'. Arendt, *Wahrheit gibt es nur zu zweien* (2013).

15 I could not find any information about this exchange programme in the letters, but Tony Kushner made me aware of the work of the Inter-Aid Committee which brought children from the continent to Britain from 1936 on.

16 I was unable to find out anything about this school. Marcus Roberts has written on the wider history of Jewish boarding schools and hotels in Brighton and Hove that 'Jewish schooling has been historically important in Brighton and Hove and by the 1930s Brighton and Hove and its environs may be considered to be perhaps the centre for Jewish education in the country. There have been a number of both Jewish schools and private Jewish boarding schools, in Brighton, starting with Emanuel Hyam Cohen's school, which operated from *c.* 1792 to 1816.' Roberts, *National Anglo-Jewish Heritage Trail*.

17 On the history and workings of the committee see the files of the German Jewish Aid Committee: General Situation and Individual Cases. London Metropolitan Archives, Board of Deputies of British Jews, Ref.: ACC/3121/E/03/533.

Chapter 4

1 A documentary to mark '40 Years since the "Reichskristallnacht" in Heilbronn' was my first bit of political activity as a schoolboy at the Justinus-Kerner grammar school in Weinsberg in 1978. Under the direction of our history teacher, Ulrich Maier, we collected, exhibited and published documents and recollections of the events of that night. The testimony of communist Walter Vielhauer, who explained in great detail how the 'Aryanization', which we knew about in theory, was a way for some 'good' Heilbronn families to profit mercilessly from others, made a particular impression on us.

2 Jacobi, *Mitbürger waren Täter und Opfer* (07.11.2008). See Schrenk, *Die Chronologie der sogenannten 'Reichskristallnacht' in Heilbronn* (1992).

3 Franke, *Geschichte und Shicksal*, Online edition, 132. Several people were charged after the November pogrom of 1938. 'In total three people were convicted.

In Landauer's case a local district commander was sentenced to one year's imprisonment for trespass and a group leader was sentenced to two years' imprisonment (minus four months' investigative custody) for trespass and criminal assault; he died before he could begin his sentence. In Henle's and Rosenthal's case another district commander was sentenced to ten months' imprisonment for trespass.'

4   Franke, *Geschichte und Schicksal*, Online edition, 130.
5   Entry Heimann, Dr Harry, in: *Biographisches Handbuch der Rabbiner, Part 23: Die Rabbiner im Deutschen Reich 1871–1945* (2009), 273.
6   Franke, *Geschichte und Shicksal*, Online edition, 37.
7   Franke, *Geschichte und Shicksal*, Online edition, 141.
8   Fink, *The Ninth Life* (1938, manuscript).
9   Talk given on Radio 2GB, October 1939 (as reference in *The Ninth Life*).
10 It would be useful to investigate more thoroughly the role of intermediaries like Jakob Wertheimer, who played an important role in the transnational support network of refugees by using their Swiss citizenship to help relatives and friends with money, guarantees and hospitality. Together with Kristina Schulz from the University of Bern I organized a conference on the topic of 'Exile – Asylum – Diaspora. The role of Switzerland in the twentieth century' (February 2015).
11 Email from Julia Neuberger (14.06.2013).
12 This Lincoln House had witnessed a bit of world history: 'When Haile Selassie was obliged to leave Ethiopia in 1936, one of the first places he stayed was at Lincoln House, on Parkside, Wimbledon Common. His hosts were Sir Richard Seligman, a leading metallurgist and entrepreneur, and his wife Hilda, a sculptor and active campaigner against British appeasement of the Italian invasion. During his stay, the Emperor sat for a bust done by Hilda, which stood for many years in Cannizaro Park, just across Wimbledon Common.' Knight, *Haile Selassie Returns to Wimbledon*.
13 Franke, *Geschichte und Schicksal*, Online edition, 306.
14 Franke, *Geschichte und Schicksal*, Online edition, 318.
15 Email from Julia Neuberger (14.06.2013).
16 *Heilbronn (Stadtkreis). Jüdische Geschichte/Synagogen bis 1938*. In: *Alemannia Judaica*.
17 Lilla Eisig refers to what was known as the 'Small ones' scheme, allowing entry to Britain if one had an onward permit to elsewhere. Ludwig's and Hermine's passports were signed by Arthur Dowden; this could explain the importance of the Uruguay permission.
18 Franke, *Geschichte und Schicksal*, Online edition, 318.
19 I grew up in Eschenau. In the village there was a castle, which had belonged to author and alchemist Alexander von Bernus, where one of my classmates lived with her family. Neighbours sometimes spoke of what had happened there 'in the war', but it was only in 2013 that an exhibition – held in the former synagogue in neighbouring Affaltrach – together with a carefully edited book accompanying it provided conclusive answers. Bernus rented the castle out to Eschenau Council and the City of Stuttgart paid for it to be converted into a 'provisional home for the elderly'. The Jewish Cultural Association of Württemberg had to pay the council 10,000 Reichsmarks, of which Bernus received half, and the Reich Security Office in Berlin approved the whole process. More than two-thirds of the ninety-three residents of the home were women; most came from Stuttgart, others from Heilbronn, Freudental and many other places in Württemberg. Twelve people died at Eschenau,

and all the others were deported to Theresienstadt. See Ritter/Ulmer, *Das jüdische Zwangsaltersheim Eschenau* (2013).

20 Schmidt, *Wege ins rettende Exil*. He goes on: 'The country was one of the few remaining states which offered entry and residence permits for Jews. As a rule emigrants came over by ship straight to Montevideo, either from German ports or from intermediate countries like Italy, France, Belgium, the Netherlands, Spain and Portugal. Some emigrants also came via Argentina and Brazil. For others Uruguay was the starting point for a further journey to other South American countries. During the Second World War fewer and fewer German-speaking Jews managed to reach Uruguay.' See Wegner, *Exil in Uruguay 1933–1945* (2013).

21 Florsheim Family. In: Loeb family tree. On the subject of his book see Meen, *Finding Julius Kahn*: 'September 6, 2010 was the 70th anniversary of the landing of HMT Dunera in Sydney Harbour, Australia. The ship carried close to 2000 Jewish refugees of Nazi oppression from Germany and Austria, plus about 500 German Prisoners of War and Italians. Owing to the appalling treatment of the refugees on the 8-week voyage from England, this voyage is now known as The Dunera Scandal.'

22 Minni Stern. In: Central Database of Shoah Victims' Names.

23 Jordan/Leff/Schlör, *Jewish Migration and the Archive* (2014), 5.

24 The US census of 1940 lists Kurt Jeselson: First Name: Kurt, Middle Name: E., Last Name: Jeselson, Age at Time of Census: 28, Gender: Male, Race: White, Ethnicity: American, Est. Birth Year: 1912, Birth Location: Germany, Residence: Assembly District 1, Richmond, New York City, Richmond, NY, Relationship to Household: Head, Other People in Household: Karl Jeselson, 65 years, male; Sidonia Jeselson, 49 years, female; Lotte Jeselson, 25 years, female; William Katz, 81 years, male; Jenny Katz, 74 years, female.

25 Max Samuel-Haus: *Wir über uns*.

26 Email from 23 December 2016.

27 Redmond Till, *Zuviel Hochdeutsch auf der Zürcher Bahnhofstraße?* (1985); Larsen, *Die Welt der Gabriele Tergit* (1987), 119ff. (According to the introduction, Kurt Maschler inspired Larsen to write this book).

28 Website of the Kurt Maschler Award.

29 See, for example, the notes on the S Frankfurt exchange control office for the taking of personal effects by Jewish emigrants in 1939.

30 Schlör, *Means of Transport and Storage* (2014).

31 The first edition of the online journal *Mobile Cultural Studies* was published on this topic – 'The journey by ship as a transitional experience in migration' – in July 2015. David Jünger dedicated a chapter of his dissertation 'Before the year of destiny. Questions of Jewish emigration in Nazi Germany 1933–1938' to journeys by ship; Björn Siegel is working on a project 'A Maritime Place of Resignation or Hope? Individual Experiences of Journeys to/from Palestine during the Holocaust' and has also published *The Maiden Voyage of the 'Tel Aviv' to Palestine in 1935* (*DieJungfernfahrt der 'Tel Aviv' nach Palästina im Jahre 1935*) (2014) on this topic.

32 Alroey, *Bureaucracy, Agents and Swindlers* (2003); Ibid., *Aliya to Early Twentieth Century* (2002).

33 Adler-Rudel, *Jüdische Selbsthilfe unter dem Nazi-Regime 1933–1939* (1974), 86ff; PHILO-Atlas. *Handbuch für die jüdische Auswanderung* (1938); Jünger, *Vor dem Entscheidungsjahr* (2013).

34 See Exilforschung. Ein internationales Jahrbuch 31 (2013): *Dinge des Exils*.

35 Schlör, *'Solange wir an Bord waren, hatten wir eine Heimat.'* (2014).

36 Hirche, *Die jüdische Wanderung und ihre Schwierigkeiten* (1939), 6-7.
37 Hirche, *Die jüdische Wanderung und ihre Schwierigkeiten* (1939), 7.
38 Hirche, *Die jüdische Wanderung und ihre Schwierigkeiten* (1939), 7.
39 Hirche, *Die jüdische Wanderung und ihre Schwierigkeiten* (1939); on Evian see Tomaszewski, *Die Asyl-Konferenz von Evian-les-Bains* (2002) and the online exhibition www.evian1938.de
40 Hirche, *Die jüdische Wanderung und ihre Schwierigkeiten* (1939), 7.
41 See Broder/Geisel, *Premiere und Pogrom* (1992).
42 See Benz, *Auswandern aus Deutschland* (1998), 164.
43 The 'Living Online Museum' of the German Historical Museum provides a good overview of this.
44 To illustrate the problems of translation, I quote the German original here: 'Nun wären wir in einem Teil soweit, aber der Andere ist schwierig. Nun höre lb. Lisel, bis jetzt konnte noch gar nichts wegkriegen von unserem Mobil[i]ar. Ich verschenke sehr viel, aber der l. Papa ist der Meinung, Bücherschrank & Schreibtisch zu behalten. Sag mal lb. Lisel, könntest evtl. Du etw. von den herrl. Möbeln bei Dir stellen? Ich habe die Absicht das Schlafzimmer mitzunehmen, das Büfett, das wir in zwei Kommoden zerteilten, Tisch & Stühle, dann das kleine Schränkchen v. Salon & die schöne Garnitur. Jetzt ist der springende Punkt das Klavier. Ein jeder ratet mir das fabelhafte Stück zu behalten & lb. Papa kann sich absolut nicht entschließen das Prachtstück so billig herzugeben, unterstützt vom Klavierstimmer den er deshalb letzte Woche bestellte. […] Nun habe auch den Waschtisch als Kommode schon machen lassen & da wir uns keine Couch noch Bettstellen anschaffen wollten, so wären doch die Bettladen, wenn Ihr bei uns wohnen wolltet, am Platze, besonders da Eure Betten & Matrazen habe. […] Sage bitte umgehend Bescheid, möchtest Du den reizenden Spieltisch behalten? Dafür hätte Liebhaber für 4 RM: Er stand im Speisezimmer & ist sehr schön. Heute war in Stuttgart betr. Besprechung weg. Lift. Alles kann noch lange dauern.'
45 I contacted the Kirchhausen family in America and received the following answer: 'I have no information about the Rosenthal family since I was but 6 years old when I was placed on the Kindertransport (July 1939). I am reasonably sure that my parents would have known the family since my father was also a businessman and well known in the Heilbronn community. He and my mother subsequently got visas for the U.S. and managed to leave in May 1941. My two sisters (one of whom is deceased and the other 89 years old with memory problems) might also have known the Rosenthal family, particularly their daughter. I am sorry not to be of further help. Best regards, Martin Kirchhausen.' (Email from Martin Kirchhausen, 18.08.2013).
46 Selling a business – 'Welfare office' – Emigration 1941. As told by Julius Kirchhausen, Baltimore, USA, in Franke, *Geschichte und Schicksal*, Online edition, 256-60.
47 Schlör, *Endlich im Gelobten Land?* (2003); Ibid., *Dinge der Emigration* (2005).
48 Brückner, *Dingbedeutung und Materialwertigkeit* (1995).
49 But see recent work, for example, Moser/Steidl (Eds.), *Dinge auf Reisen* (2009).
50 Csikszentmihalyi/Rochberg-Halton, *Meaning of Things* (1981), 308.
51 Bentham, *The Principles of Morals and Legislation* (1907) [First edition 1780], 111.
52 Améry, *Wieviel Heimat braucht der Mensch?* (1966), 96.
53 Bischoff/Schlör, *Dinge des Exils* (2013), 15; Schlör, *Mesussot entfernen – Türschilder entfernen* (2006).
54 Kerr, *When Hitler Stole the Pink Rabbit* (1974), 23-4. Doerte Bischoff interprets these scenes: 'While on the one hand a home – no matter the territorial or political context

– can materialise in the objects rescued for exile, the objects torn from their context will always be evidence of alienation and loss. Similarly, the lost objects, as long as they continue to be objects of desire and memory, create a special relationship to things which transcends a simple understanding of material ownership. As many texts suggest, when displacement is experienced person-object relationships come to the fore, along with their relativity, and that means that both the contingency and the materiality of what is accepted as home, what is taken for granted, can be felt. If exile can be described as a condition which demands or enables a particular perception of objects, then objects frequently become key objects of reflection for emigrants, who recognise and reflect their own experience of being discarded and of being completely cast adrift in the mobile nature of the objects' (Bischoff/Schlör, *Dinge des Exils*, 15).

55 On the motivation of those who wanted to 'stay', see Alenfeld, *Warum seid Ihr nicht ausgewandert?* (2007) as well as the lovely obituary to Irène Alenfeld by Keller: *Irène Alenfeld (geb. 1933)* (14.02.2014).
56 Email from Julia Neuberger (09.10.2013).
57 Pause for Thought. With Baroness Julia Neuberger, Senior Rabbi at the West London Synagogue.

Chapter 5

1 Berghahn, *Continental Britons* (1988).
2 Belsize Square synagogue website; see also Godfrey, *Three Rabbis in a Vicarage* (2005). Until a few years ago members of Club 1943, an expressly non-socialist society of culturally active emigrants, held their meetings in rooms at the synagogue. The German-language library was curated by Henry Kuttner.
3 See *The Yearbook of the Research Centre for German and Austrian Exile Studies 3* (2001).
4 Schwab, *In Memoriam – Mrs. Anna Schwab*. In *AJR Information*, May 1963, 9.
5 Reiter, *Refugee Organizations in Britain 1933–1945* (2008). For further Research Centre publications, see the Exile Centre Publications website.
6 Bollauf, *Dienstboten Emigration. Wie jüdische Frauen aus Österreich und Deutschland nach England flüchten konnten.* (2009), 187–90.
7 I thank Hannah-Lotte Lund, who read the manuscript with great care and a keen critical eye, for this lovely turn of phrase.
8 Affaltrach, neighbouring Eschenau, was one of the 'Jewish villages in Württemberg' which my tutor Utz Jeggle examined in his dissertation in 1969 (Jeggle, *Judendörfer in Württemberg*, 1999). For the history of the Jews in Affaltrach, see the following entry in Alemannia Judaica, which also reveals that Ernst Selz and his wife Civie were unable to 'get out': 'Between 1941 and 1943 the last six Jewish residents were deported, including Hugo Levi and his wife as well as Ernst Selz and his wife Civie. Ernst Selz was a highly decorated sergeant from the First World War.' (*Affaltrach (Obersulm District, Heilbronn Region)*. In: Alemannia Judaica). The former synagogue was restored in the late 1980s and became a memorial. See *Feierstunde 1988* (1989).
9 'In 1919 Basil and Rose Henriques started the St Georges Jewish Settlement in Betts Street. They lived on the premises and ran the clubs there. They were affectionately

known as The Gaffer and The Missus. The clubs were not just social. They were educational, and taught sports, acting, ballet, physical education, First Aid, etc. They helped to prepare the boys and girls to enter into the British way of life and so helped them in eventually seeking careers. At the same time they gave them a modern outlook upon Judaism and their Jewish heritage. [...] During the 2nd World War 600 old boys and girls served in the British forces.' (The Oxford and St. George's Clubs website).
10 Following Horkheimer's invitation, Adorno and his wife moved to the United States in February 1938. They rented an apartment at 290 Riverside Drive, not far from Columbia University, which had provided a building for the Institute for Social Research. The couple set up home with the furniture they had shipped from Germany. See Müller-Doohm, *Adorno* (2003), 369ff.
11 Noah Isenberg writes: 'As of yet, now 8 years into my post at the New School, I've never encountered Hermann Igersheimer's name.' (Email from Noah Isenberg, 18.09.2012).
12 Journal of Jewish Studies, vol. LXVIII, no. 2, Autumn 2017, 436–8.
13 Franke, *Geschichte und Schicksal*, online edition, 115.
14 Franke, *Geschichte und Schicksal*, online edition, 87.
15 Katell Brestic and Emilie Oleron-Evans organized a conference in November 2013 in Paris where these questions were discussed: 'Partir pour mieux rester? L'exil allemand du XIXè siècle à 1945 au prisme du transnational Journée d'études internationale' ('Leaving and staying at the same time: German exiles from the 19th century to 1945 from a transnational perspective').
16 Bindernagel et al., conference report, *Rethinking the 'Auslandsdeutsche'* (19.10.2013).
17 Ibid.
18 Dwork/van Pelt, *Flight from the Reich* (2009), XIII.
19 Fischer-Defoy, *Marlene Dietrich Addresbuch* (2003); Ibid., *Heinrich Mann* (2006); Ibid., *Walter Benjamin* (2006); Ibid., *Hannah Arendt* (2007); see also Schlögel, *Im Raume lesen wir die Zeit* (2003), 329–46.
20 Zuckerkandl, *Österreich intim* (1988), 12–13.
21 Clavin, *Defining Transnationalism* (2005), 422.
22 Lowenthal, *Bloomsbury House*, 278–9.
23 Herzog, *Meine Lebenswege* (2013), 156.
24 Lowenthal, *Bloomsbury House*, 277.
25 Grenville, *Jewish Refugees from Nazi Germany and Austria in Britain* (2009); Kushner, *Remembering Refugees* (2006); cf. also London, *Whitehall and the Jews, 1933–1948* (2001).
26 See Dove (Ed.), *Totally un-English?* (2005).
27 The Manx National Heritage Society has put together a collection of sources on the policy of internment: *Internment during World Wars 1 & 2: The Isle of Man's role*. Warth Mills was the most notorious of the temporary internment sites, a disused factory near Bury which was rat infested.
28 Gloscat Home Front: *Life in the London Blitz*. BBC History website.
29 Richards, *The Blitz*.
30 Lowenthal, *Bloomsbury House*, 275.
31 See *Die Programme des Lehrhauses*. In: *Der Jude* 7.2 (1923), 121.
32 Category 'C' stood for 'no security risk' and applied to 64,000 people, of whom around 55,000 had fled Nazi persecution. See *WW2 People's War, Fact File: Civilian Internment 1939–1945*.

33 Heilbronn City Archives, Foreign Heilbronners Section (*Bestand Auslandsheilbronner*), B021: Victor, Max.
34 Max Victor: *Die Juden in Heilbronn und unsere Geschichte bis 1941*. Manuscript, March 1984. In: Heilbronn City Archives, Foreign Heilbronners Section (*Bestand Auslandsheilbronner*), B021-42.
35 Klaus Jetz writes in a review of the 2006 exhibition 'Home and Exile' at the Jewish Museum in Berlin: 'The Dominican Republic played a particularly important role. Dictator Trujillo announced at the Évian Refugee Conference in 1938 that his country was prepared to accept 50,000 to 100,000 European Jews. By the outbreak of war, however, only 500 people had reached the Caribbean island. Hans-Ulrich Dillmann […] traces […] the problems pianists from Vienna, drapers from Darmstadt and scientists from Berlin had dealing with climate of northern Dominica, with its heat and aridity.' (Jetz, *Zuflucht in Lateinamerika* (2006/2007); see also Kaplan, *Zuflucht in der Karibik* (2010), Newman, *Nearly the New World* (2019).
36 Schwab, Walter Manfred Moshe, The Williams Family Tree website.
37 Medoff, *How America First Learned of the Holocaust* (11.06.2012).
38 *Who coined the term Holocaust to refer to the Nazi 'final solution' for the Jewish people?* English Language & Usage Stack Exchange website.
39 See Rohrwasser, *Der Stalinismus und die Renegaten* (1991). For Koestler's Jewishness and his attitude towards Zionism, see Buckard, *Arthur Koestler* (2004).
40 In 2001 Routledge published *Judaism, Philosophy, Culture: Selected Studies* by EIJ Rosenthal, with an introduction by Oliver Leaman.
41 Email from Margarita Munk (31.12.2013).
42 See Bill Williams, Jews and other foreigners. Manchester and the rescue of victims of European fascism, 1933-1940. Manchester: Manchester University Press 2013.
43 While writing this I saw the news of Thomas's death in *The Guardian*. Ion Trewin writes: 'In his prime, with his coloured shirts, red braces, bright bow ties and big cigars, there were few more flamboyant London publishers than Tom Rosenthal, who has died aged 78. […] Rosenthal was born in London, the son of Erwin and Elisabeth Rosenthal, who had fled Germany when Hitler came to power. The Rosenthals lived first in a suburb of Manchester and later in Cambridge, where Erwin became a reader in oriental studies. […] Thomas Gabriel Rosenthal, publisher and writer, born 16 July 1935; died 3 January 2014.' (Trewin, Tom Rosenthal obituary, 06.01.2014).
44 'Georg Schwarzenberger was born in Heilbronn on 20 May 1908. After studying law he gained his PhD in 1930. As a member of the SPD he was energetic in his opposition to the Nazi party in the elections of 1932/33. In December 1933 he was dismissed from his traineeship as a lawyer on racial and political grounds. In 1934 he emigrated to Great Britain. From 1938 to 1975 he worked at University College London, where in 1962 he became Professor of Human Rights. His best-known works on human rights are *Power Politics* (1941) and the four-volume treatise *International Law* (1945-1986). After the Second World War Schwarzenberger travelled to Germany on numerous occasions, including visiting Heilbronn. He died near London on 20 September 1991.' *Georg Schwarzenberger 1908-1991*, Heilbronn City Archives website. See also Steinle, *Völkerrecht und Machtpolitik* (2002).
45 The Society for Exile Research's working group 'Women in Exile' organized a conference on the subject of wartime exile in cooperation with the Erich Maria Remarque Peace Centre in Osnabrück on 27-29 March 2015. 'Discourses on war, peace and pacifism are seen in a new light when people are driven out of a

totalitarian society. And the front lines move again when this country of origin wages war on the countries which had provided shelter up to that point. […] For many living in exile a new phase of uncertainty, of being torn apart and of ever greater isolation from acquaintances, friends and family began. In the countries which had so far offered them refuge they were now declared "enemy aliens". […] The wish for Nazism to be destroyed was accompanied by fears that their former homeland would be destroyed. For those persecuted by Hitler's regime the end of the war represented a turning point, but did it also mean an end to their exile? […] What material need and pangs of conscience did those in exile experience as a result of the collapse of the Third Reich, and what considerations were involved in their decision to stay in their country of exile or to re-emigrate to Germany?' (Häntzschel/Hansen-Schaberg/Schneider, CfP, *Exil im Krieg (1939–1945)* (25.02.2014).

Chapter 6

1. Heigold, *Der 4. Dezember 1944 als Unterrichtsthema.*
2. *Der Luftangriff auf Heilbronn 1944.* Heilbronn City Archives Website.
3. In her letters, Lotte Fink frequently talked about her book *The Child and Sex*, 'a book for all parents who have the moral and physical well-being of their children at heart' as it is described in the blurb. It was published by Angus & Robertson in Sydney in 1944 and can still be found in second-hand bookshops. See Wyndham, *Norman Haire and the Study of Sex* (2012), 311.
4. My colleague Suzanne Dorothy Rutland in Sydney wrote to me: 'Dr Lotte Fink was a well-known Jewish personality in Sydney who was very active in the Jewish community. I have written about her in my history of the NSW Jewish Board of Deputies. […] Dr Fink, a medical practitioner who left Germany in 1938 was unable to obtain registration in Australia and worked in the family planning field with Ruby Rich, helping to educate women about population control. She was active in the Women's International Zionist Organisation and chairman of the Overseas Jewry Committee of the New South Wales Jewish Board of Deputies till her death in 1960.' (email from 22.12.2014).
5. *The Liberation.* Bergen-Belsen Foundation website. See also Cesarani/Kushner et al. (Eds.), *Belsen in History and Memory* (1997).
6. This could refer to Karl Wilhelm Erik August Nölting (1892–1953), a social democrat politician who since 1923 had worked at the Frankfurt Akademie der Arbeit. He had made a living for himself in Nazi Germany as an author and became politically active again after 1945, though not in Hesse – he became North Rhine-Westphalia's first Economics Minister.
7. http://www.jewage.org/wiki/he/Article:Julia_Neuberger,_Baroness_Neuberger_-_Biography [28.12.2014].
8. In 1938 a group of thirty-five families from Rexingen, in Württemberg, had emigrated to Palestine and founded the medium-size settlement of Shavei Zion under the leadership of Manfred Scheuer, a lawyer from Heilbronn. See Högerle/Kohlmann/Staudacher (Eds.), *Ort der Zuflucht und Verheißung* (2008).
9. On 8 March 1961 Moritz Pfeil wrote an article in *Der Spiegel* entitled 'A Present We Have Not Come to Terms With': 'According to future CSU Chairman, would-be

chancellor and former National Socialist Motor Corps man Franz-Josef Strauss, we should be allowed to ask [Willy] Brandt what he did for twelve years outside Germany, "as we know what we did inside Germany"'.

10   'When Momik was still a child he often played with a toy his aunt and uncle had given him: a glass ball which contained a farmer with a "lovely, sad face" and "a mouth open as if he were screaming". When he shook the ball it began to snow. One day, however, he accidentally smashed it to pieces, freeing the farmer. Perhaps this was the beginning of his resistance to the silence, the no touching rule, which people from the country they called "there" had imposed on their past as they wanted to hide their wounds from their children, the "new Jews". But this new world, which was to know nothing and be a world of hope, is a frozen world, and at night, when his parents' nightmares returned, Momik Neuman went to sleep with a gentle smile on his face, like any other happy child'. (Meyhöfer, *Im Keller der Phantasie*. In: Der Spiegel, 18.02.1991). See also Buchwald, *David Grossman und das Land 'Dort'*. In: *Die Welt*, 09.10.2010.

Chapter 7

1   *Aufgeschnappt*. In: Heilbronner Stimme, 16.04.2004.
2   Heilbronn City Archives, E001-171, 3 letters from Theodor Heuss to Ludwig and Hermine Rosenthal, London.
3   Pikart, *Heuss, Elly Heuss-Knapp, geborene Knapp* (1972).
4   Heilbronn City Archives, E001-171, 3 letters from Theodor Heuss to Ludwig and Hermine Rosenthal, London.
5   Merseburger, *Theodor Heuss: Der Bürger als Präsident* (2012); Radkau, *Theodor Heuss* (2013).
6   'Antisemitische Anklänge bei Heuss' is the title of chapter V2 in Kuschel, *Theodor Heuss die Schoah, das Judentum, Israel* (2013).
7   Kuschel, *Theodor Heuss die Schoah, das Judentum, Israel* (2013), 41.
8   Krauth, *In Heilbronn Demokratie gelernt*. In: Heilbronner Stimme, 10.05.2014.
9   Heilbronn City Archives, E001-171.
10 Braun-Ribbat, *Lebendige Begegnungen* (2009), XIV.
11 Heuss, *Weinbau und Weingärtnerstand in Heilbronn a. N., Vorwort zum ersten Nachdruck* (Bad Godesberg, 6 January 1950), 2.
12 Heuss, *Weinbau und Weingärtnerstand in Heilbronn a. N., Vorwort zum ersten Nachdruck* (Bad Godesberg, 6 January 1950), 2.
13 This and the following letters are from the Heilbronn City Archives, Foreign Heilbronners section, B021-48: *Correspondence with foreign Heilbronners (ended in 1978), R-Sa*.
14 Heilbronn Metropol Cinema Theatre website.
15 Soja, *Thirdspace* (1996); see Schlör, *The Land 'Here', the Land 'There'* (2008).
16 Speech given by Mayor Manfred Weinmann on the occasion of the reception for Jewish guests and the award of the Gold Medallion to Mrs Clara Wahl on 24 June 1985, 23.
17 See Marchtaler, *Georg Peter Bruckmann (1778–1850) und seine Söhne* (1948); *Silber aus Heilbronn für die Welt* (2001).
18 See Heilbronn City Archives, Foreign Heilbronners section, B021-119: Article 'Der gute Bürgermeister von Heilbronn' (OB Meyle) by Victoria Wolff in the Züricher Weltwoche newspaper and the reactions to it.

Chapter 8

1   Heilbronn City Archive, B033-49 (Land and Property Department; Compensation Files). The following quotes all come from here. Julia Neuberger remembers the lawyer's first name as Edwin.

Chapter 9

1   Reis, *Der Eiserne Steg* (1987), 205f.
2   Reis, *Der Eiserne Steg*, 144; see Schlör, *Endlich im Gelobten Land?* (2003), 141f.
3   Gal Engelhard, An 'in between' heritage: Organized visits of former German Jews and their descendants in their cities of origin. PhD dissertation Haifa University 2013; See Hilgert, *Germans and Americans in Israel: Israelis in Germany and the United States* (2013).
4   See Nikou, *Zwischen Imagepflege, moralischer Verpflichtung und Erinnerungen* (2011).
5   Kräutler, 'Dieselbe Stadt – und doch eine ganz andere' (2006), 26.
6   *Wolff, Victoria*. Heilbronn City Archive website; see also Franke *Geschichte und Schicksal*, online edition, 215–16; Heimberg, *Emigration ist eine Entziehungskultur* (2005); Ibid., *'Schaffen, Schaffen, Schaffen' – Victoria Wolffs Jahre in Heilbronn und ihre Zeit im Exil* (2008), 405–20; Bayrischer Rundfunk broadcast the documentary 'Wir waren unerwünscht [We were not wanted]: Victoria Wolff, Jakob Gimpel, Marta Feuchtwanger' on 1 October 1979. Wolff, a second cousin of Albert Einstein, lived with her first husband Alfred Wolf at 21 Moltkestraße. Her novel *Gast in der Heimat* (*Guest in her Homeland*), published in 1935, is set in Heilbronn and amongst other things describes the day Jewish institutions and shops were boycotted on 1 April 1933.
7   Alfred Wolf, *Erinnerungen*. Heilbronn City Archive, Contemporary History Collection 15251.
8   Will Schaber, *Weltbürger aus Heilbronn* (1986); Groth, *Eine deutsche Biographie* (18.05.1985); Ibid., *The Road to New York* (1983); see also Bartels, *Findbuch zum Nachlass Will Schaber (1905–1996)* (2005) and in particular the collection of his most important articles: Schaber, *Profile der Zeit: Begegnungen in sechs Jahrzehnten* (1992), with the remarkable epilogue from noted researcher Manfred Bosch, whose initiative led to the creation of Alemannia Judaica: *Exil als Weltgewinn*.
9   Groth, *Eine deutsche Biographie* (1985); see also Schaber, *Eine Zeitung als Heimat* (1984).
10 Will Schaber, *Weltbürger aus Heilbronn*, 9.
11 Berkholz, *Auch in New York bleibt sich der Schwabe treu. Der Publizist Will Schaber wird neunzig*.
12 Will Schaber, *Weltbürger aus Heilbronn*, 22.
13 Schwinghammer, *Als die Kulturwüste eine erregende Oase war* (07.03.1979).
14 Heilbronn City Archive, Foreign Heilbronners section B021-34: Correspondence with foreign Heilbronners (cases still open in 1978).
15 Heilbronn City Archive, Foreign Heilbronners section B021-145: Correspondence with foreign Heilbronners A-H.
16 Heilbronn City Archive, Foreign Heilbronners section B021-36: Correspondence with foreign Heilbronners (cases still open in 1978), Scheu-Schl.
17 Heilbronn City Archive, Foreign Heilbronners section B021-36: Correspondence with foreign Heilbronners (cases still open in 1978), Scheu-Schl.

18 Jacobi, *Die vermißten Ratsprotokolle* (1981); Ibid., *Heilbronn – Die schönsten Jahre?* (1984); Ibid., *Das Kriegsende. Szenen 1944/45* (1985).
19 Benz, *Rückkehr auf Zeit* (1991), 196–207; see also Schlör, *Exil und Rückkehr* (1995), 94–112.
20 Heilbronn City Archive, Foreign Heilbronners section B021-44.
21 Heilbronn City Archive, Foreign Heilbronners section B021-0, alphabetical section F-L.
22 Heilbronn City Archive, Foreign Heilbronners Section B021-62: Correspondence with Victoria Wolff, née Victor.
23 Heilbronn City Archive, Foreign Heilbronners section B021-29: Correspondence with foreign Heilbronners (ended in 1978).
24 Reis, *Speech given by Mr Arthur Reis* (1985), 28–9.
25 For more detail on Franke himself, see Schwinghammer (Ed.), *Heilbronn und Hans Franke* (1989). Schwinghammer calls Franke 'the writing conscience of the city'.
26 See Gräf, *Steine zum Reden gebracht* (1987).
27 1985 Week of Encounter (Woche der Begegnung), 51.
28 All the following information comes from the Heilbronn City Archive D 107: Rolf Palm estate.
29 Heilbronn City Archive D 107: Rolf Palm estate. The following quotes also come from letters to Rolf Palm which were kept in this file.
30 Heilbronn City Archive, Foreign Heilbronners section B021-33: Correspondence with Foreign Heilbronners (cases still open in 1978), Pl-Re.
31 Heilbronn City Archive, Foreign Heilbronners section B021-33: Correspondence with Foreign Heilbronners (cases still open in 1978), Pl-Re.
32 Letter from mayor Weinmann to Rolf Palm, 16.12.1985. Heilbronn City Archive D 107: Rolf Palm estate.
33 Speech given by Rabbi Joel Berger welcoming the Jewish guests (1987).
34 Heilbronn City Archive, Foreign Heilbronners section B021-0. See the note in the HEUSS database: 'The foreign Heilbronners were at first the group of Jewish residents who emigrated during the Third Reich, with whom mayor Paul Meyle resumed contact in 1949/50. It is now mostly their descendants or people who moved abroad after 1945 (e.g. women who married American soldiers).' (http://heuss.stadtarchiv-heilbronn.de/ [05.11.2014]).
35 Heilbronn City Archive, Foreign Heilbronners section B021-34: Correspondence with foreign Heilbronners (cases still open in 1978), Ri-Ro.
36 Heilbronn City Archive, Foreign Heilbronners section B021-113: Individual visits by former Jewish citizens to Heilbronn.
37 Heilbronn City Archive, Foreign Heilbronners section B021-74: Correspondence with James May, New York/Florida.
38 Pacheco, *It's a Wonderful Life: Keeping Faith in Humanity* (14.08.2010).
39 'May's mother, Thekla Sänger May, was the founder and chairperson of the "Heilbronner Nachmittage", a social get-together of German refugees held semi-annually at the Beacon Hotel in New York. She was assisted by Walter Strauss and Will Schaber.' Schlottmann, *Guide to the James May (1921–2012)*. See also the letters from and to James May in the Heilbronn City Archive, Foreign Heilbronners section B021-74: Correspondence with James May, New York/Florida.
40 Heilbronn City Archive, Foreign Heilbronners section B021-36: Correspondence with foreign Heilbronners (cases still open in 1978), Scheu-Schl; see also B021-63:

CV of Dr Manfred Scheuer of Heilbronn and the story of the settlement he founded, Shavei Tzion.
41 Heilbronn City Archive, Foreign Heilbronners section B021-117: Correspondence with Dr Fritz Wolf, Nahariya (Israel). The individual letters are unsigned, but are ordered chronologically. All the following quotes from Fritz Wolf are from letters in this file.
42 For images of the city before its destruction, see *Nostalgischer Spaziergang durch Heilbronn in den 30er Jahren*, http://www.youtube.com/watch?v=joLjl8of2B4 [25.01.2014].
43 Mayor Meyle to Fritz Wolf, 13.11.1957, Heilbronn City Archive B021-177
44 This letter, the manuscript of the speech given during Heuss's visit, the following account from Frielinghaus-Heuss and Wolf's CV can all be found in the Heilbronn City Archive, Foreign Heilbronners section B021-117: Correspondence with Dr Fritz Wolf, Nahariya (Israel).
45 Kreppel, *Deutsch, jüdisch, israelisch* (2012); the film *Nahariyade* (Israel 2006: directed by David Vitzthum) tells the story of Fritz Wolf, the city of Nahariya and the Yekkes who built the city as they look back on those years in conversation with the schoolchildren from Bielefeld.
46 Wolf, *Das Sülmer Tor* (2001), 33.
47 Wolf, *Das Sülmer Tor* (2001), 33, 35.
48 Fritz Wolf to Dr Manfred Weinmann, 25.02.1984. Heilbronn City Archive, Foreign Heilbronners section B021-117: Correspondence with Dr Fritz Wolf, Nahariya (Israel).
49 This and the following letters are from the Heilbronn City Archive, Foreign Heilbronners section B021-117: Correspondence with Dr Fritz Wolf, Nahariya (Israel).
50 RDC, *Obituary: Alice Schwab* [RDC = Ronald Channing].

Bibliography

ADLER-RUDEL, Salomon (1974), *Jüdische Selbsthilfe unter dem Nazi-Regime 1933–1939*. Tübingen: Mohr Siebeck.
ALENFELD, Irène (2007), *Warum seid Ihr nicht ausgewandert? Überleben in Berlin 1933 bis 1945*. Berlin: Verlag für Berlin-Brandenburg.
Aliens Restriction (Amendment) Act 1919, in: National Archives. http://www.legislation.gov.uk/ukpga/Geo5/9-10/92/contents [07.11.2014].
ALROEY, Gur (2002), 'Aliya to Early Twentieth Century Palestine as an Immigrant Experience', *Jewish Social Studies* 9, 2 (2002), 28–64.
ALROEY, Gur (2003), 'Bureaucracy, Agents and Swindlers: Hardships Faced by Russian Jewish Emigrants in the Early Twentieth Century', *Studies in Contemporary Jewry* 19, 214–31.
AMÉRY, Jean (1977), 'Wieviel Heimat braucht der Mensch?' In: IBID, *Jenseits von Schuld und Sühne. Bewältigungsversuche eines Überwältigten*. Stuttgart: Klett-Cotta, 74–101.
Ansprache von Herrn Oberbürgermeister Dr. Manfred Weinmann anläßlich des Empfangs für die jüdischen Gäste und der Überreichung der Goldenen Münze an Frau Clara Wahl am 24. Juni 1985 im Großen Ratssaal des Rathauses, *Woche der Begegnung 1985. Besuch ehemaliger jüdischer Mitbürger aus Heilbronn von 22.-29. Juni 1985*, ed. Stadtverwaltung Heilbronn. September 1985, 20–4.
ARENDT, Hannah (2013), *Wahrheit gibt es nur zu zweien. Briefe an die Freunde*. München: Piper Verlag.
Aufgeschnappt (von ff [d.i. Franziska feinäugle]), in: Heilbronner Stimme, 16.04.2004. http://www.stimme.de/heilbronn/nachrichten/stadt/sonstige-Aufgeschnappt;art1925,305244 [17.01.2014].
BARTELS, Claudia (2005), Nachlass Will Schaber (1905–1996). Dortmund: Institut für Zeitungsforschung, http://www.dortmund.de/media/p/institut_fuer_zeitungsforschung/zi_downloads/nachlaesse_1/Findbuch-Willi_Schaber.pdf [23.09.2014].
BasqueChildren.org. http://www.basquechildren.org [21.12.2014].
BAUSINGER, Hermann (2002), *Die bessere Hälfte. Von Badenern und Württembergern*. München: Deutsche Verlags-Anstalt.
Befreiung. Webseite der Bergen-Belsen-Stiftung. http://bergen-belsen.stiftung-ng.de/de/geschichte/konzentrationslager/befreiung.html [12.01.2014].
Begrüßung der jüdischen Gäste durch Herrn Landesrabbiner Joel Berger, Stuttgart, am 22. Juni 1987, *Woche der Begegnung 1987. Besuch ehemaliger jüdischer Mitbürger aus Heilbronn vom 20.-27. Juni 1987*, ed. Stadtverwaltung Heilbronn, 19–20.
Belsize Square Synagogue Webseite: About us. http://www.synagogue.org.uk/about-us [02.01.2014].
BENTHAM, Jeremy (1780/1948), *The Principles of Morals and Legislation*. New York: Hafner Publishing.
BENZ, Wolfgang, ed. (1998), Auswandern aus Deutschland. Einwandern in Palästina. *Tribüne* 37, 145, 164–74.

BENZ, Wolfgang, ed. (1991), Das Exil der kleinen Leute. Alltagserfahrungen deutscher Juden in der Emigration. München: DTV.
BENZ, Wolfgang (1991), 'Rückkehr auf Zeit: Erfahrungen deutsch-jüdischer Emigranten mit Einladungen in ihre ehemaligen Heimatstädte', *Exilforschung. Ein internationales Jahrbuch* 9, 196–207.
BERGHAHN, Marion (2007), *Continental Britons. German-Jewish Refugees from Nazi Germany*. New and revised edition. New York and Oxford: Berghahn Books.
BERKHOLZ, Stefan, Auch in New York bleibt sich der Schwabe treu. Der Publizist Will Schaber wird neunzig. http://www.erich-schairer.de/biogr/will_sch.html [25.01.2014].
BINDERNAGEL, Franka et al., 'Tagungsbericht, Rethinking the 'Auslandsdeutsche'. Respatializing Historical Narrative. 10.07.2013–12.07.2013, Berlin. In: H-Soz-u-Kult, 19.10.2013. http://hsozkult.geschichte.hu-berlin.de/tagungsberichte/id=5081 [22.09.2014].
Biographisches Handbuch der Rabbiner, ed. BROCKE, Michael/CARLEBACH, Julius (2009), Die Rabbiner im Deutschen Reich 1871–1945, bearb. v. Katrin Nele JANSEN. Berlin: de Gruyter.
BISCHOFF, Doerte/KOMFORT-HEIN, Susanne (2012), 'Vom anderen Deutschland zur Transnationalität. Diskurse des Nationalen in Exilliteratur und Exilforschung', *Exilforschung. Ein internationales Jahrbuch* 30: Exilforschungen im historischen Prozess, 242–73.
BISCHOFF, Doerte/KOMFORT-HEIN, Joachim (2013), 'Dinge des Exils. Zur Einleitung', *Exilforschung. Ein internationales Jahrbuch* 31: Dinge des Exils, 9–20.
BOAS, Jacob (1986), 'The Shrinking World of German Jewry, 1933–1938', *Leo Baeck Institute Yearbook* 31, S. 241–66.
BOLLAUF, Trude (2009), *Dienstboten-Emigration. Wie jüdische Frauen aus Österreich und Deutschland nach England flüchten konnten*. Dissertation Universität Wien 2009, othes.univie.ac.at/6563/1/2009-08-18_9609238.pdf [08.01.2014].
BOSCH, Manfred: Exil als Weltgewinn. http://www.dortmund.de/media/p/institut_fuer_zeitungsforschung/zi_downloads/nachlaesse_1/Findbuch-Willi_Schaber.pdf [21.01.2014].
BOURDIEU, Pierre (1985), Sozialer Raum und 'Klassen'. Zwei Vorlesungen. Frankfurt a.M.: Suhrkamp.
BOURDIEU, Pierre (1998), Die biographische Illusion. In: Praktische Vernunft. Zur Theorie des Handelns. Frankfurt am Main: Suhrkamp, 75–82.
BRAUN-RIBBAT, Dorothea (2009), 'Lebendige Begegnung mit Menschen und Geschichten'. In: *Theodor Heuss. Weinbau und Weingärtnerstand in Heilbronn am Neckar*, ed. Christhard Schrenk/Reinhold-Maier-Stiftung Baden-Württemberg. Heilbronn: Stadtarchiv 2009, XIII–XXI.
BRINSON, Charmian / KACZYNSKI, William (2011), *Fleeing from the Führer. A Postal History of Refugees from the Nazis*. Stroud: The History Press.
BRODER, Henryk. M./GEISEL, Eike (1992), Premiere und Pogrom. Der Jüdische Kulturbund 1933–1941. Texte und Bilder. Berlin: Akademie der Künste.
BRÜCKNER, Wolfgang (1995), 'Dingbedeutung und Materialwertigkeit. Das Problemfeld', in *Anzeiger des Germanischen Nationalmuseums Nürnberg*, 14–21.
BUCHWALD, Christoph: David Grossman und das Land 'Dort'. In: Die WELT, 09.10.2010. http://www.welt.de/print/die_welt/vermischtes/article10169472/David-Grossman-und-das-Land-Dort.html [23.09.2014].
BUCKARD, Christian (2004), *Arthur Koestler. Ein extremes Leben. 1905–1983*. München: C.H.Beck.

CACCIOTTOLO, Mario: Nazi Persecution Saw Jews Flee abroad as Servants. In: BBC News, 08.03.2012. http://www.bbc.co.uk/news/uk-16942741 [20.12.2014].
CESARANI, David / KUSHNER, Tony et al., ed. (1997), Belsen in History and Memory. London, New York: Routledge.
Chronologie des Holocaust (1938). http://www.holocaust-chronologie.de/chronologie/1938/mai/01-31.html [21.12.2013].
CLAVIN, Patricia (2005), 'Defining Transnationalism', *Contemporary European History* 14, 4, 421–39.
COHEN, Susan (2010), *Rescue the Perishing: Eleanor Rathbone and the Refugees*. London: Vallentine Mitchell.
CRAIG-NORTON, Jennifer (2019), *The KIndertransport. Contesting Memory*. Bloomington: Indiana University Press.
CSIKSZENTMIHALY, Mihaly / ROCHBERG-HALTON, Eugene (1981), *The Meaning of Things: Domestic Symbols and the Self*. Cambridge: Cambridge University Press.
DOVE, Richard, ed. (2005), 'Totally un-English? Britain's Internment of "Enemy Aliens" in Two World Wars', *The Yearbook of the Research Centre for German and Austrian Exile Studies*, 7. Amsterdam u. New York: Rodopi.
DWORK, Deborah / Van Pelt, Robert Jan (2009), *Flight from the Reich. Refugee Jews, 1933–1946*. New York u. London: W. W. Norton.
e.g.l.: Jews in the German Wine Trade. Memoirs from a Trade Journal. In: AJR Information February 1965.
EREL, Shlomo, ed. (2004), *Jeckes erzählen. Aus dem Leben deutschsprachiger Einwanderer in Israel*. Wien: Lit Verlag.
FABER, David (2009), *Munich. The 1938 Appeasement Crisis*. London: Simon & Schuster.
Feierstunde zur Übergabe der ehemaligen Synagoge Affaltrach an die Öffentlichkeit am 9. November 1988, ed. Verein zur Erhaltung der Synagoge Affaltrach, April 1989.
Festreden, gehalten zum 50jährigen Synagogen-Jubiläum, am 21. Mai 1927. Heilbronn 1927.
FETSCHER, Caroline, 'Deutsche Geschichte: Die eigene Familie als NS-Archiv', *Der Tagesspiegel*, 20.05.2013
FINK, Ruth: The Ninth Life. Chapter 2: The Escape from Frankfurt on 10 November 1938 (Manuscript, undated).
FISCHER, Ernst (2012), 'Der Sortimentsbuchhandel', in IBID./FÜSSEL, Stephan, eds., *Geschichte des deutschen Buchhandels im 19. und 20. Jahrhunderts, Bd. 2, 2:Weimarer Republik 1918–1933*. Berlin, Boston: de Gruyter, 335–412.
FISCHER, Stefanie (2012), 'Vertraute Handelspartner – geächtete Handelspartner. Jüdische Viehhändler in Rothenburg o.d.T. und Umgebung 1919–1939', in KLUXEN, Andrea M./KRIEGER, Julia, eds., *Geschichte und Kultur der Juden in Rothenburg o.d.T.* Würzburg: Ergon Verlag, 99–126.
FISCHER-DEFOY, Christine (2003), *Marlene Dietrich Adressbuch*. Berlin: Transit Buchverlag.
FISCHER-DEFOY, Christine (2006), *Heinrich Mann: Auch ich kam aus Deutschland. Das private Adressbuch 1926–1940*. Leipzig: Koehler & Amelang.
FISCHER-DEFOY, Christine (2006), '... wie überall hin die Leute verstreut sind ...' *Walter Benjamin – das Adressbuch des Exils 1933–1940*. Leipzig: Koehler & Amelang.
FISCHER-DEFOY, Christine (2007), *Hannah Arendt. 'Mir ist, als müsste ich mich selbst suchen gehen': Das private Adressbuch 1951–1975*. Leipzig: Koehler & Amelang.
Florsheim Family. In: Loeb family tree. http://www.loebtree.com/flor.html [28.12.2013].
Forging Ahead. Wolpert and Gumbel. Israeli Silversmiths for the Modern Age. Exhibition catalogue [23.11.2012–06.04.2013], Jerusalem 2012.

FRANK FOLEY: Documents from the British Archives. Documents relating to the Exploits of Frank Foley: a Passport Control Officer Who Helped Hundreds of Jews Escape Nazi Germany before the Outbreak of World War Two. http://issuu.com/fcohistorians/docs/hpdfba_5 [20.12.2013].

FRANCIS FOLEY, Great Britain. The Righteous among the Nations. Vad Vashem. http://www.yadvashem.org/yv/en/righteous/stories/foley.asp [20.12.2013].

FRANCIS, Paul: WWII Internment Camps in the Isle of Man. http://www.airfieldinformationexchange.org/community/showthread.php?6891-WWII-Internment-Camps-in-the-Isle-of-Man [07.01.2014].

FRANKE, Hans (1963), *Geschichte und Schicksal der Juden in Heilbronn. Vom Mittelalter bis zu der Zeit der nationalsozialistischen Verfolgungen (1050–1945)*. Heilbronn: Stadtarchiv. Online edition 2011: http://www.stadtarchiv-heilbronn.de/publikationen/online_publikationen/_files/03-vr-11-franke-juden-in-heilbronn.pdf [17.09.2014].

FRANKE, Julia (2000), *Paris – eine neue Heimat? Jüdische Emigranten aus Deutschland 1933–1939*. Berlin: Duncker & Humblot.

Frankfurter Biographie: Personengeschichtliches Lexikon, hg. v. KLÖTZER, Wolfgang/HOCK, Sabine/FROST, Reinhard. Bd. 2: M–Z. Frankfurt am Main 1996.

GEBHARDT, Miriam (1999), *Das Familiengedächtnis. Erinnerung im deutsch-jüdischen Bürgertum 1890 bis 1932*. Stuttgart: Franz Steiner Verlag.

GESTRICH, Andreas (1988), 'Einleitung: Sozialhistorische Biographieforschung', in IBID./knoch, Peter/MERKEL, Helga, eds., *Biographie – sozialgeschichtlich*. Göttingen: Vandenhoeck & Ruprecht.

GILBERT, Shirli (2017), *From Things Lost: Forgotten Letters and the Legacy of the Holocaust*. Detroit: Wayne State University Press.

GODFREY, Antony (2005), *Three Rabbis in a Vicarage. The Story of Belsize Square Synagogue*. London: Larsen Grove Press.

GOLDBERG, Kevin D. (2014), 'Wie der Wein in Mitteleuropa jüdisch wurde', in LEHNARDT, Andreas, ed., *Wein und Judentum*. Berlin: Neofelis Verlag 2014, 229–46.

GOMBRICH, Ernst H. (1965), Gertrud Bing, 1892–1964, in Gertrud Bing in Memoriam. London: The Warburg Institute, 1–3.

GRÄF, Hartmut (1987), 'Steine zum Reden gebracht. Schüler dokumentieren den jüdischen Friedhof Heilbronn', *Woche der Begegnung 1987. Besuch ehemaliger jüdischer Mitbürger aus Heilbronn vom 20.–27. Juni 1987*, ed. Stadtverwaltung Heilbronn. September 1987, 92–8.

GREGORY, Derek (1994), *Geographical Imaginations*. Oxford: Blackwell.

GRENVILLE, Anthony (2009), *Jewish Refugees from Nazi Germany and Austria in Britain, 1933–1970: Their Image in AJR Information*. London: Vallentine Mitchell.

GRENVILLE, Anthony (2009), 'Underpaid, Underfed and Overworked: Refugees in Domestic Service', *AJR Information*, December 2008. http://www.ajr.org.uk/index.cfm/section.journal/issue.Dec08/article=1463 [26.01.2014].

GROSSHANS, Albert (1981), *Das nationalsozialistische Regime und seine Auswirkungen auf Heilbronn*. Heilbronn: Distel.

GROTH, Michael (1985), 'Eine deutsche Biographie. Weltbürger – Bürger der Welt in New York', *Frankfurter Allgemeine Zeitung*, 18.05.1985.

GROTH, Michael (1983), The Road to New York: The Emigration of Berlin Journalists 1933–1945. Dissertation, University of Iowa.

Häntzschel, Hiltrud (2013), 'Der Brief – Lebenszeichen, Liebespfand, Medium und Kassiber', in IBID./ASMUS, Silvia et al., eds., *Auf unsicherem Terrain. Briefeschreiben im Exil*. Munich: edition text und kritik, 19–32.

HEIGOLD, Martin, Der 4. Dezember 1944 als Unterrichtsthema. http://www.stadtarchiv-heilbronn.de/stadtgeschichte/unterricht/bausteine/4_dezember_1944/ [10.01.2014].
Heilbronn Metropol-Lichtspieltheater, Website: http://allekinos.pytalhost.com/kinowiki/index.php?title=Heilbronn_Metropol-Lichtspieltheater [29.01.2014].
HEIMBERG, Anke (2005), 'Emigration ist eine Entziehungskur. Leben und Werk der Exilschriftstellerin Victoria Wolff', ed. John M. Spalek and Joseph Strelka, in *Deutschsprachige Exilliteratur seit 1933*, vol. 3: USA. Munich: de Gruyter Saur, 271–301.
HEIMBERG, Anke (2008), '"Schaffen, Schaffen, Schreiben" – Victoria Wolffs Jahre in Heilbronn und ihre Zeit im Exil', in SCHRENK, Christhard/WANNER, Peter, eds., *heilbronnica 4. Beiträge zur Stadt- und Regionalgeschichte*. Heilbronn: Stadtarchiv, 405–20.
HELA-Langzeitprojekt: Heilbronn deine Dichter – Dichterhäuser in Heilbronn. http://www.hlarshn.de/index.php?option=com_content&view=article&id=153&Itemid=43 [26.01.2014].
HELBICH, Wolfgang, Tagungsbericht, Reading the Emigrant Letter: Innovative Approaches and Interpretations. 07.08.2003–09.08.2003,Ottawa, Ont. In: H-Soz-u-Kult, 17.09.2003. http://hsozkult.geschichte.hu-berlin.de/tagungsberichte/id=288 [25.02.2014].
HERZOG, David (2013), *Meine Lebenswege. Die persönlichen Aufzeichnungen des Grazer Rabbiners David Herzog*, ed. HALBRAINER, Heimo/LAMPRECHT, Gerald/SCHWEIGER, Andreas. Graz: Clio.
HEUSS, Theodor (2009), Weinbau und Weingärtnerstand in Heilbronn a. N. [first edition 1906, first reprint 1950], ed. Reinhold-Maier-Stiftung Baden-Württemberg and Stadtarchiv Heilbronn. (Kleine Schriftenreihe des Archivs der Stadt Heilbronn 50).
HIRCHE, Walter (1939), Die jüdische Wanderung und ihre Schwierigkeiten, unter besonderer Berücksichtigung der Verhältnisse in Deutschland (Altreich) von 1933 bis 1939, dargestellt anhand der jüdischen Publizistik des Altreiches. Dissertation, University of Leipzig.
HÖGERLE, Heinz/KOHLMANN, Carsten/STAUDACHER, Barbara, eds. (2008), *Ort der Zuflucht und Verheißung. Shavei Zion 1938–2008*: Begleitbuch zur Wanderausstellung. Stuttgart: Konrad Theiss.
Institutions, Monuments & Structures in India Contributed to by the Jews. Jews of India. http://jewsofindia.org/forum/index.php?action=printpage;topic=10.0 [29.01.2014].
JACOBI, Uwe (1981), *Die vermißten Ratsprotokolle. Aufzeichnung der Suche nach der unbewältigten Vergangenheit*. Heilbronn: Heilbronner Stimme Druckerei und Verlagsanstalt.
JACOBI, Uwe (1984), *Heilbronn – Die schönsten Jahre? Nachkriegszeit in einer deutschen Stadt*. Heilbronn: Heilbronner Stimme Druckerei und Verlagsanstalt.
JACOBI, Uwe (1985), *Das Kriegsende. Szenen 1944/45 in Heilbronn, im Unterland und in Hohenlohe*. Heilbronn: Heilbronner Stimme Druckerei und Verlagsanstalt.
JACOBI, Uwe (2008): Mitbürger waren Täter und Opfer. In: *Heilbronner Stimme*, 07.11.2008. http://www.stimme.de/heilbronn/nachrichten/region/sonstige-Mitbuerger-waren-Taeter-und-Opfer;art16305,1388929 [23.09.2014].
JEGGLE, Utz (2009), *Judendörfer in Württemberg*, with a foreword by Monika RICHARZ. Tübingen: TVV.
JESSEN, Caroline (2012), '"Vergangenheiten haben ihr eigenes Beharrungsvermögen … " Josef Kastein and the Troublesome Persistence of a Canon of German Literature in Palestine/Israel', *Leo Baeck Institute Yearbook* 57, 35–51.

JETZ, Klaus: Zuflucht in Lateinamerika. Eine Ausstellung zur Emigration der deutschen Juden nach 1933. In: ila 301 (Dezember 2006/Januar 2007). http://www.ila-web.de/kult urszene/301juedischeemigration.htm [26.01.2014].

Jewish Migration: Aliens Act. In: Jewish Virtual Library. http://www.jewishvirtuallibrary. org [20.12.2013].

JORDAN, James / LEFF, Lisa / SCHLÖR, Joachim (2014), 'Jewish Migration and the Archive: Introduction', *Jewish Culture and History* 15, 1–2, 1–5.

JÜNGER, David (2017), *Jahre der Ungewissheit: Emigrationspläne deutscher Juden 1933–1938*. Schriften des Simon-Dubnow-Instituts, 24. Göttingen: Vandenhoeck & Ruprecht.

KAPLAN, Marion (2010), *Zuflucht in der Karibik. Die jüdische Flüchtlingssiedlung in der Dominikanischen Republik 1940–1945*. Göttingen: Wallstein.

KEIL, Hartmut/ZILLIEN, Felix (2010), Der deutsche Wein 1930 bis 1945. Eine historische Betrachtung. Worms: IATROS.

KELLER, Claudia: Irène Alenfeld (geb. 1933). In: Der Tagesspiegel, 14.02.2014. http://www.tagesspiegel.de/berlin/nachrufe/irene-alenfeld-geb-1933/9477688.html [22.09.2014].

KERR, Judith (2017), *When Hitler Stole Pink Rabbit*. Essential Modern Classics. London: HarperCollins.

KNIGHT, Andrew: Haile Selassie Returns to Wimbledon. http://www.anglo-ethiopian. org/publications/articles.php?type=A&reference=publications/articles/2006summer/ selassiewimbledon.php [27.12.2013].

KORFF, Gottfried 2002), 'Aporien der Musealisierung. Notizen zu einem Trend, der die Institution, nach der er benannt ist, hinter sich gelassen hat', in IBID, *Museumsdinge. Deponieren. Exponieren*. Cologne: Böhlau.

KRÄUTLER, Anja (2006), *Dieselbe Stadt – und doch eine ganz andere. Kommunale und bürgerschaftliche Besuchsprogramme für ehemalige Zwangsarbeiter und andere Opfer nationalsozialistischen Unrechts*. Berlin: Fonds Erinnerung und Zukunft.

KRAUTH, Kilian In Heilbronn Demokratie gelernt. In: Heilbronner Stimme, 10.05.2014. http://www.stimme.de/heilbronn/nachrichten/region/In-Heilbronn-Demokratie-gelernt;art16305,2966104 [23.09.2014].

KREPPEL, Klaus (1999), Wege nach Israel. Gespräche mit deutschsprachigen Einwanderern in Nahariya. Bielefeld: Westfalen Verlag.

KREPPEL, Klaus (2002), Israels fleißige Jeckes. Zwölf Unternehmerportraits deutschsprachiger Juden in Nahariya. Bielefeld: Westfalen Verlag.

KREPPEL, Klaus (2005), Nahariyya – das Dorf der 'Jeckes'. Die Gründung der Mittelstandssiedlung für deutsche Einwanderer in Eretz Israel 1934/35. Tefen: The Open Museum.

KREPPEL, Lena (2012), *Deutsch, jüdisch, israelisch. Identitätskonstruktionen in autobiographischen und essayistischen Texten von Erich Bloch, Jenny Cramer und Fritz Wolf*. Würzburg: Königshausen & Neumann.

KRÖHNKE, Karl/WÜRZNER, Hans, ed. (1994), *Deutsche Literatur im Exil in den Niederlanden 1933–1940*. Amsterdam: Rodopi.

KRUSEMARCK, Götz (1938), Die Juden in Heilbronn. Heilbronn: Stadtarchiv.

Kurt Maschler Awards. http://www.bookawards.bizland.com/kurt_maschler_award_for_children.htm [07.11.2014].

KUSCHEL, Karl Josef (2013), *Theodor Heuss, die Schoah, das Judentum, Israel. Ein Versuch*. Tübingen: Klöpfer & Meyer.

KUSHNER, Tony (1991), 'An Alien Occupation: Jewish Refugees and Domestic Service in Britain, 1933–1948', in Werner E. Mosse & Julius Carlebach, eds., *Second Chance: Two*

Centuries of German-speaking Jews in the United Kingdom. Tübingen: J. C. B. Mohr [Paul Siebeck], 553–587.

KUSHNER, Tony (2006), *Remembering Refugees: Then and Now*. Manchester: Manxchester University Press.

KUSHNER, Tony (2017), *Journeys from the Abyss. The Holocaust and Forced Migration from the 1880s to the Present*. Liverpool: Liverpool University Press.

LAMPRECHT, Gerald (2001), *Feldpost und Kriegserlebnis. Briefe als historisch-biographische Quelle*. Innsbruck: Studienverlag.

LARSEN, Egon (1987), *Die Welt der Gabriele Tergit. Aus dem Leben einer ewig jungen Berlinerin*. Berlin: Arani.

'Lebendiges Museum Online' des Deutschen Historischen Museums. https://www.dhm.de/lemo/kapitel/ns-regime/ausgrenzung/nuernberg/ [03.09.2014].

Leo Baeck Institute London: Kindertransport Conference am 25. Juni 2013. http://www.leobaeck.co.uk/archives/3318 [1.11.2014].

London, Louise (1990), 'Jewish Refugees, Anglo-Jewry and British Government Policy, 1930-1940', in David Cesarani, ed., *The Making of Modern Anglo Jewry*. London: Basil Blackwell, 163–90.

London, Louise (2001), *Whitehall and the Jews, 1933–1948: British Immigration Policy, Jewish Refugees and the Holocaust*. Cambridge: Cambridge University Press.

LSE [London School of Economics] History. http://www.lse.ac.uk/aboutLSE/LSEHistory/lseHistory.aspx [24.04.2014].

LOWENTHAL, Ernst G. (1986), 'Bloomsbury House. Flüchtlingsarbeit in London 1939 bis 1946: Aus persönlichen Erinnerungen', in Ursula BÜTTNER, ed., *Das Unrechtsregime, Bd. 2: Verfolgung – Exil – Belasteter Neubeginn*. Hamburg: Christians, 267–304.

Der Luftangriff auf Heilbronn 1944. Webseite Stadtarchiv Heilbronn: https://stadtarchiv.heilbronn.de/de/kontrast/stadtgeschichte/geschichte-a-z/123/04121944.html [10.6.2015].

Manx National Heritage Society: Internment during Wold Wars 1 & 2. The Isle of Man's Role. http://www.manxnationalheritage.im/wp-content/uploads/2013/08/CG4-Internment_Web.pdf [08.01.2014].

MARCHTALER, Kurt Erhard von (1948), 'Georg Peter Bruckmann (1778–1850) und seine Söhne', in Württembergische Kommission für Landesgeschichte, ed., *Schwäbische Lebensbilder*, vol. 4. Unknown Binding, 15–31.

The Marriage Issue. In: *AJS Perspectives. The Magazine of the Association for Jewish Studies* (spring 2013). http://www.ajsnet.org/ajsp13sp.pdf [19.09.2014].

MATTHEWS-SCHLINZIG, Marie Isabel/SOCHA, Caroline: CfP, What is a Letter? An Interdisciplinary Approach. Was ist ein Brief? Eine interdisziplinäre Annäherung. Internationales Symposium, 02.07.2014–04.07.2014, Oxford. http://h-net.msu.edu/cgi-bin/logbrowse.pl?trx=vx&list=H-Germanistik&month=1401&week=e&msg=lzcZXiZfU14F2fUMBss9cA [25.02.2014].

Max Samuel-Haus: Wir über uns. http://www.max-samuel-haus.de/wir/index.html [08.01.2014].

MEDOFF, Rafael: How America First Learned of the Holocaust. In: The Algemeiner, 11.06.2012. http://www.algemeiner.com/2012/06/11/how-america-first-learned-of-the-holocaust/ [09.01.2014].

MEEN, Sharon: Finding Julius Kahn. http://www.judeninthemar.org/?p=472 [28.12.2013].

Merkblatt der Devisenstelle S Frankfurt für die Mitnahme von Umzugsgut durch jüdische Auswanderer 1939. http://www.ffmhist.de/ffm33-45/portal01/portal01.php?ziel=t_jm_dokumente_auswanderung01 [06.06.2014].

MERSEBURGER, Peter (2012), Theodor Heuss. Der Bürger als Präsident. Stuttgart: Pantheon.
MEYHÖFER, Anette: Im Keller der Phantasie. In: Der SPIEGEL, 18.02.1991. http://www.spiegel.de/spiegel/print/d-13489421.html [23.09.2014].
MIRON, Guy (2013), '"Lately, Almost Constantly, Everything Seems Small to Me". The Lived Space of German Jews under the Nazi Regime', Jewish Social Studies 20, 1, 121–49.
MIRON, Guy (2015), '"The Politics of Catastrophe Races On. I Wait." Waiting Time in the World of German Jews under Nazi Rule', Yad Vashem Studies, 43, 1, 45–76.
Minni Stern. In: Zentrale Datenbank der Namen der Holocaustopfer. http://db.yadvashem.org/names/nameDetails.html?itemId=2031661&language=de [28.12.2013].
Mobile Culture Studies. http://unipub.uni-graz.at/mcsj [14.08.2015].
MOSER, Johannes/STEIDL, Daniela, eds. (2009), Dinge auf Reisen. Materielle Kultur und Tourismus. Münster: Waxmann.
MOYA, José C./MCKEOWN, Adam (2010), 'World Migration in the Long Twentieth Century', in Michael ADAS, ed., Essays on Twentieth Century History. Philadelphia: Temple University Press.
MÜLLER-DOOHM, Stefan (2003), Adorno. Eine Biographie. Frankfurt am Main: Suhrkamp.
NETER, Mia (1930), 'Die jüdische Wohlfahrtspflege in Mannheim im Jahre 1929/30', in Jüdische Wohlfahrtspflege und Sozialpolitik 1, 9, 10, 361–9.
NEUBERGER, Julia (2006), Graduation Address – Akademische Abschlussfeier – Abraham Geiger College, 13.09.2006, Rathaus Dresden. http://www.zentralratdjuden.de/de/topic/282.html [14.12.2013].
NEUBERGER, Julia: Tikkun Olam – the Message of Reform Judaism. Keynote Speech for Chagigah 2012, http://news.reformjudaism.org.uk/assembly-of-rabbis/tikkun-olam-the-message-of-reform-judaism.html [21.12.2013].
NEWMAN, Joanna (2019), Nearly the New World: The British West Indies and the Flight from Nazism, 1933–1945. New York: Berghahn Books.
NIKOU, Lina: Zwischen Imagepflege, moralischer Verpflichtung und Erinnerungen. Das Besuchsprogramm für jüdische ehemalige Hamburger Bürgerinnen und Bürger. Munich, Hamburg: Dölling und Galitz.
NIKOU, Lina (2020), Besuche in der alten Heimat. Einladungsprogramme für ehemals Verfolgte des Nationalsozialismus in München, Frankfurt am Main und Berlin. Berlin: Neofelis Verlag.
OCHS, Thomas (2009), Vicki Baum zwischen Wahrheit und Inszenierung in den USA. Einige Aspekte eines schwierigen Verhältnisses. Munich: GRIN Publ.
OLDFIELD, Sybil (2004), '"It Is Usually She": The Role of British Women in the Rescue and Care of the Kindertransport Kinder', Shofar: An Interdisciplinary Journal of Jewish Studies 23, 1, 57–70.
Otto Schiff Dies in London; Aided Jewish Refugees. In: JTA Archive, 18.11.1952. http://www.jta.org/1952/11/18/archive/otto-schiff-dies-in-london-aided-jewish-refugees#ixzz2rKeeXexQ [24.01.2014].
The Oxford and St. George's Clubs, Website: http://www.exploringeastlondon.co.uk/stepney/settlement/ostg.htm [03.01.2014].
PACHECO, Ana: It's a Wonderful Life: Keeping Faith in Humanity, The New Mexican, 14.08.2010.
PAUCKER, Arnold (2017), 'Speaking English with an Accent', The Leo Baeck Institute Year Book, 62, 9–19.
PEDERSEN, Susan (2004), Eleanor Rathbone and the Politics of Conscience. New Haven: Yale University Press.

PFEIL, Moritz: Unbewältigte Gegenwart. In: *Der SPIEGEL* 08.03.1961. http://www.spiegel. de/spiegel/print/d-43160078.html [08.11.2014].

Philo-Atlas. Handbuch für die jüdische Auswanderung (1938, Reprint 1998), with an introduction by Susanne urban-fahr. Bodenheim: Philo Verlag.

PIKART, Eberhard (1972), 'Heuss, Elly Heuss-Knapp, geborene Knapp', *Neue Deutsche Biographie* 9 (1972), S. 56–57; Online version: http://www.deutsche-biographie.de/ pnd118704397.html [04.11. 2014].

POST, Anna-Maria/STRUCK, Wolfgang: CfP, Workshop Schreiben in die alte Heimat – Auswandererbriefe in der Kultur des 19. Jahrhunderts. Forschungsbibliothek Gotha, 12./13. Juni 2014. http://www.uni-erfurt.de/fileadmin/public-docs/ RaumZeitForschung/Workshop_Auswandererbriefe_Konzeption_0114.pdf [25.01.2014].

PRINZ, Arthur (1936), Voraussetzungen jüdischer Auswanderungspolitik, *Der Morgen* 12,1 (1936), 10–17.

PRITZKER-EHRLICH, Marthi (1998), Jüdisches Emigrantenlos 1938/39 und die Schweiz: Eine Fallstudie. Bern: Peter Lang.

Die Programme des Lehrhauses (1923), *Der Jude* 7, 2, 121. (http://sammlungen.ub.uni-frankfurt.de/cm/periodical/tpage/3107808?lang=en [08.01.2014].

RADKAU, Joachim (2013), *Theodor Heuss*. Munich: Carl Hanser.

RDC [d.i. Ronald Channing], Obituary: Alice Schwab. http://www.ajr.org.uk/index.cfm/ section.journal/issue.Jul01/article=594 [02.02.2014].

REIS, Arthur (1985), Rede von Herrn Arthur Reis, Hod Hasharon/Israel am 24. Juni 1985 auf dem Wartberg, *Woche der Begegnung 1985. Besuch ehemaliger jüdischer Mitbürger aus Heilbronn von 22.–29. Juni 1985. Ansprachen, Bilddokumente, Zeitungsausschnitte*, ed. Stadtverwaltung Heilbronn. September 1985, 28–35.

REIS, Arthur (1987), *Der eiserne Steg*, ed. Bürgerkomitee für die Begegnung mit ehemaligen jüdischen Mitbürgern und politischen Emigranten aus Heilbronn. Heilbronn: Heilbronner Stimme Druckerei und Verlagshaus.

REITER, Andrea (2007), *Die Exterritorialität des Denkens – Hans Sahl im Exil*. Göttingen: Wallstein.

REITER, Andrea: '"I didn't want to float, I wanted to belong to something". Refugee Organizations in Britain 1933-1945. Introduction', *The Yearbook of the Research Centre for German and Austrian Exile Studies* 10 (2008), vi–xvi.

REITMANN, Roland (1971), *Die Allee in Heilbronn. Funktionswandel einer Straße*. Heilbronn: Stadtarchiv.

RICHARDS, James, The Blitz: Sorting the Myth from the Reality. http://www.bbc.co.uk/ history/british/britain_wwtwo/blitz_01.shtml [07.01.2014].

RITTER, Martin/ULMER, Martin, eds. (2013), *Das jüdische Zwangsaltersheim Eschenau und seine Bewohner*. Horb-Rexingen: Barbara Staudacher.

ROBERTS, Marcus, National Anglo-Jewish Heritage Trail. http://www.jtrails.org.uk/trails/ brighton-and-hove/history?page=8 [26.01.2014].

ROHRWASSER, Michael (1991), *Der Stalinismus und die Renegaten. Die Literatur der Exkommunisten*. Stuttgart: J.B.Metzler

ROSENTHAL, Bernard M. (1986), Continental Emigré Booksellers of the Thirties and Forties and Their Impact on the Antiquarian Booktrade in the United States. Institut d'Histoire du Livre, http://ihl.enssib.fr/the-gentle-invasion [25.02.2014].

ROSENTHAL, Gabriele (1994), 'Zur Konstitution von Generationen in familienbiographischen Prozessen. Krieg, Nationalsozialismus und Genozid in Familiengeschichte und Biographie', *Österreichische Zeitschrift für Geschichtswissenschaften* 5, 4: Biographie und Geschichte, 489-516.

SAHL, Hans (1991), *Memoiren eines Moralisten. Darmstadt u.* Neuwied: Luchterhand.

SARAGA, Esther (1988). *Berlin to London: An Emotional History of Two Refugees*. Foreword by Tony Kushner. London: Valentine & Mitchell.

SCHABER, Will (1984), 'Eine Zeitung als Heimat (Ansprache anläßlich der Ausstellung "50 Jahre Aufbau" im September 1984 im Deutschhof Heilbronn)', *Heilbronner Vorträge* 21, 10-12.

SCHABER, Will (1992), *Profile der Zeit. Begegnungen in sechs Jahrzehnten*, ed. Manfred BOSCH. Eggingen: Edition Isele.

SCHLÖGEL, Karl (2003), *Im Raume lesen wir die Zeit. Über Zivilisationsgeschichte und Geopolitik*. München: Carl Hanser.

SCHLÖR, Joachim (1995), 'Exil und Rückkehr', *Tribüne* 135, 94-112.

SCHLÖR, Joachim (2003), *Endlich im Gelobten Land? Deutsche Juden unterwegs in eine neue Heimat*. Berlin: Aufbau.

SCHLÖR, Joachim (2005), 'Dinge der Emigration. Eine Projektskizze', *Exilforschung. Ein internationales Jahrbuch* 23: Autobiografie und wissenschaftliche Biografik, 222-38.

SCHLÖR, Joachim (2006), 'Mesussot entfernen – Türschilder entfernen. Die Emigration der Gegenstände von Deutschland nach Palästina', in SCHMALE, Wolfgang/STEER, Martina, eds., *Kulturtransfer in der jüdischen Geschichte*. Frankfurt, New York: Campus, 153-72.

SCHLÖR, Joachim (2008), 'The Land "Here", the Land "There": Reflections on Returning'. Opening of the Exhibition "Ort der Zuflucht und Verheißung", Mishkenot Shaananim, Jerusalem, 21.08.2008. http://www.irgun-jeckes.org/?CategoryID=344&ArticleID=745 [20.01.2014].

SCHLÖR, Joachim (2012), '"Menschen wie wir mit Koffern." Neue kulturwissenschaftliche Zugänge zur Erforschung jüdischer Migrationen im 19. und 20. Jahrhundert', in Ulla Kriebernegg et al., ed., *"Nach Amerika nämlich!" Jüdische Migrationen in die Amerikas im 19. und 20. Jahrhundert*, Göttingen: Wallstein, 23-54.

SCHLÖR, Joachim (2014), 'Means of Transport and Storage: Suitcases and Other Containers for the Memory of Migration and Displacement', *Jewish Culture and History*, 15, 1-2: Special Issue: Jewish Migration and the Archive, S. 76-92.

SCHLÖR, Joachim (2014), '"Solange wir an Bord waren, hatten wir eine Heimat". Reisen als kulturelle Praxis im Migrationsprozess jüdischer Auswanderer', *Voyage. Jahrbuch für Reise-und Tourismusforschung* 10: Mobilitäten!, 226-46.

SCHLÖSSER, Susanne (1997), '"Was sich in den Weg stellt, mit Vernichtung schlagen …". Richard Drauz, NSDAP-Kreisleiter von Heilbronn', in KISSENER, Michael/SCHOLTYSECK, Joachim, eds., Die Führer der Provinz. NS-Biographien aus Baden und Württemberg. Konstanz: UVK 143-59.

SCHLÖSSER, Susanne (2003), 'Die Heilbronner NSDAP und ihre "Führer". Eine Bestandsaufnahme zur nationalsozialistischen Personalpolitik auf lokaler Ebene und ihren Auswirkungen "vor Ort"', in SCHRENK, Christhard/WANNER, Peter, eds., *heilbronnica 2. Beiträge zur Stadt- und Regionalgeschichte*. Heilbronn: Stadtarchiv, 281-318. http://www.stadtarchiv-heilbronn.de/publikationen/online_publikationen/heilbronnica_2/_files/08-heilbronnica2-08-schloesser-fuehrer-281-318.pdf [17.09.2014].

SCHLOTTMANN, Kevin: Guide to the James May (1921-2012) Collection, AR 5110, processed by Kevin Schlottmann. Leo Baeck Institute New York. http://digifindingaids.cjh.org/?pID=475620 [09.11.2014].

SCHMIDINGER, Veit Johannes/SCHOELLER, Wilfried F. (2007), *Transit Amsterdam. Deutsche Künstler im Exil 1933–1945*. Munich: Allitera.
SCHMIDT, Till: Wege ins rettende Exil. In: http://tillschmidt.wordpress.com/2013/08/14/wege-ins-rettende-exil [14.08.2013].
SCHRENK, Christhard (1992), 'Die Chronologie der sogenannten "Reichskristallnacht" in Heilbronn', *Jahrbuch für schwäbisch-fränkische Geschichte* 32. Historischer Verein Heilbronn, 293–314.
SCHRENK, Christhard (2013), 'Heilbronn um 1933. Eine Stadt kommt unter das Hakenkreuz', in IBID./WANNER, Peter, eds., *heilbronnica 5. Beiträge zur Stadt- und Regionalgeschichte*. Heilbronn: Stadtarchiv, 263–85.
SCHRÖDER, Christoph (2014), 'Gutes Haus, schiefe Bahn, SS-Karriere', *Der Tagesspiegel*, 24. 02.2014. http://www.tagesspiegel.de/kultur/per-leos-roman-flut-und-boden-guteshaus-schiefe-bahn-ss-karriere/9531124.html [19.09.2014].
SCHWAB, Walter, 'In Memoriam – Mrs. Anna Schwab', *AJR Information*, Mai 1963, 9.
SCHWAB, Walter Manfred Moshe. Website The Williams Family Tree. http://www.williamsfamilytree.co.uk/tree/getperson.php?personID=I13879&tree-wft [15.01.2014].
SCHWARZENBERGER, Georg (1908–1991), Website City Archives Heilbronn: https://stadtarchiv.heilbronn.de/stadtgeschichte/geschichte-a-z/s/schwarzenberger-georg.html [10.05.2015].
SCHWINGHAMMER, Gerhard, 'Als die Kulturwüste eine erregende Oase war', *Heilbronner Stimme*, 07.03.1979.
SCHWINGHAMMER, Gerhard, ed. (1986), *Will Schaber. Weltbürger aus Heilbronn*. Foreword by Albert Großhans. Heilbronn: Verlag Heilbronner Stimme.
SCHWINGHAMMER, Gerhard, ed. (1989), *Heilbronn und Hans Franke. Publizist, Dichter und Kritiker 1893–1964*. Heilbronn: Verlag Heilbronner Stimme.
SHATZKES, Pamela/SHERMAN, A.J. (2009), 'Otto M. Schiff (1875–1952), Unsung Rescuer', *Leo Baeck Institute Yearbook* 54, 243–71.
SIEGEL, Björn (2014), 'Eine "Besinnliche Fahrt ins Land der Juden"?', in GILLIS-CARLEBACH, Miriam/VOGEL, Barbara, eds., *"Ihre Wege sind liebliche Wege und all ihre Pfade Frieden" (Sprüche 3, 17). Die Neunte Joseph Carlebach-Konferenz. Wege Joseph Carlebachs. Universale Bildung, gelebtes Judentum, Opfergang*. Munich: Dölling und Galitz, 105–25.
Silber aus Heilbronn für die Welt. P. Bruckmann & Söhne (1805–1973), ed. Karlheinz FUCHS, Städtische Museen Heilbronn 2001.
SLUZKI, Carlos E (1979), 'Migration and Family Conflict', *Family Process* 18, 4, 379–90.
SMITH, Michael (1999), *Foley. The Spy Who Saved 10,000 Jews*. London: Hodder & Stoughton.
SOJA, Edward (1996), *Thirdspace. Journeys to Los Angeles and Other Real-and-Imagined Places*. Oxford: Wiley-Blackwell.
SPRINGER, Jerry: How We Did It. In: http://www.bbc.co.uk/whodoyouthinkyouare/new-stories/jerry-springer/how-we-did-it_1.shtml [20.01.2014].
STEINITZ, Renate (2008), *Eine deutsche jüdische Familie wird zerstreut. Die Geschichte eines Steinitz-Zweiges*. http://www.renate.steinitz.net/Eine%20deutsche%20juedische%20Familie.pdf [17.09.2014].
STEINLE, Stephanie (2002), *Völkerrecht und Machtpolitik. Georg Schwarzenberger (1908–1991)*. Baden-Baden: Nomos.
TILL, Ernest REDMOND (1985), 'Zuviel Hochdeutsch auf der Zürcher Bahnhofstraße? Interview mit dem 87-jährigen Kurt L. Maschler in London', *Börsenblatt für den deutschen Buchhandel (Frankfurter Ausgabe)* 41, 22, 823–4.

TOMASZEWSKI, Jerzy (2002), Die Asyl-Konferenz von Evian-les-Bains: Das 'jüdische Problem' auf internationaler Ebene, in IBID., Auftakt zur Vernichtung. Die Vertreibung polnischer Juden aus Deutschland im Jahre 1938. Osnabrück: fibre Verlag.
Transcaolloy India PVT LTD. Firmenprofil. http://www.translloy.com/company_profile.php [29.01.2014].
transversal. Zeitschrift für Jüdische Studien 14, 1 (2013): Zur jüdischen Historiographiegeschichte
TREML, Martin/flach, Sabine/schneider, Pablo, eds. (2014), *Warburgs Denkraum. Formen, Motive, Materialien*. Munich: Wilhelm Fink.
TREWIN, Ion, Tom Rosenthal Obituary, *The Guardian*, 06.01.2014. http://www.theguardian.com/books/2014/jan/06/tom-rosenthal [12.1.2014].
TROLL, Thaddäus. In: (Deutschlandradio Kultur). http://www.deutschlandradiokultur.de/typisch-schwaebisch.1001.de.html?dram:article_id=268636 [12.11.2014].
USBORNE, Cornelie (2002), 'Ärztinnen und Geschlechteridentität in der Weimarer Republik', in LINDNER, Ulrike/NIEHUSS, Merith, eds., *Ärztinnen – Patientinnen. Frauen im deutschen und britischen Gesundheitswesen des 19. und 20. Jahrhunderts*. Cologne etc.: Böhlau, 73–94.
WARBURG Institute London. http://www.warburg-haus.de/texte/london.html [24.04.2014].
WEGNER, Sonja (2013), *Zuflucht in einem fremden Land. Exil in Uruguay 1933–1945*. Berlin: Assoziation A.
WerkstattGeschichte 60 (2013): Korrespondenzen. http://www.werkstattgeschichte.de/index.php?ref=60_editorial.html [31.10.2014].
Wertheimer, Simon. In: Wertheimer family database. http://www.wertheimer.info/family/GRAMPS/Wertheimer/ppl/b/1/b11232d88d7257dae90.html [29.01.2014].
Who coined the term Holocaust to refer to the Nazi 'final solution' for the Jewish People? http://english.stackexchange.com/questions/106031 [03.11.2014].
Woche der Begegnung 1985. Besuch ehemaliger jüdischer Mitbürger aus Heilbronn von 22.–29. Juni 1985, ed. Stadtverwaltung Heilbronn.
WOLF, Fritz (1986), Das war mein Heilbronn. Aus einem zerrissenen Bilderbuch. Die Zeit eilt, teilt, heilt. Mit Federzeichnungen von Rudolf GABEL. Heilbronn: Stadt Heilbronn.
WOLF, Fritz (2001), 'Das Sülmer Tor', *Mnemosyne. ZEIT-Schrift für jüdische Kultur* 27, 33–57.
WOLFF, Victoria, Website City Archives Heilbronn. https://stadtarchiv.heilbronn.de/de/stadtgeschichte/geschichte-a-z/w/wolff-victoria.html [10.05.2015].
World ORT News. ORT India a Year on from the Mumbai Massacre, 09.12.2009. http://www.ort.org/news-and-reports/world-ort-news/article/ort-india-a-year-on-from-the-mumbai-massacre [19.09.2014].
WW2 People's War, Fact File: Civilian Internment 1939–1945. http://www.bbc.co.uk/history/ww2peopleswar/timeline/factfiles/nonflash/a6651858.shtml [03.11.2014].
wyndham, Diana (2012), *Norman Haire and the Study of Sex*. Sydney: SydneyUniversity Press.
The Yearbook of the Research Centre for German and Austrian Exile Studies 3 (2001): German-speaking Exiles in Great Britain. Amsterdam: Rodopi.
ZEICHNER, Saul: Kolomea Research Group Names of Interest: Heilbronn. http://kehilalinks.jewishgen.org/kolomea/nameorigin.htm [31.10.2014].
ZUCKERKANDL, Bertha (1988), *Österreich intim. Erinnerungen 1892–1942*. Frankfurt am Main, Berlin: Amalthea Signum.

Archives

German Jewish Aid Committee: General Situation and Individual Cases. London Metropolitan Archives, Board of Deputies of British Jews, Ref.: ACC/3121/E/03/533
Kaplan Centre Archiv, University of Cape Town
London Metropolitan Archives
Senatskanzlei Berlin
Stadtarchiv Heilbronn

Data collections

1940 U.S. Census. http://www.archives.com/1940-census [29.01.2014]
Alemannia Judaica. http://www.alemannia-judaica.de [22.09.2014]
The Central Database of Shoah Victims' Names, Yad Vashem, https://yvng.yadvashem.org/ [04.03.2020]
HEUSS-Datenbank. http://heuss.stadtarchiv-heilbronn.de [17.05.2014]
Jewish Virtual Library. [20.12.2013]

Video/Film

Heilbronn - Eine Filmreise in die Vergangenheit (Trailer) by Manfred Naegele and Anita Bindner, https://www.youtube.com/watch?v=gITIMnCl128 [04.03.2020]
Nahariyade (Israel 2006, R: David Vitzthum)

Index

Adelaide 106
Adler, Max 37
Adorno, Theodor W. 127, 237
Aerdenhout 98, 149
Affaltrach 124
Aliens Restriction Act 38
Allgemeine Zeitung des Judentums 13
Alroey, Gur 102
Amberg, Alex 203
Améry, Jean 108
Amsterdam 24, 28, 30, 39, 54–5, 65, 72, 98, 101, 103, 119, 121–2, 126, 138, 148, 179
  - 52 Michelangelostraat 115
Arendt, Hannah 77, 129, 131
Argentina 94, 105
Association of Jewish Refugees 33, 221
  - AJR Information 37, 120, 222
Auschwitz 92, 95, 125, 127, 163, 171, 211
Australia 1, 2, 59, 87, 90, 95–7, 101, 103, 105, 106, 112, 124, 128, 133, 135, 145, 147, 163, 170
Avnon, Gerda 209

(Bad) Cannstatt 2, 13, 31–2, 100, 168
Bad Kissingen 30, 164
Bad Nauheim 92, 94–5, 105, 112, 123
Bar Mitzvah 28, 34, 39–40, 78, 84, 165
Barron, Sam 70, 172
Baum, Vicki 9, 144
Beermann, Rabbi Dr Max 203
Benjamin, Walter 129
Bentham, Jeremy 108
Benz, Wolfgang 104, 205
Bergen-Belsen concentration camp 153, 163
Berger, Rabbi Dr Joel 187, 210
Berlin 1, 22, 27, 39, 44, 48, 78, 83, 92, 99, 101, 103–6, 119, 124–5, 127, 129, 132, 156, 170, 173, 182, 184, 199, 201, 208, 223
  - Charlottenburg 92
  - Romanisches Café 22
Bernhard Baron St. George's Jewish Settlement Organisation 125
Beutinger, Emil 24, 75, 185
Bingen am Rhein 29, 36
Birmingham 2, 16–17, 19, 21, 30, 33, 35, 38, 41, 49, 69, 82, 89–90, 92, 116–17, 132, 134, 143, 146, 164
  - Hudson's bookshop 38–9, 42, 51
Blackburn 98, 131
Bloomsbury House 33, 69, 121, 123–4, 129, 131–2, 138–9, 145, 165, 223
Boas, Jacob 25
Bollauf, Trude 121
Bombay 30, 37, 45–59, 61, 63–4, 68, 70–1, 75, 83, 97, 99–100, 127, 147, 151
Bonfeld 107
Bookselling 16, 21, 27, 38
Bourdieu, Pierre 5
Brighton 69, 76, 78, 83, 88, 119, 135, 137, 164
  - Beaconsfield College 78, 88, 164
  - County School for Boys, Holmes Avenue, Hove 135
British Embassy Berlin 39
British Library, National Life Story collection 3
British Mandate in Palestine 2, 11, 25, 129, 169
Buber, Martin 16, 156

Cairo 168, 174
Cape Town 24, 39, 42, 174
Cassirer, Ernst 66
Central Association of German Citizens of the Jewish Faith (CV) 25
Chamberlain, Nevill 64, 119

Churchill, Winston 169
Cologne 16, 105
Coray, Marfa 9
Craig-Norton, Jennifer 17
Csikszentmihalyi, Mihalyi 108

Dachau concentration camp 26, 86, 89, 91, 94, 124, 135
Derby 146
Determann, Dr Julius and bookshop 16, 32, 135, 175-7, 185
Dobbs, Patrick 17, 19, 21, 27, 33-4, 37, 41, 51, 117, 147, 164
Dornacher, Emma 91, 114, 185, 195
Dornacher, Josef 85, 182, 196
Dover 16
Dunera 95
Durban 24, 39

Eckert, Johanna (Hannele) 34, 174, 182
Eisig, Hans 124, 185
Eisig, Lila 81, 92
Ellern, Harold 159, 163
Emergency Committee for German Scientists Abroad 34
Engelbert, Dr Moses 13-14, 131, 186
Erez (Israel) 23, 25
Eschenau 92
Evian conference 1938 104

Feibusch, Lisbeth 52, 57
Fetscher, Caroline 6
Fink, Lotte 21, 28, 87, 88-9, 135-6, 147, 162-3, 170
Fischer, Klaus 36
Fischer, Samuel 16
Fischer, Stefanie 36
Fischer-Defoy, Christine 129
Flegenheimer, Bella 40, 78
Flegenheimer, Max (Mäxle) 78
Foley, Frank 39
Franke, Hans 18, 25-6, 73, 85-6, 91-2, 127, 184, 190, 202, 204, 208-9 215-16
Frankfurt am Main 9, 16, 19-20, 21, 28, 33, 38, 48, 66, 78, 83, 87, 90-1, 95, 98, 106, 119-20, 127, 147-8, 162-3, 167, 170, 173, 175, 195, 220
 - Strauss'sche Buchhandlung 16, 147

Freudental 107
Freudenthal, Margaret 83, 96, 157
Fritsch, Theodor 36

Gabriel, Gerhard 30, 37, 39, 47-9, 63, 67-8, 69, 72, 77, 99, 133, 139
Gabriel, David 99
Gellmersbach 183
Genoa 52-3, 55
German-Jewish Aid Committee 100, 121
Gestrich, Andreas 5
Gilbert, Robert 178
Gilbert, Shirli 5
Goldberg, Kevin 35-6
Gräf, Hartmut 208
Graf, Oskar Maria 202
Gregory, Derek 25
Grenville, Anthony 135
Grossman, David 177
Grossmann, Atina 202
Großhans, Albert 208
Gry, Rabbi Hugo 47
Gryn, Naomi 48
Gumbel, Abraham 203
Gumbel, Dr Siegfried 25-6, 203
Gumbel, Erich 173, 203
Gumbel, Heinz David 10, 19, 116, 121-2, 148, 155, 173, 203, 223
Gummers, Richard F. 206

Hätzschel, Hiltrud 4
Haganah 122
Hahn, Joachim 31-2
Haifa 209
Hakhshara 16
Halton, Eugene 108
Hamburg, Kati 9
Hamlyn, Joan 58, 134, 146, 152, 154-5
Hanukkah 10, 41, 160
Hartmann, Wilfried 221
Hayek, Friedrich 66
Hebrew 10-11, 64, 72, 165, 164, 208, 215
Heilbronn
 - Adlerkeller 64, 72
 - Allee 32, 83-4, 175, 186-7, 205, 218
 - Bergstraße 91, 148
 - Bismarckstraße 24
 - Böckingen 36, 205

- Bruckmann & Söhne 10, 191, 203
- Cäcilienstraße 183, 211
- City Archives 24, 148, 161, 180, 183, 185, 193, 211, 223
- Götzenturmstraße 6, 85, 95, 100, 116, 162, 181-3, 193-6, 209
- Käthchen von Heilbronn 17
- Karlsgymnasium 148, 215, 220
- Klarastraße 85
- Mozartstraße 73-4, 182
- Neckargartach 36, 161, 186, 205
- Staufenbergstraße 13, 15, 18
- Sülmer Tor 218, 221
Heilbronner Stimme 204-5, 212
Heine, Heinrich 11
Herzog, David 130
Heuss, Dr Ludwig 25
Heuss, Theodor 36, 161, 179, 182-3, 187-8, 190, 215-16
Heuss-Frielinghaus, Hanna 219-20
Heuss-Knapp, Elly 182
Heymann, Rabbi Dr Harry 72
Heymann, Werner Richard 178
Hilfsverein der deutschen Juden 21, 67
Hindenburg, Paul von 2
Hirche, Walter 103-4
Hirsch, Dr Julius 26
Hirsch, Els 9
Hirsch, Otto 204
Hitler's *Mein Kampf* 16
Hönigsberger, Justin 176
Holocaust Memorial Day 117-18
Homesickness 21, 136, 163
Horkheimer, Max 126-7
Horovitz, Alfred 95, 97, 132, 135, 137, 145
Horrowitz, Heinrich 206
Houghton Library, Harvard University 126

Igersheimer, Hermann 126, 131, 136
Igersheimer, Otto 127
Inter-Aid Committee for Children from Germany 44, 124

Jacobi, Uwe 83-4, 204, 208
Jerusalem 9-11, 17, 19, 23, 26, 116, 121-2, 155, 203, 209, 211
- Bezalel School 10, 168, 173
Jeselson, Kurt 21-2, 29, 97, 146, 173

Jewish Chronicle 121
Jewish Refugee Committee 33, 135
Jewish Relief Association 99
Jewish Restitution Successor Organization 187
Johannesburg 24
Jordan, James 95
Jüdischer Kulturbund 104
Jüdisches Nachrichtenblatt 104

Kästner, Erich 101
Keren Keyemet (Jewish National Fund) 121
Kern, Hermann 203
Kern, Hugo 203
Kirchheimer, Eugen 19, 68
Kirchheimer, Mathilde 148
Kleist, Heinrich von 17
Koestler, Arthur 155
Koppe, Dr Max 174-5, 177, 179
Koppe, Johanna 174-5, 177, 179, 182
Kräutler, Anja 200
Künzelsau 107
Kuschel, Karl Josef 183
Kushner, Tony 135

Latukefu, Dr Ruth 87-8
Leff, Lisa 95
Leo Baeck Institute 102
Leser, Ruth 99-100, 127-8, 130
Lichtenstern, Leopold 16-17, 19-20, 24, 28, 40, 58-9, 65, 131, 136, 138-9, 142-3, 146-7, 150, 163, 165, 175
Lion, Alice (née Adler) 211
Loeb, Luise 24, 45, 55, 72, 113, 138, 154, 169
Loeb, Richard 28, 113, 115, 138, 154
Lloyd Triestino 52, 55
London
- Belsize Square synagogue 119-20
- Goldhurst Terrace 120, 131, 152
- Greencroft Gardens 55
- Hampstead 2, 42, 120, 139, 144
- Kenilworth Avenue, Wimbledon 185
- Lincoln House 111, 116, 123, 125
- Lissenden Mansions 155, 159, 162
- Liverpool Street station 116
- London School of Economics 65, 134

- Marks & Spencer 69–70, 141, 145, 151, 176, 223
- Messrs. A Cohen & Co., Great Dover Street 53
- Paddington Spanish Aid Committee 63
- Thomas Cook & Son 51, 53
- Thurlow Road 2, 67, 69–70, 79, 90, 132–4
- Union of Girls' Clubs 125
- Warburg Institute 65–6, 223
- Worple Road, Wimbledon 3, 134, 141–2, 144, 152

Lowenthal, Ernst G. 129–30, 145

Mai, Heinrich 212
Mai, Julius (= James May) 212
Manchester 145, 156
- 31 Oak Road 156
Marseille 14, 117, 127
Marx, Leopold 183
Maschler, Kurt 100–1, 136, 145
Mayer, Hans 109
Mayer, Lola 44, 64
Mayer, Oskar 218
Meyer, Andreas 6
Meyer, Betty 52
Meyle, Paul 185–6, 188, 193, 203, 208, 213
Montevideo 2, 68, 88, 91, 97, 109, 140
Munich 156, 183–4, 217
Munk, Margarita 156

Nahariya 6, 23–4, 173, 211, 215–6, 218, 221
Nahariyade 24, 218
Neckar-Zeitung 184
Neuberger, Julia 3, 6, 14, 20, 31, 33, 70, 89, 91, 101, 116–17, 147, 151, 193, 213, 223
New School for Social Research 127
Niklasch, Eva 220–1
Nikou, Lina 200
Nuremberg 17, 193, 200
Nuremberg Race Laws 61, 105

Öhringen 107
Offenbach 30, 48–9, 50, 56, 61, 69, 167
Onchan internment camp, Isle of Man 140
ORT India 47
Oz, Amos 177

Palestine 82, 95, 102, 105, 121–2, 128, 148, 151, 153, 155, 157, 159, 168–9, 186, 218
Palestine Pavilion, New York World Exhibition 121
Palm, Rolf 85, 181, 204, 208–9, 210, 216
Paris 25, 82–3, 86, 93, 109, 126, 129, 147, 155, 165
- Hotel de Calais, rue des Capucines 83
Paynton, Jack 45, 95, 112, 135
Paynton, Olive 45, 53, 68
PEN Club 101
Philo Atlas 103
Port Elizabeth 42
Port Said 63
Prinz, Artur 21

Rathbone, Winifred 90, 111, 114–15, 141
Reches, Lotte 209
Reich Citizenship Law 26, 61
Reichskristallnacht pogrom 85
Reis, Artur 199, 207–8, 209
Rexingen 200
Rosen, Pinchas (Felix Rosenblüth) 199
Rosenstein, Roman 31
Rosenthal, Babette 13, 193–4, 195
Rosenthal, Erwin 122, 156, 159–60, 163, 168, 170, 173, 209, 211
Rosenthal, Gabriele 5
Rosenthal, Gina (Eugenie), 97, 116
Rosenthal, Lazarus 181, 183
Rosenthal, Max 85, 91, 125, 185, 194–5
Rosenthal, Willy 37
Rostock 98
Roth, Cecil 160
Rothschild family 2, 13, 31–2, 48, 100, 139
Royal Air Force 160
Rüdesheim 29
Rubinstein, Raschela 135, 139, 142
Rypinski, Philipp 41, 203

Sänger-Mai, Thekla 203, 212
São Paulo 41
Sahl, Hans 22, 102, 155
Salzberger, Rabbi Dr Georg 120
Samuel, Max 98, 131
San Francisco 27
Saraga, Esther 5
Saxl, Fritz 66

Schaber, Will 201–2, 203, 205
Schaffhausen 81
Schatzki, Walter 38
Scheffler, Kurt 208
Scheffler, Susanne 208
Scheuer, Julius R. 204
Scheuer, Manfred 183, 204, 213
Scheuer, Paul 24, 148, 155, 206
Schwab, Anna 33–4, 41, 65, 69, 77–8, 90, 97–8, 111, 120–1, 130–1, 135, 144, 149, 152, 159, 168, 223
Schwab, Harry 144, 150, 161
Schwab, Walter 3, 120, 151, 221
Schwarzenberger, Georg 157, 160
Schwarzenberger, Suse 58, 122, 150
Schiff, Otto M. 22–4, 121, 130–1
Schloss, Hans 19, 28, 82, 89, 92–3, 124, 157, 219
Schupbach, Fred 96, 100, 137
Seligmann, Richard 90, 111, 116
Selz, Ernst 124
Shavei Zion 173, 183
Ship brothers and sisters 43
Silone, Ignazio 155
Sluzki, Carlos 43, 152
Söhner, Willi 208
Sontheim 36, 107
Southampton 5–6, 17, 19, 95, 135
Sperber, Manès 155
Springer, Jerry 33
Sprißler, Georg 17
Stern, Alfred 95, 105, 112, 131–4, 135, 139–40, 145–6, 147, 178
Stern, Minni (née Florsheim) 92, 94–5, 98, 105, 112, 116, 131–2, 140, 152, 154, 170
Stuttgart 13, 16, 19, 25–6, 28, 57, 65–6, 67, 72, 77, 82, 91–2, 97, 100, 106–7, 114, 123–4, 153, 161, 176, 178, 181, 185
 - Israelite Welfare Office, 36 Hospitalstraße 124
Sussmann (Sußmann), Martha 37, 42, 67, 93, 163
Swabia, Swabian 2, 6, 18–19, 30–1, 40, 67, 106, 183, 189–90, 193, 201–2, 205, 212–13, 214–5, 219

Talheim 107
Tel Aviv 121, 128, 159, 199–200, 207, 213
 - Bialik House 199
 - Idelsohn Street 199
Theresienstadt 24, 91–2, 95, 164, 168, 170–1, 176, 195
Toronto 76–7

Uruguay 89–90, 91, 93–4, 97, 101, 105, 128, 140

Van Pelt, Robert Jan 129
Venice 170
Verein zur Abwehr des Antisemitismus 7
Verner, Rose 141, 151
Victor, Eugen 24
Victor, Liesel 24, 30, 39, 42, 162
Victor, Max 148, 155, 159, 223
Victor, Trude 30, 98, 123, 147–8, 155, 160, 169
Vitzthum, David 218

Wahl, Clara 189, 208
Wallas, Armin A. 6, 218
Wegner, Sonja 93
Weinmann, Dr Manfred 189, 204–5, 219–20, 221
Welzheim concentration camp 26
Wertheimer, Jakob 31–2, 40, 68–9, 112, 114, 154
Westerbork 24, 153
Wiener Library 5, 102
Wine merchants 13, 18, 35–6, 37, 174, 223
Winegrowers 18, 36–7, 183, 202
Woburn House 33–4, 65, 67–8, 69–70, 77, 79, 88–9, 90, 92, 100, 111, 120–1, 123–4, 129–30, 131, 135
Württemberg 13, 23, 25, 31, 37, 72, 107, 156, 195, 202–3, 204, 211, 217
Wolf, Alfred 201
Wolf, Cäcilie 218
Wolf, Fritz 6, 23–4, 160, 173–4, 188, 201, 213–19, 221
Wolff, Victoria 219, 221
Wolpert, Yehuda 10

Yekkes 208, 216
Yemenite Jews 11
Yishuv (Jewish community in Mandate Palestine) 10–11

YIVO Institute for Jewish Research 102
Yom Kippur 11, 30, 35

Zandvoort 9, 131
Zionism 11, 199, 216
Zoppot 52

Zuckerkandl, Berta 129
Zurich 23, 25, 28–9, 30–1, 32, 40, 56, 68, 72, 75, 88, 109, 111–12, 113, 127, 133, 137–8, 139, 151, 164, 176
- 1 Tödistrasse 31, 176
Zwickauer Neueste Nachrichten 184

www.ingramcontent.com/pod-product-compliance
Lightning Source LLC
Chambersburg PA
CBHW072133290426
44111CB00012B/1867